THE MAKING OF HOLY RUSSIA

The Making of Holy Russia

The Orthodox Church and Russian Nationalism before the Revolution

John Strickland

Holy Trinity Publications
The Printshop of St Job of Pochaev
Holy Trinity Monastery
Jordanville, New York
2013

Printed with the blessing of His Eminence,
Metropolitan Hilarion First Hierarch
of the Russian Orthodox Church Outside of Russia

The Making of Holy Russia
© 2013 John Strickland

HOLY TRINITY PUBLICATIONS
The Printshop of St Job of Pochaev
Holy Trinity Monastery
Jordanville, New York 13361-0036
www.holytrinitypublications.com

Cover Art: *Easter Procession* by Illarion Michajlowitsch Pryanishnikov, 1893.
Source: DIRECT MEDIA ©Zenodot Verlagsgesellschaft mbH.
Cover Design: James Bozeman

ISBN: 978-0-88465-329-5 (paperback)
ISBN: 978-0-88465-346-2 (hardback)
ISBN: 978-0-88465-347-9 (ePub)
ISBN: 978-0-88465-348-6 (Mobipocket)

Library of Congress Control Number 2013938140

CONTENTS

For my parents
Gordon and Jananne Strickland
My professional training in history would have been inconceivable
without their unconditional love and support,
and it is to them that I dedicate this book.

FOREWORD

This work originated as a doctoral dissertation researched in libraries and archives of St Petersburg, Russia, where the author lived for two years in the late 1990s. It takes the form of an extended commentary upon ideas and teaching about national identity advanced within the Orthodox Church in Russia in the closing decades of the nineteenth century and the early twentieth century leading up to the tragedy of the Bolshevik Revolution in 1917.

In particular it draws attention to the voices of those whom the author terms "Orthodox patriots," both clergy and laity, who advocated for the place of the Church as a unifying force, central to the identity and purpose of the increasingly diverse Russian Empire. Their views were articulated not only in numerous publications and administrative decisions, but through art and architecture. They sought to realize a vision of a both temporal and transcendent Holy Russia that could be God's instrument for the salvation of all nations and overcome the limitations of the sociopolitical entity known as the Russian Empire.

These voices were both persistent and widely expressed, yet have received little attention in studies of the history of Russia during this period. This is perhaps because they are less readily understood by writers more intrinsically sympathetic to the Western intellectual traditions of modern nationalism or liberal thought.

Grounded in original research, this study is nevertheless intended for a broader audience than that of most academic works. It is written in light of the historical path Russia has taken since the fall of communism in 1991, and the significant role the Orthodox Church now plays in defining and leading national life.

Such a role is reflected very clearly in the concluding statement of the February 2013 Bishops' Council that met in Moscow. In it the Bishops declared,

> Orthodoxy is being reborn as the foundation of national self-consciousness, uniting all the healthy forces in society—those forces which strive for the

transformation of life on the basis of a sure foundation and the spiritual and moral values that have entered the flesh and blood of our peoples.

Notwithstanding this declaration, many questions remain as to the extent to which Orthodoxy is being fully embraced in contemporary Russian life both in the homeland and abroad. Furthermore, the exact relationship between the Church as the universal earthly manifestation of a heavenly society and post-Enlightenment conceptions of nationhood remains problematic in practice and presents an ongoing pastoral and missionary challenge.

It is therefore to be hoped that this historical study might ignite a contemporary debate that can lead to greater clarity and prayerful action in conveying the everlasting Gospel of salvation in Christ through His Church to all peoples.

Holy Trinity Monastery
Jordanville, New York

INTRODUCTION

HOLY RUS AND MODERN RUSSIA

On July 20, 1914, Tsar Nicholas II stepped out onto the balcony of the Winter Palace in St Petersburg to announce the Russian Empire's entry into the First World War. Below him on Palace Square stood a great crowd of patriotic Russians, who fell into a hush as he began to read the war manifesto. The scene was similar to those in other European capitals during the first days of the war. In each case, rulers appealed to national traits that would sustain the sacrifices ahead. And in each case the news was received with broad support, uncanny in light of the catastrophe that the war ultimately brought.

In St Petersburg, the tsar solemnly spoke of a national community called "Holy Rus" (*sviataia Rus*). This community represented the core of "Russia" (*Rossiia*), he suggested, and was constituted by a self-conscious devotion to Orthodox Christianity and a common ethnic ancestry. It was constituted, in other words, by "faith and blood." Tsar Nicholas said that in the coming time of war, ultimate victory would depend on the conviction that modern Russia was in fact equivalent to Holy Rus. The words of his war manifesto were deeply moving to those assembled below. As he finished reading it, they sank to their knees and began singing the patriotic Orthodox hymn, "O Lord Save Thy People."[1]

Nicholas II (r. 1894–1917) was compelled to invoke the image of Holy Rus because Russia and her imperial system, which for decades had been plagued by instability, lacked the unity needed for total warfare. As such, his war manifesto drew upon a long tradition that can be called "Orthodox patriotism." It claimed that Russia possessed a national character rooted in the Orthodox Christian faith, which it was her destiny to preserve and disseminate. The First World War did not bring about the fulfillment of the ideals of Orthodox patriotism, and less than three years after the tsar's Palace

Square address, revolution swept away the hope that modern Russia was indeed Holy Rus.

Though never subjected to a comprehensive study, Orthodox patriotism has profoundly shaped the history of Russian culture and thought, and its manifestations are often a part of even the most cursory historical surveys.[2] Significantly, the earliest proponents were members of the Orthodox clergy. Within a century of the foundation of Christianity under Grand Prince Vladimir (r. 980–1015), for example, Russia's first native Church primate, Metropolitan Ilarion of Kiev (r. 1051–1055), declared that the Russian people were the successors to the ancient Israelites in that they were a national community that had become the bearers of the true faith in history. Following the collapse of the Byzantine Empire in 1453, the Pskovian monk Filofei (1460–1542) embellished the ideal further by claiming that the Muscovite state, as the "Third Rome," had been given a messianic destiny to preserve the Orthodox faith in the face of the apostasy of Rome and the fall of Constantinople, the "Second Rome." Filofei's doctrine was supplemented by other Muscovite Church leaders such as Metropolitan Macarius (1482–1563), who in the sixteenth century wrote influential works about the state's Orthodox character and promoted the canonization of large numbers of national saints. Likewise, the leadership of the Old Believers, when confronted by the Church reforms of Patriarch Nikon during the seventeenth century, claimed to preserve Russian national character by retaining unaltered what they considered the true faith. In short, there can be little argument that the identification of Russian nationality with the Orthodox faith found its earliest elaboration among representatives of the clergy.

When historians have studied Orthodox patriotism in modern Russia, however, the role of the Church has drifted into obscurity. This is not due to a decline in the status of religion as a symbol of Russian national self-consciousness. Orthodox Christianity constituted the core of nationality for well-known lay intellectuals such as Alexei Khomiakov (1482–1563) and Fyodor Dostoevsky (1821–1881).[3] In fact, the latter could go so far as to suggest through the words of one sympathetic character that the true faith was only manifested fully in Russian national self-consciousness. "The aim of all movements of nations, of every nation and in every period of its existence," declared Shatov in *Demons,*

> is solely the seeking for God, its own God, entirely its own, and faith in him as the only true one. God is the synthetic person of the whole nation, taken from its beginning and to its end. It has never yet happened that all

or many nations have had one common God, but each has always had a separate one. It is a sign of a nation's extinction when there begin to be gods in common. The stronger the nation, the more particular its God. . . . The only "god-bearing" nation is the Russian nation.[4]

Similar statements about the religious foundation of Russia's national character circulated widely among the nineteenth-century laity and represent one of the most familiar cultural currents before the Revolution.

Nevertheless, historians have continually ignored the Orthodox clergy's attitude toward modern Orthodox patriotism. Even the study that came closest to offering a comprehensive interpretation of it, Michael Cherniavsky's *Tsar and People,* neglected to consult a single ecclesiastical source in its treatment of the period following the Great Reforms.[5] In light of the influence of Orthodox patriotism in modern Russian thought and culture, it is ironic that so little attention has been directed to the leadership of what proponents believed was the leading source of nationality, the Church.

This may be explained in part by the fact that until the middle of the nineteenth century the Orthodox clergy were not a natural ally to those who promoted a modern model of nationality. Administratively, the Church suffered from a variety of weaknesses that impeded its ability to act as a force for national leadership. It was stifled by the bureaucratic authority of the Holy Synod, and its parish priests often lacked a high level of education measured in relation to lay society. Its close relationship to the imperial state, coupled with a commitment to obey earthly authority, also imbued it with an innate suspicion of politically disruptive forces such as nationalism. And finally, a model of nationality in which culture and ancestry assumed leading roles threatened its conception of the "universal Church" (*vselenskaia tserkov*).

Orthodox doctrine had, in fact, often deemphasized and even disparaged national particularism throughout the history of the Church. The New Testament taught that, as with all human differences, ethnic identity was an insignificant factor in the ultimate matter of ecclesial identity. The tension between ecclesial universalism and national particularism had been addressed and resolved by the earliest Christians, who were forced to confront the fact that the multinational Church of the first century lacked the ethnic unity of its prototype, Old Testament Israel. The authors of the New Testament therefore placed special emphasis upon the universal scope of the Christian faith. In the closing lines of the Gospel of Matthew, for instance, Christ commissioned what was then only a Jewish Church to "make disciples of all the nations."[6] Statements such as this established a principle of

universality that guided the activities of Church leaders among the nationalities of the ancient Roman Empire. It was this principle that led St Paul to
declare to the church at Colossae that "there is neither Greek nor Jew, cir-
cumcised nor uncircumcised, barbarian, Scythian, slave nor free; but Christ
is all and in all."[7] Thus the particularism of ethnic identity (whether Greek,
Jew, barbarian, or Scythian) was subsumed and in a sense rendered irrelevant
by the universalism of Christ's Church.

Indeed, throughout the centuries, Christianity was able to expand in
part because missionaries tolerated ethnic differences and focused primary
attention on the larger Church, which, according to the fourth-century
Symbol of the Faith (or Nicene Creed), could only be "one." Slavic peoples
were baptized through the mission of Cyril and Methodius and encouraged
to preserve their native tongues through the creation of the Cyrillic alphabet. When the Slavs of medieval Rus were in turn baptized in 988, they too
adopted the Cyrillic alphabet and preserved a form of culture distinct from
that of their Greek evangelists. The Orthodox clergy of imperial Russia
inherited this universalistic principle in all its fullness. It was manifested during the nineteenth century, for instance, in leading works of theology.[8] And it
was expressed in the practices of missionaries such as Innocent (Veniaminov)
of Alaska, Nicholas (Kasatkin) of Japan, and the Bishop of North America,
the future Patriarch Tikhon (1865–1925), himself, all of whom made use of
the vernacular languages of the non-Russian peoples to whom they brought
Orthodox Christianity.

Nevertheless, after the Great Reforms[9] a small but influential group of
Church leaders came to embrace Orthodox patriotism, and they began to
direct Church activities toward the formation of a modern Russian national
community. In doing so, they were engaged in what Geoffrey Hosking
has described as a project of "nation-building."[10] Conscious that the Great
Reforms had failed to resolve the problems of empire, they believed that Russia could be strengthened by mobilizing the population to embrace national
ideals such as social unity, cultural tradition, and a common ancestry.[11] Like
many representatives of the state and educated society, they believed these
ideals were embodied particularly within the empire's dominant nationality,
the Russians. As the overseers of the official Church, however, they insisted
that the most important Russian national ideal was Orthodoxy. Acting on
this conviction, they dedicated themselves to a project of unprecedented
scope and ambition, the making of Holy Russia.

This book is a study of that project. It is designed to address two broad
issues. The first is the role of the Church in the cultural life of late imperial

Russia—the period between the end of the Great Reforms in 1881 and the Revolution of 1917. The second is the relationship between Orthodoxy and modern nationalism.

The conventional estimate of the cultural influence of the Church during the nineteenth century is summarized in the observation that the greatest representative of Orthodox spiritual culture, Seraphim of Sarov, and the greatest representative of secular culture, Alexander Pushkin (1799–1837), lived as contemporaries but never knew of the other's existence.[12] A condition of extreme isolation between religious and secular culture did, in fact, characterize the imperial period up through the reign of Nicholas I (r. 1825–1855). However, with the coming of the Great Reforms under Alexander II (r. 1855–1881), these cultures became increasingly interconnected, partly because of what Gregory Freeze has called a "decisive watershed in the history of the Church."[13] New issues began to dominate Church life during the decades following the reforms, and the activities of clerical Orthodox patriots were closely linked to them. Most significant was the Church's growing engagement with the affairs of a secularized civil society. Robert Nichols has noted how the Church accepted "the need for closer contacts with society going beyond its earlier narrowly understood task of enlightenment."[14] As the Church began to broaden its relationship to civil society, it addressed a number of issues ranging from socialism to educated public opinion.[15]

It also became increasingly conscious of nationalism. The 1870s and 1880s were the years of Dostoevsky, Michael Katkov (1799–1837), and pan-Slavism, and as the Church began to address secular culture, it could not help but note the influence that ethnic nationality exerted over conservative elements in Russian society. Among the clergy, many were repelled by this feature of the modern world, and it would appear that up until the Revolution the majority of parish priests remained, along with the peasants to whom they ministered, largely untouched by ethnic nationalism. For conservative Church leaders, however, it offered a useful instrument for preserving and strengthening the frequently beleaguered imperial Church. In fact, missionaries and other Church officials close to missionary affairs proved to be the most receptive to Orthodox patriotism. In part learning from growing currents in secular society, they developed a model of the nation that was designed to strengthen Russia while simultaneously enhancing the influence of the official Church.

They called their model of the nation "Holy Rus." The history of this epithet is complex. Its earliest recorded use is in the famous correspondence between Ivan Kurbsky (1528–1583) and Ivan the Terrible (r. 1547–1584). The former, furious at the tsar's suppression of boyar authority, employed the term "holy Russian land" in opposition to the emerging autocracy of the sixteenth century. As Cherniavsky noted, Holy Rus thus had an initially "anti-tsarist" rhetorical function.[16] By the early seventeenth century, in the aftermath of the Time of Troubles,[17] the epithet had entered Russia's popular vocabulary, and it shows up in a wide range of manuscripts documenting contemporary folk songs and legends. From this body of evidence Cherniavsky concludes once again that it lacked a conscious attachment to the state. "Russia could be 'Holy Russia,'" he concluded, "whether there was a tsar or not." In the early nineteenth century, educated Russians reintroduced the epithet, ultimately making it "a commonplace in all kinds of writing."[18] In the vocabulary of Slavophiles like Constantine Aksakov, it became indispensable in debating the Russian Empire's so-called accursed questions.[19]

With the expansion of the Church's ecclesiastical press after the Great Reforms, its presence became increasingly common on the pages of missionary publications and religious journals. Within this body of official Church literature, Holy Rus was usually defined imprecisely. This may explain why historians have never undertaken a study of its meaning in a clerical context. In all cases of which I am familiar, the ecclesiastical writers who used it did so primarily to describe a primeval national community that was distinct from the empire as such. In this it resembled what Anthony Smith has called an "ethnic core." It offered a "tradition of images, cults, customs, rites and artifacts" that constituted the most integral part of the nation.[20] As the ethnic core of modern Russia, Holy Rus could serve as an instrument to bring about national unity. What is more, the Church claimed with some justification that this complex of images, rituals, and events was her special possession. The content of the ethnic core of Holy Rus was located in a historical past, medieval Rus, that had been largely shaped by the Orthodox Church.

One influential missionary priest who made an effort to define Holy Rus was the future new martyr John Vostorgov (1864–1918). He claimed that Holy Rus was much more than a complex of ethnic symbols. The standard by which one belonged to the Russian nation was what he and other clerical Orthodox patriots called the "national faith."[21] This standard excluded all members of non-Christian religions (such as Muslims), as well as any Russians who adhered to heterodox Christian confessions (such as Baptists) or religious sects (such as Dukhobors).[22] Admittedly, the case of Russian Old Belief was more complex. As schismatics who had broken from the Church in the seventeenth century, Old Believers were in one sense necessarily excluded from a national community that was defined by the Church. However, their adherence to a native form of Orthodoxy located in the medieval past presented a challenge to the standard of the national faith. With the important exception of Old Belief, then, Vostorgov's Orthodox patriotic argument could be used by the Church to appeal to the empire's remaining heterodox and non-Christian religious bodies. For while Holy Rus was exclusively defined by the national faith, he claimed, it possessed a missionary character that acted as a leaven among the other peoples of the empire. It has been set apart from these other peoples and "chosen to preserve and to disseminate the uncorrupted faith" among them. By first preserving and then disseminating the national faith throughout Russia, Holy Rus could bring spiritual as well as cultural unity to her. In consideration of this goal, it was possible to claim that the very destiny of modern Russia was Holy Rus. In Vostorgov's words, "Russia . . . is Holy Rus" (*Rossiia . . . est sviataia Rus*).[23]

There was, of course, an important difference contained in the words *Russia* and *Rus*, and patriotic Church leaders were conscious of it. The first signified the multinational and multireligious empire that arose in the sixteenth century and was finally consolidated under the secularized state system of Peter the Great during the eighteenth century. The second was associated with the medieval state, which possessed considerably more homogeneity in its culture and, most importantly, its religious makeup. Clerical Orthodox patriots were some of the first cultural figures in modern Russia to exploit the semantic differences between the two words. The Slavophiles, to be sure, had also disseminated an ideal of medieval Rus, but their romantic philosophical idiom limited its circulation to relatively confined intellectual circles.[24] With their position of social influence, on the other hand, Church leaders were able to disseminate their model of the nation to a much wider popular audience. Since the community associated with the word *Russia* was in their opinion threatened by secularization and religious apostasy, they began extensively to employ the word *Rus* to form a more Orthodox community.

This was true especially when they spoke of Holy Rus, for which Rus by itself simply served as an abbreviation. Unlike lay poets and writers who had used the epithet in the past, in ecclesiastical discourse Holy Rus signified a community that was measurable according to the ecclesial standards of the canonical Orthodox Church alone. As such, it was not a romantic "myth" describing the people's alienation from the state and the intelligentsia, as Cherniavsky argued. [25] It was rather a model, or "icon," of what the Russian people themselves must become. It was an instrument for shaping the increasingly multireligious and secularized empire into a national community that would better serve the missionary goals of the Church.

Clerical Orthodox patriots mobilized a movement to disseminate their model of Holy Rus to a broad audience during the decades following the Great Reforms. This was possible for several reasons. First, as the leadership of a large ecclesial community, the clergy possessed considerable experience in the matter of monitoring and shaping collective self-consciousness. They drew from centuries of apologetical and missionary practice to guide their activities. They also had considerable administrative resources at their disposal. The Great Reforms, while in many ways disappointing to the clergy, had helped to create the largest missionary infrastructure in the history of the Orthodox Church. This and the expansion of the ecclesiastical press offered a specialized medium through which to address the public. Furthermore, a growing percentage of the higher clergy were able to obtain an advanced education and to follow developments among secular intellectuals. While virtually all were dismayed by the rise of contemporary European nationalism, they hoped that national self-consciousness could be assimilated to ecclesial self-consciousness and thus make the latter stronger in the modern world. Finally, the synodal system of Church government, which often served as an instrument of state interference in Church affairs, could at the same time be utilized to organize empire-wide public commemorations.

In 1888 the first such commemoration was organized to honor the nine-hundred-year anniversary of Russia's baptism. In his monumental study of tsarist political culture, Richard Wortman has described this event as the "most important" religious celebration of the late imperial period.[26] At its center was a baptism festival held in the "mother city" of medieval Rus, Kiev. The year 1888 is a convenient date by which to mark the emergence of Orthodox patriotism within the Church. Due to the success of the baptism festival, other public commemorations of Holy Rus were staged in subsequent years, honoring such medieval figures as St Sergius (d. 1392) and Patriarch Germogen (r. 1606–1612).

Historians of modern Russia have customarily dismissed the Orthodox clergy as an isolated estate lacking vital connections with the secular public. By examining the organization and outcome of such public commemorations, this book will demonstrate that, on the contrary, the Orthodox clergy established an ever stronger connection with Russian culture during the decades before the Revolution of 1917.

The second issue addressed by this study is the relationship between the Orthodox Church and modern nationalism. Traditionally, historians have tended to diminish the role of Christianity in forming modern national communities, seeing the confessional concerns of priests as obstacles to nation-building. At best, the clergy are assigned a minor role as an agent of something Eric Hobsbawm calls "proto-nationalism."[27] This argument, while good for explaining the historically unprecedented influence of nationalism within modern secular societies, is frequently wedded to the claim that secularization is an inevitable process in modern history and that the growth of national self-consciousness serves to consolidate this process. This "secularization thesis," finding its origins in the sociological studies of Emile Durkheim, has been challenged by a growing number of historical and sociological inquiries.[28] Nevertheless, it continues to influence conclusions about the role of religion in the emergence of modern European nationalism. Hans Kohn's classic *The Idea of Nationalism,* for instance, placed considerable emphasis on the role of secularization during and after the French Revolution.[29] Benedict Anderson's more recent account of modern nationalism is also based on the presupposition that a process of secularization was necessary before the "imagined community" of the nation was possible.[30] Perhaps the strongest argument that nationalism superseded religion in a modern secularized world was Carlton Hayes's study, *Nationalism: A Religion.* It argued that nationalism came to fill a "religious void" created by the processes of the Enlightenment and industrialization.[31] An interesting exception to the traditional diminution of the Church's role is Salo Baron's *Modern Nationalism and Religion,* a work that devoted an entire chapter to the role of Orthodoxy in shaping modern Russian nationalism.[32] In more recent years, a small number of monographs have also begun to explore the way that the Roman Catholic Church of France and Poland contributed to the rise of nationalism.[33] The role of the Orthodox clergy in Russia, however, has been ignored.

Important distinctions should be borne in mind, however, when comparing Russian Orthodox patriotism to other cases of European nationalism. First, the Church never accepted many of the ideals proclaimed by nationalists in the West. They explicitly attacked Western nationalism as an aberration of true national feeling because of its tendency to place secular culture and racial descent higher than the ideals of the universal Church. They were aware, for instance, that nationalism arose in countries such as revolutionary France where secularization had advanced the furthest. Just as importantly, Russia's conservative clergy were deeply uncomfortable in courting the sort of popular political forces that played a role in nationalist mobilization in the West. While the October Manifesto of 1905 led some to join nationalistic political unions such as the Union of the Russian People, a deep distrust of mass politics continued to mark Church activities up until the collapse of the tsarist regime. The result was that the clergy produced an ideal of the nation that lacked the democratic character of nationalism in western Europe. For this reason, clerical Orthodox patriotism offers an important alternative case study for the analysis of nation-building in modern Europe.

In fact, the Church's model of the nation was directed in part toward upholding the autocracy. And there was a simple reason for this. The tsar provided the official Church with substantial financial subsidies and, until the Paschal Edict on religious toleration in 1905, protected it with the laws of the empire by banning apostasy and the missionary activities of both heterodox and non-Christian religious bodies. As a result, Holy Rus came to embody an ideal of the tsar as an apostle-like leader. The title Equal-to-the-Apostles (*ravnoapostolnyi*) was applied by the Church to the figures St Constantine (r. 312–337) and St Vladimir (r. 980–1015) because each had used his political power as ruler to form an Orthodox state and to advance the Orthodox mission within it. As Church leaders elaborated their ideals of the Russian nation, they emphasized the need for a tsar who would rule according to these examples. When clerical Orthodox patriotism emerged after 1881, they thought they had this in the person of Alexander III (r. 1881–1894), who contributed much to the expansion of the mission. The accession of Nicholas II, who was widely known for his piety, only reinforced this commitment. When Nicholas was forced by political necessity to partially surrender legal protection of the Church in 1905, however, the ideal of the apostle-like tsar became increasingly dissonant. This was complicated further by the rise of nationalistic political unions, which attracted the support of frustrated missionary leaders. But while the ranks of the nationalists were joined by conservative Church leaders, the latter nevertheless continued to insist that the political influence of the Russian nation within the empire be subordinated to and ultimately serve the missionary goals of the Church.

For the most part, Church leaders who embraced Holy Rus as a model of nationality came to draw an explicit distinction between "nationalism" (*natsionalizm*) and "Orthodox patriotism" (*pravoslavnyi patriotizm*). Only the latter, Archbishop Antony (Khrapovitsky) of Volynia claimed, assigned primary loyalty to the universal Church. It was intended to strengthen a "national self-consciousness" (*natsionalnoe samosoznanie*) conditioned first of all by "ecclesial self-consciousness" (*tserkovnost*). In light of this and the Church's putative commitment to the universal faith, I have therefore decided to use the phrase "Orthodox patriotism" instead of "nationalism" to describe the Church's activities throughout most of this study.

Finally, the history of clerical Orthodox patriotism in late imperial Russia offers an interesting search for an alternative to the ideology of nationalism.

While the movement was overcome by a war caused by nationalism, only to be suppressed by a revolution motivated by socialism, it explored a way for Orthodox Russians to enter the world of modern ideology while retaining their traditional religious self-consciousness. Yet it forever suffered from a weakness embodied in the tension between Church universalism and national particularism. The chapters that follow record a difficult, sometimes inconsistent, and even painful effort to fuse these two elements. Much of the tension grew from the fact that a high valuation of ethnic nationality represented an innovation in the history of the Church. As I have noted, the New Testament offered a formidable barrier against this tendency. Clerical Orthodox patriots, however, while aware of the aforementioned universalistic passages in Matthew and Colossians, began to interpret Scripture in a very particularistic spirit. In their hands, even Jesus Himself could be depicted as a patriot devoted to the unity and interests of His own national community. For while it may be true that He never promoted national self-consciousness explicitly, one ecclesiastical writer reflected that in reading the Gospels attentively we see that the Lord Jesus Christ sincerely loved His native fatherland and His people. In His life he showed all of His followers the example of true patriotism.

Certain passages in the Gospels were said to reveal this especially. By ordering the disciples "do not go into the way of the Gentiles" early in His ministry (Matt 10:5), for instance, Jesus manifested an ideal model of self-consciousness that was both ecclesial and national. What is more, in stating that He was sent "only to the lost sheep of the house of Israel" (Matt 15:24), He showed that this self-consciousness produced a loyalty to one national community before all others. As a result of such conclusions, the universalistic principle was diminished to such an extent that nationality began to appear to some Church leaders as an element of Christian teaching. Consequently, a New Testament passage expressing Jesus's devotion to universality, such as the blessing of the Samaritan woman by the well (John 4:26), could be dismissed as an "exception."[34]

Patriotic exegesis of the New Testament, which frequently appeared in the religious journals of the period, revealed the rise of clerical Orthodox patriotism. Yet it did not serve as its cause. In the end, such works offered little more than highly selective passages (and often no more than a clause) to support an argument that had clearly been formulated in advance. In fact, the innovation of Orthodox patriotism arose out of forces that were for the most part unique to the often tortured circumstances of late imperial Russia.

The chapters contained in Part I of this book address these forces. First and most generally, Russian theological tradition provided a rich soil for the flowering of national self-consciousness. Claims about a Holy Russian land, about a unique status for the Russian Church within the larger universal Church, and about a God-chosen national destiny were only possible because they had roots in the Church's intellectual heritage. Nevertheless, theological traditions that supported such claims could not spawn national self-consciousness by themselves.

The most immediate condition for the rise of clerical Orthodox patriotism was the historically unprecedented scope of the Russian Church's missionary movement, which created an environment in which conservative Church leaders were compelled to address secular culture and adapt their message to it. Many became familiar with the Slavophile tradition and sympathized with conservative models of the nation.

Traditional Russian religious culture itself also offered conditions under which nationality could flourish. Here the example of Old Testament Israel played a particularly significant role. Widely disseminated through liturgy, homiletics, and icons of such figures as the Archangel Michael, the image of ancient Israel offered a biblical prototype for Holy Rus, its national faith, and its apostle-like ruler. Thus it gained a central and recurring presence in the clergy's model of the nation. National festivals and patriotic sermons employed Old Testament symbols extensively, and some Church leaders went so far as to claim that modern Russia herself was a "new Israel."

No sooner did clerical Orthodox patriots mobilize, however, than they began to encounter the limitations that were inherent in any attempt to fuse Church and nation. These limitations, which seemed relatively minor during the baptism festival of 1888, resulted in greater and greater inconsistencies after 1905.

The chapters of Part II narrate this process. Three forces external to but closely related with the movement served to reveal its inconsistencies. First, Nicholas II severely undermined the clergy's model of Holy Rus when he issued the Paschal Edict on religious toleration in 1905. The edict declared that apostasy from the official Church would no longer be punishable by the state and that all nonofficial religious bodies were free to practice their faith and even to disseminate it among the Orthodox faithful. Now Old Believers were free to claim openly that their religious community preserved the "national faith" in greater purity than the official Church. The Paschal Edict also suggested that an apostle-like tsar had ceased to be a viable element for the nation.

The second external force was ethnic nationalism. As dismayed Church leaders tried to respond to the Paschal Edict, they were confronted by an onslaught of secularization from left-wing parties that had arisen in the State Duma as a result of the October Manifesto of 1905. In a number of cases their response was to embrace political parties on the extreme right that claimed to offer protection to the official Church. "Patriotic unions" such as the Union of the Russian People, or Black Hundreds, attracted conservative Church leaders by their ability to blend ethnic nationalism with the rhetoric of clerical Orthodox patriotism. Like the loss of the apostle-like tsar, however, the lure of nationalism revealed the inconsistencies of Orthodox patriotism by undermining its commitment to the universal Church.

Inconsistencies were also revealed by leading intellectuals who were actually sympathetic to the clergy's model of Holy Rus. Lay Orthodox patriots such as Vladimir Soloviev, Mikhail Nesterov, and Sergei Bulgakov claimed in their works that Holy Rus was indeed the destiny of Russia, and even placed the national faith at its center. Their model of the nation, however, was one in which an official Church and an apostle-like tsar were largely absent.

In the difficult years before the Russian Revolution, the increasingly reactionary proponents of clerical Orthodox patriotism did not resolve the inconsistencies revealed by the tsar, the nationalists, or sympathetic lay intellectuals. In fact, their growing numbers after 1905 only served to imbed these inconsistencies more deeply within the activities of the Church. In 1913 the movement culminated when Patriarch Germogen was canonized as a national saint. The festival that accompanied the canonization was in some ways a triumph of clerical efforts to promote national self-consciousness. Never before had so many Church leaders been so articulate in advancing the claims of Orthodox patriotism. Yet it also exposed the movement's limitations. On the eve of the war and revolution that would, for most of the twentieth century, suspend the making of Holy Russia, the tensions between Church universalism and national particularism that had characterized clerical Orthodox patriotism for the past generation manifested themselves more than ever. In fact, the Germogen festival and its aftermath revealed that these tensions were deep indeed, and perhaps irresolvable.

PART I

CULTIVATING HOLY RUSSIA

CHAPTER 1

―✦―

Russia's Faithful Remnant

Modern Orthodox patriotism entered the life of the Russian Church in 1888 when the clergy organized a commemoration of the baptism of medieval Rus. This nine-hundred-year anniversary celebration was the first time in the history of the Church that the baptism of 988 was honored as an event in itself.[1] It was also the first time the clergy organized an "all-Russian," or national, commemoration of any kind. As such it would establish a precedent for subsequent national commemorations such as those honoring St Sergius (d. 1392) in 1892, St Seraphim (d. 1833) in 1892, and St Germogen (d. 1612) in 1913. Its greatest significance, however, was revealed in a festival held in the city of Kiev. In addition to drawing over twenty thousand pilgrims and official celebrants, the baptism festival aroused considerable interest among the educated public and demonstrated that the Church had emerged from the Great Reforms as a vital force in Russia's modern culture. Eager to arrest the growth of secularization and apostasy in a missionary age, Church leaders used the baptism festival to promote the formation of a national community defined by the symbols and rituals of Orthodoxy.

RECOVERING A USABLE PAST

The historical baptism had been conducted nine hundred years earlier on the banks of the Dnieper River, where Grand Prince Vladimir (r. 980–1015) ordered his people to accept the Orthodox faith from Byzantine churchmen. Vladimir established the Orthodox faith as the official faith of his realm and placed the state in the service of protecting it. He also ordered that the pagan idols of Perun, which had formerly been worshiped by the Russians, be hurled into the river.

The consequences of this act in the shaping of Russian national identity were enormous, as Nicholas Riasanovsky has pointed out in his recent historical survey of the subject.[2] Subsequent decades and centuries witnessed the flowering of a distinctively Russian form of Orthodox Christianity. A native clergy was established, native holy places such as Kiev's Pecherskaia Lavra were built, and a distinctively native style of church architecture and icon painting emerged. As the Orthodox faith was consolidated, the civilization of medieval Rus was strengthened and finally centralized by the Muscovite state. The importance of the baptism in giving rise to this national experience had of course long been acknowledged, yet even during the nineteenth century such great lay historians as Nicholas Karamzin (1766–1826) and Sergei Soloviev (1820–1879) had placed primary emphasis on the activity of the state and the creation of the empire when describing the rise of Russian national strength.[3] Against this statist view of the nation, Church leaders after the Great Reforms began to advance an ecclesiastical one. For them, the baptism demonstrated that it was ultimately the Orthodox faith that established the historical destiny of Russia, indelibly shaping her identity.

These clerical Orthodox patriots argued that the event embodied two central national ideals. First, it revealed a "national faith" (*natsionalnaia vera*). Medieval Rus, they argued, had assimilated the universal faith of Orthodoxy to a particular form of Russian national life at the moment of the Kievan baptism, and this assimilation had produced the Church customs and Church art that later served as the content of Russia's national character. Because this national faith was a manifestation of the universal faith, however, it was not exclusive to the nation that bore it. Along with the baptism, the nation received an "ecumenical," or universal, calling to disseminate its spiritual treasure to the other peoples and tribes in the world.

The second ideal embodied in the baptismal event was that of an apostle-like ruler. Grand Prince Vladimir, canonized by the Church with the title "Equal-to-the-Apostles," had himself fulfilled the national calling by promoting its missionary destiny. He also served as a prototype for subsequent grand princes and tsars, all of whom protected the national faith through apostle-like statecraft. This was the chief function of the ruler, and he occupied a legitimate place in the national life to the extent that he preserved and disseminated the national faith. The twin ideals of a national faith and an apostle-like tsar emerged during the baptism festival of 1888 and continued to dominate clerical Orthodox patriotism until the Revolution.

Both ideals, then, were part of a "usable past" that served the goals of the clergy. Clerical Orthodox patriots were not, of course, the only cultural leaders in nineteenth-century Europe to search the past for national ideals that could be used as instruments of increased social influence. The formation of national communities in Russia and elsewhere would have been impossible without a collective imagination, and many historians of European national-ism have shown that this imagination was largely shaped by carefully dis-seminated narratives of history. An effective way of spreading such narratives was to organize public commemorations of symbolic events that featured the idealized collective experience. Such commemorations enabled cultural lead-ers to select the content of the past and, by doing so, to inscribe meaning upon it. They were, as John Gillis has noted, "largely for, but not of, the people."[4]

National commemorations gained importance in Russian political life during the Great Reforms. As early as 1862, for instance, the state organized a one-thousand-year anniversary commemoration to honor the founding of the Rurik Dynasty. Richard Wortman describes the monument erected in Novgorod for the event as a "representation of the elusive word *nation* that would encompass groups outside the state and suggest the unity of mon-archy and people."[5] As the state struggled to harness national feeling, the public also turned to commemorative activities. In 1885 a commemoration was organized by the St Petersburg Slavic Benevolent Society, a public body representing pan-Slavic opinion, to honor the one-thousand-year anniver-sary of the mission of Saints Cyril and Methodius. The Orthodox clergy fol-lowed these precedents with interest and used them as models for their own national commemoration in 1888.

By directing historical memory toward the baptism, the clergy believed they could compete with secular and heterodox forces in society to recover some of the influence they had lost in modern times. But for them the recov-ery of a usable past was not the same thing as the invention of that past.[6] As Anthony Smith has shown, the "appropriation of antiquity" often represents more than an instrument to increase the influence of elites. It also provides a model of nationality that can be disseminated among the masses by its ability to refer to real symbols, artifacts, and legends that retain a popular resonance.[7] This point has considerable importance for any study of the Orthodox Church in nineteenth-century Russia. With considerable justification, the clergy believed that the symbolism of Orthodox patriotism introduced in 1888 was recognizable to contemporaries. In their minds, a sort of "faithful remnant" of what they considered the authentic Russian nation, Holy Rus, continued to exist in modern Russia. This remnant, like that of ancient Israel in times of national peril, would serve as the basis for the making of a Holy Russia.[8]

THE IDEALS OF CLERICAL ORTHODOX PATRIOTISM

In 1888 the Holy Synod included two prelates who particularly influenced the emergence of clerical Orthodox patriotism. These were Archbishop Nikanor

(Brovkovich) (1827–1890) of Kherson and Metropolitan Platon (Gorodetskii) (1803–1891) of Kiev. Each was a strong supporter of the spiritual mission after the Great Reforms and to a significant extent had defined his hierarchical ministry within it. Both had experience working with sectarianism and Old Belief, and both were later regarded by conservative clerical admirers as model patriots.[9] After their deaths in the early 1890s, they were remembered as pioneers in harnessing nationality to serve the mission. One of Platon's biographers, for instance, stated that his early missionary work among Baltic Lutherans had been strengthened by efforts to serve as a "representative of Russian nationality."[10] Likewise, Nikanor was praised for "his complete devotion to all truly Russian and truly Orthodox people" when conducting missionary activities.[11] By supporting the organization of Russia's first baptism commemoration in 1888, Nikanor and Platon hoped to forge a national self-consciousness that would strengthen Orthodox ecclesial self-consciousness.

The timing was auspicious, for the year 1887 had witnessed the gathering of the first All-Russian Missionary Congress in Moscow, and in 1888 itself the Church began publication of its leading ecclesiastical organ, *Tserkovnyia vedomosti (Church News)*. Archbishop Nikanor, writing in the journal's first issues, indicated what he and other prelates intended the upcoming commemoration to signify. His three-part article opened with a discussion of the culturally and religiously homogenous people of ancient Israel as an example of what he called "Holy Rus." God Himself had shaped the national self-consciousness of Israel, he stated, "to protect her from intermixing with other peoples" and to ensure that "her faith would not in turn be intermixed." Following the example of ancient Israel, Nikanor claimed, "patriotism" became a "natural and holy duty" for modern Russians, who had been and continued to be surrounded by alien peoples with "alien faiths." Thus, more than any other source, the Orthodox Church should be the object of patriotic feeling for Russians, because it alone provided the confessional faith that created the "integrity of national self-consciousness." Nikanor did not leave the matter of patriotism with the national faith alone, however, but assigned considerable importance to the state. Its laws protecting Orthodoxy as the national faith and its activities in restricting alien faiths such as Roman Catholicism and Protestantism had been invaluable. As a result, his model of the nation was shaped to include a tsar as faithful as King David or, more recently in the history of God's chosen peoples, St Vladimir Equal-to-the-Apostles. For him, Holy Rus was inconceivable without a national faith and an apostle-like tsar.[12]

These two ideals had limited precedents in the history of the Church. In Russia and other states of Europe, the ruler historically had been given responsibility for protecting the faith, but only in the East were there hagiographical models for an apostle-like propagation of that faith. More innovative was the concept of a national faith. Christianity by definition was universal, and assigning a particular form of Christianity to one national community presented great theological difficulties. According to St Paul's assertion that "there is neither Greek nor Jew," the Orthodox Church considered herself a multinational community.[13] Historically, it had upheld this idea as an ecclesiological axiom.

The universalistic identity of traditional Christianity was elaborated in the metaphor of the "new Israel." The old Israel of the Old Testament had been exclusive to a single nation, but the new Israel of the New Testament was, following Christ's command, to "make disciples of all nations," universal in scope. As I will show, however, the universalistic principle upon which the new Israel metaphor rested could be modified by the emphasis Russia's patriotic clergy placed on a national faith and an apostle-like tsar. For some of the Church leaders who organized the baptism festival of 1888, in fact, the historical entrance of medieval Rus into the universal Church signaled a revival of national exclusivity within the new Israel. A few even suggested that Holy Rus had acquired an exclusive status as the new Israel itself.

Archbishop Nikanor used the metaphor in this way during an address delivered in Odessa while the festival occurred in Kiev. Telling his audience that the commemoration offered a unique opportunity for recovering a healthy collective "self-consciousness" (*samosoznanie*), he conveyed a historical narrative of Old Testament Israel that culminated, significantly, in Kiev. It was here in 988, he argued, that God's chosen people had finally been reconstituted as a Christian national community. Its status, he emphasized, was still borne by those Russians who in modern times remembered, as a kind of faithful remnant, their national roots. "Who is the new Israel at present?" he asked rhetorically. "Among a host of heterodox peoples, it is the Orthodox Christian Russian people. We are the new Israel."[14]

Such an exclamation conformed well with efforts to elaborate the ideals of a national faith and an apostle-like tsar. Even more, the claim that Russia was a national community comparable to ancient Israel was, as we shall see, a leitmotif in a festival that sought to fuse nationality and ecclesiality in a single model of community.

GATHERING THE FAITHFUL REMNANT

The process through which the commemoration was organized reveals how the Church sought to introduce its model of the nation into contemporary culture. The earliest steps were taken in 1886 by the Holy Synod, which had been petitioned by the St Petersburg Slavic Benevolent Society to consider the idea of honoring the upcoming nine-hundred-year anniversary of the baptism. The society, inspired by its recent success in commemorating the Cyril-Methodian anniversary in 1885, believed that a public commemoration honoring Russia's entrance into the spiritual community of southern Europe would offer another occasion for promoting a pan-Slavic model of nationality. The hierarchs who served in the Synod, however, realized that such a commemoration could also offer the Church an excellent opportunity for public leadership.

In fact, their ultimate decision to choose Kiev as the main commemorative site was made partly because they regarded the lay leadership of the society, based in the imperial capital, as a potential rival for cultural influence. Their fears were confirmed later by Chief Procurator[15] Constantine Pobedonostsev (1827–1907), who complained in a letter that during the festival Church organizers such as Metropolitan Platon had found themselves in competition with members of the society, such as the volatile Count Ignatiev, who had come to Kiev to deliver pan-Slavic addresses.[16] Remote from modern St Petersburg, Kiev, with its revered holy places, offered an explicitly medieval image of the national topography.

It also offered an opportunity for contesting the empire's ethnic and religious pluralism. The city, after all, featured large communities of Roman Catholic Polish noblemen and Jewish merchants.[17] It was also a focal point for growing Ukrainian national self-consciousness, which itself found much about the medieval Orthodox past to celebrate but in an explicitly anti-Muscovite form. Still in its infancy, Ukrainian nationalism did not formulate an alternative to the clergy's model of Holy Rus in 1888; however, as we will see, one of the empire's "Orthodox patriotic others," the Old Believers, would.[18]

Organizers of the festival hoped that the monumental St Vladimir Cathedral being built in the city might be completed in time for the celebration and serve as a focal point.[19] Decorated with icons by artists of the Russian national school such as Victor Vasnetsov (1848–1926) and Mikhail Nesterov (1862–1942), the cathedral would announce the rebirth of Holy Rus in modern Russia.[20]

Thus there was little debate among the Synod's members about where to hold the festival when they attached their signatures to the bottom of the protocol ordering the commemoration.[21] The protocol called upon "all faithful children of the Russian Church" to observe the national commemoration. In accordance with this invitation, the increasingly literate and educated public entered the celebration and even participated partly in its organization. This was especially true in St Petersburg, where the Slavic Benevolent Society was eager to assert its leadership. The society was the empire's largest public association for promoting self-consciousness of Russia's ethnic ties to European Slavdom, and in the past it had served as a center for pan-Slavic agitation.[22] Snubbed by the Synod's monopolization of the main celebration, it used the capital's anniversary ceremonies in part to disseminate its own model of the nation. Its most significant activity toward this end was a series of addresses by society members during the week when the Church's festival was taking place in Kiev. While these addresses generally conformed to the Synod's protocol by directing attention toward the Orthodox faith, they also tended, significantly, to promote the ideals of secular Russian nationalism and pan-Slavism. Such at least was the observation of local newspapers.[23]

Nevertheless, through its participation in the commemoration, the society also came to promote the goals of clerical Orthodox patriotism. An example is its decision to commission a saint's life of Vladimir from a Church historian at the Kiev Spiritual Academy, Ivan Malyshevskii.[24] The society ultimately produced 350,000 copies of this work, which was later regarded as one of the year's most noteworthy publications and was largely shaped by the Church's patriotic vision. Malyshevskii opened with a narrative describing the transition of God's chosen people from ancient Israel to the new Israel. The universal Church, he claimed, though by definition not limited to a particular nationality, was nevertheless centered upon the experiences of particular peoples. History had shown this. The first dominant Orthodox nation had been the Greeks after the baptism of St Constantine Equal-to-the-Apostles. Then came Holy Rus, which, having rejected paganism after the baptism of St Vladimir Equal-to-the-Apostles, became the universal Church's new eschatological center. To help fellow Russians grasp the import of their nation's destiny, the author called on them publicly to celebrate the baptism anniversary "in all corners of the Holy Russian land."[25] The publication of Malyshevskii's life was one of several activities by the society that served the goals of clerical Orthodox patriotism. Other publications were also issued, and members played an active role in scheduling the capital's religious ceremonies.[26]

In Kiev, Church organizers were also successful in mobilizing the public behind their program.[27] The university and theological academy played important roles, rallying their faculties and organizing public exhibits that informed visitors about the Russian Church and its medieval past. A group of professors from the academy organized and published a symposium discussing various issues surrounding the baptism event that was designed for broad public distribution.[28] The most active public body was the city's municipal government. Since the passage of a municipal statute in 1870, Russia's cities had gained greater self-administration, and though this freedom began to wane in the 1880s, city governments such as Kiev's had come to enjoy a limited sphere of public initiative in which to direct local affairs.[29] The announcement by the Synod that Kiev would be the center of the 1888 baptism celebration appears to have met an enthusiastic response among the elites who constituted the Kiev city duma. The body subsequently took many responsibilities for managing the festival and raised funds to cover some of the costs.[30] It also established a special "festival commission" that was designed to serve a variety of important functions.[31]

The many telegrams received by the office of the festival's nominal overseer, Metropolitan Platon, similarly suggest a high level of public interest. In all, 270 of these telegrams were received and later printed by the Kiev Theological Academy.[32] Often they were simple and brief and did not represent more than a handful of sympathizers. In some cases, though, they registered a sizable response. One of many telegrams from Moscow, for instance, was issued from several public organizations representing different social estates and claimed over twenty thousand signatures.[33] The telegrams sent to support the festival frequently included rhetorical constructions of clerical Orthodox patriotism, such as "the baptism of the Russian people" and "Holy Rus." What such expressions meant exactly in the minds of the professors, municipal authorities, and lawyers who issued them is difficult to determine. But read in the context of 1888, they can be taken as a sign of support for the same sentiments being elaborated in more detail by festival participants.

For these participants, Kiev became a "Russian Jerusalem," the center of pilgrimage and worship that expressed a national faith.[34] From places throughout the empire and even abroad, pilgrims traveled to the holy city to take part in the religious ceremonies being conducted among its "holy objects" (*sviatyni*)—its monasteries, churches, shrines, icons, and relics. In addition to a large percentage of the local townspeople, over twenty thousand pilgrims made the trek.[35] While this figure is rather modest in comparison with later Church festivals such as the canonization of Seraphim of Sarov in 1903 (which attracted more than one hundred thousand pilgrims), it was still considerable in an age unaccustomed to rail travel.[36] In fact, the level of attendance quickly exhausted the city's ability to provide shelter. As hotels overflowed, spare rooms in school dormitories were opened and Kievans were compelled to offer their homes and apartments as accommodations. Along with the common pilgrims, official delegations from important cities attended. Moscow, Murmansk, Odessa, Minsk, Kazan, and many others sent representatives to deliver greetings and to join in prayers for the nation. A notable delegation also came from St Petersburg headed by Pobedonostsev himself.

Finally, a host of foreigners were on hand to witness the gathering, having journeyed from both the Orthodox East and the non-Orthodox West. A clerical source listed no fewer than fourteen Orthodox prelates from eastern European lands, including Serbia, Montenegro, Bulgaria, and Romania.[37] A group of Orthodox priests even traveled from Japan. Others who could not make the journeys from cities such as Jerusalem, Antioch, Venice, and Karlsbad simply sent telegrams. From the non-Orthodox world, the most prominent delegation was a group of priests representing the Church of England, who came bearing the greetings of Archbishop Edward of Canterbury.[38]

The effect of this global attention was intoxicating for festival participants. A message of greetings sent from the recently converted Japanese Orthodox captured the mood. Bearing names such as Sergei Suzuki, Ignatii Mukoyama, and Foma Ono, it testified to what was then a highly successful missionary effort by Russian Bishop Nicholas (Kasatkin) (1836–1912) in Japan. It also expressed the strange mixture of universality and particularity characteristic of Orthodox patriotism and its image of the new Israel. Russia was disseminating the universal faith, the message read, but only a vital sense of national destiny enabled her to do this. "As spiritual children of the Russian Church," it therefore declared, "we implore St Vladimir and all the Russian Church to represent us before God."[39]

This nationwide and worldwide attention had a powerful effect on those who came to Kiev to attend the festival. A priest delivering a sermon on the eve of the opening ceremonies remarked that Kiev,

> as the mother of all Russian cities, was the place whence the saving light of the Christian faith radiated across all the Russian land. And now, toward the hills of Kiev, the former cradle of Russian Orthodoxy, the sympathetic gazes and feelings of everyone who lives in unbounded Russia are directed. What is more, warm sympathy is conveyed to us from other countries by fellow Orthodox, by members of our race living beyond the boundaries of the fatherland, and even by countries that are not connected to us by the confessional faith.[40]

With the nation assembled and the rest of Christendom looking on, then, Russia's first baptism festival began.

THE BAPTISM FESTIVAL

The baptism festival was strongly influenced by the aims of the spiritual mission, which will receive extensive attention in a later chapter. Here it is enough to note that a year after Russia's first All-Russian Missionary Congress, missionary leaders used the first baptism festival as an opportunity to extend their activities far into the sphere of public life. Many attended the festival itself, and many more sent greetings from various missionary fields in Russia and abroad. Representatives of the "internal mission" (*vnutrenniaia missiia*), which was designed to combat secularization and apostasy, sent greetings along with representatives of the "external mission" (*vneshniaia missiia*), whose purpose was to disseminate Orthodoxy among Muslims and other non-Christians in places such as Central Asia, Siberia, and the Far East. The Brotherhood of St Gurii, the Orthodox Baltic Brotherhood, the head of the Japanese mission, and Church leaders in Jerusalem were a few of the many participants in the celebration. Their patriotic statements encouraged Russians to frame thoughts about national destiny around the goals of the Orthodox mission.

The atmosphere of the festival vividly reflected the symbolism of clerical Orthodox patriotism. Since the festival was subsequently recorded in newspapers, religious journals, and even photographs, it is possible to describe the dramatic ceremonies and addresses in detail.[41] In the course of the busy week, numerous public readings of St Vladimir's life were presented in the hall of the city duma, and exhibits were organized at the university and the theological academy to inform the people about Russia's place in Church history. Each day religious processionals bearing icons and gonfalons (iconographic banners) moved through the streets, and when darkness fell the medieval churches and monasteries resounded with all-night vigils. On July 15, the feast of St Vladimir, the festival culminated in a large religious procession from the city's center to the place on the banks of the Dnieper River where, nine hundred years before, the "baptism of the Russian people" had occurred.

The main procession began from the ancient St Sophia Cathedral (originally modeled upon Constantinople's great cathedral of Hagia Sophia) at the conclusion of a public sermon by Metropolitan Platon about the national faith. As it moved through the streets and squares, past lines of spectators and military bands, it was joined by processions from the city's other holy places. It moved forward in spite of the hard July sun, gathering strength as the clergy and people walked together behind icons and beneath the national flags waving from the city's balconies. Finally, having passed through the city and under the monument to St Vladimir standing in the hills, a concourse numbering several thousand converged on the shores of the Dnieper. There, with icons and gonfalons aloft, they surrounded a chapel that had been built for the event on a pier over the river's water. With the people looking on and the Russian tricolor flapping over a public observation stand nearby, the Orthodox clergy performed the festival's climactic ceremony—the sanctification of what observers called the "Russian Jordan," or Dnieper River.

In addition to its dramatic liturgical imagery, the festival included a series of public addresses during the course of the week that were later published and discussed in the press. Most were delivered within the walls of monasteries and churches whose atmosphere sanctified their patriotic content. The Monastery of the Caves, for example, which repeatedly drew crowds of over eleven thousand, was described in one pilgrims' guidebook as the "richest depository of the fatherland's holy objects" anywhere.[42] Among the holy objects given special prominence were icons of St Vladimir. As addresses were read in the lavra and elsewhere, the "unquenchable icon-lamp" that hung before his image, as well as the pilgrims' tapers burning below it, offered vivid testimony that a living remnant of medieval Rus could still be found in modern Russia.

The message contained in the festival addresses was also designed to promote the goals of clerical Orthodox patriots. One of the most highly attended and widely discussed addresses was the sermon delivered by Metropolitan Platon in St Sophia Cathedral on the feast of St Vladimir.[43] Immediately before leading the religious procession toward the Dnieper, he argued that the faith that had passed through baptism to Rus nine hundred years earlier was the only true faith. This argument in itself was not remarkable and was consistent with Orthodox apologetical tradition. What is noteworthy is the way in which Platon described the universal faith as a particular feature of the Russian people. In his account, Orthodoxy in its Russian setting constituted a national faith.

"Beloved brothers, Orthodox Russians," he began, "presently we are celebrating the greatest event of our fatherland, the baptism of the Russian people into the Christian faith." Since the moment of the baptism event in 988, "Russia, once a barbarian and pagan country, has been made into a holy Christian country. Our ancestors bowed to false gods . . . but we, their descendants, now have the fortune to be, in Christ, the chosen family of God. . . . And this is why we celebrate today." In discussing the national history of "Russia," Platon here purposely used the image of medieval Rus as a challenge to the modern empire. The latter existed, he indicated, only to the extent that it embodied the character of the former. Even the slightest infusion of alien confessions was a grave threat to its national existence. In the course of Russia's recent history, he explained, "there have entered into her different heretics and rationalists, spreading the tares of their teaching. And now there are schismatics, Stundists, and other sects who are disseminating their false wisdom to the Russian people."

Salvation from these threats was a matter not of the universal Church, however, but of a national community united by a single ecclesial faith. In facing its challenge, the collective—which Platon called "the Russian people" (and not simply Orthodox persons living in Russia)—should turn for assistance to the greatest witnesses to its faith, the national saints. "Look at how many of them are associated with our city alone," he exclaimed. "In this very temple the holy martyr Macarius sleeps imperishably, in Mikhailovskii Monastery there reposes the Great Martyr Barbara, and within the lavra itself there is an entire host of God's monastic saints. So how many of them exist in all of Russia?" The proliferation of saints in medieval times was contrasted, however, to the meager number revealed since the time of Peter the Great (r. 1682–1725). A reinvigorated national community, therefore, would mark itself with the canonizations of new national saints.[44]

To conclude his address, Platon asked his listeners to follow the example of the medieval saints and to preserve Orthodoxy from schism and sectarianism. This meant, first of all, remembering the founder of Holy Rus himself. "St Vladimir Equal-to-the-Apostles," he reminded them, "prayed during the baptism of our ancestors in Kiev that the Lord would succor his newly enlightened people and maintain their faith in truth and incorruptibility." Vladimir thus became both a historical symbol and, through his heavenly intercessions, a living source of Russian national unity.[45]

Platon's discussion of saints reveals the way he and others used them as images of Holy Rus (a feature of Orthodox patriotism that will be discussed in greater detail in Chapter 2). Those he discussed had long been canonized by the Church, yet his words invested them with a significance that was expressly patriotic. They are described not as the miracle workers of a local community, not as representatives of the universal Christian community, but as Russian compatriots dwelling in heaven who care for their national community as it struggles to uphold the apostolic faith in the modern world.

Other Orthodox patriots in Kiev elaborated this argument. One was a priest by the name of Zlatoverkhovnikov who delivered a sermon during one of the week's divine liturgies. Standing at the ambo with the iconostasis rising behind him, he drew upon a wealth of Orthodox imagery to shape his audience's national imagination, asking those assembled before him to consider what an Orthodox baptism had yielded in the "history of our fatherland." The event, he claimed, had given Russia the "leaven" of her nationality, which served as the "foundation of our country and her people." The subsequent historical narrative of medieval Rus, he told his listeners, should likewise invoke a feeling of patriotic pride on the anniversary of the baptism. "The soul rejoices," he exclaimed, "the heart pounds and the head bows, for it is you, Holy Rus, whom we honor here today." As with other Church leaders, however, the presence of alien faiths and a secularized educated society induced a feeling of apprehension in the priest about the modern condition of the community. Thus he concluded his address on an eschatological note, appealing to a transcendent Holy Rus in which, he claimed, past generations continue to live with the national saints. "In the future," he asked gravely, "how will you remember us and how will we appear before you?"[46]

An eschatological theme was also presented in a sermon by a priest named Pevnitskii. After highlighting the fact that all of Russia and even the world were represented in Kiev at that moment, he reviewed Russia's role in the history of the universal Church. "In the person of the Russian people," he declared, "all-gracious providence chose a new vessel which it filled in order that the holy deposit of faith should be preserved." God had broken into the course of human history, he asserted, to create a national community to whom the universal faith would be principally entrusted. The people's collective experience thereafter bore witness to its leading role in the eschatological plan. For when the "external strength of the Greek Church weakened," he claimed, "the Lord elevated and strengthened the Russian Orthodox kingdom, and at present all zealots of Orthodoxy gaze upon Russia with manifold hope. She stands before the eyes of all as a fortress, as a strong protector and mighty defender of the holy Orthodox faith." Significantly, in a commemoration to which public bodies representing pan-Slavic opinion contributed, the object of Russia's protection was not the Slavic race and its ethnic culture as such, but the Orthodox faith. For all who confess this faith, he claimed, modern Russia is the center of worldly attention. Despite her vitality, however, she faced a challenge to preserve her faith and therefore her national character. Pevnitskii emphasized the peril of forgetting the national faith passed down from the generation of St Vladimir.[47]

Festival orators drew especially upon Old Testament imagery to describe a national community constituted by religious customs acquired in a primordial historical event. A priest named Favorov, for instance, opened his address by quoting Deut 4, where Moses, confronting Israel in the wilderness before it entered the promised land, warned the people to hold fast to the religious customs and laws being entrusted to the present, primordial generation. In fact, Nikanor had himself alluded to this important Old Testament passage in his new Israel address. The key to ancient Israel's favor in the eyes of God, Favorov now reminded his audience, had been the preservation of its ancestral faith among the surrounding nations. When, under the influence of these peoples, Israel began to slip into apostasy or indifference, prophets were called "to restore historical memory in the chosen people about the days when they were called." Assuming the voice of a national prophet himself, Favorov appealed to those assembled to preserve the testament handed down by Russia's medieval founders and, in short, to honor the memory of 988. "We remember now," he stated, "the first days of our fatherland, moments worthy of eternal memory. God created us to be great and glorious. He enlightened our ancestors with the true faith and by doing so deposited this light in the Russian people. . . . All the past of our fatherland," he concluded, "is an unbroken sequence of testimony about the powerful and gracious activity of the holy Orthodox faith in our national life and destiny. We must always remember and steadfastly preserve the testament of our fathers."[48]

CONSTANTINE POBEDONOSTSEV'S HOLY RUS

While the addresses of the clergy dominated the baptism festival, the voice of the state was also expressed by the Chief Procurator of the Holy Synod. Pobedonostsev supported the festival project and made a point of traveling from St Petersburg to attend. To the extent that he was able, he no doubt hoped to supervise the commemoration. He brought along a number of prominent synodal officials, such as Vladimir Sabler, a supporter of missionary activity and Pobedonostsev's future successor. Pobedonostsev busily attended the main events throughout the week, and his tall, emaciated figure was observed at many of the liturgical services. On the final day, he attended Metropolitan Platon's sermon in St Sophia Cathedral, and when it was finished he marched at the head of the lay contingent of the religious procession (which, according to tradition, was situated behind that of the clergy), toward the Dnieper River. After the blessing of the waters he returned to the city's center to attend the ceremonial banquet organized and hosted by Kiev's merchant association. There, in the hall of columns of the Merchant's Club, he rose before 450 honorable guests to convey his vision of the baptism's significance.

In his address Pobedonostsev paid lip service to the clergy's model of "Holy Rus" but brought considerably more emphasis to the place of the state within it. He began by acknowledging the baptism of 988 as the "greatest event in our nine hundred years of history." From a "coarse and scattered Slavic tribe," he stated, "a great state has sprung up, national consciousness has grown, and the Russian land has been gathered from Kiev to Moscow." The most significant signs of God's favor toward Holy Rus, he said, had been manifested in the centralization of the state and the territorial achievements that resulted. The course of Russian history had been characterized by the incorporation of many Slavic peoples, expansion to the east, and defense against incursions from the west. As a result, the Russian people had been able "to advance to the sea, to become powerful through the force and glory of Russian arms, and to maintain the faith prescribed by our ancestors in unshakable firmness."

Pobedonostsev's state-centered account of the baptism event brought primary attention to the role of the ruler. It was "under the leadership" of "St Vladimir the Faithful Prince," he stated, that the national faith had been established. Here the Church's apostle-like title for Vladimir was conspicuously absent. Considering his responsibility to Emperor Alexander III (r. 1881–1894), it is not surprising that Pobedonostsev laid particular emphasis on the role of the ruler in commemorating the baptism. "A time or place can scarcely be found," he remarked, "when by such peaceful and bloodless means a national leader led his people to the Christian faith." Thus, "the Russian people have believed—and since ancient times have obeyed—their prince and later their sovereign. A united government, growing within us together with the Church, strengthened, gathered, and preserved the state integrity of the Russian land. It created the Russian state [*Rossiiskoe Gosudarstvo*]."

Holy Rus was thus subordinated to a Great Russia. It was in describing the autocratic destiny of Holy Rus that Pobedonostsev chose to close his enthusiastic speech: "Under the sign of a united government and autocracy we came of age. Under this sign we stand, and under it we constitute a single body and preserve a single will. In it we see, in the future, a testament of justice, order, and welfare for our land." With this he raised his glass to offer the banquet's first toast. "Long live our Pious Sovereign!" he cried, "to all of us a Father, an Older Brother, the Supreme Defender on earth of the Orthodox Church—the Emperor Alexander Alexandrovich!" The guests shouted "hurrah" and the orchestra broke out with the imperial hymn, "O God Save the Tsar" (*Bozhe Tsarya khrani*).[49]

CLERICAL ORTHODOX PATRIOTISM
AND OFFICIAL NATIONALITY

Pobedonostsev's baptism address presented the "dynastic vision" of Official Nationality.[50] In describing the baptism event, he placed principal emphasis on the role played by the state. Vladimir for him bore the title of "faithful prince," a proto-autocratic ruler whose beneficent rule was responsible for the Russian people's salvation. What is more, the place of the Orthodox Church, to which the ruler "led" his people, was itself diminished by the importance of fulfilling the state purpose of autocracy. While this model of Holy Rus contained ideals that were not central to clerical Orthodox patriotism, it was not incompatible with the rhetoric of the other festival addresses. The clergy had much in common with Pobedonostsev and Official Nationality in 1888.

Until the momentous Paschal Edict on religious toleration in 1905, the Russian tsar appeared as a champion of the Orthodox mission. Alexander III in particular appeared as the fulfillment of the apostle-like ruler represented by Vladimir, and his reign had been accompanied by eschatological themes. The coronation cantata, for instance, composed by Peter Tchaikovsky with a text by the poet Maikov, concluded with the legendary lines "Two Romes have fallen and the third still stands—/But a fourth shall never be."[51]

The first tsar to wear a beard since the seventeenth century, Alexander III also endorsed the revival of medieval cultural symbols and rhetoric. His support for the baptism celebration was consistent with this stance. Despite his apparent intention to attend the Kiev festival personally, he was detained in the capital by a state visit from Kaiser Wilhelm II. Nevertheless, with his Chief Procurator there to represent him, he was able to declare his sympathy for the event by sending a widely publicized telegram.[52] He also personally participated in the commemorative military parade organized for the capital.[53]

Perhaps more important than Alexander's participation in the baptism celebration itself was his generous support for the contemporary Church. The scope of the late imperial mission was being greatly broadened under his rule, and he and the royal family made a special point of patronizing missionary projects and societies such as the Imperial Orthodox Palestine Society, established in 1882.[54] Early in 1888, readers of the ecclesiastical press learned that the Orthodox Missionary Society, a central institutional body, was establishing a branch in the capital under the tsar's direct patronage.[55] To a degree, then, patriotic Church leaders could agree with Pobedonostsev when he declared in Kiev that the tsar is the "Supreme Defender on earth of the Orthodox Church." They regarded the state as a vital institution of the visible kingdom of God. In the tradition of Vladimir, the present ruler was not only responsible for preserving the faith in a condition of purity but was also regarded as an important instrument of its dissemination.

The Russian ruler's participation in the historical experience of Holy Rus, then, was implicit in the 1888 celebration. After all, there would have been no baptism without the will of Grand Prince Vladimir. Archbishop Macarius of the Don, one of many Church leaders to recognize this fact, hailed Vladimir as the "spiritual father and enlightener of the Russian people."[56] Since the time in which the celebration was organized was dominated by missionary activity, the image of the Grand Prince as an apostle-like ruler was captivating. In the collective memory of the clergy, his status was greater than that as secular head of state. One priest, in fact, went beyond the festival's convention of describing Vladimir as a "second Constantine" and, quoting the saint's chief liturgical hymn, or troparion, declared him to have been a "second Paul."[57]

By making the ruler's image conform to their missionary definition of Holy Rus, however, the clergy acted to imply that conditions existed for his participation in the national experience. They honored the present tsar as a modern Constantine, tracing Alexander's lineage back through Vladimir as the leader of a missionary state. They considered him "one of the most important instruments for the dissemination of the kingdom of God on earth."[58] These eschatological expectations for the modern tsar were reflected particularly well by a group of Petrozavodsk priests who sent a statement of greetings to Kiev that spoke more of Alexander and modern Russia's missionary achievements in Eurasia than of Vladimir and the Church of medieval Rus.[59]

Alexander's publicized patronage of the late imperial mission and his active enforcement of laws against non-Orthodox religions enabled priests to integrate their model of Holy Rus with Official Nationality. The state's commitment to the defense of Orthodoxy against the intrusion of western Christendom, in fact, had been publicly demonstrated on the very eve of the celebration. A western European ecumenical Christian society known as the Evangelical Union had used the baptism anniversary to issue a petition to Alexander asking that he restore freedoms within Russia that had been enjoyed during the period of the Great Reforms but that had lately been curtailed by the new regime.[60] Pobedonostsev was assigned the task of answering the society's request, which he did by publishing an open letter of rebuttal in the ecclesiastical press. The Russian state's protection of Orthodoxy, he stated, expressed itself in the empire's laws that restricted the official faith to the Orthodox Church. These laws were inviolable, and a Western vision of "freedom of religion" was totally incompatible with the ideals of Russia. "Russia cannot permit them [alien confessions] to disseminate propaganda for the tearing-away of her confessional sons to other religious camps. She will not lay down her ancient weapon against them. She says this openly, directly, in her very laws. And in doing so she entrusts herself and the destiny of the kingdom to the highest judgment."[61] There can be little doubt that the Chief Procurator's declaration before the clergy, the public, and even God never to sacrifice the status of the national faith as the single official faith was calculated to take advantage of the national celebration scheduled later in the year. Yet the importance of this statement for the larger history of the Russian Empire is considerable. By issuing it, the regime not only assured the commemoration's organizers that the tsar continued to be an integral part of the nation and an heir to St Vladimir Equal-to-the-Apostles, but it also declared to Russia's Orthodox clergy as a whole that it would never submit to demands for complete religious freedom. As Chapter 5 will show, it would soon be forced to compromise on this principle.

For the moment, though, Holy Rus and Official Nationality appeared as mutually reinforcing models of Russian nationality. Their compatibility can be seen in an address by a priest named Yakov Chepurin, a brief excerpt of which highlights the interconnected ideals of the Church and the state. "Because the Russian Church and her Orthodox faith constitute a purely national faith," he stated, "it is embodied in the flesh and blood of the Russian people and produces their essential and unchangeable characteristics. Without the national faith the Russian people and the Russian state are unthinkable. Orthodoxy, autocracy, and nationality lie at the foundation of the Russian land. With them it grew, developed, became strong, and now exists as that great colossus, the name of which is Holy Rus."[62] Here the patriotic priest managed in a few blunt sentences to encompass the entire range of ideals embedded in the national faith, Official Nationality, and Holy Rus.

THE PUBLIC RESPONSE

While the festival addresses were being delivered in Kiev, Russia's expanding periodical press helped to carry their message to a broader public throughout the empire.[63] Louise McReynolds has shown how newspapers at this time were beginning to make a significant contribution to "the formation of a national self-consciousness" among educated Russians.[64] The fact that many newspapers took a strong interest in the festival indicates that clerical Orthodox patriots were successful in their effort to bring the Church into contemporary debates about nationality. While a survey of these newspapers cannot reach final conclusions about public reception, it can measure the extent to which the Church's definition of Holy Rus circulated as a model of nationality. Significantly, discussion of the festival in the newspapers relied heavily on the content of religious periodicals, whose coverage of the festival naturally tended to be the most extensive.[65] In some cases ecclesiastical sources were simply quoted verbatim, as in the following patriotic statement originally published by the *Tserkovnyi vestnik* (*Church Messenger*) and later reprinted in the dailies *Den* (*Day*), *Novoe vremia* (*New Times*), and *Syn otechestva* (*Son of the Fatherland*): "[The Russian people] have preserved Orthodoxy within their character, they feel pride before all non-Orthodox because of this, and with justification consider themselves to be the greatest Christian people in the world. Pointing to the schism or to sectarianism among particular Russians does not invalidate the fact that the Russian people's collective religiosity is higher than any other."[66] Such descriptions of a national faith challenged by apostasy but still integral to the character of Russia were common in many newspapers during and after the festival, and they echoed the claims made by Church leaders in Kiev. Other newspapers that made such assertions included the *Sankt-Peterburgskiia vedomosti* (*St Petersburg News*), *Peterburgskii listok* (*Petersburgh Chronicle*), *Novosti* (*News*), *Grazhdanin* (*The Citizen*), and *Moskovskiia vedomosti* (*Moscow News*).

Conservative newspapers were the most sympathetic toward clerical Orthodox patriotism. Even when they did not cite ecclesiastical sources, it is possible to discern the influence of the Church's model of Holy Rus. *Sankt-Peterburgskiia vedomosti* discussed the historical meaning of 988 by stating that the Russian land before the baptism was inhabited only by diffuse Slavic tribes and that "the Russian people in reality did not exist."[67] The formation of Russian "self-consciousness," *Moskovskiia vedomosti* agreed, can be dated precisely at the moment the people of Kiev were immersed by Orthodox priests in the Dnieper. Accepting an Orthodox baptism gave these earliest Russians a constituent national culture in the form of Church rituals and customs. If national self-consciousness depended on these traditions, the editors added, the logical conclusion was that "any barriers between Russian patriotism and the Russian Orthodox faith are impossible."[68]

Newspapers also echoed the eschatological imagery of Kiev's clerical orators. Writers situated the baptism within a historical narrative that began in ancient Israel. For them the history of the Russian people, following a trajectory set during medieval times, was the latest stage in God's plan for the salvation of the world. This fact, many claimed, had been true especially since the fall of Constantinople in 1453.[69] The collapse of the only other people in history to manifest the legacy of Israel, argued the newspaper *Den*, left Russia as the only nation to occupy the missionary field. The baptism was thus a reminder that "Russia now sows the seeds of Orthodoxy on earth alone."

Even so, her ambitious "external mission" had "already come to penetrate the womb of high-cultured America, the islands of half-civilized Japan, the lonely tundra of Siberia, and the wild steppes of Central Asia."[70]

While conservative newspapers for the most part were prepared to give Orthodoxy primacy in shaping the character and destiny of Russia, the influence of clerical Orthodox patriotism reached its limits on the pages of newspapers with liberal sympathies. Those such as *Golos* (*The Voice*) and *Birzhevye vedomosti* (*Stock Market News*) were far more reluctant to repeat the claims made in the festival addresses and in general expressed reticence about the festival's significance. *Russkie vedomosti* (*Russian News*) offered a representative account. While acknowledging the importance of religion in shaping national cultures, its editors rejected the claim that each nation possesses an exclusive national faith. Russia is constituted by millions of non-Orthodox, they observed, and to exclude them from the national community would only serve to weaken it. In fact, the editors regarded Orthodoxy as only one of several Christian confessions that played a productive role in shaping the character of nations. Far more important, they argued, was participation in a universal process of civilization. The simple acceptance of Christianity (without an explicitly Orthodox definition) had given medieval Rus the opportunity to enter into "the community of European peoples." Only since the time of Peter had Russia, by embracing secular values such as "European enlightenment and civil society," begun to take advantage of this opportunity. As a result she now served as a "pioneer of European culture in the East" and a "sower of civil society in wild and barbaric lands." Contradicting the historical narrative of Metropolitan Platon and other conservative Church leaders, the editors concluded that "Russian self-consciousness" was shaped mainly by a process of "Europeanization" (*evropeizatsiia*).[71]

The editors of liberal newspapers were not the only Russians to deviate from the model of nationality promoted in Kiev. Lay intellectuals close to the Slavophile tradition welcomed the commemoration of the baptism event but expressed ideals that undermined those of the official Church. One of these lay Orthodox patriots was the philosopher Vladimir Soloviev (1853–1900), whose contribution to Orthodox patriotism will be discussed at length in Chapter 7. He wrote two commemoration articles whose content was sufficiently controversial to necessitate their publication abroad. In them Soloviev elaborated his own definition of Russia's "national faith" but claimed that the role of an apostle-like tsar was secondary to the life of the national community. He even used the commemoration to attack the imperial system of government and the model of Official Nationality that was designed to support it.[72]

Even conservative lay Orthodox patriots at times failed to conform their commemorative statements to the interests of the official Church. In one notable case, zeal for Russia's new Israel status sparked a public debate that threatened to aggravate relations between the Russian clergy and the larger universal Church. General A. A. Kireev (1833–1910), a regular contributor to *Moskovskiia vedomosti* and a guiding light of the St Petersburg Slavic Benevolent Society, proposed to the Russian hierarchy that the baptism commemoration include nothing less than an "ecumenical council" (*vselenskii sobor*), to be convened in Kiev at the very time the festival was taking place.[73] The fact that an ecumenical council had not been convened for over eleven hundred years, and that a great council drawing together representatives of all canonical jurisdictions of the Orthodox Church throughout the world required enormous planning—to say nothing of a mutually relevant purpose—did not dampen Kireev's patriotic enthusiasm. He believed the anniversary of Russia's entrance into the universal Church would be a fitting moment for a revival of one of Byzantium's chief ecclesio-political institutions. For example, he suggested that such a council would be in a position to reconsider the question of Russia's Old Believers, whose devotion to a national faith appeared in his mind to surpass even that of the synodal Orthodox.

Though Kireev's proposal provoked dismay and even embarrassment among many of Russia's clergy (most notably missionaries themselves), a number of secular newspapers took it seriously.[74] Even the editors of the ecclesiastical *Moskovskiia tserkovnyia vedomosti* (*Moscow Church News*) respectfully discussed it and agreed that an ecumenical council "would impart to the upcoming festival a most solemn and important character." It would, they stated, "inscribe the event deeply upon the national memory and national consciousness." Even so, the patriotism of the editors was overruled by their loyalty to ecclesiastical tradition and its principle of universality. In the end, they concluded that a convocation under the present circumstances would "belittle the very significance of a council."[75] The question was too serious for the official Church to treat carelessly, and in 1888 Kiev did not become the site of the Eighth Ecumenical Council.

THE CHALLENGE OF OLD BELIEF

Even more frustrating for the Church leaders who embraced Orthodox patriotism was the continued apostasy of Old Believers. Many missionaries had hoped that the celebration of medieval religiosity would capture the sympathy of Russia's schismatics and demonstrate that they were not the only adherents of native religious traditions. However, no representatives of Old Belief participated in the Kiev festival or, apparently, any other commemorative celebration throughout the empire. Indeed, Old Believers and their lay sympathizers were in a position to challenge clerical Orthodox patriots who claimed that the official faith represented the national faith. Old Believers were well known for their refusal to accept the official Church's Greek-oriented reforms, and throughout the nineteenth century they had been praised by Afanasy Shchapov (1830–1876) and other ethnographers as the truest bearers of the national spirit. For this reason it is not surprising that they had attracted the attention of lay Orthodox patriots such as Kireev, who believed they might provide an effective symbol for celebrating the grandeur of Holy Rus. Interest was also stirred within some of the ecclesiastical journals that took the occasion of the baptism to report on missionary discussions organized between official Orthodox and Old Believers.[76] For its own part, the Belokrinitskoe Concord of Old Belief had in fact used 1888 to schedule the convocation of a Church council in Moscow.[77]

Old Believers, however, would have to wait for the relaxation of press censorship in 1905 before they could participate on their own terms in the definition of the national faith. In 1888, the ecclesiastical press had mostly disparaging things to say about their place in Russian national life. The Brotherhood of St Peter the Metropolitan, an anti-schismatic missionary society, noted their absence from the commemoration ceremonies and suggested that their claims to an identity "primarily as Russians" were unfounded.[78] Another ecclesiastical writer also reported their absence from the "national celebration." The reason, he informed his readers, was that Old Believers are in fact alien to the national community.

> Correspondents reporting about the events from different locations throughout Russia . . . quite pass over in silence the responses to these celebrations from the side of our Old Believers and sectarians. And this is not because correspondents wish to ignore the Old Believer world, but simply because the Old Believers on their own volition have broken away, in the course of these days, from the multimillion-member family of the Orthodox Russian people. Covered by an impenetrable armor of fanatical ignorance, they do not wish to participate in the general joy of the Russian people.[79]

Even Metropolitan Platon chose the festival's aftermath to issue a polemical address against Russia's schismatics. Significantly, however, the erstwhile proponent of the national faith found nothing to say about the incompatibility of Old Belief with Russia's national character, and he directed his attack toward the negative effect that multiple faiths have upon the strength of the national community.[80] Furthermore, he condemned Old Believers for violating the Church's principle of universality, which the official Church could still claim to uphold. This brought attention, however, to the limits of clerical Orthodox patriotism. As a standard of religious conformity, it was powerless in the face of Old Belief. What is more, the absence of Old Believers from the anniversary celebrations revealed that even when the official Church emphasized native religious tradition, it could not win the sympathy of these other adherents to the national faith.

UNRESOLVED TENSIONS

Thus the results of Russia's first baptism festival were, in the end, mixed. A considerable number of educated Russians and commoners traveled to Kiev or expressed their support for its ceremonies from a distance. Most of the empire's leading conservative newspapers also expressed strong approval, conveying the image of a national community defined by the Orthodox faith to a large public audience. Newspapers expressing liberal opinion, however, often dissented from claims about an exclusive religious character and destiny for Russia, even while promoting a secular model of nationality. Likewise, lay intellectuals who supported efforts to recover historical memory about medieval Rus did not always support the official model of the nation. Nevertheless, what is most noteworthy is that even when clerical Orthodox patriots failed to convince their audiences, they provoked a wide-ranging debate about the character of modern Russia and the role of the Orthodox Church within her. In a period of secularization, this in itself was an encouraging achievement for many Church leaders.

In light of the fact that the Church's definitions of Holy Rus were mostly determined by her missionary goals, it is possible to conclude that the Church's interest in modern Orthodox patriotism, itself only just emerging, was ultimately designed to serve an ecclesial goal. Nevertheless, even those Russians who were potentially the most sympathetic to the celebration of the national faith, the Old Believers, appeared to remain unmoved by the baptism festival. Furthermore, the clergy's devotion to autocracy established a model of the nation that could not easily stand without an apostle-like tsar. In 1888 the example of Alexander III and his defense of the mission, expressed so explicitly by Pobedonostsev, made the clergy's model of Holy Rus seem consistent. If the tsar should cease to defend the national faith through rule of law, however, this model might appear incoherent.

More damaging than the standard of the national faith and the potential inconsistency of the apostle-like tsar was the clergy's fusion of ecclesial loyalty and Russian nationality, which undermined the fundamental logic of Holy Rus. Because it represented an innovation that deviated from leading conventions of the Orthodox Church, it could, as Archbishop Nikanor's "new Israel" address indicated, lean toward a departure from Christian theological tradition. In other cases, such as the ecumenical council episode provoked by Kireev, it simply engendered an ecclesial self-consciousness that was highly parochial and, in light of coming events, tragically complacent.

The result, as we shall soon see, was an element of tension that plagued clerical Orthodox patriotism until 1905. When, in the wake of the Paschal Edict on religious toleration and the October Manifesto of that year, the conservative majority of the Church's clerical leadership failed to adapt its model of the nation to new circumstances, this tension would lead to growing dissonance. In most cases, however, clerical Orthodox patriots distinguished sharply between the value of a religious community that appropriated nationality, on the one hand, and the value of a national community that appropriated religion, on the other. It was with the former that their commitments principally lay. They sought to "restore" the community they called Holy Rus because doing so would help them to restore the Orthodox Church.

And for many who attended the baptism festival of 1888, the innovation appeared to work. Among the images of a Holy Russia disseminated throughout the empire from Kiev was that of an unnamed newspaper correspondent as he stood on the banks of the Dnieper River that feast day of St Vladimir. With the religious procession gathering around him to observe the culminating act of water blessing, he became a witness to the return of Russia's faithful remnant. "At the very moment the blessing of the waters was performed at the font below," he related to his readers,

> I involuntarily lifted my eyes to the monument honoring St Vladimir. It towered above us on the hill, peacefully, majestically, triumphantly. Near his face, which was directed toward the Dnieper, his cross was suspended over all of those present, raised high in the air. Long did I marvel at the remarkable effect of that image. It appeared as though with your own eyes you could see St Vladimir there himself, praying with the people, praying for the people: "Succor them from heaven, O Lord, and plant your vineyard within them."[81]

CHAPTER 2

-ᛞ-

The Theology of Orthodox Patriotism

The chief intellectual resource for clerical Orthodox patriotism was Russian theological tradition. Theology was a mandatory topic of study both in the country's four major theological academies and in the many seminaries that increased in number throughout the nineteenth century. It permeated virtually every sphere of a priest's life. It had also begun to influence the thought of Russia's lay intellectuals. Vladimir Soloviev (who as a member of the secularized intelligentsia had stunned contemporaries by attending the Moscow Spiritual Academy) and his "Silver Age" disciples of the early twentieth century all attained at least a basic proficiency with Christian theology and frequently incorporated it into their works. Thus, while modern models of nationality had begun to circulate among intellectuals such as the Slavophiles since the early nineteenth century, it is against the backdrop of Orthodox theology that the rise of national self-consciousness among the clergy must be studied.

From the wealth of this tradition, three concepts lay at the center of clerical Orthodox patriotism and provided it with an indispensable intellectual resource. These concepts were the ecclesial community, the kingdom of heaven, and the sanctification of the world. A discussion of them can be arranged according to the branches of theological knowledge that concerned them. These are, respectively, ecclesiology, eschatology, and pneumatology. Using the technical terms loosely, this chapter will explore the background of these theological concepts and trace how they were interpreted during the nineteenth century in ways that provided a foundation for clerical Orthodox patriotism.

ECCLESIOLOGY AND THE NATIONAL SAINTS

For clerical Orthodox patriots, the national community was inseparable from the ecclesial community. Intellectual traditions issuing from Orthodox ecclesiology, or the understanding of the Church, therefore shaped the way in which they understood nationality.[1] Canonical Orthodox ecclesiology unambiguously rejected national particularism in its definition of the Church. As one standard textbook from the late imperial period put it, "Being one, the Christian Church encompasses the whole world: for it there exist no spatial or national borders. The Old Testament brought an end to a single limited Jewish nationality. . . . Christ was sent to the world and not to the Jewish people alone."[2] But while rejecting nationality as a defining feature of ecclesial self-consciousness, theological tradition placed strong emphasis on belonging to a delineated community called the "true Church" (*istinnaia tserkov*). This ecclesial self-consciousness, then, was itself particularistic. As theologians insisted, it served to unite the ecclesial community not only from an unseen, mystical perspective, but also from one that was visible and psychological.[3] Accordingly, "the life of every person, his external activity, is located in the most intimate connection with his self-consciousness."[4] Imperceptible to measurable human experience, "the Church is not a phenomenon of the natural worldly order. . . . Therefore it can be said that Church self-consciousness is experienced [only] by those who live in the Church, those who are vital members of the living Church organism."[5] The process of cultivating and sustaining ecclesial self-consciousness thus became a matter of great importance to the Church and its missionary leaders.

In contrast to Roman Catholicism, Orthodoxy was institutionally organized into self-governing or autocephalous ecclesiastical branches. The Third Ecumenical Council of 431 at Ephesus ruled that each jurisdictional branch should possess certain prerogatives, such as the appointment of bishops to the hierarchy. This element of ecclesiological tradition is important in considering the emergence of a particularistic national self-consciousness. The Russian Church had gained practical autocephaly under Metropolitan Jonah (r. 1448–1461), and its status as the largest community of faithful ruled by an Orthodox sovereign after the fall of Constantinople in 1453 created a strong sense of leadership and self-determination. In fact, the sixteenth century was a watershed era for the growth of a specifically Russian ecclesial self-consciousness.

The canonizations of Russian saints at the Moscow councils of 1547 and 1549 were key events in facilitating this development. Metropolitan Macarius of Moscow (1482–1563), acting in accord with the wishes of Ivan IV, sought to create a body of Russian saints who would symbolize Moscow's leadership within the Orthodox world. As Evgeny Golubinskii (1834–1912) noted in his history of Russian canonizations, since the baptism of 988 no more than seven

Russian saints had been formally glorified.[6] To this group—which included Saints Vladimir, Boris, Gleb, and Sergius of Radonezh—Macarius added Alexander Nevsky (1220–1263) and twenty-two others.[7] This enlarged communion of Russian saints created a bridge between national self-consciousness and ecclesial self-consciousness and became an increasingly significant element of ecclesiological thought in the late nineteenth century. Its influence is demonstrated in part by a series of historical studies, including Golubinskii's, that appeared at the time. Russian saints distinguished the nation from the larger ecclesial community of the universal Church and were increasingly designated by Church leaders as "national" (*narodnyi*). This trend represented a change in emphasis from the traditional designation of a saint as "Churchwide" (*vsetserkovnyi*), which had been used for any with more than a local following.

In addition to the large number of specifically Russian saints enrolled in the *menaion,* or calendar of saints, customs of commemorating them served as a resource for Orthodox patriots. As Church leaders explored ways of defining recognizable images for Holy Rus, they inevitably came to the rich legacy of Orthodox iconography. In the Russian language the word for "image" (*obraz*) is exchangeable with the word for "icon" (*ikona*), and iconography had long sought to provide the imagery needed for the development of ecclesial self-consciousness. A particularly significant icon for the origins of Orthodox patriotism was that of the Synaxis of Russian Saints that dated from medieval times. The balance between the universal and the particular was maintained in the iconography, which typically depicted the respective national saints below a top register including such universal figures as the apostles, the archangels, the Mother of God, and Christ Himself.

In the Orthodox Church a saint was a departed member of the ecclesial community whose sanctity was recognized by a formal act of canonization. The key question in deciding whether to canonize an individual hinged upon whether he or she, abiding with Christ in heaven, continued to intercede for members of the Church abiding with Christ on earth. If confirmation was made that intercession had occurred, then canonization could be enacted. Since the Church considered the reposed to be members of the Church who continued to live in heaven, their intercession before God helped the Church on earth maintain her communion with God. Thus, the persons of the saints participated in the experience of the earthly ecclesial community.[8] When these saints were regarded as particular to a given national community, however, they could be made to serve as symbols or images of nationality. Each saint could even become a focus for different models of the nation. During the baptismal festival of 1888, for instance, the image of St Vladimir had been upheld by both Metropolitan Platon and Constantine Pobedonostsev as they defined distinct though compatible models of Holy Rus.

A more modern saintly figure was St Seraphim of Sarov, whose canonization in 1903 reveals how ecclesiological tradition became a source for clerical Orthodox patriotism. Historians in the West have only recently begun to take an interest in the canonization of Seraphim. Robert Nichols, for instance, has used the event to demonstrate the important role that religious historical memory played during the reign of Nicholas II.[9] In general, however, there is little recognition that the canonization event represented a truly significant development in the life of the late imperial Church. This is a surprise, as many contemporaries regarded it as one of the most important events of their generation. Gregory Freeze has tended to dismiss its influence on the Russian public, claiming that it "left no lasting impression" on any but elites.[10] This seems too dismissive an evaluation. In fact, the canonization demonstrated that national saints were assuming greater importance in the activities of Church leaders.

To alert the public to the upcoming opening of the saint's relics, scheduled for July 19 in Sarov, Church leaders printed a large number of saints' lives and pamphlets about St Seraphim. Most were intended for a popular audience and frequently included maps showing the location of Sarov to assist prospective pilgrims (who in the minds of the authors apparently lacked knowledge about the nation's geography). Virtually all publications emphasized to common readers that the saint served especially the faithful of Russia. One broadsheet opened by stating that "the great Sarov hermit Seraphim warmly loved the Russian people throughout his life." Thus,

> from all corners of Russia many thousands of pilgrims from among the Russian people have come to celebrate the opening of his relics. . . . Death, which took the wonder-working elder from his admirers, seemingly separating him from the Orthodox-Russian people, did not diminish his glory, did not weaken the love felt toward him by the Russian people. The people continue to receive his assistance, not only in Sarov, but in all corners of Russia.[11]

St Seraphim was not just an Orthodox holy man, to be honored by the universal Church, the broadsheet suggested, but a model of the national faith whose intercession in heaven preserved the national community.

St Seraphim's relationship to the whole of the Russian people was repeatedly emphasized. Saints' lives published for popular consumption stated that his social origins were humble.[12] His father was a common merchant and his mother a model of humble piety. One life noted that his fame had ultimately inspired top members of society such as Grand Duke Mikhail Alexandrovich to seek his council. "But to the holy elder," it added, "there appeared many simple people especially." So close to the nation was he, in fact, that "during the last ten years of his life the people flowed to him daily by the thousands, though usually only at about two at a time."[13] The sanctification he offered to the nation was described in mystical terms by another version of his life. "To the people," it stated, "he issued their vital will, their heart, their very essence. He gave the people their image, that is, the image of God that they had forfeited."[14] Seraphim, in the accounts of patriotic Church leaders, became a model Russian. And, as "he stands for Russia in heaven," the life concluded, the nation gains direct access to the greatest and most universal of all saints, the Mother of God. The "connection" between the newest national saint and the greatest of all saints was described as a sign of Russia's unique status in the ecclesial community, the "mystique of Russia."[15]

The effect of such statements upon the minds of the masses can only be a matter of speculation. But it is clear that to some of Russia's Orthodox leadership the canonization of Seraphim was regarded as both an ecclesial and a national event. The publications of 1903 and after contained relatively little emphasis on the universal Church and indicated that St Seraphim's blessings would be received primarily within Russia's borders. Not only did the saint pray particularly for the national community, but he also sanctified the physical territory it inhabited. Some accounts of the canonization celebrations stressed how his relics would be carried throughout several regions of the Russian land, sanctifying them along the way. Finally, a multitude of popular processions would converge on Sarov, "from all ends of Rus," representing a national pilgrimage.[16] One enthusiastic writer even claimed that the canonization endowed the Russian land with a third holy city and placed Sarov on an order with Kiev and Moscow.[17]

This is not to say, of course, that the Orthodox faith was being reconfigured in exclusively Russian national terms. But even those sources that discussed the Church suggested that its Russian branch acted particularly to fulfill its universal destiny within the modern world. "The Orthodox East has been since ancient times the source of light for the grace of Christ in all of the universe," began a priest-monk by the name of Alexander.[18] But with the rise of Kiev and the establishment of the Pecherskaia Lavra, the lands of

Rus became the main prism of that light.[19] In the nineteenth century, it was the Russian people who first began to stir the interest of the schismatic West, producing in some a "striving for intercourse with the Orthodox Church."[20] In "our time," the author implied, the Russian people, alone within eastern Christendom, preserved and disseminated the true faith. Therefore their national saints served as guides for a mission that was both universalistic and particularistic. As the newest among them, St Seraphim represented the perfect fusion of these two principles. "Being a true son of the Orthodox Church and with all of his heart striving for the heavenly fatherland, St Seraphim in his time was a true son of his earthly fatherland, an ardent patriot, and with all of his soul loved Orthodox Rus."[21] Father Alexander's account thus concluded by refracting the universal light of Christ through the prism of Russia's national saints.

The canonization of St Seraphim is a good example of how ecclesiological tradition provided intellectual soil for a Christian vision of Russia's particularistic destiny. The publications that accompanied the event show that during the late imperial period, definitions of the Orthodox Church were sufficiently flexible to allow the universal nature of ecclesial self-consciousness to be directed toward the definition of a national community. The national saints, more than any other element in the ecclesial community, provided an important focus for this process of fusion. But reflections on the issue of community raised questions about Russia's relationship to divine providence. Here Orthodox eschatology offered an answer.

ESCHATOLOGY AND THE NATIONAL TSAR

Eschatology is the branch of theological knowledge concerned with "end things," as its Greek root suggests. Here the ends are ultimate; eschatology is knowledge about the Church's participation in human salvation. This participation can be considered historically, where attention often focuses on the foretold Parousia (or second coming) of Christ and the final consummation of God's order on earth at the end of time. It can also be understood immediately, whereby the Church is related to a presently experienced divine order. In both cases the condition or experience in which members of the ecclesial community participate in the divine order is commonly known as the "kingdom of heaven" or "kingdom of God."[22]

Within Orthodox theology there exists a close relationship between ecclesiology and eschatology. Beginning particularly with St Cyprian of Carthage (d. 258), Church fathers sometimes taught that the Holy Spirit was present only in the true Church. Thus, only Orthodox believers could fully experience the Divine, and the history of human salvation became centered upon the life of the Church. In fact, many Russian theologians customarily equated the Church with the kingdom of heaven. As one put it, "the kingdom of God—this is the Church."[23] But the fact that the Church was defined as a community, whereas the kingdom of heaven was defined as the condition under which that community lived, yielded a distinction between the two. This distinction centered on the Church's temporal experience in the world and her relationship to divine providence. One study proposed the following formula: "The kingdom of God is that order or structure of life on earth in which the will of God is manifested through the activities of man on earth."[24] Here, the most significant feature of the divine order is its notion of human activity. Ruled from heaven, inhabitants of the kingdom of heaven are directed in their historical experience by divine providence. What is more, the kingdom of heaven itself is not an invisible part of this experience, but an "order or structure of life on earth" that logically manifests particular features.

The New Testament recounted how the kingdom of heaven was established on earth in the first century among a diversity of pagan religions and under a political system that frequently persecuted the faithful. An important event occurred in the fourth century that changed these circumstances. Emperor Constantine converted to Christianity and granted Christians toleration in what has become known as the Byzantine Empire. This act was formalized in 313 by a law known as the Edict of Milan and ultimately led to the establishment of Christianity as the only official state religion. Constantine himself was canonized with the title "Equal-to-the-Apostles," serving as a later example for Grand Prince Vladimir of Russia. In response, Byzantine Christianity, which was still being formulated at the time, came to place considerable emphasis on the role of the ruler in preserving the kingdom of heaven on earth. Influential figures such as Eusebius of Caesarea (ca. A.D. 263–339), a contemporary of Constantine responsible for the first fully developed conception of a Christian state, invested the emperor with the responsibility of preserving the key features particular to the divine order and even helping to disseminate them among pagans. A century later, Augustine (354–430) laid out a sophisticated theology of the interaction between the divine "city of God" and the earthly "city of man," which under ideal circumstances sought to emulate the former. Augustine's vision of the Christian state facilitated the later rise of papal supremacy over "secular" rulers, leaving Byzantium as the main power in Christendom in which the ruler legitimately initiated "apostle-like" policies such as the calling of episcopal councils and the conducting of missionary activities. So when Constantinople, the Byzantine capital, fell to the Muslim Ottoman Turks in 1453, the Russian state remained the only Orthodox kingdom that was ruled in accordance with this Constantinian principle. What is more, Muscovy (Russia) expanded in the seventeenth century to include Kiev, that major center of Orthodox learning and spirituality. The grafting of Kiev into the Russian state enhanced the prestige of the latter as the center of Church life and, in eschatological terms, providential activity.

Many Russians in the nineteenth century sustained this eschatological theme in their conception of history. One of the most influential prelates of the time was Metropolitan Macarius of Moscow, whose scholarly achievements were recognized by contemporaries such as Sergei Soloviev and continued to be recognized by Orthodox theologians in the twentieth century.[25] In writing his study of Orthodox theology, Macarius divided its history into three periods, the last of which was dominated almost entirely by Russian learning. "Not without cause," he told his readers, "in speaking about the development of Orthodox dogmatic theology as a science during the whole of the final period we are limited to our fatherland alone. Within Greece and all the East since the fall of Constantinople, enlightenment has gone into decline."[26] Such a statement manifested the eschatological self-consciousness that the Russian Church cultivated at the time. By the late imperial period, however, this self-consciousness was being challenged by the apparent decline in Russia's spiritual well-being. Church leaders therefore took a renewed interest in eschatology in order to interpret contemporary historical events.

One of the most interesting cases of this renewed interest is the work of a priest-professor at the University of Kiev named P. Y. Svetlov. In the turbulent year of 1905, he published a major study of the subject that opened by claiming that the "idea of the kingdom of heaven stands as the central and root idea in the Christian worldview."[27] The study offered a critical assessment of what he considered a purely ascetical consciousness that failed to manifest itself in earthy institutions. This the author dismissed as "Byzantine Christianity," which began to flourish in Russia only with the creation of Peter the Great's "bureaucratic state mechanism." True Christian self-consciousness, he argued, affirmed the vital participation of God in worldly experience. In his opinion it was Russia and her modern culture, just then beginning to shed the Petrine yoke, that most fully expressed this proper eschatological self-consciousness.

Drawing on Orthodox tradition, Svetlov argued that the kingdom of heaven is recognizable where human culture and politics participate in a "divine intercourse" (*bogoobshchenie*). "The kingdom of God," he stated, "manifests itself and exists in the external order of reality, embracing not only the invisible inner life of the faithful, but all regions of earthly relations and conditions of earthly human existence. All human activity (culture) and institutions (the state) are embraced. . . . This transfiguration and inclusion of all the world in the creation of the kingdom of God is the final purpose toward which providence directs us in history."[28] Not only do human institutions become transfigured by the divine presence, but also the kingdom of God is a condition that is "created" through man's historical activity in cooperation with God. "Here and nowhere else is where the end of civilization lies. Here is the natural ideal of historical progress, meriting heavy labor that is directed by mankind in his search for the best future."[29] Again, the divine order realized in the kingdom of heaven is neither invisible nor dictated, but the visible product of divinely inspired human activity.

Svetlov's purpose in writing was not purely academic. Like that of many other Church leaders of the period, his work was actively engaged with a perceived decline of religion in modern culture. In the apocalyptic atmosphere of 1905 especially, he believed Russia was facing a serious crisis and that reflection on Orthodox eschatological tradition would serve in the work of its redemption. At several points in his text he referred to the debates then occurring over the restoration of the patriarchate and the liberation of the Russian Church from state domination. His active engagement with these issues, for instance, led him to propose the abolition of the ecclesiastical censorship.[30] As his ideas suggest, he sided strongly with liberal ecclesiastical opinion and favored reforms.

Svetlov's principal concern was not church governance, however, but Russian culture. He likened Russia's Church leaders to the legendary *bogatyri* of medieval Rus, the heroic figures who were devoted to the preservation and defense of the Russian land.[31] Cultural bogatyrs like Svetlov were summoned by a modern "time of troubles" to witness the rich Orthodox heritage among their wayward fellow countrymen. It is in this context that he invoked Christ's missionary summons to his disciples in Matt 5:13—Orthodox Russians should go to their people, and ultimately to all the peoples of the world, acting as the salt of the earth. "The Christian Church, with its wealth of evangelical light and goodness, is naturally predestined to serve as the means toward the transfiguration of the world on an evangelical basis and to become its leaven, the very heart of the kingdom of God, the salt of the earth."[32] Eschatological tradition thus served to fuse a belief in providential activity with the Church's particular historical experience.

This fusion is revealed most in Svetlov's discussions of Russian culture. One of his study's remarkable features is that in addition to giving a learned exposition of Orthodox theology it devoted considerable space to reflections on modern European history and culture. The "pitiable position of the modern European world," he believed, was contrasted by the growing vitality of Russia's national culture.[33] His discussions included passages on the patriotic vision of Vladimir Soloviev and a chapter on "the kingdom of God in the outlook of Gogol, Dostoevsky, and Tolstoy." In discussing Russian literature, he took special interest in Fyodor Dostoevsky's vision of a European future in which Russia's national "mission" was to witness the truth of Christianity to an apostate West. Considerable attention was given in this regard to an extended discussion of the novelist's *Diary of a Writer*. The key element in Dostoevsky's vision, he concluded, was his belief that the Russian people, as a particular national community, were endowed with a messianic character of "human universality" (*vsechelovechnost*).[34] The space Svetlov devoted to Dostoevsky and other national writers demonstrated a strong interest in the role of nationality within modern culture. It also demonstrated an effort to assimilate this feature of modern culture to the standard of the national faith.

In his consistency with Eastern Christian tradition, Svetlov also assigned considerable importance to the role of the state. According to him, "the state bears a great service to the kingdom of God on earth. To it especially, divine providence entrusts a lofty mission for the preparation of the kingdom of God on earth and its actual realization."[35] The role of an Orthodox ruler was central to this tradition. "If according to Christian teaching each earthly tsar is the servant of God, the executor of the plan of divine providential will, then such an organ of divine will on earth must be a Christian sovereign. . . . The state, fully assimilating Christianity within itself, must be the bearer of the kingdom of God on earth."[36] Thus Svetlov, a liberal in matters of Church reform, regarded the status of the earthly ruler with complete fidelity to the "apostle-like" ideal. The image of St Constantine Equal-to-the-Apostles occupied a central place in his eschatological national vision. His study of the kingdom of God was a recognized standard of scholarship among contemporaries.[37] As such, it serves as an important source of information about eschatological thought at the time. More importantly, however, it demonstrates how theological tradition provided Church leaders with an intellectual resource by which to interpret Russia's particular national experience.

An eschatological vision of the nation and its apostle-like tsar was not limited to academics such as Svetlov, but circulated among a wide section of the late imperial clergy. An interesting case in which it was manifested was the coronation of Nicholas II in 1896. This event received broad attention in the periodical press and provided enormous symbolism for Russians concerned with their nation's relationship to providence. Many of the articles that preceded the ceremony in Moscow—performed on the day of Pentecost—contextualized the event within the history of eastern Christendom.

One article in the missionary journal *Vera i razum* (*Faith and Reason*), for instance, viewed the coronation as the culmination of a nation-specific, providential plan centered upon the apostle-like principle of Constantine. The author, P. Butsinskii, opened by claiming that "supreme state author-ity" is given to rulers so that their peoples obey God and answer "His calling according to their national traditions." The ruler was therefore responsible to the people for the level of their national piety. "But if the ruler governs these people according to a false path, God punishes him along with his subordi-nates and delivers authority to another." Having elaborated this historical dynamic, Butsinskii reviewed the experience of eastern Christendom up to the baptism of Russia. Special attention was given to the example of Con-stantine, who was the first to integrate Christianity with statecraft. However, he concluded that subsequently "few of the Byzantine emperors ruled their peoples in a Christian manner. . . . In the end it came to pass that the patri-arch, with his bishops, and the emperor, with his courtiers, sold off the faith of their fathers to the Latins for political reasons." The politically expedient betrayal of its ancestral faith at the Council of Florence (1447) was the last act of a state that no longer participated in divine experience. "Thus, in the middle of the fifteenth century it was conquered by the Turks. But before it fell," Butsinskii remarked, "the light of Christian teaching already shone in our Russian land." Grand Prince Vladimir's conversion of the people, he concluded, was the act that brought Russia's historical experience into union with divine providence. "From that time forward, Christianity became the state religion of the Russian land. Among the [Kievan and Muscovite] suc-cessors to Vladimir, there could not be found a single traitor to the new faith, as had been known in the Byzantine state."[38]

A national faith and an apostle-like tsar were thus central to this expres-sion of the Third Rome doctrine. They were emphasized in many other pub-lications during the year of the coronation, especially those concerned with the Orthodox mission. For these writers the Orthodox tsar served as a sym-bol of a single national faith.

V. M. Skvortsov (1869–1932), for instance, the editor of *Missionerskoe obozrenie* (*Missionary Review*) and a leading lay missionary, proclaimed to his readers that the coronation represented Russia's "struggle for a native

Orthodoxy."[39] Columns chronicling events throughout Russia brought attention to the unifying effects of the coronation. One story, for instance, reported how a wave of "patriotic animation" had "seized ahold of the schismatics" of a remote Old Believer village.[40]

The coronation also symbolized the fulfillment of Russia's universal mission. In another missionary journal, Professor A. D. Beliaev produced a long discussion of relations between Orthodoxy and Roman Catholicism that was intended to explore the possibility of ecumenical reunion. Russia stands ready as the voice of Orthodoxy, he suggested, but is repeatedly rebuked by the apostate peoples of the Roman Catholic West.[41] The journal *Missionerskoe sbornik* (*Missionary Compendium*) also used the year to reflect on Russia's role as the bearer of the true faith in modern Europe. In an article that treated the ecumenical question, a priest recorded with pride that Russia's witness had begun to turn Western Christians away from heresy. He quoted the warm praise of a sympathetic Anglican: "To it and it alone, since the schism with Rome, this great state Russia has dutifully occupied itself with the Christian faith. Indeed, it is Russia—with her bishops, clergy, monks and hermits, with her ancient order, her zealots, penitents and icons, and with her holy objects—who testifies irrefutably to the Eastern Church."[42] Testimony of Western Christian opinion such as this assured Orthodox Russians that in a nation-specific world their state occupied a central position in the kingdom of heaven on earth. It also resembled the praise offered to Russia by non-Russian Orthodox during the baptism festival.

The eschatological vision of clerical Orthodox patriotism was also appropriated by pan-Slavs. General A. A. Kireev, who had gained notoriety in 1888 for his ecumenical council proposal, contributed an article to *Russkoe obozrenie* (*Russian Review*) that used the coronation's symbolism to outline Russia's missionary role in the Orthodox East. "We cannot retire from active participation in this," he argued, "because the history of the Orthodox East is our history." He continued, "The Russian state is the expression of providential activity within the true Church." Such matters raised the question of what forces shaped Russian national self-consciousness. "What is Russia?" he asked.

> What constitutes her particularity, what is the essential feature of her character? It is that . . . she is Orthodox Holy Rus, that she is part of the universal Church and only clothed in the garment of a national state. Every one of us Russians, or at least the huge majority of us, understands and feels this! I feel myself to be first a son of the Orthodox Church, and only

subsequently a citizen or subject of the Russian state. I for my part stand on the side of Metropolitan Filipp and not on the side of Ivan IV.[43]

Here, Kireev's content definition of Russian nationality was consistent with clerical Orthodox patriotism. Ecclesial identity preceded and determined national identity, and not the other way around. His vision of the central place Russia occupied in the history of the Church reveals the way that Orthodox eschatology was beginning to yield a broader vision of national destiny.

However, most of the discussion that accompanied Nicholas II's coronation did not express Russia's centrality in the politically expansive terms of pan-Slavism. In most cases, only the tsar's relationship to the presently existing kingdom of heaven in Russia was the topic of discussion. This was especially true in the coverage given to the coronation liturgy in the Moscow Kremlin's Uspensky Cathedral, a theme that was encouraged by references to the kingdom of heaven in the prayers. Yet the accession of the Russian tsar was an event that clerical Orthodox patriots were eager to use as a symbol of their nation's role in the history of modern Christendom. Drawing on eschatological tradition, they claimed that in an increasingly nation-specific world the "apostle-like" Russian tsar continued to protect the national faith and served to disseminate it. What is more, the fact that he was crowned on the day of Pentecost pointed to another theological theme that was entailed in the coronation event, pneumatology.

PNEUMATOLOGY AND NATIONAL CULTURE

Nicholas II was crowned on May 14/26, the Sunday of Pentecost in the Church's liturgical calendar for 1896. As we have seen, one current of eschatology taught that the kingdom of heaven is a condition whereby the Church participates in the eternal experience of the Divine. In the Church's eyes, an important result of this experience is that members of the Church become sanctified by God through the action of the Holy Spirit, the third person of the Holy Trinity. In his coronation address, the new tsar appealed to the Russian people to pray that God might enter into him and "pour out upon us the gift of His Holy Spirit."[44] This element of the coronation rite was no different from earlier Russian coronations such as that of Alexander III, and indeed was consistent with the tradition of monarchical coronation in western Europe as well. But it brings attention to the significance of the branch of theology known as pneumatology, the understanding of the Holy Spirit's activity within the world. Orthodox pneumatology was the third source of Orthodox patriotic thought.

The New Testament taught that the Holy Spirit came upon the Church on the day of Pentecost, an event recorded in the second chapter of the Acts of the Apostles. The early Church regarded the presence of the Holy Spirit as the necessary condition of her continued faithfulness on earth, and subsequent Church councils explicitly appealed to the third person of the Trinity for guidance.[45] Orthodox theologians brought special attention to the Holy Spirit's participation in the life of man and man's subsequent participation in the life of God, a process known as "deification." One of the earliest of these was St Gregory the Theologian (d. 389), a Cappadocian Father and a contemporary of Emperor Theodosios the Great (r. 379–395). Gregory wrote a number of works that discussed the Holy Spirit, his relationship to the Church, and the deification of man.[46] Following the Filioque controversy with the Western Church—which, because of its reputed diminution of the Holy Spirit within the Trinity, more than any other theological issue underlined the Great Schism between Orthodox and Roman Catholics—the Orthodox Church has been said to place comparatively more emphasis than the West on the role of the Holy Spirit in elaborating the Christian experience.[47] The doctrine of deification assumed a central position in the teaching of St Gregory of Palamas (1296–1359), the definitive theologian of the tradition of prayer known as hesychasm. For him deification was the process whereby the Holy Spirit made faithful Christians godlike by imparting His "energies" to them. According to a leading Orthodox theologian of the twentieth century, Vladimir Lossky (1903–1958), the "ultimate end" of the Christian life "is union with God or deification."[48]

Canonical Orthodox pneumatology taught that the Holy Spirit is the person of the Holy Trinity who enters members of the Church on earth through the sacrament of chrismation and sanctifies them. Since sanctification of the corrupted world entailed its transfiguration, deification focused particularly on the nature of humanity. In Michael Pomazansky's words, through Christ "our humanity also is deified, for He also Himself likewise took part in our flesh and blood, united Himself in the most intimate way with the human race, and consequently united it with the Divinity."[49] The principle of deification thus brought attention to the sanctified person, but within the context of the natural world. Although in most renderings it concerned only the mystical experience of persons, rather than human institutions or natural objects, it also provided an intellectual source for reflection upon the natural world that could be used to interpret the cultural and terrestrial surroundings of the faithful as well.

In a matter closely related to the principle of deification, the Seventh Ecumenical Council of 787 judged that the use of sanctified material objects such as icons played an important role in transfiguring the natural world. As "in the holy churches of God," it declared, this process occurred everywhere in the terrestrial environment, even in "houses and on roadways."[50] It affirmed the teaching of St John of Damascus (d. 749), who argued that since "the Word made flesh has deified the flesh," icons can assist in the deification of the fallen world.[51] The Church's teaching about icons, in the words of Leonid Ouspensky, "shows that in the consciousness of the Church the role of the icon [is] dynamically creative." Therefore, "icons are placed everywhere as the revelation of the future sanctification of the world, of its coming transfiguration, as the pattern of its realization, and, finally, as the promulgation of grace and the presence in the world of holy objects, which sanctify."[52] "Holy objects" (*sviatyni*) could be any objects offered by the Church to God, especially icons. As "dynamically creative" matter that serves to focus divine grace, then, they constituted an important element in the Orthodox pneumatological tradition.

Within the Russian Church, this tradition began to make claims about the sanctity of the Russian land in the centuries after the baptism of 988. As *The Chronicle of Nestor* relates, Grand Prince Vladimir chose Eastern Christianity in response to his emissaries' testimony that the Church's liturgy transfigured nature, leading them to exclaim "We did not know whether we were in heaven or on earth, for surely God dwells there among men." The eschatological theme of heaven on earth continued to characterize the religious culture of medieval Rus. As George Fedotov argued, Kievan spirituality exhibited a strong attachment to the sanctified material world. Quoting the writings of the eleventh-century Metropolitan Ilarion (r. 1051–1055), he offered evidence of how the Russian land was seen as a transfigured natural environment. In Ilarion's words, "they adorned all the sanctuary and vested holy churches with beauty. Angel's trumpet and Gospel's thunder sounded through all the towns. The incense rising toward God sanctified the air. Monasteries stood on mountains. Men and women, small and great, all people filled holy churches."[53] Here the material air, along with the entire natural order that has now been brought into contact with the life of the Church, is sanctified.

Yet it was one thing to believe that the natural world had been sanctified by the presence of the Holy Spirit, and quite another to regard that world in nationally exclusive terms. Consciousness of a sanctified land did not lead the medieval Russian Church to emphasize national particularism. "No one in Russia in those centuries," to quote Fedotov again, "conceived of their country as the center of the Christian world, or the land of the truest faith, or of the greatest saints."[54]

The principle of sanctified nature continued to characterize certain elements of Muscovite spirituality as well. The arrival from Greece of the hesychast movement was particularly influential here, as the movement emphasized intense and intimate communion with God through the presence of the Holy Spirit. Examples of Feofan the Greek's (ca. 1340–ca. 1410) iconography and church architecture, such as the Church of Our Savior in Novgorod, expressed the hesychast striving for transfiguration.[55] Again, however, a belief that certain cultural and material media of worship such as icons, shrines, and temples represented the divine presence did not in itself inspire Orthodox Russians to emphasize national particularism, despite a growing belief among some that the Muscovite state was the "Third Rome" and the "new Israel."

By the end of the nineteenth century, the transfiguration principle gained even greater influence within Russian streams of religious thought, especially among lay intellectuals. Vladimir Soloviev's interest in the deification of humanity and the principle of God-manhood, while deviating from patristic theology in important ways, was the most influential expression of this trend.[56] Soloviev and his religious philosophy were regarded with ambiguity by clerical theologians of the era. Some discovered in his work an "oasis" of Russian theological wisdom.[57] Others, such as Archbishop Antony (Khrapovitsky) (1864–1936), dismissed it as a "typical example of the religious materialism that is being explored in our time."[58] Much more unambiguously suspect was the religious thought of Nicholas F. Fedorov (1829–1903), who also elaborated pneumatological tradition in his focus on the transfiguration of the earth.[59] Finally, the late-nineteenth-century interest in pneumatology strongly influenced the patriotic thought of free-thinking lay intellectuals such as Dmitry Merezhkovsky (1865–1941) and Nicholas Berdiaev (1874–1948) during the subsequent Silver Age.

Within the late imperial clerical establishment, pneumatological reflection also exercised an influence. Evidence of this is found in the literature accompanying the canonization in 1903 of St Seraphim, whose contemplative life was renowned for its focus upon communion with God. As an edition of his conversations with the disciple Motovilov emphasized, the hermit urged the faithful toward transfiguration by claiming that "the true purpose of our Christian life is contained in the acquisition of the Holy Spirit."[60] Various theological works published at the time also demonstrated an interest in "the universal union of heaven and earth in the Church."[61]

Further evidence can be found in the period's literature on liturgical architecture. Here in particular the teaching of St John of Kronstadt

(1829–1908) is relevant, as he was one of the most highly regarded priests of the time and published an enormous body of sermons and other reflections on Orthodox spirituality. His description of temples reinforced the theme that the sanctified natural environment represented heaven on earth. "Entering into a church," he reflected, "whether during the divine service or not, you enter, as it were, into a world that is somehow incomparable with the sensual." The Church's holy objects make this other dimension tangible. "You see the icons of the saints according to their faces when they lived on earth . . . you see the remarkable image of the God-man Jesus Christ . . . you see the image of His Most Pure Virgin Mother . . . you see the faces of the holy angels, those ardent inhabitants of heaven."[62] By transfiguring the natural world, these holy objects turn it into a heaven on earth. "A temple," he concluded, "is a terrestrial heaven [*zimnoe nebo*], a place of the most immediate communion with divinity."[63]

As both a symbol of and an instrument in the deification of man, a temple also played, as Vera Shevzov has noted, "a pivotal role in the expression and formation of individual and corporate Orthodox self-understanding."[64] It was here that the people assembled on a regular basis according to the liturgical calendar of the Church. It was also here that the understanding of persons as members of collectives such as the village, the nation, and the Church was cultivated. The parish temple thus played a central role in collective self-consciousness. And when it came to the quasi-official chapel (*chasovnia*)— often built on private initiative and distinct from the parish church, whose numbers nearly doubled in the period between the Great Reforms and the Revolution—the same could hold true. Interestingly, however, ambiguities of the collective self-consciousness—especially that concerning identification with the official Church—could also be cultivated in the Orthodox Church's "chapelscape," leading some Church leaders to regard chapels as "nests" in which sectarianism could hatch.[65] This ambiguity of the chapel as distinct from the parish temple will be seen later in discussing the contributions of Nesterov to Orthodox patriotism.

The principle of sanctification, then, when applied to the Church's holy objects and holy places, produced a belief that God's presence was experienced through the sanctified media of the natural environment. In the late imperial period this element of Orthodox pneumatology became increasingly important to Church leaders as they searched for ways to alter Russia's national culture. By focusing attention on temples, shrines, and icons located in Russia, they infused national self-consciousness with the sanctity of the universal faith. This had been the effect in Kiev in 1888, when the temples and monasteries there were presented as symbols of a modern Holy Rus. The ceremonial blessing of the Dnieper River at the end of the festival had reflected the sanctity of the Russian land even more vividly. In subsequent years, Church writers and publicists frequently described the holy objects of medieval Rus as the source of a modern national self-consciousness. Kiev's Pecherskaia Lavra, Sergiev Posad's Trinity-Sergius Lavra, and the Moscow Kremlin served as leading symbols whose domes and icons were associated with the destiny of the Russian people.

Bishop Nikon (Rozhdestvenskii) (1851–1918) of Vologda, a prelate who would become especially influential in the Orthodox patriotism movement after 1905, portrayed these holy objects and holy places as the embodiment of Russian national character. "They say that Moscow is the heart of Russia," he claimed in an address at a public gathering in 1904. "If that is so, then the Trinity Lavra is the most vital nerve of the heart. More strongly here than anywhere else one can feel the national heartbeat, one can commune with national life, and be filled with a consciousness of the purely Russian principles and ideals of this life."[66]

Orthodox pneumatology thus combined with eschatology and ecclesiology to produce a rich and influential source for Orthodox patriotic thought. More than any other intellectual resource, the combination of these three themes nourished the minds of the clergy who began to lead the Church into public debates about nationality during the period after the Great Reforms. No other tradition, not even Slavophile romanticism, explains how the universal scope of the Christian faith could be directed toward the formation of a modern national community.

But intellectual resources alone were insufficient to inspire this innovation. It was necessary to have a dynamic setting in which the clergy could employ Orthodox patriotism in its pursuit of cultural leadership. This setting was the spiritual mission.

CHAPTER 3

To the Lost Sheep of the House of Israel

If theology provided the chief intellectual resource for clerical Orthodox patriotism, the missionary movement of late imperial Russia provided its setting. As Svetlov and others suggested, modern Holy Rus was the salt of the earth, a missionary nation called to witness the universal truth of Orthodox Christianity in a critical time of secularization and apostasy. Developments during the period were revealing how urgent this calling was. Beyond the empire's borders the mission faced unprecedented opportunities and challenges. The expansion of modern communications and transport enabled nascent Russian Orthodox missions in Eurasia and the Holy Land to begin their most active period of growth. The trans-Siberian railroad built under the influence of Sergei Witte (1849–1915) gave encouragement to missionaries operating in Japan such as Bishop Nicholas (Kasatkin) (1836–1912), while the rise in steamship traffic out of southern ports such as Odessa facilitated a boom in pilgrimages to Palestine. Within European Christendom itself, the Orthodox peoples of the South were beginning to break free of the Turkish yoke while the Roman Catholic and Protestant peoples of the West seemed, to Russian observers, to sink ever deeper into religious indifference. Historical developments in the world had never revealed the destiny of Holy Rus with such clarity.[1]

Within the empire, the acquisition of large territories populated by Muslims and pagans during the past century presented new opportunities for conversion while challenging Orthodox Russians to defend the privileged status of their faith. As they did so, however, they were increasingly conscious of the presence of sectarians and the schismatic Old Believers. The latter in particular had begun to use freedoms gained in 1883 to expand their public worship. Within the official Orthodox Church itself, urbanization was transplanting the Russian peasant to an environment that lacked a strong ecclesiastical infrastructure and was creating the first experience of mass secularization since 988.² Finally, Russia's educated elite continued to patronize a secular high culture with roots in the West. Statistical data about the empire's religious makeup was fragmentary until the first census of 1897.³ Nevertheless, it was clear to Orthodox Church leaders in the years after the Great Reforms that the modern Russia in which they lived was a pale image of the medieval prototype commemorated in 1888.

This missionary dynamic played an important role in the emergence of clerical Orthodox patriotism. As the Orthodox mission grew in scope, cultivation of a national culture fell into the hands of prelates, priests, and publicists whose intellect was shaped to a significant degree by Orthodox theology. Many of these Church leaders were active in or close to missionary activities. As mentioned in Chapter 1, the Russian Church divided missionary activities into an "external mission" (*vneshniaia missiia*) and an "internal mission" (*vnutrenniaia missiia*). The former was directed toward non-Orthodox (*inoslavnye*) peoples within the empire and abroad and played a minor role in introducing patriotism to the Church. The internal mission, on the other hand, was directed toward the Orthodox community, and it was here that clerical Orthodox patriotism was strongest.

Preserving this community and recovering the "lost sheep" who wandered from its fold were the most basic tasks of the internal mission. Its goal was to engage indifferent, sectarian, and schismatic Orthodox in a public dialogue about ecclesial self-consciousness.⁴ The means of doing this varied, but from the start the temptation existed to adapt the internal mission's strategies of persuasion to trends that dominated contemporary secular culture. Since national self-consciousness was beginning to flourish among Russia's literate public, the clergy frequently chose to address their audience in this idiom. After all, St Paul had spoken of being "all things to all people" in order to advance the Gospel. For asmall but influential group of Church leaders the emergence of Orthodox patriotism offered an instrument for advancing the mission and the ideals held by the conservative Church leadership. The present chapter will explore the cultural dimension of the internal mission and its role in promoting Orthodox patriotism.

ORTHODOX PATRIOTISM AND THE MISSIONARY MOVEMENT

The promotion of national culture was for the most part alien to the practices of the Church mission. Nevertheless, the mission called upon symbols and ideals found in Church tradition and redeployed them to characterize its activities within a patriotic secular culture. This strategy was highlighted in the early issues of *Missionerskoe obozrenie*, the official organ of the internal mission. There on the cover an epigraph appeared regularly that sought to characterize the internal mission in Russia by quoting the Church's responsibility "to the lost sheep of the house of Israel."[5] The journal's programmatic statement in 1896 interpreted this New Testament passage for its clerical readership. The passage, it declared, applied particularly to the Orthodox community of modern Russia. As the editors asked, "in the home of the God-chosen new Israel—our national Church—who are these lost sheep if not the legions of our blood brothers who have broken away from us?"[6] The ideal of Russia as the new Israel will be discussed in the next chapter, but the statement suggests that "blood" and therefore national ancestry were beginning to play an important role in defining the character of the mission. For its leaders, in other words, the boundaries of the sheepfold were not just ecclesial. They were also national.

The feeling of crisis that precipitated the promotion of nationality was expressed in the speeches and reports of the Third All-Russian Missionary Congress a year after the founding of *Missionerskoe obozrenie*, in 1897. Convened in Kazan, whence the external mission to pagan Siberia and Muslim Central Asia was directed, it also registered the voice of those responsible for the internal mission to Russia's Orthodox. The bishops, parish priests, and journalists who attended constituted the largest missionary gathering to date, a fact that underlined their growing concern with the Orthodox community.[7] The mood of the congress was expressed by a special synodal liaison and by the editor of *Missionerskoe obozrenie*, V. M. Skvortsov, who, though not a member of the clergy, was to become one of the leading lights of Orthodox patriotism. Skvortsov produced a book-length account of the gathering written in dark tones. The Orthodox Church in Russia, he warned, faced a "grave illness" of apostasy and indifference that had begun to assume the "characteristics of an epidemic."[8]

Addresses and debates delivered during the course of the congress's two weeks confirmed this somber impression. Some delegates described the inactivity of the parish clergy in defending the faith among their flocks.[9] Some lamented the insufficiency of parish libraries and reading rooms for disseminating apologetic literature.[10] Still others called for the organization of a greater number of popular pilgrimages and other activities to deepen the common people's loyalty to the official Church.[11] Reflecting the specter of secularization, a missionary from Kherson provided a colorful account of the "abnormal condition in the religious-moral way of life among workers in factories."[12] As a whole, the congress's discussions revealed a feeling of deep concern about the condition of the faith among Russia's Orthodox. Significantly, virtually all of the addresses touched on matters that were strictly ecclesial, and deviations by the Orthodox flock were measured by the conventional standards of biblical, patristic, and canonical precedent. Nevertheless, the clergy sought innovative activities that would effectively permeate the other spheres of modern Russian life.

One of these spheres was culture. Skvortsov himself attended the congress, and as one of the leading authorities in missionary affairs he took the opportunity to outline the Church's relationship to culture in the opening ceremony. He spoke to the missionaries about the "cultural-historical tasks" of Russia, which, he argued, consisted of the preservation and dissemination of the Orthodox faith. Russia's Orthodox destiny would "fully depend upon the solidity of her cultural-historical foundation." The Orthodox mission, in short, could not exist outside and independently of the national culture that surrounded it. This idea, after all, was consistent with the Church's eschatological tradition described in the previous chapter. For Skvortsov, it was necessary that missionaries incorporate patriotic rhetoric and feeling into their appeal to the masses. He himself called upon the triad of "Official Nationality" (Orthodoxy, autocracy, nationality) to characterize true patriotism. But whereas another orator, Deputy Chief Procurator Vladimir Sabler (1847–1929) (who with Pobedonostsev himself had been present in Kiev for the baptism festival), sought to emphasize the leading role of the state in national life, Skvortsov, while giving the state a position of high respect, brought greater attention to Orthodoxy as the constituent element of national culture.[13] "It is necessary to conclude," he insisted, "that Orthodoxy, as the foundation of Holy Rus and in light of its ancient services to her, constitutes the primal influence upon the development and consolidation of national self-consciousness."[14] The nation's destiny, he insisted, must be guided by "Orthodox-national and truly-Russian ideals" of cultural life.[15]

Skvortsov's concern about Russia's "cultural-historical foundation" indicates that, to some leaders of the internal mission, culture represented a missionary field. They were conscious that the empire had ceased to be the pious and homogeneous community found in representations of medieval Rus. The Russia of the late nineteenth century, on the contrary, possessed an increasingly divisive and secular modern culture.

In the wake of the Enlightenment, all European societies had to some extent witnessed the emergence of secular communities of debate that were critical of the traditional religious order. In Russia, where an isolated nobility and a repressive censorship had kept this debate to a minimum, an increasingly educated public had existed for the better part of a century.[16] It generally resembled its western counterparts by looking to secular reasoning for its standards of justice and order. Among its principles was the improvement of social institutions, though the autocratic regime and Church censorship prevented a fruitful pursuit of this goal. Barred from influence, the educated public valued the secular realm all the more, for it was here that it found both justification for its goals and the hope of implementing them in the future. Spurred by a spirit of openness and progress in the wake of the Great Reforms under Alexander II, the educated Russian public began to turn to the peasants and urban masses in an effort to bring them under its influence and promote social improvement. It sponsored an effort to educate and in some ways to indoctrinate these social elements to conform to its secular social ideals. A result of this enterprise, especially among conservatives, was the promotion of a mutually recognizable system of cultural symbols that would bridge an otherwise broad social chasm between it and the people.

Jeffrey Brooks has explored this "search for cultural unity" and has discerned within it a project to propagate a secular model of nationality among the people.[17] Independent of both Church and state, the secular public located the symbolism for the national community especially in the literary works of great nineteenth-century writers such as Alexander Pushkin (1799–1837), Nicholas Gogol (1809–1852), and Leo Tolstoy (1828–1910). The attitude of these writers toward the official Church ranged from loyal to ambivalent to even hostile, yet as a whole their works presented cultural leaders with a source for the national self-consciousness that exchanged the preeminence of Orthodoxy with secular criteria of culture and ancestry. In the hands of the patriotic writers and publishers who directed the public appeal to the masses, therefore, such sources constituted a model of nationality to rival that of the official clergy. In Brooks's words, the public threatened "to forge a new sense of national consciousness as an alternative to popular identification with the tsar and the Orthodox Church."[18]

Conscious of this secular challenge, the missionary clergy began to participate in the period's project to define a Russian national community. They believed they were in a good position to do so because they possessed close links with the masses in the form of parish priests and their legal status as guardians of the empire's "predominant and preeminent" (*gospodstvuiushchaia i pervenstvuiushchaia*) faith.[19] Furthermore, they were an important force in conducting a literacy program among the people that, by 1914, had helped considerably to raise the empire's overall level of literacy.[20] The clergy's close contact with the newly literate masses provided an opportunity to seek a leading role in the formation of national self-consciousness. Even more fundamentally, the question of who constituted the nation was of vital importance to an institution that had long claimed moral leadership of the people. The state-formulated model of Russianness, Official Nationality, had granted first place to the role of Orthodoxy and placed autocracy close behind. As long as the imperial model remained unchallenged, the Church had been content with these two constituent elements, leaving the vaguely conceived third element of nationality in the background. Statements about Russian nationality by the clergy before the Great Reforms generally did not emphasize culture or ancestry.

In the missionary context of the decades after the Great Reforms, however, Church leaders close to the mission propagated a model of the nation that placed great emphasis on ethnic character. In this way they sought to establish what Charles Taylor has called a "horizon" for defining the self, in this case a collective and religious self.[21] Fearful that ecclesial identity was declining among the Orthodox community, Church leaders supplemented it with symbols of nationality in order to strengthen it. For them, the symbolic horizon of nationality would provide a point of orientation for the Orthodox faithful and lead them away from secular models of community—nationalist as well as socialist—then emerging in Russia. A visual expression of this project was recorded in one of the period's missionary journals, *Strannik* (*Wanderer*). The cover of each issue depicted an Orthodox "wanderer" (*strannik*), presumably with his back to modern society, searching the horizon for his point of orientation. In the distance toward which he gazes rise Orthodox crosses and onion domes. Holy Rus, the suggested object of his attention, was intended to serve as a symbolic horizon for those whom the conventional Church sheepfold could no longer enclose.

CULTURAL MISSIONARIES

The cultural field of the internal mission has not been adequately explored by historians. The few accounts of the late imperial mission that exist consider only its strictly defined religious activities.[22] When leaders described the Church's "cultural mission" (*kulturnaia missiia*), they identified nationality as a programmatic element. In 1910, for instance, the editors of *Tserkovnyi vestnik* discussed a "project to spread Russian culture to distant places of Siberia." As the editors related, the leader of this project believed that Orthodox peasant settlers in the East could be protected from sectarianism and the schism if the local clergy worked to implant a feeling of national self-consciousness among them.[23]

The missionary to whom they referred was Archpriest John Vostorgov (1864–1918), one of the most active and influential clerical Orthodox patriots of the period. A graduate of Stavropol Seminary in 1887, he was ordained to the priesthood two years later and became a dedicated servant of the internal mission, spending several years among the masses of displaced Orthodox settlers in Siberia who had appeared in response to Prime Minister Peter Stolypin's (1862–1911) program to alleviate European Russia's land hunger.[24] Later he made a tour of eastern dioceses and in 1909 published his impressions in a series of articles appearing in Moscow and St Petersburg newspapers. Passing through dioceses such as Tomsk, where in two years he claimed that almost two million settlers had gathered, he lamented the weaknesses of conventional Church authority.[25] In Cheliabinsk, he was shocked at the "absence of churches and priests" and regarded this as a cause of the people's growing religious indifference. Orthodox settlers neglected to baptize their children, he noted, and a growing number were succumbing to the appeals of sectarians, who "fill the wagons of settlers with their literature." One of Vostorgov's measures to oppose these developments was to take part in the "free distribution of eight hundred thousand brochures and books with a religious-patriotic content."[26] Many of these publications originated in publishing houses such as Vernost, a missionary press of which Vostorgov himself became editor.

Indeed, one of the methods of gathering the Church's lost sheep in the late imperial period was the dissemination of inexpensive or free missionary publications. A survey of the literature from several of these publishing houses indicates that while conventional Orthodox apologetics continued to constitute the average missionary appeal, publications such as those distributed by Vostorgov were beginning to employ the symbolism and rhetoric of nationality to make their case among the newly literate masses. Evidence can be found in the catalogs published for popular audiences by the printing house of the Orthodox Missionary Society. Alongside catechisms, expositions of the New Testament, and other standard works treating the universal Church, historical accounts of Russia's medieval past (the baptism of 988 in particular) and national saints were frequently issued.[27] For its part, the Church's Commission of General-Educational Readings for Moscow Factory Workers also established a press with works intended to instill Christian virtue and combat secularization through the development of Russian ethnic self-consciousness. Publications here emphasized the glory of medieval Russian history, Russian geography, modern Russian composers, and artists of the "Russian school."[28] In turn, culturally engaged missionary societies such as the Society of Lovers of Spiritual Enlightenment, also in Moscow, sponsored public readings where the audience might listen to these and other patriotic works. Auditors of the readings in 1904, for instance, were informed not only of the perceived evils of Old Belief and Friedrich Nietzsche (1844–1900), but also of the wholesome national vision of Slavophiles such as Alexei Khomiakov (1804–1860).[29] The Society of Lovers of Spiritual Enlightenment also promoted interest in Russian national culture by funding research, publications, and readings on medieval icon painting.[30]

The Vernost publishing house, a leader in the dissemination of patriotic literature,[31] issued a range of cheap brochures that ranged in price between one and thirty-five kopecks. Launched in the divisive and politically charged atmosphere of 1905, it strongly promoted both statist and cultural definitions of the Russian nation. Its programmatic statement appeared on the back page of publications and declared a goal of solidifying loyalty to the "monarchical state." While individual works endorsed the official formula of "faith, tsar, and fatherland," however, the literature often celebrated Russia's cultural particularism. As its editor, Vostorgov made frequent contributions. Under titles such as *Patriotism and Christianity* and *Orthodoxy in the History of Russia*, he outlined for his simple audience how a modern Holy Rus possesses one encompassing national destiny, "the bearing of Christianity and its sanctified culture."[32] Like Skvortsov, he acknowledged the tsar as an inseparable participant in the fulfillment of this destiny. But, again like Skvortsov, he also argued that without a strong national self-consciousness based on culture and ancestry the people would be unfit for their task. In his view the most dynamic proponent of the national faith was not the tsar but the Russian people, who he regarded as the "God-bearing people."[33] In his Vernost publications and the four volumes of moral and pedagogical addresses published during his career, this model of the Russian nation was promoted incessantly.[34]

In his struggle to advance the internal mission, Vostorgov placed considerable weight on the role of culture. His early addresses of the 1880s and 1890s claimed that the condition of Russia's culture must be a matter of concern to the Church. An address delivered in 1899 on this theme argued for a close union between Orthodoxy and the worldly order that includes economic life, social relations, and symbolic culture. Framing his argument within eschatological tradition, he stated that man's participation in the providential design is impossible without a transfiguration of the worldly environment. It was necessary, in other words, that the worldly order possess institutions conducive to the dissemination and preservation of the true faith. Here a religiously based culture was crucial, for its symbols and customs provided the soil in which that faith could be planted and flourish. As he put it, the Church must affirm culture because it serves as the "instrument and location for sowing the kingdom of God" on earth.[35]

As an instrument in the hands of the Church, it could also be used to shape ecclesial loyalty. By appropriating a culture shaped by nationality, Vostorgov and other missionaries believed they could frame a symbolic horizon of Orthodox identity for a public who appeared to be drifting more and more toward religious heterodoxy and indifference. Orthodox patriotism, then, was less an expression of clerical conservatism, as historians have always claimed, and more a product of missionary ambition. Its dominant rhetorical construction, Holy Rus, was neither a "myth" (Cherniavsky) nor a "reactionary utopia" (Zyrianov), but a model of nationality designed to change the face of Russia's secular culture. Indeed, its goal was to transfigure that culture into a religious one.

Having considered the ecclesial function of Holy Rus, it is now possible to analyze various manifestations of the cultural mission in more detail. Orthodox patriotism expressed itself in the years after the baptism festival in three particularly notable projects: the cultivation of a medieval historical memory, the canonization of national literature, and the dissemination of a Russian style of religious art. Each project illustrates the Church's effort to elaborate a national culture based in Orthodox tradition.

THE HISTORIOGRAPHY OF HOLY RUS

The internal mission's sense of crisis was closely associated with a belief that the modern Church had fallen from a standard of piety set in medieval Rus. Recognizing the challenges that this presented, Church leaders looked to the past for standards of ecclesial loyalty. While they may have overestimated the piety of the period prior to Peter the Great the distant medieval past offered an appealing picture of Church self-determination and popular religious life to contrast with the synodal system and secular culture of the empire. As the baptism festival showed, medieval Rus offered a "usable past" from which to shape a modern self-consciousness. It was not enough to admonish people simply to turn to the ecclesial example of their ancestors. Cultural missionaries sought to create links to that past that were based upon nationality. In this they were influenced by the activity of contemporary cultural leaders. The secular public used historical memory during the period to develop what Seymour Becker has called a "sense of shared national identity."[36] Regarding the medieval past as their own inheritance, the clergy competed jealously with the public for control of the collective historical imagination.

To this end the clergy utilized the expanded Church press of the time to publish and distribute narrative accounts of the national community written in the form of Church histories.[37] According to one narrative, "ecclesiality" (*tserkovnost*), was embodied in the historical experience of a particular "nation" (*narod*). Thus the "Church life of medieval Rus" presented a rich source for framing the national community. This was true especially for the seventeenth century, when the Russian people were undivided by religious schism and had come to possess a strong state and independent culture. The seventeenth century was also remembered as a time when "the life of the Russian people was [not yet] taken from the hands of the Church."[38]

This common image of a seventeenth-century Russian nation had an interesting corollary. If the model of nationality was found in pre-Nikonian Rus, then contemporary Old Believers, whose communities and culture maintained many medieval customs more intensely than the official Church, were logical candidates for membership in the national community. Such was the conclusion of Evseev. "Our contemporary Old Believers" he admitted, present "a vital witness of church self-consciousness. . . . Their ideals, their strivings—their entire way of life—all of this was what constituted the world-view of the seventeenth century."[39] The missionary argument about the medieval past was thus a knife that cut both ways. As we shall see, Old Believer intellectuals were aware of this and would be quick to use it to challenge the official Church.

In addition to the short works on historical topics produced by missionary presses and spiritual journals, large surveys of Church history provided a comprehensive vision of how national culture had been shaped in the medieval period by Orthodoxy. A two-volume account written by A. Beliaev in 1894 was an example. Illustrated profusely, it sought to communicate with its simple audience by employing an appealing format and simple prose. Rather than follow scholarly standards of criticism, it affirmed what even at that time were dubious legends of Russian Christianity, such as the first-century missionary journey of St Andrew to the hills of a future Kiev. The author's goal was not scholarly inquiry, however, but cultural influence. The history of the Russian Church was told as the history of the "Russian nation" (*russkii narod*), a construction that appears in all places throughout the narrative. Moreover, Beliaev made little distinction between the nation of medieval Rus and that of modern Russia, consciously seeking to fuse the two communities. This rhetorical practice, resembling the clerical addresses of 1888, underscored the Orthodox patriotic argument that modern Russia found her ideals and standards of community in the religious order of the past. Disregarding what to a trained historian must have been blatant anachronisms, he employed "Rus" to describe the modern Church and "Russia" to describe the state of the sixteenth century.[40]

Rhetorical devices aside, Beliaev's aim was to convince simple readers that a Russian national community had existed since the time of the baptism in 988 and that Orthodoxy served as its constituent system of symbols, values, and beliefs. He described in great detail Russia's national saints such as Sergius of Radonezh, presenting them as manifestations of the national faith. As the "father of monasticism in Muscovite Rus," Sergius and his piety were linked closely to the Russian people, whose "love of monasticism flowed from the Christian faith."[41] Summing up the medieval period, Beliaev described how "the Russian people were brought to maturity under the beneficent influence of the Orthodox faith. Orthodoxy became the distinct feature of Russian nationality, the soul of the Russian people."[42]

Nor did he close his narrative without casting an ambivalent glance over the post-Petrine period. While the imperial Church order enjoyed greater administrative strength and missionary activity than its medieval predecessor, it had experienced a constant spiritual atrophy as the "material logic" of the state had come to overshadow it.[43] "The Russian people," on the other hand, continued along a spiritual path "by which [they had] traveled for centuries."[44] As evidence of the survival of the national faith, Beliaev cited modern holy men such as Seraphim of Sarov, Tikhon of Zadonsk (1724–1783), and Feodosii of Chernigov (d. 1696).[45] The narrative ended by acknowledging weaknesses in Church life but affirming a national community that continued to embody its medieval teachings. The lesson of this narrative was clear: the modern Church must turn to her national past in order to survive.

Beliaev's depiction of a vital national culture in medieval Rus was repeated in other popular histories. A book titled *Medieval Rus in Great Days* devoted its longest chapter to the fading culture of the community it called "Holy Rus." It explained to the reader how "our time is primarily a time of external culture and external good-order." With the rise of this secular culture in the nineteenth century, however, Russia's "modern man" had been severed from the source of his nationality, which for the pious inhabitants of medieval Rus had consisted in Church customs and religious services.[46]

A PILGRIMAGE TO THE PAST

Popular Church historiography served the cultural mission of Orthodox patriotism by directing the historical imagination back to a time when Orthodoxy appeared as the source of nationality. The clergy were not content with the publication of histories alone, however. As the baptism festival of 1888 had revealed, public commemorations of the medieval past offered another opportunity for the Church leadership to direct the public mind toward what it regarded as the genuine national community. The baptism anniversary had its share of historical reflection, witnessed by the Kiev Spiritual Academy's public lectures and discussions in the press about the origins of Russian national self-consciousness. Church leaders thus came to use the lesson of 1888 to organize a number of national commemorations in subsequent decades. Channeling the popular intellect toward distant events in medieval Rus, these commemorations served as quests of the historical imagination. In most cases they actually included a Church-organized journey to one of Russia's holy places. The essence of the pilgrimage remained intellectual, however. It was designed before all else as a pilgrimage to the past.

With the exception of the Germogen commemoration of 1913, the most significant such pilgrimage occurred in 1892, which marked the five-hundred-year anniversary of the repose of Russia's revered national saint, Sergius of Radonezh. Sergius was a fourteenth-century holy man who abandoned the world to seek knowledge of God and salvation in the woods north of Moscow. His reputation for holiness and brotherly kindness had created a following, and before the end of his life a hermitage had been established with him as its spiritual leader. After his death this hermitage, the future Trinity-Sergius Lavra, grew to become the center of monasticism in medieval Russia and a yearly destination for thousands of common pilgrims. It remained so until the Revolution. Sergius's single most famous act occurred well before his death, however. In 1380 he blessed the army of Muscovite prince Dmitry Donskoi (1350–1389) as it set off for battle with the Mongols. Dmitry's subsequent victory on Kulikovo Field marked the beginning of the end of Tartar domination. Sergius had prophesied in that troubled time that "health will return to the fatherland," and this saying must have inspired the Church's decision to organize its commemoration more than five centuries later. According to Scott Kenworthy, the event represented "the most massive single pilgrimage event at Trinity-Sergius in the nineteenth century."[47]

To promote popular participation, news of the celebration was distributed throughout the empire's dioceses in the months before the anniversary days of late September. Pilgrims began to arrive in the monastery town of Sergiev Posad well in advance of the opening ceremonies and religious services on September 25. Some had journeyed from remote corners of Russia, while many more were merely from the environs of nearby Moscow. But whether they arrived in bast shoes by foot or first-class train compartments by rail, the people and their interest told Church organizers that the struggle for cultural leadership had not yet been lost to the secular public. The ceremonies themselves were much more modest than the baptism festival, and participation by an empire-wide audience was in this case notably lacking. In the absence of local parades and speeches, most of the events took place in Moscow or Sergiev Posad. The high point of the festival was on September 25, when a large-scale pilgrimage from Moscow arrived at the monastery and a series of public addresses were read in the hall of the Moscow Spiritual Academy there. A number of Church historians delivered rousing speeches about the medieval cultural order and St Sergius's influence in shaping it. They included the eminent Church historian E. E. Golubinskii, who prepared a speech that contrasted the culture of modern Russia with that of medieval Rus.[48]

The most substantial account of Sergius's significance in modern times, however, was provided by none other than Vasily Kliuchevsky (1841–1911). As the period's preeminent secular historian, Kliuchevsky exerted a great influence over the historical consciousness of late imperial Russia. His *Course in Russian History*, when completed, became a standard account among both scholars and the educated public of the Russian past. Upon his death in 1911, cultural leaders were quick to proclaim his work a "triumph of the national idea in Russian historical science."[49] Robert Byrnes has recently described the historian as a leader in the project to form a Russian nation based on culture and ancestry.[50] His prolific work, which focused especially on the experience of the common people, outlined for contemporaries how over the course of centuries a conglomeration of various tribes had been joined by customs and language to create the modern nation of Russia. With such credentials, Kliuchevsky's address at the Trinity-Sergius Lavra offers an interesting case for estimating the influence of clerical Orthodox patriotism on the contemporary public.

In front of an audience of priests and pilgrims at the monastery, Kliuchevsky presented a vision of national destiny that came remarkably close to those of the period's cultural missionaries. Standing beneath the onion domes of the holy place, surrounded by its shrines, springs, and relics, Kliuchevsky linked the many pilgrims before him to past generations of medieval Rus who had traveled there for sanctification. For five full centuries, he stated, such vital engagement with native holy places and holy objects had characterized the culture and consciousness of Russia. It had been an essential, "unchanging" element in Russian life. "If there could be rendered into writing all that has been recorded in memory of the saint," he mused, "all which in these five hundred years was silently thought and felt in front of his tomb by these millions of minds and hearts, such a testament would be the complete and deepest record of the history of our national, political, and moral life."

The "distant descendants" of an earlier Rus who now stood before the historian were not cut off from their nationality, Kliuchevsky argued, so long as they maintained a consciousness of Russia's past religious origins. In fact, by developing this consciousness they could enter into a sort of spiritual national community. "In the consciousness of these generations," he said, "all is abandoned that is temporal and local . . . when the contemporary individual transfigures these into a national idea." To promote the development of this idea, St Sergius and other national saints dwelt in the "soul of the people," preserving them as they entered each new historical epoch. For Kliuchevsky, "such persons become for subsequent generations not simply great ancestors, but eternal companions [*vechnymi sputnikami*], even their guides, and whole centuries reverently affirm their dear names not so much to gratefully observe their memory, but to ensure that their example may never be forgotten." Making an indirect reference to the book of Matthew, Kliuchevsky concluded his address by likening the saints of medieval Rus to a "leaven" that yields the "kingdom of heaven." Likewise, Orthodoxy is a leaven that yields a modern national culture, so long as each new generation of Russians preserves the memory of its "eternal companions," the national saints. This, he stated, is the nation's "spiritual reserve."[51]

Kliuchevsky's address indicates that clerical Orthodox patriotism had gained a measurable influence over the project to form a national community. It is true that the historian avoided constructions such as "Holy Rus," which he seemed never to have employed in a historical publication.[52] Nevertheless, on the occasion of the Church's commemoration of St Sergius, he showed a readiness to embrace images of Orthodox patriotism such as the national saints, the kingdom of heaven, and national holy objects. By employing them to define Russian nationality, he advanced the internal mission's goal of transforming the empire's secular culture into a religious one.

And in addition to the great historian's responsiveness, the clergy could find satisfaction in the enthusiasm expressed by common Russians who participated in the four-day pilgrimage from Moscow to Sergiev Posad. At least one hundred thousand finally turned up in the monastery town to witness the commemoration there.[53] A much larger number were reported to have gathered at the Kremlin in Moscow to launch it. One estimate claimed that as many as three hundred thousand participated in the sending-off ceremonies at Uspensky Cathedral. This gathering provoked in one clerical correspondent an outburst of optimism about the cultural mission. He took the immense size of the gathering as a sign that modern "atheistic propaganda" among the people had been a failure. The present pilgrimage to the past, he claimed, showed that the Church had recovered its earlier level of cultural influence "on the very eve of the twentieth century."

> Entering a new period of life while at the same time turning backwards to recall the lessons of the past is an act that assures that the future will not witness the repetition of former mistakes. The greatest mistake . . . was the rejection of Orthodoxy and nationality. If this doesn't bring forth the fruit of destruction for the entire Russian land, then it will be possible to say that here there was an occurrence not of the natural order, but the miraculous intercession of the saints of that Russian land.[54]

THE CANONIZATION OF NATIONAL LITERATURE

Images of old Rus were not the only expression of nationality for Church leaders. They believed that modern secular literature possessed many promising talents, despite the influence of Western tastes and interests. Another indicator of the rising function of nationality in the cultural mission was a growing body of commendations for secular writers regarded as exemplary manifestations of the national faith. Efforts to form a national community by the secular public had set a premium on the rich body of fictional literature and poetry produced during the course of the nineteenth century. Geoffrey Hosking, for instance, has illustrated efforts by the public to "weave together the torn social and cultural fabric of Russian society" with the symbolism of secular literature.[55] In his estimation, secular literature did "far more . . . than the output of state or Church to lay the foundations for a Russian national identity which could embrace both elite and people."[56] As many historians have noted, for instance, Alexander Pushkin's work was widely invoked to serve this purpose. In addition to their interest in the medieval past, composers of the national school had all but exhausted his oeuvre in their effort to establish a particularly Russian style of musical culture. Glinka, Mussorgsky, Tchaikovsky, and Rimsky-Korsakov based their most popular operas on creations of the great national poet. By the late nineteenth century, secular literature had become widely accepted as a source for defining nationality.

Cultural missionaries sought to participate in this development to ensure that Orthodoxy recovered its preeminent status. One of the first regularly to praise secular writers for their contribution to the national culture was Archbishop Nikanor of Kherson.[57] Vostorgov was also impressed by Pushkin and used Nikanor's example to deliver a series of addresses on the occasion of the poet's centennial in 1899. Vostorgov praised Pushkin for his role in providing the Russian people with values and symbols that would define their nationality. He made reference to the famous celebration of the poet in 1880 in Moscow, at which Ivan Turgenev (1818–1883), Fyodor Dostoevsky, and other cultural figures had consolidated Pushkin's place in the national literary canon. The fact that Pushkin had never been a very fervent member of the Church did not dissuade the missionary priest from recommending his works to the people. "The so-called half-hearted faithfulness of his early years," he assured the audience, "did not run deeply." Nevertheless, he spent considerable time exploring the poet's religious views and quoted his works at length. His conclusion was that the opinion of "the literary critic" who praises Pushkin for purely secular achievements incompletely grasps his significance for the nation. As part of his status as a national poet, Vostorgov insisted, he must be remembered first as a "Christian person."[58]

While Pushkin may have tested the sympathy of Orthodox patriots, the works of more religious writers were readily embraced. Gogol was frequently praised in this regard, but Dostoevsky most often served this purpose. Despite the fact that many of the novelist's sympathetic characters expressed doubts about the existence of God, his ecstatic visions of a national destiny in which an Orthodox "idea" was the guiding force appealed to the culturally engaged clergy. His appeal may also have been influenced by the clergy's universal scorn for his only rival for the status of greatest Russian novelist, Tolstoy.

Whereas Dostoevsky had died on the eve of the tsar's assassination in 1881, leaving behind a highly patriotic body of work for the clergy's appropriation, Tolstoy was at that time just turning decisively away from Orthodox Christianity. In the years that followed the publication of *Anna Karenina* (1877), his anticlerical writings and patronage of the Dukhobor sect were a scandal for defenders of the Church. Few years passed in which a spiritual journal failed to publish at least one diatribe against the embittered literary polemicist, and in 1901 he was finally excommunicated. Skvortsov, for his part, played a leading role in this effort.[59] In addition, witnessing the rise of Orthodox patriotism among the Russian clergy, Tolstoy produced a tract designed to undermine the very making of a Holy Russia. In *Christianity and Patriotism*, he attacked all manifestations of patriotism and argued that Christ's teachings in fact strongly condemned the principle of a particular love for one's fatherland.[60] Finally, his nonconformity and cosmopolitanism no doubt became all the more intolerable to Church leaders because of his status as an eminent Russian national writer among the secular public. Such a status, after all, contradicted the clergy's arguments about the preeminence of Orthodoxy in constituting Russianness.

Dostoevsky, on the other hand, delivered what the clergy was looking for. His writings, with their description of Russia as a "God-bearing people" (*narod-bogonosets*) and scorn for secular and western European culture, provided the late imperial mission with an eloquent and popular formulation of an Orthodox national destiny.[61] The didactic *Diary of a Writer*, especially, offered its readers a model of national identity and made judgments about current social and cultural issues that were sympathetic to the Church. It appears to have inspired a number of clerical open diaries of the time. One was the popular column "Moi dnevnik" of Bishop Nikon (Rozhdestvenskii), which was published in the spiritual journal *Troitskoe slovo* (*Trinity Word*) between 1910 and 1915.

An example of Dostoevsky's appropriation and the missionary turn to a national culture is found in the writings of Archbishop Antony of Volynia. This great conservative prelate with experience in missionary work among the Old Believers often referred to Dostoevsky in the course of patriotic addresses.[62] In his efforts to establish dialogue with idealistic philosophers after the turn of the century, he cited the novelist as a source of mutual inspiration around whose ideas all true Russian patriots could gather.[63] He regarded Dostoevsky's novels as a source of wisdom about social ethics and even proposed their use in pastoral work by the Church.[64] So important was the writer for Russia's national culture that in 1888 Antony recommended him as an object of yearly commemorations on the anniversary of his death, thus canonizing his ideas though not his person.[65]

ORTHODOX PATRIOTISM AND THE LITURGICAL ARTS

In addition to historical depictions of medieval Rus and efforts to canonize patriotic literature, cultural missionaries used artistic representations of the nation to strengthen ecclesial self-consciousness. Commemorative pilgrimages to the past in 1888 and 1892 had been, in fact, purposefully associated with temples, icons, and hymnography. While evangelization through spiritual beauty had always been a technique of the Church, particular features of late imperial culture encouraged the mission's appropriation of the liturgical arts. As with the revival of historical memory and the canonization of literature, the secular public initially took the lead.

First, the 1880s witnessed the rise of a "national school" of painting that directed viewers' imaginations to Russia's medieval past. An example was Surikov's *Boyarinia Morozova* (1887), a large canvas portraying its seventeenth-century subject as a noble and devout Old Believer preparing to die for her religious faith. Secular architecture of the period also began to highlight medieval and distinctly Russian motifs. Throughout the empire, public buildings appeared that used as ornamentation the tent roofs, radiating arches, and paired columns of churches from the sixteenth century.[66] Much of this enthusiasm overflowed into projects by secular artists to revive medieval styles of church architecture. In the artists' colony of Abramtsevo near Sergiev Posad, for instance, residents including Mikhail Vrubel (1856–1910) and Victor Vasnetsov constructed a mock medieval chapel in 1882 for little other reason, it seems, than to hone their creative talent. Finally, musical composition also turned to the medieval past for inspiration. A national school produced a series of successful operas, including Mussorgsky's *Boris Godunov* (1874) and *Khovanshchina* (1880), Borodin's *Prince Igor* (1887), and a string of titles celebrating historical and folk themes by Rimsky-Korsakov up until his death in 1908. Taken as a whole, these cultural developments created a "Russian style" of secular art. This term had its origins particularly in the period's architecture, but with justice it may be applied to the broad range of artistic techniques and media that promoted the formation of a culturally distinct Russian nation.[67]

Church leaders viewed the Russian style with great interest. The medieval revival that accompanied it was seen as a sign that at least part of secular society was ready to move away from the antihistorical and frequently anticlerical values of the reform decades. Some may have remembered with bitterness the social criticism contained in the works of earlier artists such as Vasily Perov (d. 1882), whose *Monastic Refectory* (1875), for instance, had depicted a bloated and indolent clergy devouring wines and delicacies while hungry peasants looked on. And, of course, the Russian style promoted nationality. The affirmation of a national community in which Orthodoxy was seen as a leading cultural symbol was a source of inspiration for those who perceived a crisis in the contemporary Church order. Church leaders thus gave their conditional approval to the Russian style, provided it conveyed a vision of national life in which Orthodox symbolism was preeminent. They employed it in a variety of artistic media to influence the ecclesial self-consciousness of the people.

The national and in most cases medieval themes of the Russian style were readily adapted to a liturgical context. Music, for instance, was a case in which Orthodox patriotism could be linked to contemporary trends in composition and taste. As secular composers experimented with historical themes in operas and tone poems, Church musical journals such as the weekly *Baian* began to appear and called for a revival of "our medieval composers." This meant, of course, musical churchmen.[68] One of the most interesting cases in which cultural missionaries influenced secular composers occurred at the Synodal School in Moscow. The school possessed one of the most talented choirs in Russia under the direction of Stepan Smolenskii (d. 1909), who actively promoted a return to medieval liturgical styles of singing such as znamenny chant.[69] Interestingly, he claimed the influence of contemporary Old Believers and based his work in part on their example. His enthusiasm bore fruit when leading composers such as Serge Rachmaninov (1873–1943) began to collaborate with the school and compose works reviving the features of medieval Russian singing. Rachmaninov's *All-Night Vigil* (1915), dedicated to the choirmaster, was notable for its use of the deep bass voices understood to be common in old Rus. A series of talented and purely liturgical composers trained at the Moscow School, including Pavel Chesnokov (d. 1944) and Alexander Grechaninov (d. 1956), whose works came to attain wide circulation and respect in the Russian Orthodox Church during the twentieth century.

A number of missionary societies also promoted research and interest in iconography that could be defined by the Russian style. Long regarded in the Orthodox Church as a proclamation of the Gospel and an instrument of worship rather than a merely aesthetic endeavor, iconography was highly esteemed in Church life. The process in which icons were produced was traditionally understood as an expression of the Church's universal faith and was not dependent on the inspiration of the individual painter or his particular cultural environment.[70]

Under the influence of Orthodox patriotism, however, cultural leaders of the Church promoted a style of icon painting that was presented as particular to Russia. Moscow's Society of Lovers of Spiritual Enlightenment established departments for the promotion of popular appreciation for icons, and its Church-Archeological Department funded a series of publications that illustrated Russian creative uniqueness. One member was a scholar by the name of D. K. Trenev.[71] In the years before the Revolution he produced a number of programmatic works arguing that, while the Russian people had in truth learned the art of iconography from the Greeks, a universal style of painting had disappeared with the formation of a culturally autonomous nation.

Universal forms of icon painting that were "passed on to us by ancient Byzantine art," Trenev stated, "became fully assimilated by the religious feeling and understanding of our people."[72] The cultural genius of the nation yielded a high point of icon production that lasted throughout the seventeenth century. But with the coming of Peter the Great, this genius was subverted. "The reforms introduced by the strong and decisive hand of Peter I," Trenev stated, "corresponded to a great intensification of everything Western. They were a most brutal and deadly blow to the successful development of our medieval Russian iconography."[73] Despairing about the synodal Church's embrace of foreign influences, Trenev looked with hope to the role of the national community in restoring Russia's past ways. The "spiritual needs of our Russian people," he claimed, "[have ensured that] our declining Russian Orthodox icon painting still lives among us and partly preserves its medieval character."[74]

It is interesting to note that in a later work comparing Russian Orthodox iconography to the secular painting of "modern educated society," Trenev was compelled to deemphasize the role of the individual in the creative process.[75] Here he affirmed Church tradition about the absence of personal genius and feeling. At the same time, though, he maintained his argument that icon painting was a national affair and went so far as to question a secular public that found no inspiration in it. As an alternative model of spirituality and aesthetic taste he even commended "modern Old Believers," who, as a rule, are "well informed about the iconography" of medieval Rus.[76] Trenev's interest in the character of icons reveals the influence of clerical Orthodox patriotism. In this case, the aims of the internal mission were served by defining a Russian style of icon and contrasting it with the tastes of secular society. The Russian style's national logic enabled him to promote it as an essential feature of the Orthodox community, the ultimate concern for his missionary society.

While Trenev's personal effect on the culture of early-twentieth-century Russia cannot be measured, the Russian style he promoted clearly had an influence on the cultural landscape. The temple architecture of the period, after all, became dominated by medieval motifs and forms. Though most were closed down, museumized, or demolished by the Communists in the decades after 1917, a large number of the temples built in St Petersburg at this time were designed in what was generally described as the Russian style. This was an architectural era dominated by Orthodox patriotism, as Chapter 5 will show.

The construction of a church not located in the capital, however, offers the best example of the way in which the artistic program of cultural missionaries was put into practice and the response from the secular public it received. This was the monumental St Vladimir Cathedral in Kiev. The project to build a large church in honor of the apostle-like Grand Prince was actually launched during the reign of Nicholas I.[77] Construction lagged due to structural problems, however, and only in the 1880s did it gain momentum. Adrian Prakhov, a professor at the university, took command of the project in 1886 with a push to finish the work in time for the baptism festival of 1888. Though this proved impossible, his demand that St Vladimir Cathedral "constitute a monument not only to the baptizer of Russia, but to Russia herself and her art," was in fact realized.[78]

Prakhov's aesthetic priority demanded the use of a distinctly national style of art. Nothing could be done about the Byzantine architectural style that dominated the exterior. It had been selected back in the 1850s, before the rise of Orthodox patriotism. The interior frescoes and icons, however, had not been started. The project directors, therefore, set out to turn the interior of the cathedral into a monument to Holy Rus. Two of the painters they recruited were in fact leading secular representatives of the Russian style. One was Victor Vasnetsov, the son of a priest whose renderings of Russian folk legends and fairy tales had already brought him wide recognition. In paintings like *After Prince Igor's Battle with the Polovtsy* (1880) and *Battle between the Scythians and the Slavs* (1881), he brought the medieval past to life and offered the educated public abundant visual images of secular nationality.[79] The second main painter was Mikhail Nesterov. He had just emerged as a young talent in the art world, and his experience in painting icons in St Vladimir Cathedral contributed to what a Soviet biographer calls a "crucial change" in his development toward a more religiously oriented commitment to the Russian style.[80] One of the most influential future proponents of Orthodox patriotism among lay intellectuals, he was beginning his renowned studies of St Sergius when Prakhov discovered him and invited him to come to Kiev to participate in the cathedral project. Along with several other less-well-known painters (though Mikhail Vrubel was actually among them), Vasnetsov and Nesterov labored on the scaffolding there for the better part of a decade. Then, in 1896, the "first national church of a new Russia" was sanctified and their murals and icons were revealed to an expectant Russian public.[81]

One of the more extended accounts of the cathedral interior was a book written by V. L. Dedlov that opened with a summary of the "culture of Great Russia" permeating the cathedral's images.[82] Emphasizing that this was a particularly religious culture, the author focused on Vasnetsov's contributions. In addition to reviewing the architecture and painting, Dedlov used the occasion of St Vladimir Cathedral's consecration to discuss what he regarded as the period's leading aesthetic and cultural questions. He contrasted what he considered the universalistic Church art of western Europe with what he regarded as the cathedral's superior example of native religiosity. For him the element of nationality was in fact the most important matter in Church art. For "when art doesn't stand in national soil," he argued, "it is not art. This we have been taught by our literature and music." Dedlov regarded a universal style of religious art to be "cosmopolitan" and therefore powerless.

This idea was borne out in his tour-like description of the cathedral's most notable murals. "Here on the wall behind the altar is a colossal representation of the Mother of God—this is a Russian Mother of God. . . . Here in the dome is Christ—this is the Russian Christ, whom you have known since childhood."[83] Predictably, the greatest praise was not for the symbols of the universal Church. Vasnetsov's depiction of the "Synaxis of Russian Saints" on the south side of the altar, including Sergius and the missionary Stephen of Perm, was for Dedlov in a way the greatest achievement of the iconographers. Vasnetsov executed the work in spatial opposition to a "Synaxis of Saints of the Universal Church." As backgrounds for the "Synaxis of Russian Saints" he used a series of onion-domed churches and for the "Synaxis of Universal Saints" he used Constantinople's St Sophia Cathedral. Predictably, Dedlov's attention was drawn toward the former. "These are not only real people," he exclaimed; "they are unmistakably Russian people. These national types are as real as the heroes of *Fathers and Sons, War and Peace,* and *The Brothers Karamazov.*"[84]

Another, more subtle account of the cathedral's significance was provided in a spiritual journal by N. V. Rozhdestvenskii. In opening he too discussed Western influences on the development of Russian religious art. Unlike Dedlov, he affirmed what he considered to be valuable contributions made "fully in the Orthodox spirit according to Western techniques." However, he also believed that the secular culture of the nineteenth century had revealed a new principle to religious artists. "The development of Russian art in all regions during the present century," he stated, "indicates clearly and eloquently that subsequent growth can be truly fruitful only under the conditions of its nationality." With this theoretical basis he turned to the St Vladimir Cathedral, where, he claimed, "one breathes Rus."[85]

Rozhdestvenskii himself saw in Vasnetsov's depiction of the Mother of God an expression of the "national spirit" and "the highest artistic representation of the Russian woman." He even quoted a verse by Pushkin to provide concrete symbolism for this impression. He also noted the juxtaposition of

Old Testament prophets and New Testament figures, considering the unity of the old Israel and the new Israel to be "one of the best-loved themes of medieval Russian preaching." Equally expressive of a particular Russian religiosity were the national saints. The image of Stephen of Perm, he said, reminds the viewer of "the enlightening tasks of the Russian clergy and the historical role of the Russian people as the disseminator of Orthodoxy among the pagans." He was especially struck by the "entirely Russian" countenances of Stephen and the others.

Before closing his three-installment account, Rozhdestvenskii surveyed the lively discussion of the cathedral's interior that had arisen in the public press. The secretary of the Orthodox Palestine Society, M. P. Soloviev, and the curator of the Imperial Public Library, V. V. Stasov, were described as two particularly affirmative critics. Indeed, the public's acclaim for the "national church" appeared, as it were, nearly universal. "And so," Rozhdestvenskii concluded, "the Cathedral of St Vladimir in Kiev, apart from all of its general significance for the whole of Russia, possesses, as a religious-historical and national monument to the Russian apostle and the most important event in the Russian past, a completely independent significance in the region of Russian art, especially religious art."[86]

Almost a decade after the baptism festival, then, clerical Orthodox patriots had managed to assert leadership in defining the symbols and imagery of Russian nationality. Their cultural mission "to the lost sheep of the house of Israel" had penetrated the spheres of historical memory, secular literature, and liturgical art. They had demonstrated beyond question that the Orthodox Church was an active participant in the life of modern Russia.

While the images found in the cultural mission offered considerable resources for defining the nation, however, Church leaders were compelled to seek an even more authoritative source for their model of Holy Rus. This they found in the imagery of ancient Israel.

CHAPTER 4

— ✝ —

The New Israel

If the tension between the universal and the particular sometimes seemed irresolvable, clerical Orthodox patriots had a powerful example from the Bible to which they could refer. This was ancient Israel. The experiences recorded in the Old Testament offered a rich source of symbolism for their vision of an ecclesially defined nation, and its canonical authority compensated for their innovative tendency to promote such a model of nationality in the cultural mission. The Old Testament recorded the formation of a primordial nation, Israel, its struggle against the pagan idolatry that surrounded it, the formation of native religious traditions, and the people's subsequent temptations and tribulations in preserving them. In spite of a wayward spiritual character, the tenacity of which repeatedly led the people and their ruler away from the faith, ancient Israel had at all times been the object of God's favor and had repeatedly received His assistance in the form of providential activity. Then, from the perspective of the New Testament, Israel ultimately fulfilled its national mission by offering universal salvation to all nations in the person of the Messiah.

For Orthodox patriots, the eschatological narrative in this experience conformed to many of the patterns they discerned in the history of Russia. What is more, ancient Israel's identity as the one true people of God and its occupation of sacred territory, centered on the holy places of Palestine and the holy objects of the Jerusalem temple, appealed to the ecclesiological and pneumatological structure of Orthodox patriots' thought. As they sought to build authority for their model of Holy Rus, therefore, they were drawn to the Old Testament in general and to the example of ancient Israel in particular.

Nevertheless, an explicit comparison of modern Russia to ancient Israel was paradoxical. While Church tradition recognized an integral relationship between the Old Testament and the New Testament, the Old Testament's authority to delineate God's chosen people was sharply circumscribed by the New Testament's greater emphasis upon universality. The issue of Old Testament authority has a long history in the Church, dating at least from the second-century Marcionite controversy.[1] Its most important expression in Russian history was the fifteenth-century Judaizer controversy, which was suppressed under Ivan III.[2] In the patriotic atmosphere of late imperial Russia, the Old Testament again attracted the interest of innovative Church leaders, who appropriated its image of ancient Israel as an ideal of national self-consciousness. Although they understood that the universalistic teaching of the New Testament seemed to negate the Old Testament's glorification of national particularism, they could facilitate the identification of Russia and ancient Israel with reference to an important ecclesiological precedent.

Ecclesiology in both the East and the West regarded the universal Church as the "new Israel" (*novyi Izrael*)—the community of believers who have been chosen by God as the people of ancient Israel had been. The doctrine imbedded in this metaphor was not particular to any one people, to be sure, but could be traced to the writings of St Paul. In his Epistle to the Romans, Paul outlined the Church's relationship to the chosen people of Old Testament Israel. In sections addressed to foreign Gentiles, he identified himself with his native Israel and vigorously affirmed God's promise to center human salvation upon that particular national community. His conclusion, though, was that with Christ's commandment to disseminate the faith beyond the limits of Israel, membership in the community had ceased to be limited by ancestry, or what he called "children of the flesh."[3] The faith was now universal, and thus all nations were entitled through it to share the status of Israel. As he put it, "if the root is holy, so are the branches."[4]

Orthodox tradition in the late imperial period continued to invoke this metaphorical vision of the Church. Ancient Israel was in fact regarded as the "Old Testament Church," which prefigured the New Testament Church. According to one contemporary Russian theologian, "Old Testament Israel offered a model to the new Israel. It was selected by God from all the peoples as the first-born to preserve and herald in the world the truth of knowledge about God. Christians are the new Israel, adopted to herald the fulfillment of the same providence that called them from the darkness to its miraculous light."[5] As the citations of Old Testament Scripture indicate, the universal Church was therefore directly related in provenance to the nation of ancient Israel.

If these theological origins of the new Israel appeared obscure, Orthodox patriots were encouraged by the fact that Russian religious culture was characterized by the emphatic presence of Old Testament imagery about the nation of Israel. Evidence of this can be found in the important place the Church assigned to the Archangel Michael. In the Old Testament, Michael was one of the greatest of the angels and was invested with personal responsibility for defending God's chosen people in their historical experience on earth.[6] His status in Russian culture was preserved by the wide use of his title in founding towns and churches, the best known examples of which were the great northern town on the White Sea and the Kremlin cathedral in which the grand princes and tsars of Muscovy were buried.[7] He also served as one of the most prominent subjects for icon painting. His image customarily occupied a leading position on the church's iconostasis, preceded from the left side of its center, the Royal Gates, only by the Mother of God, or from the right side by Christ Himself. The familiar image of Archangel Michael was an important cultural symbol that made the theology of the new Israel immediate and visible to Russia's believers and the late imperial priests who were mobilizing to guide them.

In fact, Church leaders could even find a precedent for identifying medieval Rus as the "new Israel" in Muscovite Church tradition. This tradition has received little attention from historians, though it did attract the interest of one scholar in late imperial Russia.[8] An article by Daniel Rowland, which represents one of the few modern treatments of the medieval use of the new Israel metaphor, indicates that its largely ecclesiological connotation lacked substantial emphasis upon nationality in the modern cultural sense.[9]

Among late imperial patriotic clergy, the metaphor had much to recommend it. While the new Israel epithet was seldom invoked explicitly, Church leaders frequently characterized the Russian nation by drawing from Old Testament imagery, believing that this imagery would resonate among the public. Not only was the new Israel metaphor a symbolic device that could underpin their innovative fusion of Church and nation, but it also alluded to familiar images in Russian culture and implied that the claim for national particularism being advanced was grounded in the Bible and Church tradition. The imagery of the new Israel thus offers an important key to understanding clerical Orthodox patriotism. This chapter will explore both the metaphor's explicit appropriation and the more implicit manifestations of it within the cultural mission.

ARCHBISHOP NIKANOR'S EARLY USE OF THE NEW ISRAEL METAPHOR

A good way of introducing the metaphor's role in late imperial Church life is to consider the activities of one of its most influential proponents, Archbishop

Nikanor of Kherson. His career spanned the reigns of Alexander II and Alexander III and represented one of the earliest efforts by a Church leader to embrace Orthodox patriotism. Like many prelates who came of age during the reform years, he was an active leader of the mission, and his efforts to expand it in the later years of Alexander II's reign earned him warm recognition from nascent missionary bodies such as the Orthodox Missionary Society. Like other missionaries, he pursued a career of writing and preaching that was devoted to reshaping Russian culture in response to the dominant intellectual currents of the age. He too believed that a model of nationality must stand at the center of this effort and that the most convenient construction with which to identify it was Holy Rus.[10] He regularly urged the Missionary Society and its affiliates to conduct the Orthodox mission in a patriotic spirit, believing that the mission "is called to preserve and support, to elevate and develop this eternal Russian spirit, which in the first thousand years of Rus converted all according to flesh and blood, converted them by the Russian language and temper."[11] Unlike with most missionaries, though, a premium on ethnic character and ancestry alone was insufficient. Nikanor's contribution to early Orthodox patriotism was the innovative claim that the Russian people were the new Israel.

It appears that Nikanor's first public use of the metaphor was in a sermon delivered in 1860. Subsequently bearing the title "The Russian People Are the New Israel" (*Russkii narod—novyi Izrail*) in printed editions, this sermon was addressed not so much to the immediate audience but to the entire national community that it sought to define. Nikanor opened by making a series of references to the prophesies of Moses in Deuteronomy, urging his audience and readers to ponder the destiny of ancient Israel. He stated that the experience of God's chosen people had grown out of their national faith. "At the basis of their nationality," he stated, "there was placed a loyalty to their God-fearing faith." As a result, "their Lord God placed them at the head of other peoples, and not behind them. On the other hand, when they betrayed the faith of their fathers, all vows spoken by Moses befell them. . . . God visited upon them dullness of wit and destruction." Thus the nation fell to the faithless Gentiles in the Babylonian captivity and the Roman conquest that later followed. These were signs that God had turned His back on the old Israel and had brought its history to an end. Even though later generations of Jews sought to adhere to their "national faith," and up to the present had managed thereby to "preserve their national identity," their eschatological status was irrecoverably lost with the coming of Christ.

Alluding to Paul's Epistle to the Romans, Nikanor next reviewed the New Testament's teaching about the relationship of Jews to the Church, the new Israel. Then came a significant break from the heretofore ecclesiological consistency of his speech: "Holy Rus, you Orthodox folk, you new Israel! Won't you turn your attention to this title—the new Israel—by which your priests sometimes honor you? Don't you know that it is not in your particular case a rhetorical phrase, but a word having an essential significance in your historical life? It is a name that reveals your world purpose." Several interesting issues are notable in this statement. First, Nikanor revealed his intention to use the epithet as a way of supporting a model of nationality called Holy Rus. Second, he noted that it had some currency in the tradition of the Church but suggested that it was rarely employed. Last, he claimed that it revealed the essence of Russia's national history and destiny.

Continuing his account, Nikanor related conventional Church teaching to advance his claims.

> Divine revelation indicates your high mission. Among all who have forgotten God, like so much dead wood, He has implanted the root of His own people. This is the same divinely chosen family of Abraham, Isaac, and Jacob. And from Jacob there was created, according to the flesh, the old Israel. To it, to Israel, God entrusted and deigned to preserve the divinely revealed faith. . . . Israel partly fulfilled, partly forgot her mission. Owing to this, she broke away from the root of Christ until a predetermined time. And in place of the old Israel . . . the Gentiles were engrafted as the new Israel. Then, in the tenth century of the year of our Lord, we Russian Slavs were as a people engrafted to this root.

Though the hierarch recognized the place of other national communities such as the Greeks in the Church, he brought the Bible's eschatological design to focus primarily on modern Russia. God, he claimed, "values the means of salvation, the right faith, more than we can. Yet he has assured that in a particular people it is preserved for all the world. Here is your world purpose, Orthodox Rus—the preservation of your Orthodoxy for the whole world." Significantly, he then cited as evidence the eleventh chapter of Paul's Epistle to the Romans, which he claimed applied particularly to Russia.

In elaborating his claim that the Russian people was the new Israel foreseen in the Bible, Nikanor made some interesting but unspecified allusions to what appear to have been modern theories of nationality and society in contemporary European thought. For instance, in discussing the fall of

Constantinople and the devolution of Israel's status to Holy Rus, he claimed that the Greek people had finally succumbed to historical necessity "according to the law of the development of peoples." They had, he said, "become exhausted" and could be superseded only by a "youthful people." Furthermore, he asked if it was not significant that the Russian people, their successor, gained their self-consciousness in Eurasia away from the nations of the West, which had already passed the stage of maturity and were starting to decline into a stage of "senility" (*odrakhlenie*). In this way Nikanor, a highly educated member of the clergy, appropriated notions of ethnic nationalism that were then gaining influence within the European public.

Combining innovative statements about Christian teaching with contemporary theories of nationality, Nikanor managed to formulate a vision of Russia's destiny that conformed to the aims of the late imperial mission. For those of his listeners and readers who were sympathetic, he had elaborated a vision of how a nation-specific providence brought Orthodox Russia to the leading position in world-historical development, a position formerly occupied by ancient Israel. And, provided its people preserved the national faith, they would continue to occupy this position forever. "For us," he concluded his 1860 address, "it appears that the necessity of developing in the spirit of the pure Christian faith was predestined to the Russian Orthodox people. It has been predestined that she shall teach it to others—if not to old Christian peoples, then to new peoples. And she shall preserve it for all the world until the end of time and the Last Judgment."[12]

To understand the cultural context that made the new Israel metaphor meaningful to Nikanor, it is worthwhile to consider the career of the influential prelate in some detail. Nikanor was part of the first generation of late imperial missionaries, and his professional experiences help explain how he and others came to promote a movement that could, implicitly, undermine the Church's principle of universality.

ORTHODOX PATRIOTISM IN THE CAREER OF NIKANOR

The future archbishop was born to a clerical family in 1826, in a village near the western town of Mogilev. Deciding to pursue the career of his father, he entered the seminary and did well enough to win admittance to the research-oriented St Petersburg Spiritual Academy in 1847.[13] It was here as a student that he decided to take monastic vows and adopt the ecclesiastical name Nikanor. He completed his studies in 1851, a mere four years before the end of the Crimean War in which the Ottoman empire supported by major western nations inflicted their humiliating defeat on Russia. Nikanor's career took shape against the background of the Great Reforms that followed.[14] As a young priest in the empire's capital city during these years of openness and public debate, he had the opportunity to follow the intellectual currents of the day. He read the secular journals avidly and took particular interest in the polarization between Westernizers and Slavophiles.[15]

As the reforms gathered momentum and began to influence the clergy, the deficiencies of the imperial Church began to reveal themselves in both administrative and popular spheres. While the attention of some priests such as the liberal Belliutsin was directed toward the former, many conservatives such as the young Nikanor turned their zeal toward the wayward Orthodox masses. The period marked a reawakening of the Church's social engagement and witnessed the earliest efforts to establish the mission that would outlive the reforms and grow to dominate Church life in the period following 1881. Even before the emancipation of the serfs in 1861, Nikanor had become increasingly committed to the internal mission. He sacrificed pastoral and administrative duties to pursue this mission and spent the majority of his creative energy writing apologetical studies and sermons. From his earliest works of the 1850s up to the time he took over the diocese of Kherson in 1883, this literary activity occupied his principal attention.[16] At an early point, he began to focus especially upon Old Belief.[17] According to one biographer, he was attracted to the schism because of the cultural traditions that were involved.[18] This interest is revealed in his first full-length book, a study of Old Believer literature that was an exploration of national religious culture as well as a polemic against this ecclesial rival to the official Church.[19]

As Nikanor's interest in Old Belief indicates, the writer-priest regarded Russia's missionary challenge as a matter partly of culture. At one level he made an effort to understand the philosophical currents of the day, especially those that characterized contemporary western Europe. He took great interest in theories about the development of modern society and read the works of John Stuart Mill (1806–1873) and Herbert Spencer (1820–1903), in particular.[20] The effect of these liberal secular intellectuals on his own development is difficult to determine, but the era's fascination with ethnic character almost certainly registered in the mind of the missionary priest who had lived through the Great Reforms and national humiliation of Sevastopol.[21] His opinion of Western culture was predictably negative, and some of his publishing activity was directed against what he considered to be the rising domination of philosophical positivism.[22] Significantly, however, his criticisms of modern Western culture were not directed at the rise of nationality, which through his silence he appears to have appreciated.[23]

Along with his critique of Western philosophy, Nikanor was alarmed by the condition of Russia's high culture. Like so many late imperial missionaries, for instance, he came to consider the anti-ecclesiastical thought of Tolstoy to be a major symbol of Russia's spiritual malaise.[24] As a missionary engaged with culture, though, his perspective on Russian thought was not entirely negative. He made a programmatic effort to promote certain native writers whom he regarded as paragons of Russian Orthodox spirituality. Dostoevsky was a major source of inspiration. On the occasion of the writer's death in 1881, for instance, Nikanor wrote a special sermon hailing the national visionary as a "servant of God" who personally revealed modern Russia's tribulation to preserve the national faith. The sectarians and Old Believers who threatened to sever "Rus" from this faith, he stated, would do well to consider Dostoevsky's early temptations away from Christianity. To follow such a course toward spiritual ruin would result in the fate of ancient Israel, whereas returning to it as prodigal sons would secure their own and the nation's well-being.[25] To a lesser degree, Nikanor also saw missionary potential in the work of Russia's greatest national poet, Alexander Pushkin.[26]

As the reform years passed and many of the empire's problems persisted, Nikanor felt increasingly convinced that Russia had reached a critical stage in her historical development. The failure of administrative, legal, and institutional measures to correct the ailing society was proof for the missionary priest that Russia's problems were in their nature cultural. In an article written in 1868 while serving as rector of the Saratov Spiritual Seminary, he vented his discontent with the empire's cultural order, stating that its problems had been set in motion from the very beginning by Peter the Great. Being "from youth raised toward a striving opposed to Church and national customs," the first emperor had embodied a fundamental "indifference toward the national faith." The entire sequence of emperors and empresses of the eighteenth century, he continued, followed in their predecessor's footsteps by setting a standard of religious "indifferentism" when leading cultural affairs. And though Nicholas I's example of patriotic piety had offered hope of restoring the religious culture of medieval Rus, his death and the reforms of Alexander II represented a new departure from the national faith. The rampant spread of secular and Western thinking that followed 1855 produced an order whose inherent instability was revealed by the fact that even Alexander Herzen's (1812–1870), ideas were beginning to circulate among official bureaucrats and leaders of the Church.[27] Among the works Nikanor cited as evidence for the decline of the national faith were sympathetic studies of Ukrainian nationality by Mykola Kostomarov (1817–1885), and the likewise sympathetic studies of Old Belief by Afanasy Shchapov. On the other hand, he reflected, faithful Orthodox could take heart in the emergence of proponents of Russian nationality in the public press such as Mikhail Katkov (1818–1887).[28] The missionary priest's enthusiasm for the period's leading Russian nationalist even motivated him to send at least one sermon to the offices of *Russkii vestnik* for publication, though it was respectfully turned down.[29]

Despite his conservative values, Nikanor seems to have concluded that Russia's problems would be at least partly resolved through a culture that encouraged public debate. He accepted the growing influence of the written word among the masses and began to actively promote a Church-based program to teach literacy.[30] His encounters with Western intellectual figures such as Mill suggested that the modern social order, for better or worse, was indeed a "free market of opinion," a civil society in which ideas and doctrines would have to be debated in an atmosphere that was open to more than one perspective. He therefore sought to fortify the Orthodox faith with an array of cultural symbols and rhetorical constructions that would enhance its reception among a skeptical audience. The discourse of the national faith in general and the identification with Old Testament Israel in particular enabled him to do this.

A sermon written less than a year before the assassination of Alexander II signaled Nikanor's growing sense of despair about the empire's cultural order. By this time he had reached the conclusion, in contrast to his cautiously optimistic thoughts of 1860, that Russia was "living through a critical phase of decline." To convince the public that the peril it faced was religious, he again likened Russia to ancient Israel. This time he emphasized the cultural discrepancy between the nationally unified prototype and its wayward successor. The cause of modern Russia's troubles, he concluded, grew from the cultural order that had become increasingly dominant since the establishment of the empire. "Since the time of Peter the Great and especially since the time of Catherine the Great," he lamented, "Russians have begun to turn to foreign gods, to Baal, to the god of European learning." As Old Testament Israel had drifted toward apostasy before the Babylonian captivity, so now the new Israel of Russia was forsaking the national faith and embracing the idolatry of surrounding nations to the west.[31]

The assassination of the tsar by revolutionaries in the following year justified the archbishop's gloom about Russia's destiny. In response, perhaps, the final years of his life witnessed a more vigorous appropriation of the new Israel metaphor.[32] The success of the Orthodox mission, he seemed to feel, now more than ever needed the self-conscious identification with the chosen people of the Old Testament and the devotion to nationality that went with it. Before he died of stomach cancer in 1890, he had a final opportunity to broadcast this vision in circumstances that promised to ensure its broad reception.

In St Petersburg in 1888, now a member of the Holy Synod, Nikanor attended the meeting in which the Church's highest body composed the program for the nine-hundred-year anniversary of the baptism of medieval Rus. Along with Metropolitan Platon and the Church's other leading hierarchs, he had the privilege to add his signature to the official protocol ordering the celebration in Kiev. Then, perhaps like the aged Moses standing on the threshold of the promised land before the Israelites, he delivered an address designed to convince Russia that the nation now being commemorated was indeed the new Israel.

The scene was St Vladimir Cathedral back in Kherson, the Black Sea coastal town where St Vladimir himself was said to have been baptized nine hundred years earlier. Nikanor chose to open by citing the farewell address of Moses to the Israelites in Deut 32. In that Old Testament passage, the Jewish prophet addressed the nation of Israel, the offspring of Jacob, and contrasted its divine status with that of other inferior nations. "These are the words of God's prophet Moses," the hierarch proclaimed. "He is delivering a farewell speech to his Israelite people. Take heed, though, for his words are also addressed to the Russian people. . . . In the destiny of Israel, they were realized with striking accuracy. But to the destiny of the Russian people they just as surely testify to us and will come true, though only that part of them that concerns us." In contrast to his 1860 invocation of the new Israel metaphor, Nikanor now discussed the Church's teaching about the angel-protectors who guide each people from heaven. He brought attention to the special relationship with God that Israel in particular enjoyed through the agency of its angel-protector. "This relates to us Orthodox Russians because the supreme right to be among all peoples the beloved chosen sons of God, to be his particular community, and to have the very God who served as the angel-protector of ancient Israel—this right was inherited in the New Testament period by the Russian Orthodox-Christian people." With the Archangel Michael and ultimately God as their heavenly patron, the conclusion was that "the Russian people in the New Testament period are the new Israel."

Despite the particularistic implications of the claim, the archbishop again made an effort to justify it by elaborating the Church's teaching about the new Israel. He was naturally drawn toward the Pauline metaphor of Israel as a root upon which the Gentile nations were to be engrafted after the coming of Christ. In Nikanor's words, there had indeed arisen a "new family of the new Israel, the new living branch of the great root planted by God." But he neglected to grant the status of the new Israel to the universal Church as such. Like other celebrants of 1888 who promoted consciousness of the national saints, he bypassed Greek and other adherents of the Orthodox faith. For him, the metaphor was particular to Russia. "Who is this new Israel at present? Among the many non-faithful peoples, it is the Orthodox-Christian Russian people. We are the new Israel. We are the chosen people. We are the family of God on earth. We are the beloved children of God."[33]

These claims, bold in themselves, were made bolder by the status of the man who issued them. Archbishop Nikanor had now become one of the Church's leading prelates and had earned the respect of many other contemporary missionaries.[34] His zealous patriotic preaching had earned him the reputation among some as a "Russian Goldenmouth," in reference to St John Chrysostom (d. 407).[35] Others considered his stature equal to that of the late Metropolitan Filaret (1882–1867).[36] Nikanor's vision of Russia as the new Israel thus was not a momentary and isolated curiosity rising from the euphoria of the year's baptism celebration. It was the logical extension of the Orthodox patriotic argument that his career had been devoted to developing. The fact that this vision resonated beyond the setting and time in which it was issued indicates that the movement began to exercise a vital influence over the cultural mission in the years that followed 1888.

SUBSEQUENT PROPHETS OF THE NEW ISRAEL

In subsequent years other missionary priests and prelates called upon the metaphor to elaborate the destiny of the Russian people. One was a priest by the name of Peter Smirnov, who used it to organize a 1903 sermon on the feast day of the Kazan Icon of the Mother of God, one of the Russian Church's most revered holy objects with powerful patriotic significance in the late imperial period.[37] Vera Shevzov highlighted this in a recent article.[38]

Smirnov opened by citing the same passage in Deuteronomy used by Nikanor. After discussing ancient Israel's failure to preserve the national faith bestowed to it by Moses, he turned his listeners' attention to modern times. "Who and where are these other members of God's vineyard, the new vineyard implanted by Christ, by the Savior? Where is that people that succeeded to the Kingdom of God? Where is the new Israel?" He acknowledged that the calling to bear the teaching of Christ had been intended for all the peoples of the world, and even referred to the universal principle of Matt 28:19 (where Christ called upon His disciples to go to "all the nations"). Despite God's intention, however, the nations of modern Christendom have betrayed their calling. "In the total aggregate of the Christian world," he stated, "we observe division."

> And is it not true that all of these denominations reflect the essential confusion in their understanding of the faith, and demonstrate more or less that they have deviated from the truth? So where at the present moment is the true member of God's vineyard? To what people has been entrusted the kingdom of God and who creates its fruits? Who at present is the new Israel? To this without a moment's hesitation it is possible to answer that among all modern peoples it is most fitting to give the title the new Israel to the Russian people! The many centuries of our fatherland's historical life testify to this, the confirmation of which is particularly well made by the present event, our present church-national feast day. Blessed is the new Israel, the Russian nation, for to it as to ancient Israel the word of God has been entrusted. It was chosen by providence for the preservation of the pure Christian faith.

An interesting feature of Smirnov's feast day sermon, and one that was very typical of Orthodox patriotic literature, is that it classified modern Christendom in national terms. As he suggested, each constituent confession had a particular national bearer. From such a claim, the Germans were the bearers of Lutheranism, the French of Roman Catholicism, and the English of Anglicanism. Furthermore, Russia, being in this community the bearer of Orthodoxy, was constituted as a people by that faith alone. Though he did not explicitly employ the term "national faith," his characterization of the Russian people perfectly matched that of other clerical Orthodox patriots.

> Entering the course of their history, the Russian people in distinction from the peoples of the West did not possess any preconceived elements for their essential character. The first source for this was acquired in the Orthodox faith. In this was located the very source of that culture which in the course of centuries remained uncorrupted. Through the influence of Orthodoxy the Russian people's character was thus constituted and strengthened. The Orthodox faith defined its mental, moral, and social way of life. . . . Indeed, the Orthodox faith became so linked with the Russian national spirit that both together existed as a vital and indissoluble unity.

Smirnov reviewed the entire course of the nation's history from its Kievan baptism, through the Time of Troubles, and culminating in the defense against the French in the Patriotic War of 1812.[39] "Holy Rus," he said, had frequently been "on the brink of ruin." In each case, however, "the prayerful pleas of members of the earthly Church joined with the prayers of the heavenly Church, the blessed company of heaven." In other words, Holy Rus had been preserved by her devotion to the national saints. In both the Time of Troubles and the Fatherland War, he said, the intercession of the national saints such as Sergius saved the fatherland as well as demonstrated that the new Israel, like the ancient, received special intercessions from heaven.

But like the ancient Israel, the new Israel was forever troubled by a wayward tendency to abandon the national faith. "Should we inculcate within ourselves," he asked his audience, "a haughty consciousness of our primacy and a feeling of inordinate pride before other peoples?" His answer, predictably, was no, because a threat of apostasy forever hung over the chosen nation, especially at present. Using the parable of the tares, he described a fatherland that brought forth not only healthy Orthodox works, but also such errors as Old Belief. The schism, in fact, was the nation's great religious temptation. But its vitality demonstrated that Russia bore a God-given national faith. "There exist among us," he stated, "zealots of the so-called correct or old faith. . . . These zealots of an imaginary 'old faith' even champion themselves as the most 'true' Russians, and from within them can be found faithful messengers and defenders of our so-called advanced thinkers." Like the Pharisees in ancient Israel, he believed, Old Believers were dangerous in the new Israel. Through their passionate defense of "external formality" and literal-minded devotion to ritual, they could represent themselves as champions of the national faith. But the challenges they and their liberal sympathizers had begun to advance at the time for freedom of religious practice and expression would ultimately leave the people with no single source of religious authority, and end inevitably in apostasy. He thus concluded his feast day address to the new Israel with a tone of worried, though not pessimistic, apologetical entreaty.[40]

It is not necessary to cite the appropriation of the new Israel metaphor in all its manifestations to show that it reflected a growing tendency among the clergy to identify Orthodox Russia with Old Testament Israel. What is most interesting is that when it was invoked—often on religious feast days with special patriotic significance—it expressed a strong concern with the late imperial mission. While it served to promote and even celebrate what its proponents defined as Holy Rus, it also conveyed their fear about that nation's future.

Thus the priest I. Fudel, a regular contributor to *Missionerskoe obozrenie* and other journals, invoked the new Israel metaphor to promote the mission to Russia's increasingly restless working class. Directing a public reading for workers in Moscow's Historical Museum in 1902, his invocation represented one of the more transparent manifestations of its service to the cultural mission.[41] The metaphor could also be used to preach to Russia's most privileged estate, which prophets such as Nikanor had accused of abandoning the national faith to serve the Baal of Western culture. Even the future metropolitan of St Petersburg, Antony (Vadkovsky) (1846–1912), who as a liberal prelate represented a sharp contrast to Archbishop Nikanor, was himself drawn to the metaphor in an address to a gathering of the nobility in Kazan Cathedral in 1890.[42]

THE PALESTINE SOCIETY AND ITS PATRIOTIC MISSION

Thus Old Testament imagery continued to suit the Orthodox mission. To explore its use in a context other than festal addresses, it is useful to turn to one of the most prestigious missionary projects of the period, the Imperial Orthodox Palestine Society. As a central expression of the internal mission to which many of the period's leading Orthodox personalities belonged, the Palestine Society has received very little attention from historians of Russian culture and religion.[43] The only published English-language monograph that exists is that of Theofanis Stavrou. While excellent in its focus on the tension between Greek and Russian missionaries, it is concerned mainly with the institutional structure and activities of the Palestine Society.[44] Here, an analysis of the society's vigorous publishing activity and its use of Old Testament imagery in Russia will reveal how Orthodox patriots used the new Israel image implicitly within a specific institutional context to advance their cultural mission.

Founded under tsarist patronage in 1882, the Society had the dual purpose of promoting Orthodox piety at home while serving as an agent for cultural growth among the non-Russian part of the Orthodox population of Ottoman Palestine.[45] The former task, however, naturally served as the main focus. Throughout the late imperial period, Russia's chief missionary body, the Orthodox Missionary Society, promoted pilgrimages as an effective means of instilling the kind of piety that would shield the faithful from the growing forces of sectarianism and secularization. The Third All-Russian Missionary Congress of 1897, for instance, assigned to pilgrimages a leading function in the internal mission's cultural program.[46] According to proponents of the Palestine Society, pilgrimages to Jerusalem were particularly effective. They argued that the draw of sectarianism would be neutralized if Russia's Orthodox could be made to appreciate such holy places and to venerate its holy objects, particularly the Temple of the Resurrection (known in the West as the Church of the Holy Sepulcher).[47] What is more, Old Believers, who themselves were regarded by missionaries as lovers of Orthodox holy objects, would be unable to compete with the society in organizing journeys to the Holy Land.[48] And while the sites of greatest interest were in fact those associated with the life and times of Christ, the mission's promoters frequently invoked the imagery of Old Testament Israel to appeal to the Russian public, especially its less educated classes.[49]

In fact, Palestine's holy objects were portrayed as extensions of those found within Russia, possessing a special draw on the truly self-conscious Orthodox Christian. When one of the founders of the Palestine Society decided to introduce the Russian public to the Palestine mission in 1881, for instance, he found it useful in his opening words to evoke Old Testament images and tie them to the symbols of Russian national self-consciousness. "For the majority of us Russians," wrote V. N. Khitrovo,

> there is no country more well known and at the same time less well known than the Holy Land. From early childhood, we became accustomed to pronouncing holy place names such as Jerusalem, Jordan, Nazareth, and Bethlehem. And in our childish imagination, these names flowed together mysteriously with our own native place names, Moscow, Vladimir, Novgorod. Who among us, sitting upon the school bench, did not wander in his imagination alongside the Old Testament patriarchs, did not muse upon the destiny of the Jewish people . . .?

However, lest the leap from Holy Rus to the Holy Land seem too great for the imagination of his readers, he reminded them of the many holy objects that constitute the topography of Palestine. These, he argued, were the force that drew modern Russia toward the fatherland of ancient Israel. "A longing by the Russian people for the holy objects of the East," he stated, "is a notable phenomenon that a survey of Russian life illustrates."[50]

Like Archbishop Nikanor and other members of the cultural mission, Khitrovo believed that Russia's imperial era had witnessed a sharp decline in the vitality of the Orthodox faith. This was especially evident in his perception of a recent decline in popular pilgrimages. The late imperial period has been shown by recent historians to have been a boom time for popular pilgrimage, and Khitovo was writing in 1881, just as this development was beginning to take shape.[51] He saw past indifference as an aberration, departing from the precedent of the medieval period, when pilgrimage had been one of the nation's most notable characteristics. He attributed the decline to the religious "indifferentism" that had begun to stifle Russian culture ever since the time of Peter. As a result, he estimated that the total number of Russian pilgrims to the Holy Land by the end of the eighteenth century had dropped to no more than a few score every year.[52] With the renewed missionary leadership of a patriotic and pious tsar, however, the Russian people by the end of the nineteenth century were beginning, he claimed, to pour into the Holy Land in numbers approaching nine thousand a year.[53] Much of this travel would not be possible, he added, but for the fact that the modern technology of rail and steamship transport shortened the journey from St Petersburg to Odessa and on to Jerusalem to about a fortnight.[54]

For its part, Khitrovo noted, the Palestine Society in recent years had begun to successfully establish a Russian presence in the Holy Land. It had overseen the construction of churches, pilgrim shelters, and various service buildings in the region, in turn making the arrival and acclimation of Russian pilgrims much easier. In Jerusalem itself, for instance, the accession of Alexander III to the throne in Russia had been accompanied by the construction of a large Orthodox church built in the medieval Russian style. Dedicated to St Mary Magdalene, it stood on the hillside of Gethsemane overlooking the city.[55] Near the Temple of the Resurrection, the site of Jesus's entombment and resurrection from the dead, the society had constructed a building it called simply the Russian Home (*Russkii dom*) containing a church in the name of Alexander Nevsky, one of Russia's greatest national saints. The interior frescoes of this church, Khitrovo noted in one account, were executed with the aim of emphasizing Russia's vital participation in the history of the universal Church. For along opposite walls, "the saints of Palestine and the saints of Russia are collected together to represent the spiritual unity of the Holy Land and Holy Rus. We [also] see this thought in the iconostasis, where St James of Jerusalem the Brother of the Lord and St Stephen the First Martyr stand together with the saints of the Russian land—Peter, Aleksii, Jonah, and Filipp, who himself holds the icon of the Kazan Mother of God."[56] The Russian people's ecclesial primacy and the claim to the status of the new Israel thus found an eloquent argument in the images of their national saints that adorned the walls of one of Jerusalem's newest examples of liturgical architecture.

In addition to the group of founding members and regular contributors to the society's journals, a large number of local and voluntary members
provided leadership in bringing the society's mission to the Russian public.[57]
The society kept its headquarters in St Petersburg, but a sprawling chain of
diocesan chapters brought virtually every region of the empire into contact
with its affairs. Each chapter had its local leadership, usually priests, officials of the diocesan seminary, and members of town dumas.[58] These in turn
were responsible for carrying the society's message to the local public.[59] To
fulfill the task, chapters scheduled public readings of Old Testament history and other topics appearing in official publications. Held throughout the
year, they were designed to spark interest among the masses about the Holy
Land and facilitate pilgrimages there. The readings were usually free and
were considered the chief obligation of the local leadership. Reports about
them published in the society's yearly summaries of activities indicate that the
Orthodox patriotic argument reached the ears of the provincial commoner.
A reading in Tver in 1896, for instance, directed the listeners' attention to the
importance of the Holy Land. There, it claimed,

> a new basis of life directs the course of European and even world history,
> and thus indicates the exclusive and extreme significance of the Holy Land
> for us Russians who confess the Orthodox faith. In the soil of the Holy
> Land, they say, rests the truth from which the very foundation of indi-
> vidual and social life originates for the Orthodox Russian man. The Holy
> Land has for us significance as the primordial source of our historical des-
> tiny in the past, the present, and the future.[60]

Whether the Orthodox masses accepted this argument is not known.
Yet the claim that the society expressed the popular spirit of the people was
strengthened by the fact that the majority of its financial resources came from
popular donations collected during Great Lent and other times in the year in
parish churches of participating dioceses.[61] Thus, with their connection to the
Orthodox masses, leaders of the Palestine mission sought to shape popular
self-consciousness about the relationship of Russia to the Church as a whole.
By invoking patriotic feeling about the role of Russia in the Holy Land, they
believed they would facilitate the larger task of strengthening Orthodoxy.

One historian and advocate of popular pilgrimages, Professor A. A. Dmitrievskii, reasoned that ever since their baptism in 988 the Russian people had
been drawn to the geographical source of Christianity "from the most distant
regions of our fatherland."[62] After all, he noted, pilgrimages to Jerusalem

had been a regular feature in the life of "every true son of Israel."[63] As the successor to the Old Testament's chosen people, modern Russia continued to maintain a "strong yearning toward the holy objects of the East," a feature of its "way of life" that distinguished it from the other peoples of European Christendom.[64] For the typical "wanderer of Rus," therefore, he proposed an ideal pilgrimage that began in the summer in Kiev's Pecherskaia Lavra, was followed by a trip to Sergiev Posad in the fall, and culminated at the Temple of the Resurrection in Jerusalem that winter.[65]

The association of the land of Old Testament Israel with Holy Rus was made by other clerical Orthodox patriots as well, who were in agreement that a Russian's experience in Jerusalem was sure to instill a greater "feeling of love toward the motherland."[66] The rector of the Stavropol Seminary, Peter Smirnov, was particularly interested in the relationship between pilgrimages to Jerusalem and modern Russian Orthodoxy. His opening words in a short book on that topic asserted that "each people in the world has a historical locality by whose name a complete series of recollections is excited within every member of that people."[67] As Kiev, the site of the Russian people's baptism, now served as the symbol of their nationality, Jerusalem, the "mother of Jewish cities," likewise served during Old Testament times as the embodiment of ancient Israel. But with the coming of Christ this national possession was lost. "And in the place of ancient Israel there sprang up a new one, reborn and united in the name of Christ and with the blessing of the Spirit of God for all tribes under heaven. But even if this brought portents of an era in which all would be brought into the kingdom of God, alas, such did not occur from the center, from Jerusalem, in the centuries after the apostles."[68] Instead, the new Israel was centered upon the Orthodox lands of eastern and southern Europe, lately dependent for leadership upon Russia, and its rightful center had long ago fallen under the rule of Muslims. The Russian people's present pilgrimages to Jerusalem, therefore, were evidence of their primacy in the historic mission to bring the capital of the old Israel back under Church control.[69]

While most proponents of the Palestine mission argued that the only proper role for Russia to play in the region was a cultural and religious one, they often portrayed this as a vital stage in the history of the entire Church. The pilgrimages of the Russian people in general, and their organization by church leaders in particular, were thus portrayed in eschatological terms. "Each Orthodox Russian man must passionately affiliate with the Imperial Orthodox Palestine Society," argued the Bishop of Smolensk in a ceremonial address, "for it represents the holiest and highest of our native affairs."

"Here, it is possible to say, advances the first gigantic step of the great Russian people in its world-historical evangelical task, moving in union with that multimillion member state, Orthodox Russia. Holy Rus advances toward the Holy Land, in order that the Holy of Holies might be preserved."[70]

The presence of Russian Orthodox in Jerusalem was in a sense, then, a stage in the restoration of the house of Israel, which had been prophesied in the Old Testament. The citation of Old Testament Scripture was very common in the society's pamphlets and public readings.[71] Many publications bore as an epigraph its official slogan, quoting the book of Isaiah, where the prophet foretells the gathering of all the earth's nations in Jerusalem under the restored leadership of God's chosen people. The quotation usually included only the first line of the following verse:

> For Zion's sake will I not hold My peace, and for Jerusalem's sake I will not rest, until her righteousness goes forth as brightness, and her salvation as a lamp that burns. (Isa 62:1)

The context of the passage, which the society's cultural missionaries assumed was familiar to their popular audience, was important. Subsequent verses from the same chapter of Isaiah read:

> The Gentiles shall see your righteousness, and all kings your glory. You shall be called by a new name, which the mouth of the Lord will name. (62:2)

> Go through, go through the gates! Prepare the way for the people; build up, build up the highway! Take out the stones; lift up a banner for the peoples! (62:10)

> And they shall call them, The Holy People, The Redeemed of the Lord; and you shall be called Sought Out, A City Not Forsaken. (62:12)

Although interpretation of these verses among contemporaries would be purely speculative, it may be argued that proponents of the society chose this passage in order to link the image of Russian pilgrimage to Jerusalem with the image of the new Israel's eschatological fulfillment, all of which was emphatically organized around their model of nationality.

With the attention the Palestine Society brought to the people of ancient Israel, it is not surprising that the issue of modern Judaism was occasionally invoked in public readings and publications. In all, however, the destiny

of the Jews after the incarnation and the destruction of the Jerusalem temple in A.D. 70 does not seem to have elicited more than passing references
among the clergy and lay leadership. One Chernigov priest by the name of
Efimov argued that a basic difference existed between the view of modern
Jews toward Jerusalem and the view of Orthodox. The former were as guilty
as the heretical Christian peoples of the West, he said, in viewing Palestine
with political designs, and contemporary efforts to promote Jewish settle-
ment there were contrary to the true meaning of this "center . . . of moral
enlightenment for all the world's peoples." Contrasting the society's cultural
and religious involvement with Jerusalem to the Zionist political movement
then receiving attention in the Russian press, he declared Orthodox pilgrims
to be "New Testament Zionists" who alone properly interpreted the city's
historical meaning.[72] Other proponents sometimes invoked an anti-Judaic
vocabulary, but on the whole the era's growing anti-Semitism did not find a
significant voice in this branch of the cultural mission.[73]

The overall lack of political and even anti-Semitic interest among the
society's leadership had one remarkable exception. This was the person and
career of M. P. Soloviev.[74] A founding member of the society, Soloviev acted
as a publicist and served for a time as the secretary of the society's publishing
department. A strong proponent of the pan-Slavic movement, he used his
position to advance arguments that Russia possessed a vital political future
in Turkish Palestine. Even so, his statements, while volatile, usually stopped
well short of advocating military expansion.[75] His publications included
pamphlets as well as two substantial books on the Palestine mission.[76] A mixture of religious idealism and political imperialism, his writings generally
were a contrast to the society's other publications. For this reason, perhaps,
his death in 1901 received only minor attention from the society's administrative board.[77] At the provincial level of the society's cultural mission as well,
his ideas about the aims of the society seem to have been ignored. The yearly
reports about public readings very rarely listed his publications among those
on the itinerary. Thus Stavrou's comments that Soloviev's passing witnessed
a lessening of tensions between the Russian and Greek missionaries in Palestine have an application in Russia as well.

In the end, the Palestine Society before 1905 represented an important
focus for the missionary concerns of Orthodox patriots. It revealed how their
interest in Old Testament imagery about ancient Israel was closely tied to
their direction of the Russian Orthodox mission. As other Church leaders
such as Nikanor and Smirnov show, though, it was not the peculiar circumstances of directing pilgrimages to the fatherland of ancient Israel that led

to the use of the new Israel metaphor and its accompanying imagery. It was the belief that the cultural order of imperial Russia had reached a "critical phase of decline," to use Nikanor's words. The appropriation of the epithet for God's chosen people would help Orthodox Russians focus on the national faith of what they called Holy Rus.

THE UNITY OF THE NEW ISRAEL
AND THE THIRD ROME

The metaphor of the new Israel provided Russia's official clergy with a powerful and recognizable symbol with which to characterize the national community of Holy Rus. It combined the ambitions of the universal Church with Old Testament imagery of God's particularistic chosen people, affirming a community that was partly imperial and partly national. In this way it remained a cultural paradox. It was clearly used to transform the present order. But at the same time its proponents could argue (and conservative priests such as Nikanor emphatically did argue) that the universalistic ambition it embodied—an evangelical faith radiating from a core nationality—was perfectly suited to serve the multinational and multireligious empire. Its dual application to the empire and the nation was reflected in the flexible way it was employed. Nikanor, for instance, claimed that it applied equally to the "Rossiiskii narod" and the "russkii narod."[78] Its lack of coherence was not atypical of the movement that had given new life to it. Clerical Orthodox patriotism was plagued by a tension between the universal and the particular, and while the new Israel metaphor enabled Church leaders to promote nationality with greater boldness, it did not resolve this tension.

It is interesting to recall in passing, however, that the character and historical experiences of another reputedly sacred community, Byzantium, often aided clerical Orthodox patriots in their efforts to mold public opinion. The practice usually served as a means of introducing the claim that Russia (or Moscow) was the Third Rome. This had been true during the baptism festival of 1888 especially, and subsequent decades saw frequent use of Filofei's legendary doctrine. In many ways this doctrine offered a more coherent model of community when applied to the Russian Empire. Both ancient Rome and Constantinople had been the center of empires, and the claim that Russia bore their eschatological legacy did not in itself call the multinational or even the multireligious system into question. In short, the fact that Church leaders revived the new Israel metaphor indicates that they believed that the imperial character of the Third Rome epithet lacked the necessary bonding power in contemporary Russian society.

Nevertheless, their revival of the new Israel metaphor should not be interpreted as a sign of ambivalence in the question of which historical people, Israel or Rome, best prefigured Holy Rus. For the aims of the cultural mission, the title of the new Israel was perfectly compatible with that of the Third Rome. After all, the "Israel" of the theological metaphor was that of the Christian era, that is, the era of the "three Romes." In fact, as an epithet originally intended for the universal Church, the new Israel epithet could not have been used intelligibly to signify a nationally exclusive people in the Old Testament sense of the term. This point appears to have been overlooked by Daniel Rowland, who in his excellent study treats the medieval use of the title with reference to the imagery of Old Testament Israel only, with no explanation of its Christian theological origins.[79] To be sure, it was the innovation of clerical Orthodox patriots to invest the new Israel with national particularism. But the epithet continued to express the claim that Russia was chosen to fulfill a universal destiny among many peoples, much like the Third Rome doctrine.

Thus the new Israel metaphor and the imagery that accompanied it provided an important source for the expansion of clerical Orthodox patriotism, serving not only to propagate the Church's ideals of a national faith, but also to advance the ideal of an apostle-like tsar. The Old Testament recorded the rise of a national faith located in the ancestral traditions of ancient Israel, but the ruler of the nation, while not necessarily involved with the faith's further dissemination, was responsible for preserving it against apostasy and indifference. In fact, when Israel's first king, Saul, had broken from the national faith and turned away from God, it was the religious leadership in the person of the prophet Samuel that replaced him. The order under Solomon's successor, King David, had then witnessed an ideal condition of harmony between the ruler and the clerical leadership. The example of this relationship was important to late imperial missionary leaders, who were well aware that ancient Israel had possessed an estate of official priests who enjoyed a very close and protected relationship to the ruler. Before the edict on religious toleration in 1905, this last point provided encouragement to those who felt their hold on the masses slipping. The loss of this protection, however, would upset the harmony between the ideals of the national faith and the apostle-like tsar, fundamentally threatening their model of Holy Rus.

Illustrations: Part I

Fig. 1.1 From the balcony of the Winter Palace, Nicholas II issues the War Manifesto announcing the Russian Empire's entrance into World War I on August 2, 1914. Directly opposite him on Palace Square stood the Alexander Column, the monument to the empire's victory over Napoleon in the Fatherland War of 1812. It was said that the face of the angel atop that column was modeled on Emperor Alexander I, who had declared that he would not make peace until all foreign forces had been expelled from Russia. Nicholas must have found encouragement in that face.

Fig. 1.2 Statue of St Vladimir overlooking the Dnieper River, Kiev. This statue, erected in 1853, towered over those assembled on the banks of the river for the water blessing performed during the Baptism Festival in 1888.

Fig. 1.3 The Baptism Festival of 1888. In this photograph, the Russian public, led by Orthodox clergy, gathered at the Dnieper River to participate in the blessing of the water.

Fig. 1.4 The ecclesiastical publication *Missionerskoe obozrenie* (*Missionary Review*) was the leading journal of the missionary movement within the Orthodox Church during the late imperial period. Edited by V. M. Skvortsov, it often featured articles supporting Orthodox patriotism.

Fig. 1.5 *Coronation of Nicholas II* by Laurits Tuxen, 1898. Like previous tsars, Nicholas was crowned in Dormition Cathedral in the Moscow Kremlin in 1896. The ceremony took place in connection with Pentecost (the feast of the descent of the Holy Spirit) and was an expression of Orthodox patriotism's theological understanding of the Russian state's participation in the kingdom of heaven.

Fig. 1.6 *A Meal in the Monastery* by Vasily Perov, 1876. This painting, like other contemporary realist paintings inspired by Western secular standards of art, served to cast doubts on the leadership and viability of the Orthodox Church.

Fig 1.7 Vasily Kliuchevsky, the greatest historian of the late imperial period, helped define the Russian public's sense of nationality.

Fig. 1.8 *Lev Nikolayevich Tolstoy Shoeless* by Ilya Repin, 1901. Tolstoy directly challenged the legitimacy of the Orthodox Church as well as the patriotic ideals of her conservative clergy.

Fig 1.9 *Self-Portrait* by Victor Vasnetsov, 1873. Unlike realists such as Repin and Perov, Vasnetsov led an effort in late imperial painting to return to the myths and legends of medieval Russia.

Fig 1.10 *Portrait of Fyodor Dostoevsky* by Vasily Perov, 1872. Unlike his younger contemporary Tolstoy, Dostoevsky became a strong defender of the Orthodox faith in the life of imperial Russia.

Fig 1.11 *Baptism of Saint Vladimir* by Victor Vasnetsov, 1893. Vasnetsov was commissioned to execute a series of frescoes for the Vladimir Cathedral in Kiev, which had been built in connection with the anniversary celebration of the baptism of Russia in 1888. Here Vladimir emerges from the font after baptism by an Orthodox bishop of the Church of Constantinople in 988.

Fig 1.12 *Cathedral of Saints of the Universal Church* by Victor Vasnetsov, 1895–1896. This fresco in St Vladimir Cathedral, Kiev, shows non-Russian saints such as Pope Clement of Rome assembled under a Greek dome. Opposite them in the nave of the cathedral stands the fresco of the *Russian Bishops*.

Fig 1.13 *Russian Bishops* by Victor Vasnetsov, 1895–1896. In this fresco, Russian saints who contributed to the life of the Orthodox Church and therefore Russian national character are assembled under an onion dome. The medieval missionary Stephen of Perm stands second from the right holding the cross in the air, while Sergius of Radonezh stands second from the left.

Fig 1.14 The Church of Mary Magdalene in Jerusalem was built by Russians in connection with the activities of the Imperial Orthodox Palestine Society during the late nineteenth century. With its medieval style of architecture, the church symbolized the vital missionary identity of clerical Orthodox patriotism.

Fig 1.15 Pascha in Palestine. This photo shows a group of Orthodox Christian pilgrims from Russia celebrating the feast of the resurrection of Christ at one of the centers of the Imperial Orthodox Palestine Society's activities in Jerusalem during the early twentieth century.

Fig 1.16 An icon of the Archangel Michael, associated with the Archangel Cathedral in the Moscow Kremlin, represents the angelic protector of God's chosen people, the New Israel, armed for spiritual warfare against apostasy and division.

Fig 1.17 The Archangel Cathedral in the Moscow Kremlin was built during the height of Muscovite ascendency. This cathedral became the burial place for Russia's tsars until the time of Peter the Great, when the architecturally Westernized Peter-Paul Cathedral of St Petersburg took its place.

Fig 1.18 Murals of Muscovite princes in the Archangel Cathedral, Moscow, show a group of rulers standing together honoring God and serving him in the defense of the Russian state. Below them are their tombs.

PART II

CONTESTING HOLY RUSSIA

CHAPTER 5

---†---

The Crisis of Apostle-Like Statecraft

The first part of this book described the way in which Church leaders cultivated national self-consciousness in the wake of the Great Reforms to reinforce ecclesial self-consciousness. They pursued what can be described as a cultural mission, an effort to link missionary activities to the formation of a Russian national community they called Holy Rus. However, events associated with the Revolution of 1905 severely shook their model of Holy Rus and opened a new phase in the history of clerical Orthodox patriotism. After 1905, Church leaders found that the ideals of the national faith and the apostle-like tsar, which had served them since the baptism festival of 1888, became increasingly dissonant.

During the first half of the troubled year 1905, Nicholas II, who had been hailed during his coronation ceremony less than a decade earlier as an apostle-like successor to St Vladimir, reversed the state's ancient policy of restricting the freedoms of non-Orthodox religions. Issued on Pascha, or Easter Sunday, the edict promised religious toleration (*veroterpimost*) to all of the empire's schismatics, sectarians, and pagans. These were the very groups against whom the missionary clergy had struggled and for whom in part it had developed its model of Holy Rus. While the state had in fact shown limited religious toleration in the past (especially during the eighteenth century), the Paschal Edict's scope was unprecedented. Then, before Church leaders had time to imagine a national community without an apostle-like tsar, Nicholas issued the October Manifesto. This laid the basis for the State Duma, a system in which secularistic and non-Orthodox political leaders would possess the power to act on the Paschal Edict and undermine the "preeminent and predominant" status of the Orthodox faith. The year 1905 therefore represents a turning point in the history of prerevolutionary clerical Orthodox patriotism. Where formerly there had been a sharp tension between the principles of universality and nationality, now there was also dissonance in the clergy's defense of autocracy.

THE IDEAL OF THE APOSTLE-LIKE TSAR

The Paschal Edict had a powerful effect on the minds of many Orthodox patriots. To understand their response, it is necessary first to consider the way they had come to view tsarist authority since the baptism festival of 1888. James Cunningham noted how up until 1905 the clergy had been in the habit of judging Russia's tsars according to the "hallowed tradition" of statecraft founded under Constantine. Even Peter the Great and his successors had been seen "as protectors of the Church and its interests" because they had "defended the Church before the claims of other religions."[1] For their part, clerical Orthodox patriots had been accustomed to a tsar who was a steadfast proponent of missionary activity.

This was true especially during the reign of Alexander III. Many of the most prestigious missionary societies such as the Orthodox Palestine Society had come into being under his beneficent patronage, and he had contributed enormous sums to the missionary program. What is more, he had consistently refused to consider any diminution of the state's legal ban on apostasy. He even used the occasion of the baptism festival of 1888 to reassert this commitment. As Chapter 1 showed, Constantine Pobedonostsev had at that time asserted that the Russian state would never adopt a legal principle of toleration for the heterodox. The Orthodox faith was the historical faith of the Russian people, and the religious calling of the tsar compelled him to protect it with the full force of governmental power. Certain freedoms of worship had been given to loyal subjects such as the Old Believers as recently as 1883, but this did not constitute a principle of religious toleration. Most importantly, it did not allow the heterodox and non-Christians to propagate their faith or, in the case of the Old Believers, publicly proclaim their activities with the use of crosses or church bells.[2] In fact, under Pobedonostsev, Alexander's regime had tended progressively to rescind many features of the 1883 law almost as soon as it was introduced.[3] Thus, Pobedonostsev's tenure as Chief Procurator of the Holy Synod actually brought increased restrictions upon non-Orthodox religions, so that in the year of Nicholas's coronation he could produce his most thorough statement of opposition to the principle of religious toleration.[4] For this reason, the symbolic importance of the tsar in the clergy's model of Holy Rus had been very high during the baptism festival and in the years that followed. Church leaders had readily adopted the state's formula of Official Nationality because autocracy appeared to contribute to the formation of an Orthodox national community. In their writings, Alexander III became the true successor to Constantine and Vladimir and to some was even worthy of the title of Equal-to-the-Apostles.

This feeling was expressed in a book written by Bishop Nikanor (Kamenskii) (1847–1910) of Orel. Written in memory of the miraculous survival of Alexander in a railroad accident just months after the baptism festival, it was titled *On Saint Constantine Equal-to-the-Apostles and Tsarist Authority*.[5] Revealing a concern with missionary matters, it opened by discussing the early Church's struggle against paganism. Constantine, once he had converted to Christianity, set a standard for subsequent tsarist authority by using his power to promote the spread of the faith. His most important act had been the Edict of Milan in 313, which formally granted Christians the right to worship in the Roman Empire. But rather than grant mere religious toleration, Bishop Nikanor claimed that the Edict of Milan represented Constantine's active promotion of the true faith and even the first steps toward state restrictions upon nonbelievers. It was the "birth of the Church's influence upon the state."[6]

What Nikanor and others found most significant about Constantine and his rule was his leadership in the "dissemination of the faith" throughout his empire and abroad. "Generously promoting the construction of Christian temples," Nikanor noted, "Constantine also ordered the destruction of numerous pagan temples."[7] He even invited the Church clergy to advise his rule and enter court service. Therefore, "St. Constantine Equal-to-the-Apostles in his relations to the Church was an example of a Christian tsar, and it is for this reason that the Church glorifies him." In subsequent centuries, "his model of a Christian tsar often manifested itself in our Holy Rus, beginning in the days of St Vladimir Equal-to-the-Apostles and continuing afterward with a multitude of princes, tsars, and emperors."[8] Significantly, Nikanor listed only Kievan and Muscovite rulers when discussing concrete cases of apostle-like rule, avoiding mention of Peter and his eighteenth-century successors altogether. Nevertheless, by modeling their activity on medieval statecraft, Russia's modern rulers could also achieve the true missionary ends of tsarist authority. This was most evident in the reign of Alexander III. Nikanor regarded Alexander as "the faithful successor to St Vladimir Equal-to-the-Apostles and the true preserver of the holy traditions of rule established by the original Christian emperor, St Constantine Equal-to-the-Apostles."[9] Alexander deserved the same apostle-like title as Constantine and Vladimir above all because he had refused to tolerate apostasy. In the bishop's notion of tsarist authority, "not only faithlessness, but even a religious toleration that issues from indifference to matters of the faith is virtually the same as persecution of Orthodoxy itself. Thus indifference can be the most dangerous attitude of the state toward the Church."[10]

An even more influential voice in establishing the missionary clergy's model of tsarist authority was John Vostorgov, the priest and publisher whose role in the cultural mission was discussed in Chapter 3. He also admired Alexander III and used him as a standard for imperial rule. Alexander embodied for Vostorgov all of the native traditions of old Rus while extending the Orthodox faith over a sprawling imperial territory.[11] Many of the priest's missionary activities were conducted in the imperial borderlands of Caucasia, Central Asia, and Siberia. The non-Orthodox populations there could only be won for the Church, he believed, with the assistance of apostle-like statecraft. Alexander's support of the external mission thus earned his warm sympathy. So important was the modern tsar's example that Vostorgov composed at least two separate public addresses praising Alexander and his reign that were later disseminated in pamphlet form.

The first was written at a very fateful time for the mission, in 1904, just a year before the Paschal Edict. In this address Vostorgov praised Alexander as a "faithful expression and bearer of traditional Russian principles, thoughts, and strivings expressed throughout the centuries."[12] His reign represented a correction in the direction Russian statecraft had taken since the time of Peter. "Until the time of Peter the Great," Vostorgov argued, "the Russian state and Church history were indistinguishable." The century that witnessed the consolidation of the multinational and multireligious empire, however, "was a century of mockery for all that is national" and, by association, Orthodox. Nevertheless, the national faith of Holy Rus had been kept alive in tsarist customs such as the coronation ceremony. "In the ceremony of tsarist coronation, which has been preserved unchanged, we see that state authority clearly understands the importance . . . of Orthodoxy. And could it be otherwise? Is it not true that the Russian state was born and raised in the soil of the Orthodox Church? . . . Separation from the Church would be death to the people, and the state."[13]

Vostorgov listed the many services of Alexander to the mission, including the expansion of clerical theological schooling, the establishment of clerical salaries, and the construction of over four thousand Orthodox temples. For these reasons Alexander had helped restore the apostle-like function of Russian statecraft ignored by emperors after the seventeenth century. "Not in a single reign since the time of the first Romanovs has the Russian Church experienced such a revival and creative activity," he exclaimed, "as in the blessed reign of the late Sovereign." To close, he turned his attention to the heir, Nicholas II. In 1904, he stated, the present tsar is to be commended for guiding the Russian state "by the radiant course set by His Father and His example. In these ten years, [Nicholas] has demonstrated faithfulness to His word."[14]

NICHOLAS II AS AN APOSTLE-LIKE TSAR

For his part, Nicholas II strove to live and to rule in accordance with the Orthodox faith. "There is no doubt," writes Sergei Firsov in a recent study of the Church and state during the late imperial period, "that the last Russian autocrat was a sincerely faithful Orthodox Christian who regarded his political activity as a religious duty."[15] Nicholas's official biographer, taking pains to describe this, wrote how "not one day, not one act is started by him without turning with prayer to God."[16] And since the outward expression of his faith was unquestionably sincere, Nicholas and his supporters conveyed an apostle-like image to the Orthodox clergy. He attended the divine services regularly, took a leading role in the canonization of saints, and spent an enormous sum on the construction of Orthodox churches. He supported the Orthodox mission and on occasion even personally contributed to the advancement of Russia's "native faith."[17] An anecdote relates how a group of peasants from the region of Kholm, for instance, once came to the capital to address the tsar during Bright Week (Easter Week), proclaiming as they arrived the customary greeting "Christ is Risen!" While secularized bureaucrats responded only with "hello," the tsar, once he appeared, answered properly with "Indeed He is Risen!" The peasants, impressed by this, were said to have returned home, confidently proclaiming to others that "the tsar is Orthodox, Russia is Orthodox, and Christ lives in our land."[18]

Even more effective than popular anecdotes was the impression Nicholas's piety made upon missionaries. V. M. Skvortsov, publisher of *Missionerskoe obozrenie* and a leader of the internal mission, praised his many acts of devotion. Especially noteworthy was a journey the new tsar made with the entire royal family to Kiev in 1896 to pray among its medieval holy objects. This royal pilgrimage to the past was timed so that Nicholas could also participate in the consecration of Kiev's St Vladimir Cathedral the same year. Honoring what had become Russia's greatest monument to clerical Orthodox patriotism, Skvortsov claimed, could be interpreted by the Church as a firm demonstration that the tsar would defend "native Orthodoxy" against alien faiths and would not tolerate the "possibility of an American style freedom of religion in Orthodox Rus."[19] Occurring just three months after the tsar's coronation, "the Kievan pilgrimage of Their Imperial Majesties represents a great event for the missionary movement," he concluded.[20]

And indeed, Nicholas marked the beginning of his reign with a symbolic gesture of great importance for leaders of the Orthodox mission. Like his predecessors, he was crowned in Uspensky Cathedral in the Moscow Kremlin.[21] During a ceremony attended by dozens of high prelates, he assumed, according to the traditional rite of coronation, the image of King David standing at the head of the priesthood and people of Israel. The prayers spoken by the clergy were intended to shape this image, for they drew upon Old Testament passages concerning the ruler's religious office. The presiding hierarch, Metropolitan Palladii of St Petersburg, petitioned the "God of Jacob" in the coronation prayers to help the new tsar fulfill his obligation as the "highest patron and defender" of the Orthodox faith. "As you selected your servant David and anointed him to be the tsar over your people Israel," the metropolitan read aloud, "hear our unworthy prayers now. Grant from your holy dwelling that your faithful servant, the Great Sovereign Nicholas Alexandrovich, might with your favor now be made Emperor over your people."[22]

This new Israel imagery was reinforced in the press. Spiritual journals such as *Missionerskoe obozrenie* reviewed Old Testament history to conclude that the relationship of Nicholas II to modern Russia "is similar to David in his relationship to the people of Israel."[23] Secular newspapers disseminated the same image. *Moskovskiia vedomosti* told its readers how "the sacred ritual of tsarist coronation" had passed "from the Jewish Church to the Christian Church" during the reign of the first Christian tsar Constantine Equal-to-the-Apostles.[24] Destined to be performed only in Russia, there it came to symbolize, among other things, the Russian tsar's apostolic role in the universal Church. St Vladimir Equal-to-the-Apostles, whom many newspapers remembered and discussed during the weeks preceding the coronation, served as the highest Russian example of this tsarist authority, eclipsing altogether Peter the Great. Vladimir and other medieval rulers presented a testament of the state serving the spiritual mission of the Russian people. "Enlightened by the holy faith," Russians had learned "to look to their sovereigns . . . not simply as the bearers of power, but as spiritual pastors."[25]

The prayers and publicity that accompanied the coronation highlighted the tsar's vocation as defender of the Church mission. For religiously informed participants the many references to David also carried biblical significance. As many of the articles in the spiritual press testified, the greatest "tsar" of Old Testament Israel had been chosen by God solely as a consequence of the apostasy and disloyalty of his predecessor, Saul.[26] That story is recounted in 1 Kingdoms (1 Samuel in the Western Old Testament). Saul, the initial ruler of the chosen people, had been entrusted with the preservation of its holy faith. At first he fulfilled his task perfectly, using his power to ban heretics such as sorcerers and mediums (28:3). However, when troubles shook the realm, his resolve broke and he chose to compromise the strict prohibition on apostasy by consulting a medium, the Witch of Endor (28:7–15). As a result of this behavior and his refusal to act on divine instructions after a battle, he was rejected by God through the prophet Samuel (13:9–14) to be replaced as tsar by David. While the clergy officiating the coronation of Nicholas naturally preferred to focus on David and his ultimate fulfillment of Israel's religious mission, the apostasy of Saul reminded them that the Russian tsar, as head of the new Israel, was expected to fulfill his lawful vocation as the "supreme defender and preserver of the dogmas of the ruling faith."[27] These were the expectations that accompanied the accession of Nicholas II. In little more than a decade, however, he would be forced by revolutionary political circumstances to compromise the apostle-like legacy of Russian statecraft.

A missionary leader and Orthodox patriot who had strong opinions about the apostle-like legacy was Skvortsov. In 1897, a year after witnessing Nicholas II's coronation and subsequent pilgrimage to the past in Kiev, Skvortsov had traveled to Kazan to serve as chairman of the Third All-Russian Missionary Congress. There he discussed the necessity of continued strong state support in conducting the Orthodox mission. He attacked contemporary liberal opinion, which stated that Church and state should be separate and that missionary organizations should be operated and financed privately.[28] Speaking to the assembled missionaries in the opening address of the congress, he even claimed that "all questions of faith and the Church are for us in Orthodox Rus now essentially questions of the state."[29] Skvortsov, a lay missionary serving as an official of the Holy Synod, believed strongly that state assistance was essential for the continued life of the mission. In the years before the Paschal Edict, he therefore responded to rumors about an approaching law on toleration with horror.

For him, the most foreboding sign of change came on February 26, 1903, when Nicholas issued a manifesto hinting at changes in the Fundamental Laws governing religion. Warning of "troubles" (*smuty*) that beset the civil order, the manifesto spoke vaguely but forcefully about the desirability of instituting some form of "religious toleration" (*veroterpimost*) within the empire. It stated that although official Orthodoxy should remain, as it had been defined in the Fundamental Laws, the "preeminent and predominant" (*perventsvuiushchaia i gospodstvuiushchaia*) faith, some alteration of the present legal order was favored.[30] Skvortsov responded to the implications of this statement with strong resistance. In his regular column in *Missionerskoe obozrenie* the following week, he discussed the manifesto as an "event of huge historical importance." Holding fast to Nicholas's affirmation of the preeminent and predominant status of Orthodoxy, he claimed that full religious freedom in Russia was impossible. "The Imperial confirmation of religious toleration," he insisted, "cannot extend to the existence in our state of freedom of religious confession" (*svoboda veroispovedovaniia*). Thus he attacked the "sectarian-loving organs of the press" that had already begun to interpret the 1903 manifesto as a promise of full religious toleration. "A false interpretation of these directives, as is well known, is opposed to the two main pillars of the Russian state—opposed to the autocracy of its tsar and the Orthodoxy of its Church. Both of these pillars are united in one common, great, deeply religious understanding of Russian tsarist authority." To elaborate what he meant by this statement, he, like Vostorgov, turned with praise to the reign and example of Alexander III. The implications of the 1903 manifesto were "clear," he asserted: there would be no edict granting full religious freedom.[31]

He was wrong. On April 17, 1905, Tsar Nicholas took the unprecedented step of granting religious toleration to what the official Church regarded as Russia's heretics and schismatics. Nicholas believed he had little choice. In a manifesto of December 12, 1904, he had noted that the granting of religious freedoms would work toward the "improvement of state order" within the multireligious empire.[32] With the rising tide of insurrection following Bloody Sunday[33] the following month, he therefore turned a deaf ear to the cries of Orthodox missionaries and, on Pascha itself, issued an edict on religious toleration. While stating that freedom of conscience had always been supported by Russian laws, this Paschal Edict repudiated the ancient ban on the practice of religions rival to the official faith. "We . . . order," Nicholas proclaimed, "that apostasy [*otpadenie*] from the Orthodox faith is not subject to persecution."[34] Even an individual branch of Old Belief would no longer carry the derogatory label of "schism" (*raskol*), he announced, and would be elevated to the category of an "Old Believer concord" (*staroobriadcheskaia soglasiia*).[35] Henceforth, it appeared, Russia's heterodox and non-Christians would be free to practice their faith and even to proselytize among Orthodox believers without fear of state repression. For the first time since the baptism of 988, the Russian tsar provided legal protection to his non-Orthodox subjects. The apostle-like status earned by St Vladimir, it seemed, had been shaken.

CLERICAL REACTION TO THE PASCHAL EDICT

For conservative Church leaders, the news came as a great blow. While some could have seen the writing on the wall as early as 1903, they expressed dismay that the principle of apostle-like statecraft had been abandoned so suddenly and without their consultation. The two years that had elapsed since the 1903 manifesto had witnessed repeated efforts to preclude the issue. Here Skvortsov led the way. With great consistency, and despite rumors that toleration was inevitable, *Missionerskoe obozrenie* attacked the idea of a legally sanctioned principle of religious toleration.[36] Then, after the manifesto of December 12, 1904, which hinted once again that such a law was imminent, he resignedly published an article in his column titled "On the Eve of Complete Religious Toleration."[37] Conceding that religious freedom was now inevitable, he stated that it would have disastrous consequences for the mission and suggested that his readers look to the book of Revelation for courage and insight into the dark future that lay ahead. "A kingdom of evil has opened up in front of us and is engulfing the kingdom of God," he warned. "It will now begin its struggle against the Christian Church."[38] His apocalyptic mood was recorded in subsequent issues that year, made all the more dark by the widespread social upheaval and violence around him. He spoke especially of the heartfelt sorrow that "true Russian people" felt at news of the Paschal Edict.[39] Perhaps from habit or the fact that *Missionerskoe obozrenie* still received considerable support from the state, he stopped well short of challenging the tsar himself for issuing the edict and even called upon missionaries to recognize the tsar's "idealism and humanism."[40] His tone, however, was one of deep disappointment.

Nicholas had been compelled by forces beyond his control to accept limits on his status as the apostle-like successor to Constantine, Vladimir, and even Alexander. Nevertheless, in the months that followed the Paschal Edict a degree of disaffection occurred among the conservative clergy, leading them to criticize his increasingly secularistic government. There is no evidence that any of the most influential Church leaders began directly to question the tsar's authority or their loyalty to him, though at the parish level a number of local clergy actually participated in revolutionary activities.[41] The most influential criticism of the tsar's edict came from the prelates, the majority of whom appear to have met the Paschal Edict with bewilderment and dismay.[42] They greeted the prospect of toleration with bitterness and a feeling that the Church and her interests were being sacrificed by efforts to preserve the civil order. The cause of disaffection grew most sharply out of the great uncertainty about the future of the Orthodox internal mission now that it was no longer unambiguously defended by the empire's laws.

And of course the clergy recognized Nicholas's personal devotion to the Orthodox Church. There was no question about that. But after October 1905, when the tsar was compelled to issue the October Manifesto authorizing the creation of the State Duma, political initiative was no longer entirely in his hands. Legislation affecting the place of the Church and other religious bodies could now be introduced, and the tsar maintained the unconditional power to veto. But an institutional basis for challenging Russia's historical spiritual order now existed. And during the radical period of the first two Dumas especially, a parade of such challenges were made. As a result, conservative Church leaders began to question the legitimacy of the state over which Nicholas remained the head. Before 1905, clerical Orthodox patriots had not shrunk from criticisms of the secularized state system introduced by Peter the Great. As we have seen, however, prelates such as Archbishop Nikanor of Kherson had contextualized such criticisms within what they described as the model statecraft of Alexander III. Now it appeared that secularized government might be revived under Nicholas II to assume an even more threatening specter.

The disaffection of the conservative clergy in the years following 1905 produced a significant though ultimately indecisive reevaluation of the importance of the tsarist state in the life of the national community they called Holy Rus. While maintaining unbroken loyalty to the person of Nicholas, clerical Orthodox patriots began to question the new religious order that he, albeit unwillingly and even tragically, had played an instrumental role in creating.

THE CASE OF BISHOP NIKON

The most eloquent expression of clerical disaffection toward the new Russia was Bishop Nikon, whose early career had been devoted to the revival of a more autonomous form of monasticism according to what he regarded as the spirit of medieval Rus. Nikon believed this was necessary before Russia's manifold problems could be solved. The "sad phenomenon of our day," he stated in one publication, was that monasticism, which once dominated Russian culture, no longer played a leading role in religious and social life.[43] In 1879, therefore, he had settled in Russia's most famous monastery, Trinity-Sergius Lavra at Sergiev Posad, and lived there for much of the remainder of his life.[44]

Nikon's strong sense of calling and the role of Orthodox patriotism in it is expressed in a brief passage from his spiritual autobiography. "God called me," he wrote, "to be in constant communion with these, his children. They are the simple hearts that bear the Russian Orthodox soul. And this is the place where the best people of the Russian land are found. Here is where its salt lies."[45] As noted in Chapter 3, Nikon regarded Trinity-Sergius Lavra, with its treasury of Orthodox holy objects, as one of the most tangible symbols of Russia's national faith. He had been especially impressed by the great pilgrimage to Sergiev Posad of 1892 and had helped commemorate the anniversary of St Sergius's death that year by issuing a second edition of an unusually long saint's life he had written in 1885.[46] From this famous holy place Nikon began a publishing career dedicated to advancing Orthodox patriotism and the place of an apostle-like tsar within it. He became editor of a series of moral and religious brochures titled *Troitskiia listki (Trinity Leaflets),* as well as the journal *Bozhiia niva (God's Field).*

When the Revolution of 1905 came, he began to speak of a new time of troubles for Russia and regularly compared "the Time of Troubles three hundred years ago with that of our time."[47] In particular, he began to glorify and disseminate the image of Patriarch Germogen (r. 1606–1612), whom he regarded as a prototypical Orthodox patriot who had rescued the national community from dissolution and state collapse by rallying the people behind the Orthodox clergy. Following Germogen's example, Nikon enlarged his writing and publishing duties and began to take an active role in cultural and political affairs. In addition to producing books and tracts, he now began to edit a series of brochures titled *Troitskiia tsvetki (Trinity Flowers), Troitskaia biblioteka (Trinity Library),* and *Troitskaia narodnaia beseda (Trinity Peoples' Conversation).* Even more influential was another journal over which he became editor, *Troitskoe slovo.* With this array of media at his disposal, he became a leading voice in discussions about the burning issues of Orthodoxy during the prerevolutionary period. His eagerness increased as he rose in power and influence. In 1907 he became a member of the State Council, in 1912 he became a member of the Holy Synod, and in 1913 he was elevated to the office of archbishop.

These positions of responsibility did not shake Nikon from his belief that the state order was in perilous decline. He was truly alarmed by what he regarded as an assault by "modern paganism" in past decades against Russia's Orthodox way of life.[48] Now this had resulted in religious toleration and an increasingly secularistic logic of statecraft. Each time a new bill was introduced in the Duma to realize the promises of the Paschal Edict, or even exceed them, he attacked it with vigorous political and spiritual commentary. An example is his response to a 1909 proposal to reduce the number of state religious holidays. With the government abandoning the traditions of the national faith inherited from medieval Rus, he argued, it was time for the Orthodox clergy to intervene and reassert "the Church's responsibility to the people."[49] He rejected the right of the state to interfere with Church life, stating that "holidays belong to God and not to us." In fact, he argued, those holidays that honor the civil government and in particular the anniversary of the tsar's coronation are likewise the affair of the Church, as "they establish state authority upon the principle of the Church's blessing."[50] The state in the present case not only threatens the Church, he argued, but the national community grounded in it. This was a provocative claim indeed.

Nikon stated that the people "understand that the earthly law can never stand higher than the heavenly law, that the human is not greater than the divine. Any law that contradicts the teaching of God invariably excites hostility in the heart of the faithful and undermines their faith in the legal system and in authority generally. Authority, according to a national view, must be the bearer of national ideals." Of course, Nikon here was equating Orthodox piety with the "national ideals" of the Russian people. But by doing so, by appropriating nationality to characterize the universal faith, he presented a challenge to post-October state authority based on the interests of the Orthodox national community. The missionary formula of the national faith that Orthodox patriots had employed since 1888 was now, strikingly, being directed against the government itself.[51]

Nikon's influence was greatest in the pages of *Troitskiia listki* and *Troitskoe slovo*. The latter organ of the Trinity-Sergius Lavra was placed under his control from the very first issue in 1910, and remained so until its wartime demise in 1915. Its goal, he stated in the inaugural issue, was "to oppose" (*protivodeistvovat*) the modern forces of secularism and apostasy recently unleashed in "Orthodox Rus."[52] This negative program of opposition was compensated by his positive praise for the glorious historical record of old Rus. He turned his readers' attention to the Time of Troubles, when, he argued, Holy Rus was strong and the Church led the way toward national integration as the state disintegrated. Nikon regularly contributed to the journal in the form of an open diary titled "Moi dnevnik," which resembled closely the "Writer's Diary" of Dostoevsky. Long before computer blogs, the great novelist had successfully used the serially published public diary genre as a medium in which to air publicly social and political opinion about contemporary events, and in the atmosphere of the prerevolutionary period Nikon also found such a medium highly effective for outlining his visions of Russia's national destiny. Its tone was just as controversial.

The first installment in 1910 set a polemical tenor that continued for subsequent years. The previous year had witnessed the start of construction of the great St Petersburg Mosque, the largest Islamic place of worship in all of Europe. Nikon was indignant, he informed his readers, that here, in the very capital of the Russian Empire, religious toleration had been advanced so far as to allow a "pagan temple" to be erected. He emphasized the fact that the bright blue tiled structure now stood in visual range of the Peter-Paul Cathedral where Russia's emperors lay buried. Such a desecration of the city was symbolic, he suggested, because it was the logic of empire and secularized statecraft that had led to the incorporation of Islam into Holy Rus. But even Ivan the Terrible (buried properly in the Cathedral of Archangel Michael in the Moscow Kremlin), who had been the first ruler to end the homogeneity of the national community, at least had helped to lead a missionary campaign against Islam. Now the Russian state was not only permitting "sacrifices to Satan" to begin anew but also took pride in the mosque's aesthetic appeal. What, he asked, would "our ancestors" have thought about this?[53]

Soon after the mosque episode, Nikon received a letter from a sympathetic reader complaining of another desecration in the capital, a Buddhist temple built on the banks of the Malaia Neva River. "What is this?" the reader was said to have exclaimed. "Is it the rebirth of idolatry in Rus? If so, then it is a revolution running counter to the whole of Russian history. It is a turn away from the era of Vladimir toward a new paganism." Another patriotic reader, Nikon reported, was contrasting the tsar's introduction of religious toleration with the act of Vladimir hurling pagan idols into the Dnieper River in 988. Now in the capital of the empire the image of Perun had again been erected in the form of the Buddha. What Nikon found even more troubling in the affair was that many of Russia's secular nationalists, as supporters of religious toleration, found nothing wrong with the proliferation of non-Orthodox places of worship and even promoted their construction as symbols of the empire's diversity. He focused particularly on a certain contributor to *Novoe vremia* named Menshikov. "It is time," Nikon stated, "for the Church to cleanse itself of [such] open traitors. It is time to say to them: you are not ours . . . anathema to you!" It is necessary, he continued, "for the Russian Orthodox people to pray that the Lord not punish all of our land for the sins of those who allow this desecration of our holy objects. . . . It is necessary that this unclean idol be cast into the depths of the Neva, just as Perun was cast into the depths of the Dnieper."[54] According to the intemperate Nikon, not only was Holy Rus suffering a "desecrating sacrilege" similar to that prophesied in the thirteenth chapter of the Gospel of Mark, but she was forfeiting her Christian mission. He pointed to the construction of non-Christian temples as evidence that the nation was failing its destiny of converting others to the faith.

Motivated by such thoughts, Nikon next printed an untitled poem he had received from a reader that was even more vividly intolerant in focusing on the threat of national apostasy represented in the proliferation of non-Christian places of worship in the imperial capital. Consisting of five stanzas, it told the history of Holy Rus from her origins to the present time of troubles. The two events that framed the narrative were the baptismal act of Vladimir in 988 and the Paschal Edict of Nicholas in 1905, though the latter was not mentioned explicitly. The opening stanza described a scene on the shore of the Dnieper where Vladimir has baptized the Russian people. The second stanza described the destruction, under his order, of idols such as those to Perun and climaxing in the triumphal erection of the cross over Kiev. The third stanza was set in Moscow. Over the city, it read, stand "innumerable crosses on churches / the sound of church bells ringing magnificently / which speak about a faith in God / found in the living heart of every Russian." Thus, "not without purpose," it closed, "did Rus become Holy Rus." The last and lengthiest stanza was set, predictably, in modern St Petersburg. "On the shores of the broad Neva," it began,

Stands the Russian capital,
And glorious memories about past deeds
Of the native land she keeps.
The crowning towers of God's temples,
Over her cast the holy cross,
And remind all about their God,
And about their former love for him.
Former . . . because now where the cross shines,
They are erecting a Buddhist temple!
And soon enough within it the services will commence
To a soulless host of idols and gods.
Oh, Rus! You, in olden times, *were* holy,
But now you are profaned.
And in front of Christ's very enemies,
Your children have abandoned you.[55]

In this document it is interesting to note the sharp contrast in mood with earlier expressions of Orthodox patriotism. In the historical narratives of the

1880s and 1890s, Church leaders had also presented the medieval past as a superior reflection of national destiny, but with a sense of optimism that the current Russia, with its revival of apostle-like statecraft, was returning to that course. Here the poet lacks any optimism at all, and, consumed by despair, speaks of the ruin of Holy Rus.

NICHOLAS'S RESPONSE

As the first "son of the Church," Nicholas II was clearly implicated in the censure of the final line of the poem about the decline of Holy Rus. It was his edict, after all, that had made the construction of pagan temples possible. But the apocalyptic predictions of Nikon and other contributors to *Troitskoe slovo* were not directed primarily at the tsar. With whatever disaffection Orthodox patriots may have met his decision to grant toleration, the targets of their vigorous activity were the liberal and radical factions of the Duma. Persistent efforts to bring the promise of toleration into full realization were the immediate source of the decline in apostle-like state authority. As Orthodox patriots watched the hallowed position of Orthodoxy attacked in the halls of the Tauride Palace, where the newly formed Duma assembled, they were inspired to transfer some of their hopes back to the Winter Palace, where Nicholas continued to agonize over the secularistic direction in which the Russian state was being forced to go.

And in fact the tsar gave Orthodox patriots within the Church much reason for reconciliation in the years after 1905. To begin with, he had long demonstrated his devotion to a model of nationality framed by the symbolism of medieval Rus. He self-consciously embraced the manners of a seventeenth-century tsar with complete sincerity. He had long esteemed the rule of his earliest Romanov ancestors, and while Alexander III had set the trend by reestablishing medieval symbolism at court, Nicholas went even further to forge a connection between imperial and pre-imperial symbols of rule. Not only did he wear an obligatory beard, but he openly favored costumes, singing, and iconography in the medieval style.

A good example of the role of medieval symbolism that characterized his reign was the famous costume ball held in the Winter Palace in 1903. It was organized, ironically, to commemorate the two-hundred-year anniversary of the founding of St Petersburg, Peter's "window on the West." This gala event appears to have been the last great dance of the old regime and a symbol of the cultural values that its leader embraced in the final years.

A comparison between it and Queen Victoria's roughly contemporaneous Diamond Jubilee in London in 1897 presents an interesting contrast between the meaning of empire for two of Europe's Great Powers as they entered the twentieth century. Both celebrations brought emphasis to their respective imperial communities. The Diamond Jubilee honored the sixtieth year of Victoria's rule and with it the consolidation of the British Empire. Petersburg's Bicentennial Ball honored Peter the Great's construction of a new capital and the Russian Empire it now administered. In sharp contrast to the affirmation of imperial community expressed by the British celebration, however, the Bicentennial Ball recognized only Russian nationality. Whereas in London representatives of diverse peoples and races had been welcomed by the queen in their native costumes, in the Russian capital the costume style was uniformly Muscovite. In fact, instead of honoring the founder of the Russian Empire, Peter the Great, Nicholas glorified the founder's father: the costume he chose to wear to the ball was that of the religiously pious Alexei Mikhailovich (r. 1645–1676). Thus, for an evening at least, the Winter Palace became the Terem Palace of the Moscow Kremlin, decorated accordingly and filled with a company of pseudo-boyars decked out in seventeenth-century dress. As Nicholas moved through their midst, he presented himself as a modern successor to the Tishaishii Tsar,[56] complete with pointed shoes and a fur hat.

In matters of Church culture the tsar also turned to the period that Orthodox patriots claimed had best expressed the national faith. In the very year of the costume ball, for instance, he received a letter written by a patron of the Church raising fears that traditional Russian icon painting was in danger of extinction. Icons painted by hand in monasteries, the petitioner claimed, were being squeezed out of the market by cheap, factory-produced icons imported from abroad. Thus Russians faced the "death of our art of iconography."[57] Nicholas's response was highly sympathetic. He ordered the creation of a Committee for the Defense of Russian Iconography, which directed its activity according to the principle that "national iconography" is one of the "pillars of the Russian people."[58] Here he proclaimed the same values propagated by Trenev and the other leaders of the cultural mission discussed in Chapter 3. His support of Orthodox patriotism was further expressed in his strong disapproval of the sample of non-Russian Orthodox icons that had been presented for his examination. "It is really impossible not to have the most severe reaction to these pictures," he exclaimed to the Chief Procurator, and he ordered that the synodal censorship be employed to limit their circulation within the borders of Russia.[59]

Thus, in the wake of the Paschal Edict Nicholas was prepared to meet the cries of conservative Orthodox patriots such as Bishop Nikon with a renewed demonstration of his apostle-like heritage. He continued to set a model of Orthodox piety in his private life. He also continued and in some ways even expanded the state's administrative support of what remained, for the time being at least, the "preeminent and predominant" Orthodox faith. After a period of supporting Peter Stolypin and his program to advance religious toleration in the Duma, the tsar began to reverse course. By 1909, Stolypin was forced to abandon his toleration legislation altogether. "The monarch," he announced before the Duma's delighted clerical representatives, "according to our law, is the defender of the Orthodox Church and the custodian of its dogmas . . . [and] these religious laws will operate in the Russian state and will be confirmed by the Russian Tsar, who for more than one hundred million people was, is, and will be an Orthodox Tsar."[60]

Within the Holy Synod Nicholas's reversal on toleration was expressed in his decision to appoint V. K. Sabler as Chief Procurator in 1911. Sabler served until 1915, holding the office longer than any other Chief Procurator in the years after Pobedonostsev. In fact, he did much to restore the policies of his predecessor. As the German historian Igor Smolitsch aptly put it, he was in many ways a "reincarnation" of Pobedonostsev.[61] Sabler was first of all an active supporter of the Church mission. He had attended the important Third All-Russian Missionary Congress of 1897 as Pobedonostsev's special synodal representative and had impressed the assembled missionaries with a patriotic speech about the necessity of state support in preserving Orthodoxy in modern "Rus."[62] As Chief Procurator, he also represented the Church's interests in the Duma. He opposed a broad interpretation of the Paschal Edict and claimed that the remaining restrictions upon the freedoms of sectarians and Old Believers should remain in place.[63] He was a strong opponent of the leftist deputies' efforts to advance religious toleration and thus earned the respect of many of the disaffected clergy. However, when Sabler did nothing to block the ascendancy of Gregory Rasputin (1869–1916), at court, nor his subsequent influence over Church appointments, he ultimately lost favor in the eyes of clerical leaders such as Archbishop Antony (Khrapovitsky).[64] Nevertheless, for a period he had given missionaries and conservatives hope that the tsar's beneficent influence in religious affairs could be restored.

In financial matters Nicholas did even more to win back the esteem of the Church and its missionary clergy. In spite of recurrent attacks from the Duma floor, state subsidies to the official Church did not significantly decrease in the years before the outbreak of the First World War. In fact, under his pious guidance and in the face of resistance by his own ministers, they actually increased from roughly 30,000,000 rubles in 1908 to 53,000,000 rubles in 1914.[65] Part of this sum went into an expanded spiritual press, which the clergy readily deployed after 1905 to compete with the now free voice of Old Believers and the heterodox. Nicholas's generosity was thus responsible in part for the establishment of a new range of spiritual journals and popular newspapers for commoners and the public. Two such newspapers were placed in the hands of leading Orthodox patriots. The St Petersburg daily *Kolokol* (*The Bell*) was founded under the editorial control of V. M. Skvortsov in 1905, and the Moscow newspaper *Vernost* (*Fidelity*) was assigned to John Vostorgov in 1909.

Nicholas's support for the Church was made most visible, however, in the sphere of church construction. In the period between his accession to the throne and 1908 alone, almost 6,000 new churches were built.[66] Much of this construction was either financed by the state or supported directly by funds provided by Nicholas from the crown. It is quite significant that when he intervened directly to support church construction the tsar favored the use of the Russian national style of architecture esteemed so highly by clerical Orthodox patriots. In this Nicholas had been inspired especially by the impressions of 1896. Fresh from his coronation ceremony in the Moscow Kremlin, he had followed the example of his medieval ancestors by making a pilgrimage to Trinity-Sergius Lavra, where he prayed before the same national holy objects that Kliuchevsky had commemorated during the St Sergius anniversary four years earlier. From Sergiev Posad he had then traveled to Kiev to attend the ceremonies for the consecration of St Vladimir Cathedral. The impression created by his pilgrimage to the cradle of Holy Rus and the site of the baptism festival of 1888 must have been great. At the cathedral he viewed what clerical Orthodox patriots were hailing as the truest expression since the seventeenth century of Russia's national faith. Vasnetsov's depiction of the national saints juxtaposed to those of Byzantium would have appealed strongly to the young tsar after a coronation ceremony that compared him to Constantine. Nicholas's interest in the art of Vasnetsov and his younger collaborator Nesterov, in fact, would last for the remainder of his reign.

After returning to St Petersburg, therefore, he was pleased to see them both in the following year begin working upon what became an even more outstanding monument of clerical Orthodox patriotism. This was the Resurrection of Christ Church, known popularly as the Church of the Savior on Spilled Blood. The church was dedicated to the memory of Alexander II and was built on the very site of his assassination in the capital in 1881. After a design competition in 1887, Alexander III had awarded a commission to the architect, A. A. Parland.[67] The church, whose style paradoxically bore no relation to the Westernized spirit of Alexander II's reign, was to be built with colorful onion domes, tent roofs, and bright colors that created an effect comparable to the sixteenth-century Cathedral of Basil the Blessed on Red Square in Moscow.[68]

As such, it was conceived with the purpose of bringing old Rus to the capital of modern Russia. Work proceeded for more than twenty years, and when it was finally completed under Nicholas it had consumed over 3,000,000 rubles from the state treasury. This cost was offset in part by public donations, and the response of the faithful was later symbolized by decorating the outer walls with colorful tiles bearing the coats of arms of cities throughout the Orthodox national community. The greatest part of the cost, however, was carried by the tsar.[69] Therefore, when it was formally consecrated by the clergy on August 19, 1907, Nicholas came in person with a large suite and played a prominent role in the ceremonies. As he had hoped, this display received a very warm response from the clerical community.[70] Accounts praised the construction of a church as splendorous as this and so well designed to convey an image of the national faith. It was regarded as both a high example of the "national-artistic genius" of Russia and one of the greatest modern expressions of Orthodoxy. Most commendable of all, it was "built in the medieval style."[71]

In light of the great success of the Church of the Savior on Spilled Blood, Nicholas began actively to patronize the construction of other churches in the spirit of Orthodox patriotism during the years after the Paschal Edict. Due in part to his patronage, the period witnessed a transformation in the style of Russian Orthodox church architecture. Nowhere was this more apparent than in the city of St Petersburg itself, where Church leaders such as Nikon had been watching with dismay as non-Christian places of worship were being erected. Clerical disaffection over the Paschal Edict could be contained in part, Nicholas may have thought, by honoring the cultural symbols that Orthodox patriots had assigned to the national faith.

The St Petersburg scope of this construction was impressive. Between 1905 and 1914—when war brought most current projects to a halt—church architects worked to transform the appearance of the capital from a secularized imperial metropole to the heart of an Orthodox national community. Predictably, the great churches of the seventeenth century and earlier served as models. This project of "medievalization" has been little studied by historians, for obvious reasons. Soviet historians were generally banned from a study of late imperial church culture that employed much more than a reductionist method, and for their part Western scholars tended to ignore the period's religious life altogether. In any case, by 1991 few examples of the city's medieval-style churches remained to be studied at all. The communist government regarded early-twentieth-century church construction as a grotesque exception to the Marxist-Leninist model of prerevolutionary modernization, and so representatives of the period were the first to fall victim to Leningrad's de-Christianization projects. As a member of a demolition team honestly put it after dynamiting the Church of the Savior on the Waters in 1932, the medieval style simply "did not correspond to the aesthetics of the classical architecture of the city of Lenin."[72]

Only in the late Soviet period would interest in the city's prerevolutionary church architecture be revived in unofficial spheres by patriotic associations such as the All-Russian Society for the Preservation of Monuments of History and Culture (VOOPIK).[73] Richard Wortman discusses the project of medievalization, yet he focuses solely on Nicholas's regime and largely ignores the influence of the Orthodox Church.[74]

Over seventy freestanding cathedrals, churches, and chapels were begun in St Petersburg and its surrounding suburbs alone under Nicholas, and of this number over forty were begun during or after 1905.[75] If one includes churches and chapels attached to larger buildings (such as the Church of the Intercession of the Most Holy Mother of God attached to the Polytechnic Institute in 1913), the figure would be much greater. Many of these churches were built in medieval styles that featured either onion or helmet domes, tent roofs, colorful facades, and white stone. Some were even built specifically for missionary societies and brotherhoods. The Brotherhood of the Most Holy Mother of God, for instance, finished a large medieval-style church in 1897 that served as inspiration for other missionary societies as they struggled with religious toleration after 1905. The Society for Religious-Moral Enlightenment built two churches in 1906 and 1912 to honor the recently canonized St Seraphim. The church built by the Brotherhood made an impressive sight, dwarfing the four-story apartment buildings that surrounded it with six gilded onion domes and a ten-story bell tower. Another missionary contribution to the medievalization wave under Nicholas was the Church of St Nicholas built in 1911 by the Orthodox Palestine Society. Extremely tall with a thin, square base, the white church resembled the churches of medieval Novgorod such as the Church of the Savior on Ilina Street. Symbolizing the mission of the Palestine Society, its architecture sought to remind parishioners of the intimate connection between Holy Rus and the Holy Land.

One of the most overt cases of the apostle-like tsar's desire to reexpress his patronage of the national faith was the construction of a church built to resemble one of the most famous churches of medieval Rus, Prince Andrei Bogoliubsky's Church of the Intercession of the Most Holy Mother of God on the Nerl River in Bogoliubovo near Vladimir. The Church of the True Cross, known while it stood as the Church of the Savior on the Waters, was built in memory of the Russian sailors killed at sea during the 1904–1905 War with Japan. The humiliating disasters of Port Arthur and Tsushimo had saddened and angered the Russian public, and the government under Nicholas sought to divert attention from charges of military incompetence by establishing a religious symbolism of mourning. The symbolism chosen was shaped by standards established in recent decades by clerical Orthodox patriotism. In accordance with its commemorative nature, the church was built on the premises of the New Admiralty buildings downriver from the Winter Palace. Here, adjacent to the shipyards that were to build a fleet to replace that sunk in 1904 and 1905, one of the most exact replicas of a great medieval church was erected in 1911. It stood very high upon a small base with a single, large, onion-shaped dome towering above a pure white facade. It not only channeled public memory of a national experience through the official Church, but, standing prominently on the banks of the Neva, it also stood as a symbolic counterbalance to the Buddhist temple across the city on the Malaia Neva.

THE FAILURE TO ELABORATE AN ALTERNATIVE MODEL OF NATIONALITY

The tsar's efforts to restore the autocracy's apostle-like status were made as the Duma sought to broaden the scope of religious toleration with secularistic statecraft. The October Manifesto, issued six months to the day after the Paschal Edict, had led to the creation of a partisan Duma with responsibility to discuss and vote upon legislation affecting religious life in the empire. This, too, struck a heavy blow against the Church's long-held privileges and would prove in the years afterward to be far more threatening than the declaration of religious toleration. Ironically, the creation of the Duma ultimately served to limit clerical disaffection. In general, the clergy understood that the tsar had been forced against his will to grant the irreverent institution, and its introduction came in time to reinvigorate clerical devotion to him as the patron of the Church. While revolutionaries were attacking the traditional order, then, Nicholas found the clergy rallying behind him with the hope that he would use his power to protect the Church.

One statement issued in the wake of the October Manifesto by a group of Moscow priests reflected the clergy's alarm about the political challenge to Orthodoxy and the subsequent decision to seek protection from the tsar. It opened by asking, as so many church leaders were doing, "What is to be done?" It continued: "We must regain our consciousness and rouse ourselves. Each of us is a son of the native land and a faithful subject of the Tsar. . . . They are tearing your dear mother, your native Rus, to pieces. They want to amputate her sacred holy object, the Orthodox faith, by which she has lived until now. They are defaming your Little Father Tsar and profaning his image. Can your heart be peaceful, Russian man?"[76] Such patriotic statements were a common response by the conservative clergy to the political upheavals that accompanied the October Manifesto.

However, the decision by clerical Orthodox patriots to retain the tsar as an essential component of Holy Rus was fateful. The role of Duma politics and political nationalism will be discussed in the next chapter. In what remains of this one, it is necessary to show how Orthodox patriots, most of whom were universally dismayed by the Paschal Edict, rallied to restore the place of the tsar in their model of the national community. Their decision to retain an uncompromising faith in autocracy was a sign of the movement's dislocation from political reality and its inability to offer the Russian public a viable alternative to a secular ethnic nationalism in the fateful years before the war and revolution.

Among those Church leaders who sought to restore devotion to the tsar, the missionary priest John Vostorgov, one of the era's most active missionaries, played the most influential role. Vostorgov's career would be worthy of a full-length biography.[77] Born in 1867, he came of age in the era following the assassination of Alexander II and thus witnessed the rise of secular nationalism among the Russian public at a formative time in his intellectual development. He completed his clerical training in 1887, the year of the First All-Russian Missionary Congress. During his early years as a priest, he taught the Russian language at various church schools in Georgia. After visiting St Petersburg in 1901, he received the support of Pobedonostsev and began to serve in Transaucasia as a member of the Holy Synod's Council on Church School Affairs. In 1906 he was called to the Moscow diocese by Metropolitan Macarius and given command of the missionary courses being established there.[78] Soon after that he assumed editorial control of the Church publishing house Vernost, as well as the journal published from 1905 to 1917 bearing the same name. In the prerevolutionary years, he began to participate more actively in the affairs of the external mission in Central Asia and Siberia, even traveling beyond the borders of the empire to places such as Japan, Korea, and Persia. Before war broke out in 1914, he rose to a position of considerable influence within the Church. His articles and addresses began to appear regularly alongside those of other Church leaders in religious journals such as *Tserkovnyia vedomosti,* and several conservative newspapers such as *Moskovskiia vedomosti* also published him. His success was cut short by the Revolution, however. He chose not to flee the country, and in 1918 the steadfast defender of Orthodoxy was taken by the Communists to a park in Moscow and shot to death with about eighty others.

Vostorgov's output of sermons and addresses, to judge by his collected works, increased in direct relation to the rise of the empire's troubles. Like Skvortsov, he had strongly opposed the tsar's decision to grant religious toleration. As the Paschal Edict approached, he too had reemphasized the meaning of Nicholas's coronation and his duty to protect the true faith in the kingdom.[79] Instead of accepting the edict's terms and implications, he promoted an interpretation of toleration that included conscience alone and not the broader freedom of religious practice and propaganda. To this interpretation he held steadfastly in the months after April of 1905. Then, as political forces hostile to the Church mobilized in response to the promises of the October Manifesto, he threw his commitment back in with the tsar, calling upon all Russians to maintain allegiance primarily to the tsar as the indispensable patron of the national faith. He made no effort to distance clerical Orthodox patriotism from autocracy, and even seems to have emphasized popular identification with it more strongly than before.

In a collection of sermons titled *A Pastoral Voice in Days of Revolution,* one of his earliest responses to the October Manifesto, Vostorgov revealed some of the reasons for his unshaken devotion to autocracy.[80] He remarked that a significant change in governmental authority had taken place since the Paschal Edict in April and noted how many of the political forces that would soon dominate the Duma would be hostile to the Church. Seeing virtually no advantage to severing the Church and its missionary activity from the state under such circumstances, therefore, he appealed for increased identification with the tsar in the hope that this would influence Nicholas to limit the effects of the Paschal Edict. Vostorgov gave close attention to the status of the tsar's Orthodoxy and its role in the integration of the national community. Much of Russia's present division, he claimed, was due to the activity of alien faiths that acted upon the Paschal Edict in a way that was totally at odds with the intentions of Nicholas. "In the west of Russia are found people who are accepting Catholicism, alien to the Russian man. In other places apostasy to the schism and sectarianism is occurring." He reviewed the references these people were said to be making to the principle of toleration contained in the Paschal Edict and reiterated more recently in the October Manifesto. "These references," he argued, "are groundless. It is true that freedom of conscience in the state consists of the fact that everyone freely chooses his own confessional faith. In this sense, governmental authority will no longer demand that someone betray his faith. But conscience," he insisted, "is something that remains within the individual." In other words, the open practice of one's faith, and certainly its propagation, were not necessarily guaranteed in the tsar's new dispensation. "Our sovereign himself," he continued, "is as before a Son of the Orthodox Church and its Defender, and never desired in issuing His manifesto that Orthodox faithful would become apostate from the faith. He believed before and believes now that without the help of governmental protection, sons of Orthodoxy together with Him will continue as before according to the freedom of their conscience to remain within the sheepfold of the Orthodox Church." Ultimately, Vostorgov hoped, the tsar would not be indifferent to the national faith and would with time resume his role as its defender. Recognizing that Orthodoxy "made our Rus into Holy Rus," he claimed that Nicholas would not deviate to the pattern of statecraft found among the world's "pagan tsars."[81]

It should not be overlooked, either, that Vostorgov's desire to restore Nicholas's shaken status as apostle-like tsar was closely related to the Orthodox theological traditions discussed in Chapter 2. Orthodox theologians had long supported a close relationship between the ruler and the clergy, and they called this ecclesio-political relationship "symphony."[82] Orthodox patriots made much of this ideal relationship when they discussed the national community. The people of Holy Rus, they claimed, experienced the kingdom of heaven on earth. In eschatological terms, this was not only a spiritual order, but was visible politically and culturally. So immanent was it in the minds of Church leaders, in fact, that the two sometimes became blurred. St John of Kronstadt, who did not usually choose to express himself in the Orthodox patriotic medium, occasionally spoke of the preeminent position of Russia within the kingdom of God. For him, Russia was like Old Testament Israel, through whom divine providence was channeled. "I perceive a new Israel," he wrote on one occasion. "By this I mean the Christian Israel known otherwise as the Christian Church of Russia."[83] Over this new Israel, he stated, God has placed Tsar Nicholas II as a "guard" devoted to the protection of the kingdom of God on earth. Russians should remember, then, "that the earthly fatherland with its Church is the threshold to the heavenly fatherland."[84]

Christian eschatology thus influenced the Church's view of the tsar. In a 1908 address celebrating the anniversary of Nicholas's coronation, Vostorgov echoed John of Kronsdadt by stating that "the human kingdom is not an end itself, but a means toward the manifestation of the kingdom of God." Accordingly, "the life of a Christian people's state cannot override the needs and demands of Christian conscience." What Vostorgov opposed most strongly in the state was indifference to what he called the "religious-moral" purpose of nationality. He believed that the strong self-consciousness about Russian national destiny that accompanied a patriotic evaluation of the tsar was justified only if it contributed to the advancement of the Church. "If the state lacks religious-moral principles and character," he claimed, "if it is only an economic entity or it is based only upon mutual advantage and national egoism, and is not the means toward the realization of the moral ideals of Christian individuality and the high calling of a Christian people, then in fact the tsar need not be crowned at all, nor should his authority be sanctified." If the tsar should cease temporarily from promoting the religious purpose of the people, he went on, then it was the Church's responsibility to remind him of it. "Then once again, God's Church will stand as an embodied conscience to go before tsars and peoples, showing them the path from earth to heaven. Once again this idea will be clothed before the people in the beauty of sacred rituals and sacred deeds. Once again there will be a holy coronation of tsars and the sanctification of authority."[85]

An even stronger argument for the resumption of apostle-like tsarist authority was contained in a sermon by Vostorgov commemorating the First Ecumenical Council held in Nicaea under St Constantine in 325. Notably, he opened this address by emphasizing the fact that the feast day coincided with the birthday of the tsar's wife, Tsaritsa Alexandra. Conscious that a direct challenge to Nicholas based upon the example of Constantine was danger-ous, Vostorgov used the present address as a more subtle summons to apostle-like rule. Nevertheless, in the context of 1908 his comments were clearly a critique of the Paschal Edict. St Constantine, he stated, had convened the council for the "elimination of heresy" in particular and the "strengthening of the true Orthodox faith" in general. Thus the first Christian tsar set an example of state assistance in the affairs of the Church. "While it is true that supporting the wholeness and purity of the faith is largely an affair and duty of the Church's pastors, civil authority itself has complete power in this affair and competence in union with the pastors. To this extent the Orthodox tsar is a son of the Church, duty-bound by his office to care for it precisely as a son would for his mother. It was in such a manner that St Constantine

Equal-to-the-Apostles regarded himself." To make Constantine's example even more explicit, Vostorgov went so far as to trace the line of his apostle-like rule to Russia. "Before the time of the fall of Constantinople, the Lord raised up the young, powerful, and talented Russian people. Under the new Constantine, St Vladimir Equal-to-the-Apostles, it accepted the Christian faith, was raised in it, and under its influence formed the Russian kingdom." Most important, Vostorgov claimed, Russia's later rulers fulfilled Constantine's and Vladimir's legacy.

> Of course, in Russia there existed and continue to exist schismatics and sectarians who rebelled against the Church, as well as atheists and false teachers. But so long as . . . the Orthodox Autocrat, God's chosen and crowned Tsar, guards the Church's safety and strength, then the powers of hell do not frighten us. It would be different, however, if it came to be that the power and authority of the Tsar declined, if the Tsar became limited, powerless, and constrained.

The state, he warned, "if cut off from the Church will fall just as Byzantium fell. . . . In such a way our Russia too will fall."[86]

Vostorgov's apocalyptic concerns reflected the growing sense of uncertainty among Russia's Church leaders in the years after 1905. While for some Orthodox the revolutionary changes in Russia's political and religious order inspired confidence that a better future would be reached because of them, many met the loss of the Church's legal monopoly in religious life in a growing spirit of frustration. Considering the wholesale opposition they cultivated toward the "new Russia," it is understandable that they maintained what might otherwise seem a blind devotion to the apostle-like tradition of tsarist authority. As has been shown, their devotion was anything but blind. They and other clerical Orthodox patriots insisted that the tsar was a legitimate member of the national community to the extent that he promoted its religious destiny. Thus, while they were critical of Nicholas for bending to the forces of religious diversity and issuing the Paschal Edict, to their missionary minds the autocratic heritage still presented the best hope for restoring Church life.

CHAPTER 6

~ ✟ ~

The Lure of Nationalism

So long as the Russian state remained an autocracy, the clergy's model for the national community remained relatively unentangled in public political affairs. Archbishop Nikanor of Kherson may have praised the patriotism of Mikhail Katkov, for instance, but the principles of national exclusivity expressed by this and other nationalists were criticized both as a contradiction of the universal principle of Christianity and as a threat to the authority of Russia's apostle-like tsar. However, when Nicholas II was compelled to undermine both his apostle-like status and a genuine autocracy in 1905, the relationship between clerical Orthodox patriotism and ethnic nationalism began to change.

ETHNIC NATIONALISM AND THE RUSSIAN EMPIRE

It is extraordinarily difficult to characterize nationalism in Russia during the late imperial period. The fact that Russia was a multinational empire ruled by an autocrat greatly complicated any expression of national self-consciousness. The distinction between the Russian words *russkii* and *rossiiskii* captured this complexity, as historians of the period have long been aware. The first was based on the ethnic criteria of language (*russkii iazyk*), customs (*russkii byt*), and ancestry (*russkoe proiskhozhdenie*). The word *rossiiskii,* on the other hand, was invented in the sixteenth century (and became widely applied only in the seventeenth century) to describe the imperial regime (*rossiiskoe pravitelstvo*) and the multiethnic territory (*rossiiskoe gosudarstvo*) it ruled. This distinction often prevented nationalists from speaking consistently about their ideals of statehood and culture. The result is that studies of nationalism in western Europe offer only limited insight into the Russian experience.[1]

Part of the difficulty is also due to what until recently has been a lack of studies of Russian nationalism. Geoffrey Hosking, one of the few historians to attempt a comprehensive interpretation of its development, suggests that

two "alternative strategies" can be distinguished among the forces within
the state that promoted "nation-building" after the Great Reforms. The first
was directed toward building a civic national community that would tolerate ethnic differences in exchange for a commitment to the secular ideals
of civil freedom and participatory government. The second sought to create an ethnic national community that would be founded upon the equally
secular standards of language, popular customs, and common ancestry. The
civic strategy was almost hopelessly doomed in a state with a conservative
leadership and a long tradition of autocracy. Its proponents were influential
during the liberal reform process of the 1850s and 1860s, but when the Great
Reforms failed to solve the empire's problems they were eclipsed by proponents of an ethnic strategy. Ethnic nationalism, then, remained the dominant
approach among state officials who, with varying degrees of commitment,
promoted the formation of a national community before the Revolution.[2]
Hosking assigns these strategies mainly to the state, yet they can be witnessed
among many public leaders of the period as well. Pan-Slavs such as General Kireev promoted the growth and influence of Russian ethnic nationality, for instance, and the period after 1905 witnessed an explosion of public
forces seeking to create an ethnically homogeneous national state.[3] Likewise,
civic nationalism, with its basis in the ideals of civil society and representative
government, was embraced by liberals of the Duma such as Paul Miliukov
(1859–1943).[4]

Between these two alternatives, it was ethnic nationalism that attracted
the patriotic clergy after 1905. Ethnic nationalists generally held conservative political values and believed that a strong official Church would help
to reestablish the traditional social order. To them, the Great Reforms had
shown how liberal institutions and policies only perpetuated further division
of the state. They believed that a policy of Russification directed at national
minorities and the defense of Russian national privileges were the keys to
uniting the troubled multiethnic empire, and they believed that the Orthodox Church must play a significant role in this policy. To the extent that Russification was successful, they hoped that Russia would begin to resemble the
great national states of western Europe such as Bismarck's Germany.

Nevertheless, the lure of ethnic nationalism among conservatives such
as clerical Orthodox patriots was ironic. Suppressed by the autocratic state
before 1905, nationalism in the prerevolutionary period exerted a political
influence that was often disruptive. The most successful parties to embrace
ethnic nationalism, the self-styled "patriotic unions," were capable of reck-
less demagogy and frequently incited attacks upon groups that did not meet

their ethnic criteria of nationality, particularly the Jews. The irony was not lost on the leaders of the patriotic unions themselves. "To be a conservative in this time," wrote a contemporary member of the Union of the Russian People, means to be a "radical."⁵ The appeal of the unions therefore depended in part on their proclaimed commitment to autocracy and other forces of the traditional order such as the Church. Also significant in explaining conservative support was the fact that Russia's nascent system of representative government lacked well-organized conservative institutions. Apart from the unions, no official party to the right of the Octobrists⁶ existed to offer conservatives a means of advancing their political interests. As Hosking has noted, "it was symptomatic of the monarchy's isolation that it was unable to sponsor the formation of a real conservative party for the Duma."⁷ The banner of conservatism thus passed into the hands of the patriotic unions, and those who sympathized with the traditional order—including many among the clergy—looked to them for leadership in public political affairs.

This was doubly ironic in the case of the clergy, for they had mobilized the cultural mission partly to counter the influence of ethnic nationalism. While the policy of Russification promoted by ethnic nationalists was often premised on a strengthening of the Orthodox Church, nationalists and clerical Orthodox patriots were by no means natural allies. Most importantly, the clergy's model of Holy Rus could not accommodate Russia's heterodox, who were frequently courted by nationalist leaders. Here the issue of Old Belief was especially volatile. Patriotic unions often tried to recruit Old Believers, making little distinction between these adherents to the national faith and their official rivals.

No sooner had the October Manifesto been issued than nationalist parties began to make public appeals to this effect. The Union of Russian Men declared that Old Believers were legitimate members of "the Russian people" and therefore would be welcomed as bearers of the national spirit.⁸ The editor of the right-wing *Moskovskiia vedomosti,* V. A. Gringmut, also included the Old Believers in his vision of the nation when organizing the Russian Monarchist Party. In order for Russians to assert their status as the "master of the house," he believed that Orthodoxy must play a substantial role in the process of Russification.⁹ Nevertheless, he was far less concerned with ecclesiology than the missionary clergy when it came to defining membership in the Church. In his model of the nation, Old Believers occupied a place alongside canonical Orthodox. "When we appeal to Orthodox people under the banner of the Monarchist Party," he was quoted as saying by the dismayed editors of *Tserkovnyi vestnik,* "we mean precisely you Old Believers too."¹⁰

In addition to including the Old Believers in their model of the nation, ethnic nationalists alienated the clergy by their tendency to emphasize secular standards of nationality, such as politics and ethnicity, at the expense of the universal faith. The "Great Russia" (*Velikaia Rossiia*) that many nationalists sought to build did not conform well to the Holy Rus of the Church's cultural missionaries. Here the primacy of secularized statecraft, language, and ancestry directly threatened Orthodox spiritual goals, for ecclesial self-consciousness was not a necessary element of any. This fact was demonstrated by Peter Struve (1870–1944), whose standard of nationality could be extended to persons of any religious background, including Jews, provided they maintained conformity to a culturally defined "national face."[11] As a result, the clergy frequently spoke about the threat of what it considered "pagan nationalism."

Nevertheless, the differences between ethnic nationalists and clerical Orthodox patriots were not unbridgeable. In the years after 1905, a small group of conservative Church leaders made an effort to form connections with the patriotic unions. To understand the motivation behind their activities, long misunderstood both in the Soviet Union and in the West as "typical" of the Russian Orthodox Church during this troubled time, it is necessary to consider the perceptions of conservative missionaries. They were lured toward ethnic nationalism by upheavals resulting from the Paschal Edict and the October Manifesto.

CONSERVATIVE CLERGY IN THE WAKE OF 1905

The months that surrounded the Paschal Edict were a time of great insecurity for leaders of the mission. In the wake of the tsar's declaration, a feeling of anxiety about the future spread throughout the ecclesiastical press. A writer in *Tserkovnyi vestnik,* for instance, stated that the edict "will place before the internal mission . . . heavy and demanding tasks in comparison with old times." While in the future religious freedom would "undoubtedly lift the character, ability, and influence of the mission," he went on, its leaders faced in the meantime the prospect of declining revenue and an upsurge of proselytizing heterodox.[12]

Missionaries feared the challenge of Old Belief especially because of its reputed appeal to popular religiosity. "The Russian man is drawn with love toward the schism," warned a critic of toleration in *Strannik,* "as somehow the schism captures the loyalties of his heart." Without legal privileges such as state protection for canonical Orthodoxy, therefore, "the consciousness . . . of the mass of simple people" was now in jeopardy.[13] As Firsov has noted, the challenge of Old Belief "can without exaggeration be called one of the most complicated questions of Church and state life" during the period.[14]

Missionaries in the non-Russian borderlands doubted their ability to continue the project of Christianization that had been consolidated during the reign of Alexander III. In Kazan, the editors of *Tserkovno-obshchestvennaia zhizn* (*Church Social Life*) felt that the "gloomy reality" of the official Church would now make it difficult for missionaries to address the "ten million non-Russians" who inhabited surrounding areas.[15] The edict had "put an end to governmental protection of missionary affairs," stated an article titled "What Is to Be Done?" Without the same level of state support known previously, it claimed that the Church was compelled to seek new allies in conducting its activity. In some cases this offered the opportunity for reviving the much neglected church parish. "From now on," it declared, "the Christian enlightenment of non-Russians and the establishment of faith among them must lie with local authorities. Christians are far less justified today in shrinking from activity than at any time heretofore."[16] Such calls for self-sufficiency and increased activism among the clergy and even the laity encouraged some missionary leaders to innovate new alliances outside of the official Church community.

This was especially true in the political sphere, where the formerly beneficent authority of the autocracy was by the end of 1905 displaced by a contentious State Duma. Issued just six months after the Paschal Edict, the October Manifesto that created the Duma unleashed forces that were far more threatening to the Church than the mere decline of apostle-like statecraft. The short-lived First and Second Dumas, filled with a large number of socialists and Kadets,[17] were a disaster in the eyes of conservative Church leaders. Not only did secularistic representatives demand greater freedom for heterodox Russians, but they also proposed radical measures to reduce Orthodox Church influence. Some went so far as to propose the confiscation of monastery lands.[18] The "Stolypin coup" of 1907[19] broke the influence of the extreme left, but the forces of secularization continued to assail the Church's long-held privileges. The Third Duma, in fact, became a battleground on which many of the consequences of the Paschal Edict were decided. The Duma's clerical representatives found themselves besieged by efforts to introduce legislation that expanded the edict's terms. Their adversaries, who included not only the Kadets and the Octobrists but Stolypin's government as well, sought to facilitate easier conversions away from the official Church and to grant Old Believers the right to propagate their faith.[20] In most cases it was the parties of the extreme right who defended the interests of the Church against these onslaughts. The result, as John Shelton Curtiss noted when discussing the Church's experiences in political life after 1905, was that the alignment of the clergy moved continuously to the right.[21]

This, of course, is no surprise to historians familiar with the Church's role in politics during the troubled prerevolutionary years. Nevertheless, it is important to emphasize the impact that the new political situation had upon clerical Orthodox patriotism. The experience of losing the protection of an apostle-like tsar while simultaneously gaining the protection of parties on the extreme right caused conservative Church leaders for the first time to define their activities in relationship to an organized nationalist movement.

THE PATRIOTIC UNIONS AND THE CHURCH

The reasons for this ominous turn toward ethnic nationalism were expressed in a book written by John Vostorgov after the dissolution of the First Duma in the spring of 1906. Titled *The State Duma and the Russian Orthodox Church,* it described in a bitter and harried tone the efforts of leftist political forces to advance secularization and undermine the traditional strength of the Church.[22] The priest noted that the Paschal Edict simply "did not satisfy the Duma." Deputies had not only given a broad interpretation to its principle of "religious toleration" (*veroterpimost*), he claimed rhetorically, but had also sought "complete freedom of atheism."[23] He held out hope that the effects of the edict could be reversed and that Orthodoxy could be restored to reflect its status as the "preeminent and predominant" faith, despite the contrary "logic of governmental authority" that now existed.[24] The answer, he argued, increasingly lay in the strength of Russian national self-consciousness and the political forces that promoted it. "According to a purely Slavic understanding of things," he claimed, "it is clear that the Duma project will produce not freedom of faith and conscience but the destruction of Orthodoxy in Russia. Of this there can be no doubt."[25]

Conservative priests like Vostorgov were prepared to consider a "purely Slavic understanding of things" because the political parties that defended traditional Orthodox privileges strongly extolled Russian nationality. This was true especially of patriotic unions such as the Union of the Russian People and the Union of the Archangel Michael. In seeking the support of the Orthodox Church, they played upon the anxieties of the conservative clergy. The Union of the Archangel Michael, for instance, whose very name invoked the image of Russia as the new Israel, assigned Orthodox ecclesial self-consciousness an important status in its official program. It stated that it was committed to a "political struggle" against the secularistic left to restore the Orthodox faith to its formerly "predominant" position.[26] Politics in the Duma, it asserted, must be conducted exclusively "upon an Orthodox basis."[27]

The Union of the Russian People was far more influential, owing in part to its successful wooing of disgruntled members of the weakened Church. Alexander Dubrovin (1855–unknown), its founder, actively cultivated a friendly relationship with the Holy Synod and repeatedly petitioned it for support.[28] Conscious of the clergy's anxiety about the effects of religious toleration, he attacked the Paschal Edict and the growing freedoms enjoyed by sectarians.[29] One petition sent to the Synod sympathized with missionaries in their struggle to limit the powers of heterodoxy. It stated that the Duma's "extravagant and undeserved kind-heartedness toward the enemies of Orthodoxy serves as a signal for sectarians to rebel." It referred with particular distaste to the civil administration of the capital, which, following the logic of the Paschal Edict, was "providing its own halls for use as cathedrals to Stundists[30] and other heretics."[31] Such attacks on the non-Orthodox were calculated to earn the sympathy of Church leaders such as Bishop Nikon, whose journal *Troitskoe slovo* had launched its own attacks upon the construction of "pagan temples" in the capital.

In their efforts to win support from the clergy, the patriotic unions adopted the rhetoric of clerical Orthodox patriotism. Political "catechisms" regularly described the national community as inseparably linked to Orthodox ecclesial self-consciousness. The Union of the Russian People, for its part, defined the national community simply as the "Orthodox-Russian people."[32] A ecclesial definition of nationality was also manifested in the appeals of patriotic unions to the common people. A typical but anonymous broadsheet addressed to "faithful workers and peasants" called upon them as true Russians to vote in Duma elections only "for religious and honorable people who are filled with the Holy Spirit and his wisdom."[33] This won the sympathy of many conservative Church leaders. Their requests for permission to join the patriotic unions finally yielded the Synod's official blessing on March 15, 1908. The statement notified bishops that they "should permit and bless the participation of the Orthodox clergy under them in the activities of the Union of the Russian People and other monarchical patriotic societies as long as they remain in conformity with the rules of the Orthodox Church and serve the interests of the fatherland."[34]

This gave increased impetus to a direction that was already under way to establish chapters of patriotic unions in local parishes and monasteries such as the prestigious Pochaev Lavra in the western diocese of Volynia. There the abbot, Archimandrite Vitaly, became chairman of the local chapter of the

Union of the Russian People and oversaw a highly coordinated campaign to disseminate the monastery's political and religious teachings throughout the province. To do so he needed the endorsement of the head of the diocese, Archbishop Antony (Khrapovitsky), who, as a conservative proponent of Orthodox patriotism himself, lent his support.[35]

The Staritsa Monastery in the province of Tver presents another case in which the Church actively supported patriotic unions. Under the authority of Archimandrite Pavel, the monastery established a chapter of the Union of the Russian People whose members directed nationalistic political activity toward missionary goals. With the union's support, they scheduled public readings among the common people designed to strengthen Orthodox ecclesial self-consciousness. These were often preceded by the para-liturgical pageantry of Orthodox patriotism, including public prayer services and the bearing of gonfalons and icons in processionals throughout the town of Staritsa. The topics of the readings represented the historical and cultural program developed by Church leaders since 1888. Listeners learned about the holy places of medieval Rus, the Time of Troubles, pilgrimages to Palestine, the national saints, and, of course, the baptism of 988. In a reading about the heroic defense against the Mongols offered by St Mikhail of Tver, one group of listeners was reminded of the "necessity of standing selflessly for the faith of Orthodoxy, upon which Holy Rus was built."[36] Here, as in the Pochaev Monastery, Church leaders used their affiliations with nationalists to promote missionary goals.

To be sure, many among the clergy did not support the patriotic unions, and this was true even for some who sympathized with Orthodox patriotism. Liberal priests regarded the counter-revolutionary movement with horror and blamed the unions for instigating murderous pogroms against Jews and others. The prestigious Church theologian P. Y. Svetlov, for instance, whose work had made an effort to establish an eschatological foundation for clerical Orthodox patriotism, spurned the political right.[37] Metropolitan Antony (Vadkovsky) of St Petersburg had also embraced Orthodox patriotism in many of his speeches, promoting the Church's model of "Holy Rus" and the image of Russia as the "new Israel."[38] All the same, as the most prominent liberal in the Church he issued an open refusal to associate with the Union of the Russian People, an act that provoked Dubrovin publicly to attack the prelate for what he considered "brutal and unjust words."[39] Finally, for the Orthodox clergy who welcomed the Paschal Edict and other religious reforms, and for those who found nothing useful in Orthodox patriotism, the nationalistic appeals of the unions were even more vacuous. This is why such a small percentage of the Russian Orthodox clergy actually joined. And, as Firsov has shown, "among the leaders of the Union of the Russian People the clergy were almost completely absent." Only one priest was a founding member of the organization in 1905, and by 1908 only three had joined its Head Council.[40]

The most prominent Orthodox patriots in the Church did sympathize with the unions and in many cases even became formal members. They included Archbishop Antony (Khrapovitsky) of Volynia, John Vostorgov, and V. M. Skvortsov. The activities of these three Church leaders in the tumultuous years after 1905 reflect an important turning point in the history of prerevolutionary Orthodox patriotism. Coupled with a failure to redesign the image of the apostle-like tsar, their turn to ethnic nationalism manifested the growing dissonance of the movement. Apologies for the patriotic unions could seemingly call the universal principle of Orthodox Christianity into question, and anti-Semitic statements—which all three occasionally made—could only have served to further demoralize Church life. Nevertheless, their increasingly reactionary activities can only be understood in light of the upheaval that followed 1905. For two decades they had been struggling with success against the rise of apostasy and secularization. After the Paschal Edict and the formation of the secularistic Duma, that began to change.

CONVERTING THE NATIONALISTS: ARCHBISHOP ANTONY'S DEFENSE OF THE UNIVERSALISTIC PRINCIPLE

Of the three leading collaborators with Russia's ethnic nationalists, Archbishop Antony (Khrapovitsky) of Volynia made the greatest effort to maintain the Church's principle of universality. This may have been due to his being both a theologian and a hierarch. He had been born Alexei Pavlovich Khrapovitsky, the son of a Novgorod landowner who later served in the pan-Slavic war against Turkey in 1877–1878. Taking monastic vows at the conclusion of his training at the St Petersburg Spiritual Academy, he was appointed docent of the Old Testament there a year before the baptism anniversary of 1888.[41] Soon afterward he transferred to the Moscow Spiritual Academy, where he played a leading role in the founding of the spiritual journal *Bogoslovskii vestnik* (*Theological Messenger*). It was in Kazan, however, that one of the most important experiences in his career occurred. As rector of the Kazan Spiritual Academy, the largest center for training Orthodox missionaries in the empire, he became intimately acquainted with the needs and challenges of the mission. His work with courses for the internal mission especially led him to develop strong opinions about the destiny of the Orthodox Church in Russia. He came to believe that the expansion of Russian national self-consciousness would serve as a powerful instrument for pursuing the mission. This belief was marked especially in his attitude toward the schism. Contrary to many within the Church, he esteemed the Old Believers as true Russians whose organization and way of life actually offered a positive example to the canonical Church. As James Cunningham wrote, "Antony thought the courses offered to 'refute' the Old Believers were ridiculous and that they needlessly antagonized a whole section of the Russian people whom he thought should be conciliated."[42] Much of his work from this point forward was directed at restoring unity with these other adherents to the national faith. In 1902 he was transferred to Volynia, and he remained there as bishop and then archbishop until the outbreak of the First World War, when he was transferred to Kiev.

One of Antony's earliest contributions to Orthodox patriotism was issued in 1887, the year he was appointed docent in St Petersburg. Using the feast day of the Descent of the Holy Spirit, he described the Orthodox character of "Rus" and the threat sectarians posed to her "simple people." The Holy Spirit was the source of national strength and piety, he said, as centuries of history of the "motherland" testified. Without the transfiguring power of the Holy Spirit, Russia was in danger of losing her "religious and national character, her Russian Orthodox essence."[43] Subsequent sermons further developed this pneumatologically shaped model of "Holy Rus." A speech delivered on the occasion of the unveiling of a monument to the assassinated Alexander II spoke enthusiastically about Russia's place in the universal Church and invoked the new Israel image (as well as images disseminated by the Orthodox Palestine Society) by repeating a reputedly popular expression that "Christ may have been born in Bethlehem, but he lives in Russia."[44] Some of his most enthusiastic sermons honored patriotic events such as the coronation of Nicholas II in 1896 and the unveiling of the relics of St Feodosii of Chernigov the same year.[45]

When the 1905 Revolution broke out, Antony responded to the violence and impiety with disgust. The faithless behavior of the Russian people provoked him to place even greater emphasis on the new Israel image. Again employing the expression that "Christ was born in Bethlehem but lives in Russia," he denounced those who were "perverting the Russian national character" by calling for political rebellion. Even more destructive than political rebellion, he claimed, was a general reversion to "paganism" among the people and their leaders.[46] As the Paschal Edict and October Manifesto tore the state's protection away from the Church, Antony was left with a feeling of bitterness toward virtually all of Russia's contemporary political life. His mood was symbolized by a letter he wrote in November to Pobedonostsev to console the now retired Chief Procurator and express his mutual sense of helplessness.[47]

Like other Church leaders close to the mission, Antony felt that the Paschal Edict was a disaster. As an influential prelate and a leading proponent for the revival of the Russian patriarchate, he was chosen as a representative in the Preconciliar Commission in 1906. There he disputed with others like Pavel Svetlov over the question of whether the white clergy (those who are not monastic) should participate in the council. And, in addition to presenting the views of the conservative black (monastic) clergy, he used his position to challenge a policy of religious toleration. Like others, he sought to draw a distinction between freedom of conscience and full toleration. The former was long part of the state tradition in Russia, he stated, but toleration itself would undermine the Church. He was especially adamant in opposing the freedom of non-Orthodox faiths to disseminate propaganda.[48]

Nevertheless, he made a strong effort to uphold the Church's principle of universality and to limit the influence of ethnic nationalism. "Russia," he stated,

> is identified properly as an organism, as a people, as a powerful idea flowing through history. But what is our people in its history and in its present circumstances? Is it an ethnic community? Is it first of all a community dedicated to state defense? No. Russians define themselves before all else as a religious community, as a ecclesial community, which includes even Georgians and Greeks who are unable even to speak the Russian language.[49]

Such an ambiguous characterization of the national community, common to other expressions of clerical Orthodox patriotism that focused upon the national faith, claimed that national integration was secondary to and dependent upon ecclesial unity. It thus made a coherent ethnic definition of Russia almost impossible, as anyone who was Orthodox might belong to the nation, even non-Russians. Seeking to preserve the universal self-consciousness of the Church, Antony did not offer an effective model of a ethnic national state.

His shortcomings as a nationalist were revealed in other addresses and essays. One, titled "The Universal Church and Nationality," demonstrated the dissonance between the principles of universalism and particularism especially well.[50] Written formally as a commentary on nationalist conflict in the Balkans, it spoke generally about the problems of universality for all Orthodox national communities. Nevertheless, after emphasizing that in Russia all faithful pray for Orthodox non-Russians such as the Greeks on Church feast days, he could nevertheless not avoid claiming primacy for Russia. The universal Church had been given a political example in the Russian state, the "Third Rome," he said. Furthermore, Russia served her sister nationalities as an example of Orthodox national consciousness. Though she was now suffering a new time of troubles, in her medieval history she long demonstrated primary attention to the faith. Contrary to her example, today in the Balkans was found a rising spirit of ethnic nationalism, divorced from the sanctifying influence of "universal Orthodoxy." Turning away from the Church, Serbian nationalists had embraced the "Christ-hating Renan"[51] and other Western intellectuals for secular models of the national community such as race and ancestry. Using the example of Russia as an alternative, Antony appealed to the Balkan peoples with the familiar imagery of the ancient Israelites turning away from their essentially religious calling. "In this way the old Israel was ruined," he warned, "but you are the new Israel and still you do not understand the fate of the first-born."[52] By granting the new Israel status to other Orthodox peoples, Antony thus sought to maintain adherence to the principle of universality even while he compromised this principle when addressing the issue of nationality in Russia.

Another example of Antony's failure to coherently define an ethnic national community in Russia is found in an essay titled "On Nationalism and Patriotism," which was written in 1909 and was addressed, significantly, to a meeting of the Union of the Archangel Michael. Antony, as the head of the diocese in which the Pochaev Lavra and its conservative clergy were located, felt compelled to carefully elaborate the nature and limits of Orthodox patriotism. His effort to do so reveals the weakness of the cultural mission in comparison with nationalist movements within Russia and elsewhere throughout Europe. "The popular spirit of nationalism among the tribes of Europe," he observed, "constitutes the essential basis of their social and state life. Put simply, it represents the axiom upon which all political parties endeavor to lean. For us, on the other hand, such an axiom has not yet achieved the right to full recognition." Russia, he noted, lacked a long tradition of civic participation in state affairs. She had not had the opportunity like the states of Europe to develop a politically defined sense of nationhood.

This was a great weakness, he told his listeners, as it had enabled her simple people in recent years to come under the influence of liberal and cosmopolitan ideas. Lacking a political sense of her nationality, Russia now had the opportunity to form a more solid and unified community through the assistance of her "national unions."[53]

All of this was good, he claimed. But at the present stage of developing political institutions, it was important to avoid the errors of the Western national states. Above all, Western nationalism, growing ultimately from the "foundation of Roman paganism," sold the birthright of universal Christian self-consciousness for the pottage of political glory. For Western peoples, Antony observed, the principle of nationality had culminated in collective "egoism" whereby the highest aim of state activity was the acquisition of power and competitive self-preservation. This was all quite "natural," he stated, and for that very reason it had achieved "nothing high, inspired, or holy." The Russian people, on the other hand, were animated by a different spirit. "The purpose of their activity is not to think about their own country and themselves, but about being a serving force to higher purposes that are holy, divine, and universal. Bearing within themselves a certitude of preserving the teaching of Christ, the Russian people have defended and vindicated their land selflessly, as a depository of divine truth and as the servant of evangelical piety." According to Antony, then, "Russian national self-consciousness is not a self-consciousness that is racial or tribal, but religious and ecclesial."[54] This was one of the clearest statements of the Church's defense of Christian universality. In light of the fact that it was issued to a group promoting ethnic nationalism, it demonstrates that when clerical Orthodox patriots went to the nationalists, it was not to join them but to convert them.

When definitions of Russian nationality were made, use of the new Israel imagery was usually quick to follow. Antony asked his listeners to believe that what he had to say about this topic was drawn from a national faith. "Try to persuade a Russian of the need to esteem the Jews," he started.

In light of the fact that the Mother of God, the holy Apostles, and the Prophets were all Jews and not Russians, what do you suppose he will say? He will say that it is untruth, because that was a long time ago when Jews were, in fact, Russians. He knows well enough that the ancient Jews did not speak Russian, and knew nothing about the Russians, but he considers them to be his forefathers, and himself their descendants. This is due simply to his ecclesial self-consciousness.

He explained how a Russian "feels and speaks in accord with the word of Christ, which revoked from the Jewish apostates the right to be sons of Abraham, and gathered many peoples to his bosom."

This in itself was mostly consistent with Orthodox teaching—beginning with St Paul—about the new Israel. But Antony did not rest content with theological tradition when he sought to elaborate the national faith. "I will tell you something still more significant about this sort of Russian patriotism," he stated. Here he offered an anecdote about a custom in Kiev's Pecherskaia Lavra, in which a prayer to the Mother of God praises Her for defending Her "ruling city" from foreign attack. The city in question, he explained, is Constantinople and the foreign enemy is the ancient and pagan Russians. In other words, Russian national self-consciousness is so determined by ecclesial self-consciousness and its universality that ethnic character can become irrelevant. For, as he noted in this case, "it is clear that our people consider their spiritual forefathers not the ancient Russians, but the Greek Christians, and their enemies are our enemies." It is also clear, he added, "that onto such a people it is impossible to graft racial nationalism." To conclude his address to the Union of the Archangel Michael, then, he entreated it to help the Church defend and promote "universal ecclesial patriotism" (*vselensko-tserkovnyi patriotizm*) as the basis of Russia's formative national community.[55]

As a prelate, Archbishop Antony may have felt more reluctant than other clerical Orthodox patriots to emphasize the ethnic features of the national faith. He believed Orthodoxy in its Russian setting was the strongest bond of national unity, as his praise of the Old Believers indicates. Yet he insisted that the national community was ultimately broader than many of the ethnic nationalists with whom he associated claimed. His address to the Union of the Archangel Michael shows this best of all, and it is clear in reading it that he went before nationalists not as a blind enthusiast for their program but as a critic of it, however sympathetic. A Christian missionary at heart, Antony was prepared to engage political unions because he believed they could be won over from "racial nationalism" to something he called "universal ecclesial patriotism."

JOHN VOSTORGOV AND THE ORTHODOX NATIONAL STATE

This was also true of John Vostorgov, though his statements after 1905 gave less attention to the presence of other Orthodox national communities. His missionary addresses and sermons are remarkable in that they touched upon virtually every concern of clerical Orthodox patriotism. Vostorgov characterized what he believed were the most patriotic expressions of culture and literature, finding Dostoevsky and the idea of Russia as a "God-bearing" people the most inspirational. He occasionally described Russia as the "new Israel" for whom Palestine symbolized a second native land,[56] speaking frequently of its "native Orthodoxy" and its constituent "national faith."[57] He employed the title *Holy Rus* with great frequency and looked to a medieval prototype of the national community defined by experiences such as the baptism of 988 and the Time of Troubles.[58] And to help rescue modern Holy Rus from its present "time of troubles," he extolled the patriotic deeds of medieval national saints and holy men such as St Vladimir, St Sergius, and Patriarch Germogen.[59]

As we saw in the previous chapter, the Paschal Edict did not shake Vostorgov's devotion to the autocracy, and after the creation of the Duma system he became one of its most vocal defenders among the clergy. While he continued to claim that tsarist authority must be apostle-like in its defense and promotion of the Orthodox faith, in practice he did not directly criticize the tsar's compromises with secular forces. Instead, he sought to forge an alliance between the Church and the monarchistic parties of the right, being especially drawn to patriotic unions such as the Union of the Archangel Michael and the Union of the Russian People. Although these unions embraced ethnic nationalism, they were the potential allies of conservative Orthodox patriots like himself. In defending their reputation among the clergy, he claimed that the nationalists served in the Duma alone as the "guardians of the religiosity and patriotism of the Russian people."[60] Significantly, many of his addresses in the years after 1905 were delivered at gatherings of the patriotic unions.

Yet, like Archbishop Antony, Vostorgov was not a blind adherent to the nationalist movement. He realized that nationalists could, under some circumstances, pursue interests that were far from the goals of Christianity. When expressing his political ideals, he, like other members of the clergy, therefore preferred to speak of "patriotism" (*patriotizm*), which he equated with love for the nation, rather than "nationalism" (*natsionalizm*), which he equated with competition between nations. In the inaugural issue of a newspaper titled *Patriot* he brought attention to "how we define patriotism." The statement represents one of the most concise definitions of Orthodox patriotism in the period. "It is a pity," he declared, "that even among leaders of the right patriotism is often understood in its European sense, that is, as something essentially pagan. What this constitutes is an animalistic nationalism, a nationalism that is zoological and which is based upon an attachment to and a love toward one's own people, toward one's own land, and toward one's own state to the exclusion of all else." Such a "pagan nationalism" (*iazycheskii natsionalizm*), he asserted, was distinct from a "patriotism formed by the Church" (*votserkovlennyi patriotizm*).[61] It was upon the latter principle that the political unions must stand.

Like other clerical Orthodox patriots, Vostorgov's apologetics were built partly upon highly selective passages in the New Testament that spoke of love toward the Jewish nation. In an address titled "Patriotism and Christianity," Vostorgov quoted Paul's declarations of sympathy for Israel in the Epistle to the Romans.[62] Paul's words to this effect, while not central to the message of universal salvation that occupied his attention through most of the Epistle, seem to have represented for Vostorgov a divinely inspired commandment to embrace patriotism. He claimed that this commandment had been realized particularly well in medieval "Holy Rus" and summarized the life of St Sergius as an illustration. In recent times, however, the commandment had been rejected by representatives in the Duma and in the newspapers. Many "fashionable wise men," he exclaimed, speak of a "love toward all of humanity" while spurning patriotism as an "abusive and shameful word." Such a love is quite impossible, he argued, without a commitment first of all to one's native people. Here he did not consider other New Testament passages about the insignificance of nationality within the Church (such as Gal 3:28) or the love shown for another national community (such as the Good Samaritan in Luke 10:29–37).

Interestingly, in his support for national feeling, Vostorgov did look beyond ideology to what he called the "voice of nature" that works providentially in every person, binding mankind together. This God-given voice declares "that it is impossible to love humanity understood as an abstraction. There exists no humanity as such, there are only individual persons whom we love." The same voice indicates also "that it is impossible to love one we never see and will never know just as much as one whom we know and with whom we live."[63]

Believing in the existence of a close relationship between patriotism and Christianity, Vostorgov actively courted the patriotic unions that promised to defend Orthodoxy in the Duma. His estimation of their potential as political allies was revealed in an address delivered during the course of a "patriotic evening" in early 1907. Titled "The Patriotic Unions and Their Relationship toward Religion," it represented more of a projection of the ideals of Orthodox patriotism on the nationalist movement than an accurate assessment of that movement.[64] It opened stating that

a great poverty and danger has called forth the mobilization of conservative elements of Russian society and directed them toward the defense of
the vital interests of the Russian people, the Russian state, and Russian culture. Neither political "Old Belief," a "devotion to stagnation," a "despotic
regime," nor the "bureaucracy" can respond to the tasks of a national state
[*natsionalno-gosudarstvennyia zadachi*]. Only citizens [*grazhdane*] can do
this, enabled through reason and the heart to attend to the call of civic duty.

Russia's current crisis could be solved in part through the conservative political activities of the nationalists, supported here, interestingly, by a heightened
sense of civic responsibility.

Vostorgov believed that a decline in religious faith was at the root of this
crisis. But it was not merely a matter of secularization and the influence of
what he called "cosmopolitanism." The decline of Orthodoxy, he claimed,
could not be separated from the loss of Russian dominance in political life.
"Against the destructive and anticultural influence of cosmopolitanism and
against the elimination of the Russian people [*russkii narod*], Russians have
advanced the principles of Orthodoxy and Russian nationality. For cosmopolitanism, by its very nature, is so atheistic as to be hostile to the national
basis of the state. Here is why, in essence, Russian patriotic unions in their
political programs speak first of all about religion, about Orthodoxy." Vostorgov praised the unions because they organized their nationalistic program
at least partly around the issue of ecclesial self-consciousness. "Being guardians of Russian national feeling and believing in a world-historical calling
for Russia," he continued, ". . . we cannot abandon the national faith and we
cannot ignore it. In it we see the truth for ourselves and the path to our own
salvation. Simultaneously, it offers us the single path toward a good social
order and the salvation of the people in its earthly kingdom."[65] Believing that
the patriotic unions could carry clerical Orthodox patriotism into the political arena through their programs, Vostorgov, like Antony, thus spent considerable time addressing their gatherings as a missionary seeking to influence
their ideals.

In the many addresses he delivered to the patriotic unions, Vostorgov
promoted two ideals in particular. The first was that the political integration of Russia should be based on an adherence to the faith of the Orthodox Church. This is a familiar conservative ideal in the historiography of
the late imperial period.[66] The policy of Russification undertaken since the
late years of Alexander II's reign included an effort to convert non-Russians
to the official faith and by doing so create loyal subjects. The role assigned

to Orthodoxy in this policy attracted the support of many clerical Orthodox patriots in the years before 1905, but after the October Manifesto Russification through conversion also became a theme among the patriotic unions.

Among those that Vostorgov courted, however, Orthodoxy was often associated with national exclusivity. As we have seen, he rejected the principle of such "pagan nationalism." But in the context of his engagement with the unions, he could not help speaking of the cultural and even racial differences that distinguished Russians from other peoples and tribes. As early as 1899, in the essay on the cultural mission discussed in Chapter 3, he expressed an interest in the cultural role of "Indo-European tribes" during ancient times. He went so far as to discuss the implications of recent "historical science" that had begun to demonstrate the dominant influence of "our Aryan ancestors" in establishing a Slavic culture and form of civilization.[67] Vostorgov was certainly not a "protofascist," as both his Soviet and western detractors would later claim. His use of such racial language, which was rare, is better explained as an unfortunate consequence of the clergy's decision to engage ethnic nationalists at a time in history when such language for them was common.

And whatever emphasis Vostorgov placed upon racial particularity did not prevent him from describing Russia as a community integrated before all else by Orthodox Christianity. The primacy of the faith, in fact, served him in determining national character. "Russia," he claimed to one political gathering, "is in the consciousness of her sons, Holy Rus." Since the empire contained many millions of non-Orthodox citizens, such a definition of nationality could only make sense if they actually converted to Orthodoxy. It reflected a belief, cherished by Orthodox patriots, that nations possess what Simon Franklin and Emma Widdis call an "essentialist" character rooted, in this case, in religious faith.[68] Vostorgov proposed to those who sought greater influence for Russians within the empire that they look to their own national faith to preserve the strength of its dominant nationality. "Prevent the Russian people," he pleaded, ". . . from falling away from the long-cherished form of life that is expressed in its name, Holy Rus." Doing so would not only preserve it among the many non-Russian nationalities, but would also enable it to grow greater as it converted non-Orthodox to the universal faith. By recasting the empire as a potential national community based on religious faith, Vostorgov therefore appealed to the program of his nationalist audience. "Blessed are you members of the patriotic unions," he declared warmly, "if you place at the head of your creeds and your ideals a concern that our great, dear, and limitless Russia never cease to be Holy Rus."[69]

The second ideal promoted by Vostorgov in his addresses was that the destiny of Russia be constituted as an Orthodox mission. Celebrants of the baptism festival had regarded the mission as the defining feature of Russia's national destiny in 1888. Vostorgov sought to convey this ideal to the nationalists after 1905. As other cultural missionaries had been compelled to elaborate the past into a narrative serviceable to the mission, so Vostorgov sought to present the history of Russia as an ongoing struggle to preserve and disseminate the true faith. To do so he employed a historical mythology that began at the moment of the crucifixion. According to a "touching tale" told in Russian folk legend, he stated, Christ when on the cross turned his gaze from "those native to him" standing below "toward the distant, little-known north" that became "our native country." Thus the old Israel, in Vostorgov's version of the legend, was superseded by Holy Rus as the new Israel, even without the intermediary of Byzantium.[70]

When promoting the missionary ideal among the patriotic unions, Vostorgov spoke of a special national destiny for Russia that arose inevitably from Russia's geographic position in the world. "Divine providence," he stated to a group of nationalists, "called us Russian Slavs of central Europe to the bosom of the Christian Church in that very geographical location on the border of Europe and Asia, of west and east." Here, he argued, Russia faced a "great mission":

To bring the received treasure of the pure and true faith to little-known eastern and northern Europe, and even further to the mysterious lands of Asia. This mission is to lift the darkness of paganism and Islam, and to enlighten wild and numerous tribes of non-Russians to join them with the kingdom of God and the life of civilized mankind. This, in truth, is unique in the history of man, the greatest world mission given to Holy Rus.

He related what he considered to be the great successes of this missionary destiny, focusing especially on those associated with the Kazan Icon of the Mother of God, which, as was noted in Chapter 4, was one of the most revered holy objects of the Russian people and frequently served as a focal point for Orthodox patriotism. Because of its association with the conversion of Muslims in Asia and the defense against the Roman Catholic Poles during the Time of Troubles, it possessed a "significance that is highly patriotic." The vitality of the national mission in Asia had declined in recent times, however, as evidenced by the discouraging Russo-Japanese war. Not only had the Russian state failed to penetrate Japan and open the way toward freer missionary activity there and in Korea, he noted, but in the midst of the military humiliation an unprecedented and terrible portent occurred. As civil unrest began to spread throughout Russia, the Kazan Icon of the Mother of God was stolen, temporarily depriving Holy Rus of one of its sanctifying holy objects and the symbol of its national mission.[71] In contrast to the time of the baptism festival twenty years earlier—when the celebrants of Kiev received greetings from Orthodox Japanese converted by Russian missionaries—the destiny and character of Russia were now clearly in peril. Vostorgov therefore urged the patriotic unions to place their political programs "under the banner of Orthodoxy."[72]

Vostorgov's ideal of national destiny was not limited to missionary activities alone. He believed military strength and diplomatic vitality were also important. More than most other clerical Orthodox patriots, he took an active interest in military affairs and sought to direct attention to the foreign policy achievements of the empire. This dimension of his activity is recorded especially well in the weekly journal over which he was given editorial control, *Vernost*. Described under its title as "military-national" and "patriotic" in content, it was founded in 1909 and continued publication until the demise of the empire in 1917. In addition to issuing free supplements on national holidays, it addressed matters such as the instruction of parish and military priests, the dissemination of Russian folktales, information about the geography of Russia, accounts of military affairs, and even a section titled "Rest and Fun" offering amusement for common soldiers.[73]

Under Vostorgov's control, this journal served as an organ of Orthodox patriotism. In addition to the editor's contributions, it printed addresses by conservative clergy such as Archbishop Antony and a range of material that sought to define an Orthodox national community: poems, accounts of pilgrimages to Russian holy places such as Sergiev Posad and Palestine, lives of national saints, and illustrations of national holy objects such as the interior paintings of St Vladimir Cathedral in Kiev. It even contained a regular column titled "Holy Rus."[74] Russian nationalists would have found the journal appealing, especially for its treatment of Russia's obligations to the Balkan Slavs and her past military triumphs. In 1912, for instance, the journal gave extensive attention to the celebration of the centennial of the Battle of Borodino. Tsar Nicholas attended the ceremonies on the famous battlefield west of Moscow, and *Vernost* devoted an entire issue to this event, including a thick supplement with photographs of the celebration.[75]

While this commemoration honored a largely defensive war, the journal's material could also appeal to militarists within the nationalist movement. Vostorgov himself expressed a growing sense of despair over the failure of

Russia to pursue a "world mission" with "world activities."[76] For him, however, the main missionary field was within the boundaries of the empire, particularly Siberia. He regarded Russian settlers there as similar to the Jews of the Old Testament who had been dispersed among the pagans "in the land of Canaan."[77] But like the old Israel, he warned, representatives of the new Israel are sinking into apostasy. As a result, "the Russian Church has now become overwhelmed by grief and misfortune. The faith is in decline and sectarianism spreads, all hostile forces against Christianity move toward greater unity, and the faithless rail against all that we hold dear and holy. The freedom that has been given to non-Orthodox and non-Russians has been forged into a sword with which to smite Orthodoxy."[78] Even eminent figures of Russian culture such as Leo Tolstoy participated in the destruction of the national faith. Vostorgov discussed the one-dimensional image of canonical Orthodoxy depicted in the novel *Resurrection* and warned that if cultural life continued in the same direction as the work of Tolstoy, the national faith might not survive. Here in the pages of *Vernost* and elsewhere, Vostorgov set out to define a national destiny rooted in the Church mission.

As clerical Orthodox patriotism proved itself increasingly powerless to slow the rate of secularization and apostasy, pessimism continued to spread among its proponents. In fact, Vostorgov could even allow himself to brood over the possible demise of Holy Rus. "We are afraid that a terrible sentence is being delivered upon the Russian people," he mused. It was comparable to that which "long ago was delivered upon the God-chosen ancient Israel: 'The kingdom shall be taken away from you and delivered to another people. Many shall enter the kingdom of God from the east and from the west, but the sons of the kingdom shall be cast out.' We, the Russian Church, may be cast out."[79] To interpret these apocalyptic circumstances, he turned to the book of Revelation, where he found in the letter to the church at Ephesus what he considered to be a prophesy about Russia's struggle with apostasy in the past and in the present:

> I know your works, your labor, your patience, and that you cannot bear those who are evil. . . . Nevertheless I have this against you, that you have left your first love. Remember therefore from where you have fallen; repent and do the first works or else I will come to you quickly and remove your lampstand from its place—unless you repent.[80]

For this national pastor, however, Russia after 1905 seemed a long way from repentance.

And so his mood remained apocalyptic. As he addressed patriotic unions in his political addresses and in the pages of *Vernost,* Vostorgov described a condition in which extreme measures for restoring the national faith of Holy Rus were urgently needed. His relations with the patriotic unions indicate that he regarded ethnic nationalism as a necessary substitute for the loss of an apostle-like tsar. But as he urged his audiences toward greater activism, he unwittingly invited the very forces that would contribute to the final collapse of the traditional order.

VLADIMIR SKVORTSOV AND POLITICAL MOBILIZATION

No less anxious about the condition of Holy Rus after 1905 was Vladimir Skvortsov. Before 1905 his activities had mostly been directed toward responsibilities as the chief lay missionary connected to the Holy Synod, and toward editing *Missionerskoe obozrenie*. In the months between the Paschal Edict and the October Manifesto, however, he became involved in secular affairs, and by the end of the year he took up the editorship of a newspaper titled *Kolokol*. This was a Church-financed daily that was launched amid the chaos of late 1905 and that continued publication until the Revolution of 1917. It advertised a "social, church, political, and literary" content, devoting itself especially to Russia's political troubles and the affairs of the Duma. It addressed itself to a popular audience. Skvortsov's ambition was to use this daily as a means of reaching beyond the ecclesiastical readership of *Missionerskoe obozrenie* and directly influencing the political commitments of what he called the "new Rus."[81] As he stated in the inaugural issue, the newspaper would serve as a "proponent of Christian principles in the consciousness of secular society and of the Orthodox ideals that have animated Holy Rus."[82]

To fulfill this mission, the newspaper focused especially on the political issues that erupted in the wake of the October Manifesto and that, in the mind of the editor, demanded a bold response from an Orthodox public. Skvortsov encouraged contributions from leading clerical Orthodox patriots such as Bishop Nikon, Archbishop Antony, and Vostorgov. Skvortsov himself, perhaps because of his close relationship to the Holy Synod, warmly defended the autocracy and frequently used the formula of Official Nationality to articulate his ideals for a modern Holy Rus. Even so, his version of the formula incorporated the rhetoric of ethnic nationalism.

An early editorial offered "a few words about what exactly is meant" by the newspaper's promotion of Official Nationality. In addition to a conventional devotion to the principles of Orthodoxy and autocracy, it claimed, the ideal of a "Russian Russia" (*russkaia Rossiia*) must be explicitly emphasized as the third constituent element of the formula. Thus Russian national exclusivity and political domination assumed greater proportions than they had in earlier renderings of the formula, which spoke only about the rather vague ideal of "nationality" (*narodnost*).[83]

Like other clerical Orthodox patriots, Skvortsov asserted that all patriotism must be shaped to serve the interests of the Christian faith. He and other writers in *Kolokol* believed that Orthodox patriotism could in fact rescue nationalism from its tendency toward "paganism." An article published in 1910, for instance, criticized the popular columnist in *Novoe vremia* named Menshikov (whom Nikon had likewise opposed) for embracing a form of "nationalism" that lay ambivalently "between Orthodox ecclesial self-consciousness and intelligentsia-style [religious] indifference."[84] Likewise, Skvortsov stated, the Church's principle of universality should always stand prior to nationality. As with Vostorgov, however, this principle could be muted in the actual context of some political utterances. While the Russian people must hold an ideal of human sympathy in their heart, he acknowledged, "this universal human ideal cannot carry a denial of nationality. Nationality is the necessary form by which particular peoples travel toward a universal human ideal." Thus a Russian patriot in practice is superior to a "cosmopolitan" in his devotion to the interests of humanity. What bestows Russians with a universal human ideal is the universal faith of Orthodoxy. Therefore, "parties and unions who place Orthodoxy at the basis of their programs" deserve strong support in the political sphere.[85]

The issue of politics became acute as the elections to the Second Duma approached. While the radical First Duma had been dissolved, Skvortsov and other writers in *Kolokol* realized that with no change in the electoral law the Second Duma was likely to be equally rebellious. They therefore launched a campaign in early 1907 to promote parties that they believed would defend the Church in the new Duma. The standard for reliable parties was what they defined as a truly Russian form of "patriotism." Here the newspaper's strongest endorsement went to the Union of the Russian People.[86] The nature of patriotism for this, Russia's most influential patriotic, union was totally different from that of other parties who also claimed to be patriotic, one article claimed. Unlike the conservative Octobrists, the Union of the Russian People made the defense of Orthodoxy a leading ideal of its program. Again, the slogan of restoring an ethnically defined "Russian Russia" was inseparable from such statements, and it highlighted the underlying dissonance in the newspaper's ideals.[87] In the days just before the February elections, in fact, writers in *Kolokol* regularly employed the union's nationalistic cry of "Russia for the

Russians" when appealing to their readers. The destiny of "Holy Rus," one warned, hung in the balance.[88]

"Who Is to Blame?" was the title of a characteristic article that appeared after the disastrous results of the elections were announced. It answered the question by pointing to the Jews and socialists, who, it asserted, had ensured the success of Kadets and Octobrists.[89] An analysis of the election results indicated that only 89 "patriots" had been given seats in the new Second Duma, while over 350 seats had gone to "revolutionary" and "non-Russian" parties.[90] The consequences for Orthodoxy, Skvortsov and others agreed, were grim.

Thus in subsequent months the newspaper began to give even more unqualified support to the nationalistic right. Skvortsov used the newspaper to reprint vitriolic articles from *Russkoe znamia* (*Russian Banner*), the organ of the Union of the Russian People.[91] Support for virtually all patriotic unions was given in political articles, and figures such as Vladimir Purishkevich (1870–1920) were hailed.[92] Purishkevich's quip while standing on the Duma floor—that "to the right of me stands only the wall"—increasingly characterized the editorial policies of *Kolokol* as well. Even a renegade conservative priest named Iliodor from Tsaritsyn received praise. Despite the fact that he had recently been severely reprimanded by the Holy Synod for his anti-Semitic provocations, an editorial stated that he must still be admired as "a true son of the Orthodox Church and an unflinching patriot."[93] As the defense of such a notorious figure indicates, Skvortsov was prepared to suspend Christian ideals such as obedience and even compassion in a desperate effort to advance the cause of the clerical right. Even after the "crisis" of the Second Duma had passed and Stolypin's unconstitutional electoral reform promised more conservative Dumas in the future, *Kolokol* continued to link Orthodox patriotism closely to the nationalist movement.[94]

All that was left for Skvortsov to do was to outline how the Church should incorporate the political ideals of nationalism. This he did in a book titled *Church Light and State Reason*.[95] Published in 1913, the two-volume work served as a compendium of Orthodox patriotism before the war. Skvortsov called himself simply the compiler of its contents, and to be sure many of the ideas and arguments came from other conservative leaders of the Church. Virtually all of the leaders of clerical Orthodox patriotism were here: Vostorgov, Archbishop Antony, Bishop Nikon, and Archbishop Nikanor. A consistent vision shapes the argument of the text, however, and Skvortsov clearly intended to bear the final responsibility for its content. This was evident by the emphasis placed throughout the first volume upon the "mission of the Orthodox clergy." He claimed that the clergy was Russia's most "national"

and "patriotic" force and throughout history had devoted itself to the preservation of "Holy Rus."⁹⁶ In the past, he noted, it had been protected from
foreign faiths by the state. Significantly, he remembered with reverence how
Alexander III had issued a public declaration during the baptism anniversary year of 1888 in which the issue of religious toleration was categorically
rejected. The Paschal Edict of 1905, on the other hand, has been a great set-
back for the mission.⁹⁷

Despite the emphasis given to the clergy and issues concerning the mission, the first volume concluded with a curious appendix titled "The Political
Catechism of a Nationalist." This, Skvortsov explained in the preface, was
the work of an independent writer and was offered to demonstrate the just
nature of the nationalist movement. Provided nationalistic programs such
as the present one endorsed Orthodoxy, they deserved the Church's public
support as Russia's most worthy political force. Interestingly, the "catechism"
in question said very little about the Christian faith, and much more about
the "Russian nation" (*Russkaia natsiia*) and the "Aryan extraction" of its
members.⁹⁸

Accordingly, the second volume of the work was almost entirely devoted
to a defense of patriotism and nationalism. It began with a chapter titled
"The Church and National Particularity" (*natsionalnoe obosoblenie*). Here
Skvortsov addressed criticisms from Tolstoy and other "cosmopolitan" intellectuals that Christianity has no place for an emphasis upon national particularity. Such critics of Orthodox patriotism, he noted, cite the Church's
principle of universality found in New Testament passages such as Col 3:11,
which state that "there is neither Greek nor Jew."

On the contrary, he asserted, Russia's "spiritual writers" have "written
much on the study of this question" and have shown convincingly that patriotism is a legitimate and even necessary virtue of the Christian community.⁹⁹
Not only are the nations said to have been set apart by God himself in Genesis,
but Pauline passages about the irrelevance of nationality pertain only to the
perspective of God. In considering Church tradition, the Orthodox system of
establishing autocephalous communities based largely on language had made
national particularism an essential feature of liturgy and the practice of the
faith.¹⁰⁰ After surveying these elements of ecclesiastical tradition, Skvortsov
turned to lay theologians and philosophers, favoring especially the opinion
of Slavophiles such as Alexei Khomiakov and Vladimir Soloviev. He even
consulted famous national writers. While Ivan Turgenev was anything but a
pious adherent to the official Church, Skvortsov quoted one of his patriotic
statements with marked approbation. "Cosmopolitanism," he repeated, "is

nothingness and even worse than nothingness. Outside of nationality, there is not art, there is not truth, there is not life, there is nothing."[101] Skvortsov did not explicitly apply this rule to the Christian faith, but in the context of his editorial project one could get the implication that without the content of nationality it, too, perhaps would be "nothing." Hence his conclusion that "a correct interpretation of Christianity" must entail a warm "feeling of love toward the fatherland."[102]

In a specific chapter titled "Patriotism," he sought to define a truly Christian form of patriotism. To do so he was compelled to emphasize something he called the "natural feelings of man." The natural love of one's native land, he argued, suggests that patriotism is implicitly commanded by Christ.[103] This led him to the case of Russian patriotism. He stated that "nationalism" in a secular form had become the dominant political principle among "the other tribes of Europe." Russia was different. To describe how, he employed Archbishop Antony's definition of Orthodox patriotism discussed earlier in this chapter. "Russian national self-consciousness," he quoted loosely, "is a self-consciousness that is neither racial nor tribal, but ecclesial and religious."[104]

In spite of such qualifications, however, Skvortsov attached considerable importance to "nation" and "race" and, like Archbishop Nikanor before him, even quoted western European political theorists. His final conclusion in the work was that nationalistic politics were as much the destiny of Holy Rus as the Orthodox mission. Indeed, he stated, in the new Rus the two could not be separated. "Before all modern states," he claimed, "there lies a single road, the national road, and this applies to Russia. It is necessary once and for all to assert completely that the development of the Russian state must be accomplished in a particularly Russian way." Only when the Russian people constituted the unqualified "master people" (*narod-khoziain*) of the empire, he concluded, and thereby transformed it into a national state, would Orthodoxy be restored as the national faith.[105]

For Skvortsov, as for Vostorgov and Archbishop Antony, the troubled times following 1905 demanded a closer relationship between the Church and Russia's nationalists. Departing from the purely autocratic logic of early Orthodox patriotism, they justified this relationship with arguments about the need to defend the national faith in the absence of an apostle-like tsar. Their writings and addresses, which were often presented before nationalistic audiences, therefore defined political ideals that could be shared by both the Church and the patriotic unions. As this development unfolded, however, the rhetoric of clerical Orthodox patriotism became increasingly nationalistic in tone. Greater emphasis was placed on the ethnic character and exclusivity of Russians within the empire, and imperial and military affairs beyond it also gained significance.

Nevertheless, the argument of this chapter has been that these three conservative Church leaders did not support the nationalistic ideals of the patriotic unions unconditionally. On the contrary, in addressing their members at political gatherings and in the press, they sought to redefine nationalism according to the standards of the Christian faith. The result was a definition of the Russian nation that was frequently vague, and perhaps to some would have bordered on the incoherent. As it turned out, Russia's Church leaders failed to make good nationalists.

Nor in their mission to the nationalists were they content with rhetoric alone. They made use of the entire program of Orthodox patriotism as it had been developed during the past generation. Theological resources such as the national saints and cultural engagement such as historiography and orchestrated pilgrimages to the past were used as well.

All of these were ultimately brought to a focus in the person of Patriarch Germogen. His seventeenth-century personality offered an excellent case for creating a historical image that embodied ideals common to both clerical Orthodox patriots and ethnic nationalists. Though originally a missionary among Muslims near Kazan, he had become famous as a Russian patriot during the legendary Time of Troubles. According to medieval chronicles, he had called upon Russians to rise up against the invading Roman Catholic Poles, and thus helped to preserve both national autonomy and the Orthodox faith. Furthermore, he had personally blessed the Russian army that defended the Trinity-Sergius Lavra and other holy places, and though he died in the Moscow Kremlin's Chudov Monastery before the final victory of 1613, he helped prepare medieval Rus for the founding of the Romanov Dynasty.

These deeds were especially significant to Vostorgov, who took the opportunity in an address to a patriotic union in 1907 to discuss the example of Germogen. Delivered among the "national holy objects" of the Moscow Kremlin's Uspensky Cathedral, it directed the attention of the nationalistic audience to the sepulcher in which Germogen's relics lay. Expressing regret that so illustrious a figure as Germogen was "still not glorified" as a national saint, Vostorgov recounted his service to "Holy Rus." His adherence to the twin ideals of "ecclesiality and nationality" (*tserkovnost i narodnost*) were praised and were said to have constituted a formula for the "Russian faith."

Germogen therefore offered an example to modern Russians prepared to translate Orthodox patriotism into political activity. "At present Russian troubles have again been unleashed," Vostorgov warned. Germogen's example "offers a means for conducting our struggle, and this struggle is perhaps even greater than that which was conducted by Russian people for faith and fatherland three hundred years ago."[106] Indeed it was.

In 1913, six years after this address and three hundred years after the end of the first Time of Troubles, Patriarch Germogen was finally glorified by the Church as an official national saint. Vostorgov, Skvortsov, Antony, and other Orthodox patriots all rallied to participate in the canonization festival organized in the Moscow Kremlin. Before we turn to this last act of prerevolutionary clerical Orthodox patriotism, however, it is time to consider the influence of the movement upon some of Russia's leading lay intellectuals.

CHAPTER 7

-*+*-

The Lessons of Patriotic Religious Intellectuals

The tension and later dissonance that characterized clerical Orthodox patriotism in the years after 1905 appear to have been largely ignored by the majority of conservative Church leaders. No fundamental criticisms of Orthodox patriotism appeared in the spiritual journals before the Revolution, and Church-organized national commemorations continued to disseminate the imagery of Holy Rus. As the clergy continued its activities, however, religious intellectuals who were sympathetic to some of the Church's ideals pursued their own cultural program to influence the formation of a national community. Their contributions to Orthodox patriotism, which often shared images of Holy Rus with the official Church, revealed weaknesses that were contained in the clergy's model of the nation. In this chapter, I will examine the ideas of leading members of Russia's prerevolutionary intelligentsia. Vladimir Soloviev, Mikhail Nesterov, Sergei Bulgakov, and an Old Believer named Ivan Kirillov were all deeply interested in the clergy's cultural program, and their engagement with it provides important insights into how it was received outside the official spheres of Church life. As sincere Orthodox Christians and intellectual sympathizers, they followed the activities of the clergy closely and contributed to their efforts to transform the empire into a nation called Holy Rus. However, they fundamentally reconfigured the clergy's model of the nation. For them, the "national faith" had much less of a place for a conservative Church leadership and, even more, an apostle-like tsar.

THE CLERGY AND RUSSIA'S INTELLIGENTSIA

The restoration of Holy Rus, many of the clergy believed, depended upon the Church's selective assimilation of lay culture. We have seen, for instance, how a number of nineteenth-century writers were afforded a special status by leaders of the cultural mission, with strong commendation going to figures such as Pushkin and above all Dostoevsky. In addition to canonizing a national literary tradition, efforts were made to attract Russia's contemporary intelligentsia. It is true that conservatives within the Church regarded intellectuals with deep distrust. As we saw in the previous chapter, Skvortsov had argued in *Church Light and State Reason* that the clergy were the only dependable force with "deeply national and patriotic" commitments. They alone must exercise "supremacy . . . in the face of the rootless and cosmopolitan intelligentsia."[1] Nevertheless, he and others realized that in an increasingly literate society intellectuals could profoundly influence public opinion about the clergy. The clergy's leadership thus directed their cultural mission toward the intelligentsia.

The Church's efforts to establish a dialogue with the intelligentsia during the late imperial period have received only passing attention from historians. There are some notable exceptions, however. P. N. Zyrianov has argued that after the turn of the century the Church conducted an ongoing "debate with progressive secular culture" that lasted until the Revolution. Here clerical leaders were especially sensitive to the influence of intellectuals and the "dissemination" of their thought "at the highest levels of society."[2] Gregory Freeze has also discussed the Church's interest in "educated society" (*obshchestvennost*) in an essay that focuses on the mostly amorphous "urban mission." He identifies three ideals for this public that were promoted by urban missionaries: an ideal of Christian "sociability," an ideal of Christian economic relations, and an ideal of forming a Christian "public opinion."[3] It is the last of these ideals that concerned clerical Orthodox patriots.

Like the urban mission, the mission to Russia's intellectuals lacked both a formal program and an administrative structure. Missionaries and other Church leaders discussed their activities regularly, but they never succeeded in creating a lasting dialogue with them.[4] In fact, the relationship was often marred by strong disagreement when the issue of the national faith was at stake. In the case of Leo Tolstoy, for instance, criticism of canonical Orthodoxy and support for its sectarian opponents such as the Dukhobors so threatened the cultural mission that Russia's preeminent novelist was finally declared to be excommunicated from the Church. In fact, as a guardian of the national faith Vladimir Skvortsov himself played a leading role in the excommunication process.[5]

Despite such conflicts, however, the hope for establishing a dialogue was not unfounded. As long as cultural leaders within both the laity and the clergy demonstrated an interest in the questions of faith and nationality, the possibility existed that common values and ideals could be identified. Here an important intellectual bridge between the two groups was found in Slavophil-ism, the movement founded during the reign of Nicholas I by intellectuals such as Ivan Kireevsky (1806–1856) and Alexei Khomiakov.⁶ In the wake of the Great Reforms, numerous scholars representing the official Church had begun to explore its rich legacy.⁷ Clerical Orthodox patriots such as P. Y. Svet-lov utilized Slavophile arguments extensively as they developed the theologi-cal underpinnings for their model of Holy Rus. The Slavophiles' vision of an Orthodox nation also appealed to Church leaders in the wake of the Paschal Edict, despite the fact that the early Slavophiles had defended religious free-dom. The program of the ecclesiastical journal *Khristianin* (*The Christian*), for instance, spoke of Russia's "transitory period" in the wake of the edict. "Freedom of conscience," it warned, "has served as a signal for the freedom of brutal assaults upon the Church." Appealing to Russia's fifty thousand official priests as "a huge army of intellectual leaders," it called for a reconsidera-tion of both ecclesiastical and lay intellectual traditions such as Slavophilism to form a front against secularization and apostasy.⁸ It published Orthodox patriotic poems by Khomiakov such as "We Are the Chosen People" (*My—rod izbrannyi*).⁹ It also promoted the thought of later Slavophiles such as Gen-eral A. A. Kireev, whose death in 1910 was commemorated as a "bitter loss" for all who recognized the "existence of Russia as a cultural nation."¹⁰

In addition to the Slavophile tradition, the moral principles of Christian-ity served to unite the clergy and lay intellectuals in their search for solutions to contemporary social, political, and cultural problems. The ineffectiveness of the tsarist state, the spectacle of revolutionary violence, and the impending dissolution of the empire could all be reversed, many believed, if Christian principles of compassion and brotherhood became more widely dissemi-nated. For their part, many intellectuals became increasingly attracted to religion at the turn of the century, a phenomenon that Nicholas Berdiaev named the "new religious consciousness."¹¹ The best example of the mutual interest in the social significance of Christianity among the clergy and lay intellectuals was the founding of the St Petersburg Religious-Philosophical Society in 1901. The society conducted a series of lectures and debates on issues such as freedom of conscience and Church reform, and though these ultimately proved abortive, they aroused considerable attention from clerical and lay cultural leaders. Significantly, one of the Church's representatives at the meetings was Vladimir Skvortsov. In addition to defending the principle of an apostle-like tsar against lay opponents such as Vasily Rozanov (1856–1919) and Dmitri Merezhkovsky, he claimed that Orthodoxy served as the basis of Russia's public life.¹²

Thus while no explicit structure or program for the mission to Russia's intellectuals can be discerned, it is possible to trace the mutual interests of the clergy and lay intellectuals who drew from the Slavophile tradition and were convinced that Russia's national troubles could be solved only with the application of Christian moral principles.

To be sure, important differences continued to divide the two groups. Ecclesiastical loyalties prevented the clergy from endorsing any intellectual too strongly, while a disdain for some features of ecclesiastical life—especially the conservative clergy's hostility toward religious freedom—usually kept free-thinking intellectuals from fully embracing the official Church. Nevertheless, both found themselves participants in a common cultural mission to advance Orthodoxy as the basis for Russia's national community.

VLADIMIR SOLOVIEV AND AN ECUMENICAL NATIONAL FAITH

By far the single most influential proponent of Orthodox patriotism among lay intellectuals was Vladimir Soloviev. Though read widely only after his death, as early as the 1870s he had begun to attract the attention of leading political writers and nationalists such as Nicholas Strakhov (1828–1896), Dostoevsky, and Katkov. Soloviev was influenced at this early stage by Ivan Kireevsky, and he used the early Slavophile tradition in part to form his own understanding of Russia's destiny and national self-consciousness.[13] However, a growing commitment to the Church's principle of universality caused the young philosopher to reassess the nature of nationalism and Russian nationality in the early 1880s. While his career coincided with the first period of clerical Orthodox patriotism, his ideals for the nation served as an important precedent for the other lay Orthodox patriots who followed him in the troubled years after 1905.

Soloviev's intellectual development toward Orthodox patriotism was initiated in response to the assassination of Alexander II in 1881. The idealistic rage of the revolutionaries who committed this act impressed him deeply, and he urged the new tsar to demonstrate the Christian moral principles formally endorsed by the Russian state by showing clemency and forgiving the assassins. In a letter addressed to Alexander III, he expressed a belief that "the Russian people lives in the fullness of the Christian spirit" and that the tsar is "the expression of the national soul." It would thus be proper for Alexander "to demonstrate forcefully the Christian principle of universal forgiveness."[14] In spite of his appeal to Church teaching, Soloviev's moral idealism was disappointed. Being severely reprimanded for his proposal and suspended from lecturing, he came to doubt the state's claim to be Christian. He subsequently became a critic of what he considered its anti-Christian tendencies and, as we shall see, the conservative nationalism that supported them.

Throughout his career Soloviev was animated by the social teaching of the Orthodox Church. He was a passionate idealist by temperament and directed his energies toward issues connected with religious life in Russia and the West. He repeatedly addressed himself to issues such as secularization, Polish Catholicism, sectarianism, the condition of Jews, and the Orthodox mission.[15] Thus, as one of his early biographers noted, religion constituted the "central idea for all of Soloviev's thought."[16] What concerned him was the realization of a social order based upon Christian standards of corporate love. This goal gave much of his philosophy an eschatological character. His works abound with discussions of the conditions under which the kingdom of heaven on earth can be established. One of his most famous concerns, what he called the condition of "God-manhood" (*Bogochelovechestvo*), reflected this eschatological interest best of all. By focusing on the Christian transfiguration of society, Soloviev directed his attention toward an issue that, as we have seen, concerned Orthodox missionaries as well. Whereas they measured the presence of the kingdom of heaven by the scope of the canonical Orthodox Church, however, he focused on the whole of Christian civilization, Orthodox as well as heterodox. His goal was to reunite the East and the West to establish a "free theocracy" based on brotherhood and service to others.[17]

Soloviev was a baptized member the Orthodox Church, yet as his studies of religion proceeded he became increasingly estranged from the Orthodox faith. After the tsar's assassination he turned to Roman Catholicism for inspiration. While he never repudiated Orthodoxy and by the end of his short life even began to return to its fold, the 1880s were a period when he placed most of his universalistic hopes upon Rome. Since the reunification of Christendom seemed impossible without a state to govern it, Soloviev began to develop a model of "Christian politics" (*khristianskaia politika*) to achieve this aim. "As Christian morality seeks the realization of the kingdom of God within an individual man," he stated, "so Christian politics must prepare for the advent of the kingdom of God for all of mankind, constituted by the whole array of its peoples, tribes, and states."[18]

Like Orthodox patriots among the clergy, Soloviev recognized the great influence that nationality had gained in the political life of modern Europe. He regarded the formation of modern nation states as a normal and even potentially progressive development. At the same time, he believed that ethnic nationalism was the principal barrier to his ecumenical program. Its secularized logic brought states into opposition with each other and obscured their spiritual goals. Ultimately, it degenerated into what he called "zoological nationalism." Thus, his interest in establishing a form of Christian state-craft to foster reunion between Orthodoxy and Roman Catholicism focused on what he called the "national question." This was already apparent in 1883. In that year he wrote an article that scorned conservative Russian newspapers such as Katkov's *Moskovskiia vedomosti,* which, he noted, seemed to thrive on a belligerent attitude toward Rome.[19] In a book titled *The Great Debate and Christian Statecraft,* published the same year, he manifested an even greater disillusionment with ethnic nationalism in Russia. Here he indirectly attacked lay intellectuals such as Ivan Aksakov (1823–1886), for unleashing the same "anti-Christian movement" that had long ago caused the division of the Church.[20]

Thus it was the Church's principle of universality that motivated Solo-viev's interest in Christian politics and nationalism. As Greg Gaut has recently noted in an article on Soloviev, the philosopher's "ecumenical project" must be considered the primary reason for his polemical debates with Russia's nationalists in the 1880s.[21] Most leaders of the Russian Church at that time had no sympathy for what would become the ecumenical movement. This more than any other issue divided Soloviev from Church leaders, who in the 1880s had begun to develop a Christian model of Russian nationality.[22] In principle, clerical writers acknowledged the high importance of reuniting Christendom, but they were extremely reluctant to entertain measures that would require compromises with the holy tradition of the Orthodox Church.[23] In this they behaved in a way no different from contemporary leaders of Roman Catholicism and Anglicanism, though it was from the latter that many of the earliest efforts toward reunion came.

Embracing an ecumenical program after 1883, Soloviev thus launched a systematic critique of secular nationalism and the models of nationality promoted by the state and lay intellectuals in Russia. During the five years that followed this break, he wrote a series of articles that yielded the first fruits of his critique. When completed in 1888, the same year of the baptism festival, these were published together as the first part of his major work on nationality, *The National Question in Russia.*[24] Russia's leading proponents of nationality were all brought to task here for placing the interests of the Russian nation before those of the ecumenical community he misleadingly called the "universal Church." In the six articles that constituted this first part, Soloviev now explicitly criticized Ivan Aksakov, Nicholas Danilevsky (1822–1885), Strakhov, and Kireev. Since this critique of nationalism has been carefully outlined by Gaut, it is unnecessary to summarize it here. Instead, I will focus on the main similarities and differences between Soloviev's model of nationality and that promoted by the clergy. As we shall see, his Orthodox patriotism frequently overlapped that of Church leaders, and in some cases it was even more intellectually consistent.

This was especially true in his theological treatment of nationalism. Soloviev's appropriation of Orthodox eschatological and pneumatological tradition brought him to lay great stress on the need to evaluate "nationalism" differently from "nationality." Reflecting the Russian public's increasingly common use of "nation" (*natsiia*) as a synonym for "people" (*narod*), he described how "nationality—either of the people or the nation—represents a positive force and every people has been appointed a special role to serve according to its special character." Every nation, he claimed, possessed an essential character that had been impressed upon it by God. The character given to a Christian nation demanded that it fulfill its calling to preserve and disseminate the kingdom of heaven on earth. In fact, it was justified exclusively by its fulfillment of this calling. On the other hand, when a Christian nation ceased to fulfill its mission, or worked in opposition to it, it lost the justification to act on a world-historical plane. This was true especially when it pursued the ideals of ethnic nationalism, which distorted the otherwise productive force of national self-consciousness. In such a case, Soloviev claimed, "the positive force of nationality mutates into the negative force of nationalism." The result was an "extreme antagonism" toward other nations, wherein "nationalism destroys its own people and makes it an enemy of humanity." On the other hand, "Christianity, by abolishing nationalism, saves peoples because to be supranational is not the same as to be nationless."[25] According to Soloviev, then, nationality was a legitimate, God-given form of human community. Its divine purpose was to focus the community's attention on the Christian mission to unify humanity and establish the kingdom of heaven on earth.

A second common feature between the Orthodox patriotism of Soloviev and that of the clergy was a distinction between "patriotism" and "nationalism." Here, significantly, his thoughts conformed closely to those of Archbishop Antony. Soloviev's views can be seen most clearly by considering two of the articles he wrote for an encyclopedic dictionary titled "Nationalism" and "Patriotism." In nationalism, he discerned the "transmutation of healthy national self-consciousness into an abstract principle that opposed 'the national' to 'the universal.'"[26] Patriotism, on the other hand, was merely a feeling of "love toward the fatherland." As such it possessed a "moral significance" in the life of humanity, imparting collective "duties" and "virtues." He even went further and assigned a "religious significance" to patriotism, seeing it as one of the most productive forces in history. Among ancient peoples "service to the native land constituted an active service to the gods." It was also a force for Christian statecraft during the Middle Ages. In modern times, on the other hand, it had "reached its culminating point" and had been torn free of its religious foundation. Here again Soloviev's argument was in close conformity with the defenses of patriotism promoted by the Church. Contemporary France, for instance, was criticized for harboring a "patriotism" that "has become a substitute for religion."[27]

With these basic principles of Orthodox patriotism in place, Soloviev was able to address specific issues concerning Russian nationality and Russian statecraft. Some of his views on these issues were contained in a book published in 1887 titled *The History and Future of Theocracy*. This lengthy work intended to show how statecraft should be conducted in a Christian state, which Russia reputedly possessed. Its "general purpose," he stated in the preface, was "to justify the faith of our fathers" and "to show how this medieval faith, liberating us from the bondage of local particularity and national self-love, coincides with the eternal and universal truth."[28] The work intended, therefore, to explore not only the nature of theocracy but also Russia's national faith and its relationship to that of the "universal Church" ecumenically defined. Soloviev made it clear that he believed the principal challenge to Europe's greatest Christian state at present was the divided condition of Christendom.

> A division according to peoples and national states is the reality of the Christian world. That this condition cannot be the final form of statecraft for humanity . . . here there can be no argument from a religious point of view. But the question is, how are we to free ourselves from the exclusivity of the present condition? How are we to move from national particularity to a global brotherhood of all peoples without first of all standing in the position of true disciples devoted to an international (or supranational) unity?[29]

Since this question was contained within the larger project of outlining the nature of theocracy, his conclusions inevitably reflected the importance he assigned to the relationship between the Russian tsar and the Russian people.

In considering Russia's history, Soloviev noted that the issue of Christian statecraft had been foremost in medieval times and had culminated during the Old Believer schism of the seventeenth century. That event had high-lighted a question that had continued to haunt Russia to the present day: where was the Church's "center of gravity" actually located? "Is it in government," he asked, "or is it in the people?"[30] The question was central to Soloviev's understanding of the national faith. For the synodal system established by the government of Peter the Great, he claimed, had utterly failed to establish a "kingdom of love and freedom" in Russia.[31]

He was therefore inclined to look to the people for a vital expression of the national faith. To be sure, he noted, the common people had so far failed to establish a full manifestation of the kingdom of heaven. Despite the activities of contemporary missionaries, many were slipping toward a condition of "religious indifference."[32] The greatest problem, however, was that Russia's religious life lacked a universal character. The Church did not foster contacts with the rest of Christendom, and vital expressions of the national faith such as Old Belief had also become isolated. Nevertheless, he asserted, Russia did possess a strong Christian heritage in her statecraft. This, coupled to the continued religious devotion of the people, could possibly serve as an agent in fostering reunion with the Roman Catholic Church.

Soloviev realized that the idea of an Orthodox Russia establishing unity with a Roman Catholic western Europe would sound fantastic to many of his readers. "For Russia," he acknowledged, "the reunification of the Church is an affair of the greatest difficulty." But, he added, "God did not create a great and powerful Russia for easy and simple deeds."[33] Russia possessed a healthy national self-consciousness and a historically proven ability to pursue her calling. If she were able to channel these talents toward the reunification of Christendom, she would reestablish herself as history's greatest Christian nation. With words resembling the most enthusiastic proclamations of Vostorgov, Soloviev assigned a messianic destiny to the national community. "We believe in a national-universal idea [*natsionalno-vselenskuiu ideiu*] for Russia," he exclaimed. Nevertheless, "faith without works is dead." Russia now faced the challenge of affirming or denying her very nationality. "Either a restoration of universal Church unity established by us is the true affair and duty of our historical life, or we must recognize that in spite of the one-thousand-year growth of Russia and the fruit of her centuries-old national self-consciousness, the very object of our common activity is still not clear."[34]

Soloviev failed to provide a plan for how a "free theocracy" under Russian statecraft would reunite Christendom, partly because his work on theocracy was never completed. While lengthy in itself, it was to be only the first of three separate parts. As his attention was diverted to other matters and he began to lose hope in ecumenical activities by the end of the 1880s, he never discussed the particular features of the Russian state system that would contribute to the fulfillment of the national mission. Nevertheless, by looking at what he did complete, it is possible to see some of the patriotic ideals he held.

Interestingly, most of the completed first part addressed the experience of Old Testament Israel. Its "national theocracy," Soloviev indicated, prefigured the universal theocracy that Russia would bring to all of Christendom. In discussing the exemplary features of Israel, he displayed many of the same interests as the clergy. For instance, he demonstrated an impressive understanding of the Bible. More significantly, he revealed a familiarity with the content of the official missionary journals used by clerical Orthodox patriots, such as *Vera i razum*.[35]

Nevertheless, Soloviev's discussion of theocracy showed that a national faith could be sustained without the influence of official priests or an apostle-like tsar. When discussing the origins of Old Testament theocracy, in fact, he ignored the role of Israel's priests. Instead, he focused on the time when the national faith was formed under the leadership of Moses. The holy prophet's example of a leadership accepted freely and without compulsion by the people illustrated Soloviev's definition of spiritual authority within a free theocracy. For the "essence of theocracy," he argued, "is a free union between man and God that completely excludes the despotic authority of a priesthood over the people."[36] Such a definition of the model religious order could hardly win sympathy from Russia's official clergy, despite the fact that it, too, regularly looked to the Old Testament example of ancient Israel.

In discussing the Israelite state, Soloviev also diminished the importance of the tsar, emphasizing the fact that the establishment of a king after the period of Judges required sanctification by Samuel, who was a prophet and not a priest. Furthermore, he described the "matter of appointing a supreme earthly authority" as but a "conditional necessity."[37] Such a diminution of the principle of tsarist authority was virtually unknown in clerical depictions of the old Israel, as well as the new Israel. It is noteworthy, however, that here Soloviev emphasized a form of statecraft that was very similar in aim, if not in form, to the clergy's ideal of an apostle-like tsar. When Saul himself failed to fulfill the theocratic function assigned to him, Soloviev continued, he was removed. "As the tsar of Israelite theocracy," he explained, "Saul was expected before all else to possess theocratic virtues."[38] Though Saul was soon replaced by David, his abortive example indicates that in a free theocracy the tsar constitutes only an "instrument" for maintaining the faith, and he is by no means an inseparable element in the national community. Far more significant is the voluntary union of the people under a spiritual authority that is more prophetic than ecclesiastical. In Soloviev's interpretation, "the God of Israel indicated through his prophet that the firstborn tsar of Israel [that is, Saul] was a prototype of the antireligious state in which the ruler shifted the blame for his personal arbitrariness to the 'will of the people.'"[39] In the final analysis it was an "autocratic form of statecraft" that alienated Saul from the national faith. What is more, to assign the tsar of ancient Israel an apostle-like status would have been impossible, according to Soloviev, because the "national theocracy" over which he presided was by definition exclusive.[40] Only with the coming of Christ and the new Israel could theocracy become universal. It was at this point that the role of the tsar assumed an apostolic character.

Throughout the 1880s, Soloviev's work on the unpublished sequel to the first volume of *The History and Future of Theocracy* contributed much to the content of a work titled *Russia and the Universal Church*.[41] Its effort to define Russia's national destiny and the role of Orthodoxy in shaping it also resembled in interesting ways the model of Holy Rus developed by the Church. Soloviev divided the history of universal theocracy after the incarnation into two periods, the medieval and the modern. Employing the Third Rome doctrine in all but name, he described the medieval effort to establish a theocracy in the West as a failure, though one in which the examples of Constantine and Charlemagne embodied many of the ideals of apostle-like statecraft.[42] "The question thus arises," he stated, "whether there now exists in the Christian world an authority capable of once again, and with the greatest hope of success, taking up the affair of Constantine and Charlemagne."[43] The answer, he claimed, was Russia, as her people possessed a "deeply religious and monarchistic character." What is more, the features of Russian nationality indicated that "history has predestined Russia to provide the universal Church with the political authority needed by her for the salvation and rebirth of Europe and all the world."[44] In such rhetoric there was virtually no difference between Soloviev's Orthodox patriotism and that of the most enthusiastic leaders of the Church.

A striking difference, however, was contained in his definition of Russia's national faith. He rejected altogether any claim that stated Russia preserved Christianity in its purest form. With his commitment to ecumenism and to the principle of universality, he attacked "certain Russian propagandists" who claim that the "true representative and bearer of Christianity is Holy Rus."[45] Whether he was referring to members of the clergy here or nationalists such as Katkov (whom he cited in another context) is not clear. But he made his attack upon clerical Orthodox patriots more explicit when distinguishing between "the true Orthodoxy of the Russian people" and "the false Orthodoxy of the anticatholic theologians." The latter were committed to defending an ossified state Church and had isolated themselves from both the universal Church and the Russian nation. Their definition of an exclusive national faith and the hostility toward the West that motivated it were based, he stated, on a circular argument. They justified their isolation by claiming that the universal Church provided the Russian people with a self-contained national faith and that Russian national exclusivity was in turn justified by the retention of this national faith.[46]

Here Soloviev contested the right of the conservative clergy even to claim that the official Orthodox faith was the national faith. He stated that what leaders of the Russian Church cited as essential features of Orthodoxy, such as the absence of the Filioque in the Symbol of Faith, were in fact theological trifles divorced from the deeper faith of the common people. "When asked about their religion," he argued, Russians "will tell you that to be Orthodox means to be baptized a Christian, to wear a cross or some other holy icon on one's breast, to pray to the Immaculate Virgin and to all the saints represented by images and relics." Such religiosity was the only legitimate standard for the national faith, he claimed, and not the doctrinal standards prescribed by officials in the Holy Synod. Thus if the national faith was not to be found in the "official Church," it was necessary to search for "a deeper basis" for it within the Russian people.[47]

The place to look was among sectarians and schismatics. "If you want to reduce Orthodoxy to the level of the Russian national idea," he argued, "then you must search for the true expression of this idea among the native sects and not in the realm of the official Church."[48] Simultaneously rejecting the clergy's ecclesial standard of nationality and highlighting one of the key inconsistencies of clerical Orthodox patriotism, Soloviev claimed that the national faith was in fact guarded best of all by Russia's Old Believers. He was aware of how threatening such an argument was to his clerical opponents. Not only did recognition of the rival expression of the national faith undermine their missionary goals, but the schism's rejection of the official order "obviously does not harmonize well with an extreme patriotism which presents Russia in her current condition as the second Israel and the chosen people of the future."[49]

Soloviev was of course no champion of the Old Believer schism. He regarded it as almost hopelessly isolated by the same exclusive tendencies for which he attacked the official Church. At the same time he was working on *Russia and the Universal Church,* for instance, he wrote an article on the schism that emphasized in its opening sentence that "the true essence of the Church is connected to its universal or catholic character."[50] Nevertheless, when assessing what he acknowledged was the uniquely religious character of the Russian people, he presented Old Belief as its epitome. By doing so, he redirected attention away from the priesthood and tsar of official Russia, leaving the people as the sole repository of the national character. With but one significant exception, this was consistent with all of his works on Christian politics during the 1880s.

The exception was his participation in the baptism festival of 1888. This defining event in the history of modern Orthodox patriotism attracted Soloviev's close interest, and he chose to commemorate it by writing an essay titled "Saint Vladimir and the Christian State."[51] This was one of his most significant contributions to a definition of Holy Rus. The only substantive analysis of this piece that I know of is contained within an article by Martin George, who discusses Soloviev's critical remarks about the baptism festival in great depth.[52] As he sees it, Soloviev's objections could be reduced to three main points: the "politicization of St Vladimir's image" by the state, the "blind Russian nationalism" that accompanied the Kievan speeches, and the use of the festival to strengthen Russia's system of "caesaropapism." In spite of Soloviev's clearly polemical attack on Russian nationalism, however, George properly discerns an underlying effort to promote an alternative model of Russian nationality. As he puts it, "throughout Soloviev's entire critique of the nationalistic spirit of the Kievan festival, another, subtle nationalism shines forth."[53] And this "subtle nationalism" (which, to appropriate Soloviev's vocabulary, might more accurately be called "patriotism") constituted a link between Soloviev and his clerical opponents in Kiev.

For in his commemorative essay Soloviev was as eager as the clergy to articulate a healthy form of patriotism based on the apostle-like example of St Vladimir. Much of his attention was absorbed by what he considered the impoverished example of Russia's historic statecraft, and to which he attached labels such as "Russian caesaropapism," "Petersburg bureaucracy," and "anti-Christian absolutism." Noting in his opening sentence how "official Russia has officially celebrated" the baptism festival, he attacked the government officials who helped organize the event and the secular nationalists who turned out in the press to support it. A system represented by figures such as Pobedonostsev, he asserted, had nothing in common with the Christian statecraft of the "real" Vladimir. Interestingly, he mentioned none of the festival's clerical orators and said virtually nothing about the Church's role in organizing the event. In any case, he claimed that the nationalists who supported the autocracy were deceiving the Russian people when they claimed Russia's founding Christian leader as their heritage. "If secular absolutism is a unique foundation for our national way of life," he asked critically, "wouldn't one see other festivals celebrating this foundation in Russian history?" With a mixture of sarcasm and venom, he brought attention to the tension between Christianity and the autocratic state in Russia's past. "Was it not celebrated," he sneered, "on that day when, in the person of the holy Metropolitan Filipp, Ivan IV strangled the voice of Christian conscience that had been lifted up to challenge the arbitrariness of unlimited power?" Promoting an alternative historical vision, he insisted that the statecraft of St Vladimir must be interpreted from what he called a true "Christian point of view."

> For it is historically incontrovertible that St Vladimir in the epoch of his conversion did not think about the Russification of Slavic peoples and did not think about crowning caesaropapism with the grand administration of a Chief Procurator of the Holy Synod in St Petersburg. No. Accepting baptism and inviting the people to follow his example, he wanted only to become a Christian and to create a Christian Russian nation.

The role of a national faith was crucial for the functioning of the "nation state" (*natsionalnoe gosudarstvo*) established by Vladimir. Soloviev asserted, for instance, that "the faith that replaced our national paganism was not the Greek faith" as such; that is, it was not the national faith of a people who had outlived their missionary calling. Instead, it was "a truly universal Christianity." Accepting a universal faith, however, Russians assimilated it into their own national way of life. After all, he emphasized, the year 988 came less than a century before the Great Schism of Christendom. As Russia was committed neither to the East nor the West, it alone as a great nation formed a national character capable of fostering their reunion. This ecumenical destiny was brought closer to fulfillment in the time of Peter, when Russia entered the culture and history of Europe. But what exemplified the national faith of Russia most of all, he argued, was not the tsar or the official clergy but Old Belief. Though isolated now into exclusive sects, Russia's Old Believers had refused to allow either a "caesaropapist state" or an "official Church" to deprive them of the national faith. Thus they refused to allow the "renewed idol of a pagan monarchy to overcome the faith of St Vladimir."[54]

Bestowing upon the Russian people their constituent national faith, then, Vladimir had discharged the greatest task of Christian politics. Yet his successors, Soloviev lamented, began almost immediately to stray from this course. Subsequently, "the Tatar invasion and the transfer of the national center to the north initiated a new direction in our governmental development. The Christian state, designed in Kiev, yielded its place to the Tatar-Byzantine despotism of Moscow and the Teutonic absolutism of St Petersburg." But the testament of Christian statecraft had not been lost. To illustrate Vladimir's example, Soloviev selected a series of accounts about his rule from *The Chronicle of Nestor*.[55] One in particular must have brought a grim smile to the disillusioned idealist's lips. He related the story of how on one occasion a group of men had been apprehended by the state for a particular capital offense. As a Christian ruler, Vladimir decreed that they should be shown mercy and that the death sentence should not be administered. Asked by the metropolitan why he did not inflict the death penalty, Vladimir stated: "I am afraid of sin." Perhaps it was Soloviev's way of reminding the present tsar, Alexander III, with whom he had disagreed over the issue of capital punishment years earlier, how far he had drifted from the Christian statecraft of St Vladimir.[56]

Soloviev looked almost exclusively to the people as the bearers of Russia's national destiny. The role of the apostle-like tsar, so important to the missionary clergy, was greatly minimized in his discussions of national life, even when considering theocracy. The only significant exception was the case of St Vladimir. But even when discussing his example of Christian statecraft, Soloviev noted the absence of state religious compulsion and the greater role played by a people devoted to the national faith. Vladimir was significant for the negative (one might even say kenotic) role he played in the life of the national community.

Soloviev's radical indifference to the apostle-like tsar, however, was not a complete contradiction of clerical Orthodox patriotism and even offered a solution to some of its inconsistencies. As we have seen, many among the clergy turned to the image of an apostle-like tsar in order to sustain the mission. This made good sense under Alexander III, and even after the Paschal Edict of 1905 tsarist protection of the official Church would seem to promise the continuation of its missionary activities. But in all cases in which the clergy defended the position of the tsar, he was little more than a participant in the national community and a guardian of its national faith. His statecraft might help sustain that community, but if, as Soloviev showed, the national faith and the universal destiny it prophesied were secured by the people, Holy Rus could be expected to survive his overthrow.

MIKHAIL NESTEROV AND THE SANCTIFICATION
OF THE RUSSIAN LANDSCAPE

The paintings of Mikhail Nesterov represent another interesting case in which a religious intellectual appropriated Orthodox patriotism. Because of their popularity, they were widely disseminated and remembered along with the imagery of the Church's cultural mission. Many Church publications including Vostorgov's *Vernost,* for instance, regularly used his works as illustrations. In Nesterov's paintings, medieval peasant costumes, birch trees, and the rolling landscapes of northern Russia served as dominant symbols for the nation. Like the Church leadership, natural and cultural features of the nation were insufficient. Only a model of nationality that was sanctified by the presence of the Church's holy objects could offer modern Russians a reliable image of their collective destiny. Paintings therefore included Orthodox crosses, onion domes, and rustic monasteries as their most basic symbols. Nevertheless, Nesterov's Holy Rus frequently excluded the official clergy and suggested that the people were the main defenders of the national faith. What is more, his work suggested that the Old Believers were legitimate bearers of it and that the apostle-like tsar was of only limited significance in defending it.

Nesterov's interest in Orthodox patriotism was closely connected with his career as a painter. A native of the town of Ufa in the Urals, he studied in the Moscow College of Painting during the 1880s, a time that witnessed the rise of the historical themes in Russian art discussed in Chapter 3. The ambitious young student readily employed historical subjects in some of his earliest paintings. One from 1885, painted while he was still a student, was titled *The Election of Mikhail Feodorovich to the Throne* and depicted the first Romanov tsar before an iconostasis preparing to restore the state of Rus at the end of the Time of Troubles. Its subject was significant, however, for more than its historical interest. As a young intellectual, Nesterov was conscious of the many problems that beset the empire, especially its political order. He had been in St Petersburg in 1881, for instance, when Alexander II was assassinated. While a Soviet biographer tends to exaggerate his "efforts to turn away from the pain and contradictions" of his times, she is correct to point to the young painter's desire to find an ideal that would help heal Russia's divisions.[57]

More than other historical painters of the period, however, Nesterov looked to Orthodox Christianity as the basis for his model of nationality. As he related in his memoirs, he had been raised in a devout household and at an early age developed a deep respect for Orthodox worship and Church holidays. Icons of saints such as Sergius, he claimed, "were adored by us with a special love and reverence."[58] His native religiosity was deepened considerably in 1886 when his wife, to whom he had been wed less than a year earlier, died. In his grief he painted a picture of her dressed in a white bridal gown. Finishing the emotional work, he immediately launched into another that came to constitute a turning point in his career. The work was titled *The Bride of Christ* and was finished in 1887. Its sole subject was a young woman resembling his wife dressed this time in a dark blue sarafan, looking both sorrowful and pious, and lost in thought as a peaceful river flows past behind her.[59] Covering her head is a white shawl, signifying her status as a novice in a convent. As a novice, she is neither of this world nor fully committed yet to a life in the service of God. While her calling seems to be a spiritual one, her medieval costume suggests that she will not seek it according to the standards of the contemporary Church. It suggests, one critic has argued, that at this turning point in his career Nesterov was seeking to recover for his contemporaries an "antiquity that was still preserved in Russian Old Belief." The young woman was intended to constitute a "true expression of a national soul located in pre-Petrine Rus."[60] Like the Russian people of the late nineteenth century, she too was deeply troubled by the present but was reluctant to pursue a religious destiny. The young woman of *The Bride of Christ* might therefore be interpreted as an allegory of the Russian nation. It certainly possessed great significance for the patriotic young painter. With the completion of the work, Nesterov later stated, "a transition occurred in me."[61] From this point until the Revolution of 1917, he devoted his talent to revealing the religious destiny of Russia.

Significantly, his interest in religious painting reflected an ongoing relationship with the official Church leadership. Between 1890 and 1914, Nesterov was repeatedly commissioned to participate in the decoration of church buildings. His first commission, as we saw in Chapter 3, was St Vladimir Cathedral in Kiev. After completing that work, he was appointed to the Church of the Savior on Spilled Blood in St Petersburg. In 1902, he traveled to the Georgian city of Abbas-Tuman to conduct work on the Church of Alexander Nevsky, newly built by the heir to the throne Grand Prince Georgii Alexandrovich (Tsarevich Alexei Nikolaevich having not yet been born to the royal family). Finally, in 1911, he applied his brush to the interior of the female Monastery of Saints Martha and Mary in Moscow, founded and overseen by the Grand Duchess Elizabeth Fyodorovna (who had abandoned the world after the assassination of her husband Grand Duke Sergei Alexandrovich during the Revolution of 1905). Considering that the first two of these projects occurred in what were probably the most celebrated churches built in Russia since the Cathedral of Christ the Savior in Moscow, Nesterov's official commissions earned him considerable prestige among the clergy. Painting icons and holy images according to the requirements of Orthodox canon showed a readiness to cooperate with the official Church.

As we shall see, however, Nesterov's respect for Old Belief and Russia's intellectuals (in whose company he spent most of his time) prevented him from devoting his work wholly to the life of the Church. With the exception of compositions commissioned by the ecclesiastical authorities, his works were at most paraliturgical. They constituted religious paintings and not icons. They were intended for discussion, not veneration.

Nesterov's model of Holy Rus was expressed by using two particular symbols. The first was the presence of the national saints. If one considers the painter's output between 1887 and 1917, saints were one of the most frequently encountered subjects. His official work in churches obviously played a role in this emphasis, but nonecclesiastical works also reveal this interest. As we have seen, the theological roots of Orthodox patriotism were located partly in Orthodox ecclesiology, which assigned each of the national churches self-determination in the canonization of its saints. To elaborate the character of what they called the national faith, leaders of the clergy appealed to the images of St Vladimir in 1888 and St Sergius in 1892. Likewise, when St Seraphim of Sarov was canonized in 1903, some members of the official Church also proclaimed the nineteenth-century recluse a guardian of national character.

Nesterov sympathized strongly with the promotion of national saints and dedicated numerous works to it. The first and most significant was the celebrated series of paintings on the subject of St Sergius. Nesterov spent much of his free time in the environs of the Trinity-Sergius Lavra established by the fourteenth-century saint. When he was not actually living in Sergiev Posad, he roamed the low-lying hills of the area in search of ideal subjects for his landscapes, or visited the artists' colony in nearby Abramtsevo. The monastery came to symbolize his encounters with clerical Orthodox patriotism. He was residing in Sergiev Posad in July of 1888, for instance, when he received news of the baptism festival in Kiev.[62] In September of 1892 he was also there, having come especially to participate in the St Sergius commemoration. He was deeply impressed by the latter event, he related in a letter, though because of his failure to attend Kliuchevsky's speech he was forced to read it in the press.[63]

Nesterov had good reason to appreciate the efforts made by the clergy who organized the St Sergius festival. He himself had just two years before finished *The Vision of the Boy Bartholomew* (1890), a depiction of the childhood of Sergius. This, the first in a series of five paintings of the national saint, made such a strong impression when shown in the capital the next year that it won Nesterov the offer from Adrian Prakhov to participate in the St Vladimir Cathedral project in Kiev.[64] In 1891 *The Youth of St Sergius of Radonezh* was completed, and before the end of the decade he added to it *The Labors of St Sergius of Radonezh* (1896), *St Sergius Blessing Dmitri Donskoi for Battle with the Tatars* (1897), and a final work titled simply *St Sergius of Radonezh* (1898). These works represent a fairly transparent effort by the artist to disseminate images of the medieval saint to contemporaries in order to enhance national self-consciousness.

Like that of the clergy, it should be noted, Nesterov's contribution to Orthodox patriotism was influenced by his encounter with the rise of western nationalism. This was especially true of his interest in national saints. He had made the first of several journeys to western Europe a year after the baptism festival and took the opportunity to study the works of French painters such as Jules Bastien-Lepage (1848–1884). In a letter to his family, he described the painter as the "very greatest of French contemporaries." His attraction was based largely on an encounter with one particular work, *Jeanne d'Arc,* finding in the Frenchman's interpretation of the fifteenth-century French national saint the image of an "undefiled patriotism" (*chistyi patriotizm*).[65] Nevertheless, Nesterov was decidedly uncomfortable in the secularized culture of the West. Abandoning what he called the "new Babylon" of modern Paris (where, it might be said, he claimed to appreciate only medieval artifacts), he returned home to begin painting the images of Russian national saints and the "undefiled patriotism" they revealed.[66]

The St Sergius series was certainly regarded as one of Nesterov's most successful works. Within it the most memorable painting for contemporaries was probably *The Vision of the Boy Bartholomew.* It depicted the young Bartholomew, soon to take the ecclesiastical name Sergius, standing on a low hill before a mysterious angelic figure. In the background is visible what would soon become Nesterov's standard landscape for Holy Rus: birch trees, a fertile field, and a wooden church with onion domes. The boy, dressed in traditional peasant costume, stands erect but with a humble expression characterized by the large, dark eyes for which Nesterov became famous. His hands are clasped in ecstasy, and he appears to be pondering some spiritual message being conveyed by the figure in front of him. The next painting in the series, *The Youth of St Sergius,* focused upon a youthful Sergius, now in a novice's costume with his hands clasped affectionately to his heart and a peaceful, attentive bear lying at his feet. Across the saint's face a mild, even passive expression is perceptible. The three remaining paintings, though of Sergius's adult life, also depict the saint as a mild, meditative, and passive character. And in each, physical symbols of Russian nationality such as birch forests and medieval costumes are prominent.

Nesterov's vision of a passive national sanctity was not limited to St Sergius. Some of the other subjects he chose were in fact female saints such as St Olga Equal-to-the-Apostles. He also depicted St Gleb, St Boris, Tsarevich Dmitri (1552–1553), Alexander Nevsky, and, after his canonization in 1903, Seraphim of Sarov. Many of these images possessed stereotypically feminine features or, in the case of St Seraphim, were of a bent and humble old man. St Gleb, for instance, who was painted for the St Vladimir Cathedral project, looked more like a girl than a boy, with soft broad lips, dark eyes, and earrings. Even the great warrior Alexander Nevsky reflected a feminine ideal, emphasizing humble piety far more than military power. In the Church of the Savior on Spilled Blood in St Petersburg, he stands before an icon of the Mother of God with his eyes closed and his head bowed, crossing himself and offering a devotional taper as his sword lies buried under a shield at his feet. The Tsarevich Dmitri was depicted with his arms clasped to his breast in rapture.

While Soloviev had assigned a dynamic role for Russia in European politics, then, Nesterov described a Holy Rus that was peaceful, reclusive, even passive. These reputedly feminine attributes were prominent in many works besides those of the national saints. Some depicted women exclusively, and those that featured men often included a youthful figure with soft features and a curving posture. The painter's motivation for giving feminine attributes to his model of the nation may have arisen from an effort to propagate the compassionate and forgiving principles of Christianity. While one can only speculate here because his Soviet-edited letters and memoirs lack elaborate details about his attraction to the Orthodox faith, the virtual absence of militant and nationalistic subjects in his compositions suggests an aversion toward the same sentiments being disseminated widely by conservative newspapers, and, after 1905, patriotic unions.[67]

The second most significant symbol of Holy Rus discernible in Nesterov's paintings is the sanctified national landscape. We have seen how clerical Orthodox patriots customarily drew from Orthodox pneumatological tradition to characterize the Russian land as a holy land comparable to Palestine. The same tendency is one of the most significant features of Nesterov's work. Landscape painting was in fact one of his greatest talents, surpassed during the period perhaps only by Isaac Levitan (1860–1900). Nesterov succeeded in capturing the beauty of Russian nature with the use of soft, warm colors and the absence of sharp lines His hills roll gently into meadows and plains, and the seasons are in virtually every case temperate. The freshness and fertility of spring appear to have been his preferred atmosphere, and blossoming trees and wildflowers therefore decorate a large proportion of his works.

In addition to reflecting his aesthetic sensibility, however, these landscapes were designed to serve a patriotic program. Most used as their subjects the hills and woods of central and northern Russia, the lands that constituted the boundaries of medieval Rus. His many journeys to the region around Sergiev Posad, whose beauty remains to this day one of Russia's greatest natural treasures, and to the forests on the shores of the White Sea made lasting impressions upon his vision of the nation. It was while gazing at the scenery near Abramtsevo, in fact, that the "undefiled patriotism" he attributed to St Sergius was envisioned. As Nesterov later related,

> my eyes were suddenly aware of a vision of beauty that was Russian, purely Russian: on the left—the wooded hills, and winding beneath them Aksakov's Voria; a pink glow in the distance, with a thin spiral of smoke, and closer at hand the cabbage-patches, bright emerald-green; on the right, the golden foliage of the grove. Change a bit here and there, add a bit, and a better background for *Bartholomew* you could not imagine.[68]

Nesterov was not content merely to paint the landscapes made famous by Sergei Aksakov's novels, however. Without the deifying presence of the Orthodox faith, he believed, the loveliness of central Russia—and the nobility of Russian nationality—were barren. This may be why he referred to the need to "add a bit" to the landscape for *Bartholomew*. What he added in this case and in virtually every other major landscape he executed in the years between 1887 and 1917 was a transfigured image of Russian nature. As a result, the beauty of the national landscape became unimaginable without wooden churches, onion domes, and isolated sketes.

Nesterov represented the sanctified national landscape with the use of two particular attributes. The first was the "holy object." It consisted of a physical object such as a church building, a monastery, or another recognizable Christian symbol such as a cross or an icon. Since in the world inhabited by Nesterov's contemporaries such objects were usually built or manufactured under clerical authority, their presence can be interpreted as a representation of a Holy Rus that rested firmly within the bosom of the official Church.[69] Examples of these paintings included all those of the St Sergius series and an interesting work titled *To the Chiming of Church Bells* (1895). This latter work showed two monks walking along a line of birch trees reading from devotional books. The monk in the lead is a young man in his twenties, tall in stature, but emaciated by his devotion to spiritual feats. The monk behind him, who might be his spiritual father, is hunchbacked and gray-bearded. In the background stands a church, whose bells, if we are to take the work's title literally, are presently calling them back to a liturgical service. Another work, this time emphasizing Nesterov's ideal of the peaceful and harmonious nation, was titled *Silence* (1903). It depicts two monks on a lake fishing from separate boats. Though they are separated, they appear to enjoy a fellowship in the simplicity of their mutual labor. The lake from which they gather their food lacks even a ripple, and the peace brought by the liturgical community is further symbolized by two small churches standing on a wooded hill behind them. Such works as these employed the holy objects to describe a nation grounded in an unchallenged faith and an attachment to regular liturgical worship.

The second principal attribute employed by Nesterov in his depiction of the national landscape was the holy man. In contrast to holy objects, this attribute suggested the diminution of a national faith defined by the official clergy. Nesterov's holy man often stands in immediate relationship to God and is therefore not mediated by the liturgy and the clergy who preside over it. Nesterov maintained a strong interest in Old Belief and sectarianism throughout his life and occasionally executed sanctified landscapes that suggested an ambivalence about loyalty to the official clergy. In the 1870s he had taken an interest in Andrei Pechersky (1818–1883), the writer whose novels described the lives of Old Believer communities living on the left bank of the Volga.[70] He also respected the religious views of Leo Tolstoy and, well after the writer's excommunication, even painted his portrait. The ideal for Nesterov was the holy man depicted in the novels of Dostoevsky, especially the famous elder Zosima of *The Brothers Karamazov*. In the late 1880s, in fact, he entertained the idea of executing a series of illustrations for that novel.[71]

As we saw, the turning point of Nesterov's career in 1887 had been a historical depiction of Old Belief in the form of *The Bride of Christ*. After that, he periodically produced landscapes that were sanctified not by official holy objects, but by the presence of holy people. *The Hermit* (1888), for instance, depicts an elder slowly making his way along the shore of a lake. In the landscape behind him there is no sign of holiness—whether church, hermitage, or cross. There is only the holy man, and his peaceful, bright eyes suggest a condition of deep spirituality. He alone, with his black cassock and bast shoes, seems to sanctify the beautiful landscape that surrounds him. Another example of a missing official faith was a work titled *St Simeon Verkhoturskii* (1906). This canvas, while depicting an officially canonized saint of the Church, locates him by a stream with no holy object in sight. The only visible objects apart from nature are a simple person fishing in the stream and the edge of a building that could possibly be a church, but only whose corner is ambivalently placed on the edge of the canvas. Neither a cross nor even the roof is visible, and it may as likely be a peasant's hut. All that is left in this particular national landscape, therefore, is a common man and a saint. And, since Simeon reposed in 1642 before the Old Believer schism, his presence can be interpreted as a suggestion that Holy Rus is sanctified by a national faith located only in the distant past and borne particularly by Russia's contemporary Old Believers.

Nesterov's patriotic painting reached its culmination with the completion of his most deliberate image of the nation, *Holy Rus* (1905). This work absorbed an enormous amount of the artist's care and attention, taking more than four years to complete. As such it represents a better summary of the artist's national vision than later paintings such as *The Soul of the Russian People* (1916).[72] It was used by Cherniavsky as evidence that the "myth" of a Holy Russia had become hollow during the years preceding the Revolution. Cherniavsky was certainly correct to interpret the painting as a contrived and ultimately unsuccessful effort to portray a living faith in the Russian people.[73] But in focusing on the details of the canvas, he paid little attention to the attributes Nesterov incorporated into his work that I have tried to outline above. Completed during the Revolution of 1905 and drawing wide public attention upon its display in 1907, *Holy Russia (Svyataya Rus)* represented an important moment in Nesterov's career and a major contribution to Orthodox patriotism.

The canvas, as most critics agree, is divided into two zones. On the right is represented the Russian people. On the left stand Christ and three Orthodox saints. The two groups face one another, and in the background are a rolling landscape and a number of churches with the architectural styles of medieval Rus. Unlike in most of Nesterov's paintings, however, it is clear that Holy Rus is now presented in its modern condition, and this may explain why, contrary to almost every other painting he executed, the sanctified national landscape is now covered by frost. In the wake of the military disasters and social upheavals of 1905, winter has descended upon the life of the nation. The people facing Christ include three wealthy people in western European costume. Significantly, they are obscured by bearded peasants and are intended to represent the problems of modern Russia. The face of one wearing a top hat looks utterly expressionless, while the face of another is sullen and directed away from the figure of Christ. The true nation, the canvas suggests, are those facing Christ and his saints. One woman is prostrate in front of the Savior while others, including children, stand looking him in the eyes. A hermit and what might be a holy fool are among these. And standing behind the crowd of faithful is a young woman in very fine medieval costume overwhelmed by what appears to be repentance. This is the Russian people, the canvas insists, both its faithful and unfaithful members.

In this painting, the faith that serves as a measure of the people's worthiness is a national faith. Standing at the extreme left behind Christ are some of the most popular saints of the Russian people: St Sergius, St Nicholas, and St George. The latter two, of course, were not Russian but were Greek. They had been widely revered since ancient times, however, and thus in Nesterov's mind had become as Russian as Sergius. Within the Russian Church, in fact, Nicholas was so highly esteemed that he held the status of a national saint and was considered a "patron of the Russian people."[74] For Nesterov, these three saints were as inseparable from Holy Rus as the onion domes, birch trees, and bast shoes in the painting. Nevertheless, the presence of the two Greek saints, to say nothing of Christ himself, served to weaken the impression. Nesterov, like the Orthodox clergy, could not present an image of the national faith without reference to the universal principle that necessarily undermined it.

This inconsistency was noted among some of those who viewed *Holy Rus* when it was exhibited in St Petersburg in 1907. A writer in *Russkaia mysl (Russian Thought)* recognized Nesterov as "one of the most remarkable representatives of Russian religious painting," noting especially the artist's emphasis upon a "national faith" with the use of birch trees, onion domes, and "Russian saints" in his landscapes. Unfortunately, he claimed, "all of these symbols by themselves affirm nothing." A true faith would depict Christianity not as an element of Russian nationality, but as a faith embodying "universal humanity" (*vsechelovechnost*).[75] A writer in *Vesy* likewise regretted that in painting the work "Nesterov wanted to paint a Russian Christ." By consciously ignoring Byzantine tradition, the artist had created a "contrived religious impression" constituting an example of the artist's greatest "deficiencies."[76]

Even when *Holy Rus* met with critical praise, it was viewed in a nationalistic light that undermined the status of the universal faith. A good example is the response from the popular journal *Niva,* which praised the "luminous nationalism" of Nesterov's work. It reviewed earlier paintings such as the St Sergius series, which, it claimed, reveal "how a saint, a *Russian* saint, should look." The "native Russian" character of Nesterov's paintings, it argued, had been absorbed during a childhood spent among the many Old Believers near Ufa. Nesterov was thus distinct from other national painters such as Vasnetsov, for he avoided the use of Byzantine imagery in representations of the "Russian national soul." Instead, Nesterov brought attention to the "cultural conditions" (*bytovaia obstanovka*) of Russian Christianity, which included the "influence of nature." *Holy Rus,* the journal concluded, represented the artist's "most characteristic" work to date.[77]

One of the most influential lay intellectuals of the period, Vasily Rozanov, was ambivalent but nevertheless engaged with the problems raised by the artist. After the St Petersburg exhibition, he wrote three articles about Nesterov's *Holy Rus* that constituted both an affirmation and a rejection of Orthodox patriotism. Increasingly interested in the Church, he believed Nesterov had made an important statement about nationality and religion to modern Russians. *Holy Rus,* he said, represented one possible future for the increasingly disunited empire. Its strength lay in its vision of a community unified around a religious faith. However, the national faith depicted in the painting had severe weaknesses. First of all, it was an idealized faith located in a distant past. "Nothing is said to us about the cities or the intelligentsia," he noted. Instead, the national community is limited to a "Rus before the universities" and the Western culture introduced by Peter the Great. Furthermore, the national faith of *Holy Rus* lacks a firm grounding, for the canonical Church is absent. "For some reason," he continued, "the clergy is nowhere. A sacred and religious Rus has been reduced to the monk and the peasant."[78] Without intellectuals or clergy, then, the religious life of the nation would inevitably lack vitality. It would become isolated from "universal" commitments and, finally, degenerate into a "Rus that prays to itself" (*samomoliashchaiasia Rus*).[79] Thus, Rozanov concluded that the model of nationality proposed by Nesterov was a failure. Its "pitiful" and "weak" nature, he believed, could not serve a vital role in the development of a modern Russia.[80]

SERGEI BULGAKOV AND THE CONVERSION OF THE RUSSIAN INTELLIGENTSIA

Sergei Bulgakov (1871–1944) presents a case in which the image of the apostle-like tsar, radically redefined by Soloviev and ignored by Nesterov, was consciously abandoned. Born to a priest and trained early in life for the priesthood, his "Levite blood," as he once put it, inclined him toward sympathy for the official clergy. The fact that he was ultimately ordained after the Revolution indicates that in the years between his loss of faith and his return to the Church he never lost interest in Christianity. Bulgakov's interests as an intellectual were closely connected to the socialist movement and the question of establishing a just economic and social order. It was in the baptism anniversary year of 1888 that he, like Soloviev, abandoned his native faith to search for a worldview that promised to solve Russia's modern problems. As Catherine Evtuhov notes in her biography, Bulgakov was especially moved by the famine of 1891. The primitive nature of this catastrophe—occurring long after major famines in the industrial nations of the West had become a thing of the past—inspired his decision to study political economy at Moscow University.[81] His concern for the presence of suffering and economic issues soon led him to Marxism. But no sooner did he immerse himself in economic research about capitalism and modern society than he discovered that many of Marx's scientific predictions about the development of the modern economy—especially agriculture—had failed. The result led him, as the title to a collection of his essays from the period put it, "from Marxism to idealism." His commitment to philosophical idealism was also temporary, however, and it appears that he very soon began to consider the teaching of the Church as a foundation upon which to build a just social order in Russia.

The philosopher who more than any other inspired him to do this was Vladimir Soloviev. His vision of a free theocracy under which a divided Christendom would be reunited and the first steps toward the consolidation of the kingdom of God on earth taken attracted Bulgakov's economic concerns. Arsenii Gulyga has noted that Bulgakov's interest in Soloviev was fundamentally "ontological" and not "ethical," but Soloviev's eschatological teaching nevertheless offered a vision of how the social order might be transfigured by the Church.[82] In 1903 Bulgakov wrote the first of many apologies for the late "prophet" of Russia's national destiny, claiming that his work represented "the most important future task of study for the spiritual development of our society." After a lengthy exploration of Soloviev's philosophy, it concluded with the exhortation: "Let us follow him!"[83]

Bulgakov's striving for Christian justice in economic and social affairs served as the motivation for forming a political party named the Union of Christian Politics in 1905. Interestingly, his name for the group was similar to those of the monarchistic and patriotic parties. It was a "union" designed to bring solidarity to the Russian people, not to represent class interests or to facilitate further fragmentation. This effort brought Bulgakov into the political fray and forced him to confront many of the same issues as the conservative clergy who supported the patriotic unions. For instance, he supported the argument that Russia's troubles were at their root spiritual and that a strengthening of the people's Christian self-consciousness was a necessary step toward reunifying society. Similarities between his political program and that of the clergy included the desire to base Russia's revival on a healthy "patriotism" shaped by the principles of Christianity. To disseminate his views he founded a political newspaper titled *Narod* (*People*). He also participated in public debates about political issues and even won a seat in the Second Duma. Like clerical conservatives, he believed the Duma would play a central role in deciding the fate of modern Russia.

At the same time, Bulgakov's vision of a Russian nation united by the Orthodox faith contained sharp differences. In direct contrast to Archbishop Antony, Vostorgov, and Skvortsov, Bulgakov rejected autocracy and attacked the conservative patriotic unions in the Duma who defended it. He explicitly repudiated the official model of nationality, "Orthodoxy, autocracy, nationality."[84] In an article in *Narod* he stated that "our popular representatives are faced with the prospect of saving Russia, of being the voice of the people, the nation, directed toward a stubborn bureaucracy. Really, we must have, and we do have, just one party of Russian patriots." These true patriots were the Christian socialists who sought to embody Christian social teaching in the law. They were opposed by false patriots from parties such as the Union of the Russian People, whom he sarcastically called "those truly Russian, professionally Russian, idiotically Russian people who despoil the Russian name."[85] His rejection of the patriotic unions and the priests who supported them was made even more explicit in an article he addressed to the Orthodox clergy, begging it to repudiate the patriotic unions. Here he referred to the Union of the Russian People by name, calling its members "wolves dressed in sheep's clothing" who had turned a party claiming to represent the interests of the Church into a "pogrom-terrorist organization."[86] Even more dramatically, Bulgakov welcomed the Paschal Edict and went so far as to attack Church missionaries who sought to recover state protection for the official faith. "The day of the full liberation of the Russian religious conscience," he claimed, "will be the greatest celebration of the Russian Church and the Russian people; only for the clerical bureaucracy, for the representatives of Inquisition fanaticism, for 'Orthodox missionaries' will this be a black day."[87] Clearly, Bulgakov's Orthodox patriotism had no place for an apostle-like tsar or an official faith.

Bulgakov's critical distance from the clergy resembled the stances of Soloviev and Nesterov. As with these other intellectuals, however, a tenuous relationship between him and the clergy began to develop as he searched for a Christian solution to the empire's problems. This relationship was nurtured by the mutual sympathy among contemporary lay intellectuals and the clergy for the works of Dostoevsky. Dmitri Merezhkovsky, for instance, proclaimed Dostoevsky to be one of Russia's first original writers because of his interest in Orthodoxy and its place as the spiritual foundation for nationality.[88] Bulgakov's own interest in the writer seems to have developed in connection with his turn away from Marxism and philosophical idealism toward the Orthodox Church in the years after the turn of the century. In 1901, for instance, he described Ivan Karamazov, the free-thinking youth of *The Brothers Karamazov,* as a "characteristic feature of our youth and our intelligentsia."[89]

Subsequent essays frequently referred to the novelist and his work. The most significant, perhaps, was an address delivered in 1906 at a Dostoevsky commemoration in Kiev. Here he characterized Dostoevsky as a "companion" (*sputnik*) of contemporary Russian society, a prophet who in the present time of troubles revealed the essence of its religious ideals. While critical of Dostoevsky for "incorrectly" assessing "autocracy and other political questions," Bulgakov believed that the Christian writer's "social worldview" was of great importance. In light of the previous year's revolutionary upheaval, he brought attention to the claim for an "exclusive mission of the Russian people." Despite the shocking destructiveness of the Revolution, he affirmed this eschatological vision and quoted with approval the novelist's belief that "the ideal of the people is Christ."[90]

In using the great national writer to make claims about Russia's national mission, Bulgakov indirectly contributed to the clergy's cultural mission. As if to symbolize their mutual ideals, an excerpt of his Dostoevsky address was subsequently printed by an official missionary society as a preface to several addresses in honor of the novelist by Archbishop Antony of Volynia.[91] Bulgakov's use of the Orthodox patriotic argument, which became even more marked in the years that followed, resulted partly from his frustration at the failure of Christian socialism within the Duma. The link between him and the clergy ceased to be limited to the thought of Dostoevsky alone, and it is interesting to trace his thinking beyond his Kiev address in 1906. As he turned to nationality as a means of unifying Russia's divided society, he appears to have found the vision articulated by Antony and other cultural missionaries increasingly useful.

This fact can be seen in his contribution to the famous symposium of essays titled *Vekhi* (*Landmarks*) that took Russia's intellectuals by surprise in 1909. His essay was titled "Heroism and Asceticism: Reflections on the Religious Nature of the Russian Intelligentsia."[92] Like the other essays in the volume, Bulgakov's was addressed to intellectuals as the guardians of Russia's future. Russia's budding political system, embodied in the State Duma, had been a failure, he stated. Therefore, it had left the task of leading Russia to the intellectuals. "This is why for the patriot who loves his people and suffers for the needs of the Russian state system, there is not a more compelling matter for consideration than the nature of the intelligentsia." Although he did not consider the clergy a potential force for national regeneration, he cited the mutually attractive figure of Dostoevsky as one of the few intellectuals who had divined Russia's "spiritual character" in the nineteenth century. His hopes in Russia's intellectuals, therefore, were premised upon the ability to transcend philosophical materialism. Bulgakov hoped to convince Russia's intellectuals that their tasks were primarily spiritual ones. In effect, then, he repudiated the distinction between "clergy" and "lay intellectual" and, like the clerical editors of the spiritual journal *Khristianin* cited above, called for the assimilation of intellectuals to the Church.

To further this aim, Bulgakov's *Vekhi* essay called upon intellectuals to accept what he called Russia's "national faith." This, he claimed, was the foundation of national unity and the hope for social progress. In language resembling that of official Church missionaries, he claimed that Russia's "national worldview and spiritual way of life is defined by the Christian faith." Therefore intellectuals must accommodate themselves to religious goals. Nationalism was not a legitimate means of achieving these goals, for it denied Christianity. An undefiled "national idea," he explained, "is based only partly upon ethnographic and historical foundations, and far more upon religious-cultural foundations. It is founded upon a religious-cultural messianism, into which flows every conscious national feeling." To elaborate an undefiled form of "national self-consciousness" here, he offered the example of Old Testament Israel. "This was the character of the greatest bearer of the religious-messianic idea, ancient Israel, and it remains so for each great historical people." As with the patriotic clergy, this comparison brought Bulgakov to reject the intelligentsia's "empty cosmopolitanism." For it was precisely the "absence of a healthy national feeling" that had resulted in the "alien character" (*vnenarodnost*) of the intelligentsia.

Not until it turned to the "national faith," then, could the intelligentsia regain its spiritual authority to lead Russia. Political struggle without a religious goal would only lead to further violence and alienation from the people. This idea, inevitably, had led to a struggle between the Church and the intelligentsia. "For those to whom the national faith has been a treasure and who feel compelled to preserve it—that is, people of the Church—it has been obligatory to struggle against the influence of the intelligentsia in its relations with the people for the sake of precisely that faith." National leadership, therefore, must receive its sanction to act from within the Orthodox Church. While Bulgakov acknowledged that the official Church suffered from a variety of problems, he criticized Russia's intellectuals for ignoring its many positive contributions to national life. He spoke of Russia's holy objects such as monasteries and popular icons, which attracted throngs of pilgrims every year. The national saints also played a positive role. In fact, he specifically cited the St Sergius commemoration address of Kliuchevsky in 1892 (which had deeply impressed Nesterov too) as evidence of how Russia's lay intellectuals could enter Church life for the higher interests of the nation. In light of this idea, he called for the formation of a "ecclesial intelligentsia" (*tserkovnaia intelligentsiia*) to apply "true Christianity" to the "cultural and historical tasks of the hour."[93]

For his bold challenge to Russia's intellectuals and his appeal to the national faith, Bulgakov earned the sympathy of clerical Orthodox patriots. The most notable recognition came from Archbishop Antony, who publicly congratulated the authors of *Vekhi* for their "pure, Christian, and Russian" patriotism.[94] Nicholas Berdiaev, a collaborator in the symposium, had himself conducted a correspondence with Antony, and its contents must have been conveyed to Bulgakov. At the center of one of Antony's letters was the figure of Dostoevsky, a national writer who showed how "the teaching of Christ is incarnated in the national way of life." Like the national saints of old Rus, Antony stated, the novelist could guide Russia's intellectuals as they sought a spiritual path through the present period of crisis.[95]

At the time he completed his *Vekhi* essay in 1909, Bulgakov had reached a position comparable in some ways to that of clerical Orthodox patriots. He had employed the symbolism of holy objects and national saints and had even made use of the new Israel imagery. Most importantly, he had demonstrated a belief that the Orthodox faith was the key to Russia's destiny as a nation. Evtuhov makes the argument, however, that it was only after the death of his son during the same year that Bulgakov's interest in Russian nationality assumed a leading position in his work. It was during subsequent years, she writes, that "a single preoccupation emerges—what might be termed a myth or story about Russia: this was his sense of the essential religiosity of the Russian people and Russian society."[96] Evtuhov does not choose to explore Bulgakov's Orthodox patriotism in any detail, though she does note his appeal to Russia as "Holy Rus" at the end of a published speech during the same year.[97] Bulgakov's appropriation of this model of nationality serves as a good indication of his deepening commitment to Orthodox patriotism. While I would disagree with Evtuhov by pointing to the 1906 Dostoevsky essay as evidence of an earlier turn to Orthodox patriotism, it is true that Bulgakov's most significant writings began to appear after his work in *Vekhi*.

His most significant contribution to Orthodox patriotism before the Revolution was an essay written the following year about the question of nationality in general and its role in the history of Russia in particular. It bore the simple title "Reflections on Nationality," and it expressed an even more explicit sympathy for clerical Orthodox patriotism than the *Vekhi* essay.[98] While Bulgakov did not follow the example of cultural missionaries such as Antony by excluding non-Orthodox from the national community, his essay assigned an important place to the "Church-religious mission" and its contributions to the "creation of a national culture." He even likened the "holy remnant" of Old Testament Israel to those Russians in the present who upheld the testaments of the national faith. It was the "national faith witnessed by the Jewish prophets," he claimed, that most perfectly resembled "our national faith in Holy Rus." Bulgakov used quotation marks to invoke the model of nationality here, thus expressing an ambivalence not present among most clerical cultural missionaries.

However, Bulgakov's discussion of the national self-consciousness that was shaped by the Church's "culturally creative work" revealed clear evidence of the cultural missionaries' influence. Here he endorsed the Church's symbols of nationality strongly, and like them he tended to diminish the principle of universality in exalting the national faith. "It is possible," he stated, "to speak in full seriousness and without the slightest trace of blasphemy not only about a Russian Christ, but about a Greek Christ, an Italian Christ, and a German Christ." This idea was expressed "when speaking about the national saints."

> It is a fact that, according to the character of our individual religious experience, we Russians are inwardly closer to our own particular Russian Christ—the Christ of St Seraphim and St Sergius—than to the Christ of Bernard of Clairvaux, of Catherine of Sienna, or of Francis of Assisi. And in this we by no means reduce religion to an attribute of nationality. In fact, just the opposite is true. Here nationality becomes an attribute of religion, or more precisely that particular image in which the universal truth is apprehended.

Thus, like the clergy, Bulgakov walked a fine line between exclusivity and universality when defining the features of Russia's national faith.

Like Soloviev and Nesterov, Bulgakov embraced an ideal of the national faith and the images that accompanied it to create a national community that was based on the teachings of the Church. Like these other two lay intellectuals, he also maintained considerable distance from the official Church while doing so and altered its model of Holy Rus to fit his own ideals. Most significantly, he explicitly rejected the role of an apostle-like tsar and the autocratic principle of statecraft that went with it.

Nevertheless, Bulgakov retained many of the Church's claims about Holy Rus. He gave considerable attention to the Church as a unifying force in modern Russian society and contrasted this idea with the divisive influence of the secularistic intelligentsia. Echoing some of the claims made by Vostorgov about the nature of culture, he spoke of the "crisis" that secularization had brought to the modern world. While not rejecting the humanism that had accompanied modern cultural developments (as Vostorgov did), Bulgakov stated that the "schism of life into secular and ecclesiastical spheres" had destroyed the health of human culture. Thus, he concluded, the "dissemination of Church self-consciousness is necessary for the fulfillment of the world's historical destiny."[99] His statements about the character of true patriotism also echo claims made by the clergy. By calling for an "upsurge of cultural patriotism and a decline in political nationalism" (*podem kulturnago patriotizma i oslablenie politicheskago natsionalizma*), he summarized Archbishop Antony's distinction between the healthy force of a religious culture and the pernicious force of secular nationalism.[100] Finally, his promotion of the title Holy Rus, while often conditioned by the use of quotation marks, revealed a similar ideal for an Orthodox national community. As he eloquently put it in his essay on nationality: "'Holy Rus'—this is that facet of the Russian people's soul by which the people apprehend Christ and the Church. In its relationship to all of our national life, it is the light—a light that shines in the darkness."[101] Thus Orthodox patriotism was assigned the role of bringing an apostate Russian people back into the sheepfold of the Church.

OLD BELIEVERS AND THE SCHISM OF HOLY RUS

We have seen at different points how the clergy used their definition of a national faith as an instrument in the struggle against apostasy and secularization. Religious intellectuals such as Soloviev, Nesterov, and Bulgakov were prepared to accept the existence of the national faith and even to promote it, but in a far less exclusive way than the clergy. They were reluctant to accept the argument that only within the canonical Church was it to be found, and they refused to endorse the demands of conservative priests who called for a reversal of the Paschal Edict. Rejecting altogether any claim to limit religious freedom, they thus had little or no place for an apostle-like tsar in their model of Holy Rus. Their dissent was nevertheless not a major challenge to clerical Orthodox patriotism, as mutual agreement in other areas, such as the importance of the national saints, generally drew the focus away from their differences.

There was one community of religious intellectuals, however, who tended completely to confound the argument of clerical Orthodox patriotism. These were the Russian Old Believers. Preserving an allegiance to the customs and religiosity of medieval Orthodoxy, Old Believers were in practice ideal adherents to the national faith promoted by the official clergy. The appropriation of the national faith by Old Believer intellectuals such as Ivan Kirillov represents the most challenging case of lay Orthodox patriotism before the war. More than the works of Soloviev, Nesterov, and Bulgakov, it highlighted the dissonant ideals circulating among Russia's conservative clergy.

In the hands of Old Believer intellectuals, the formula of the national faith was in fact used to confront the official Church. After all, the contradictory nature of the official clergy's medieval ideal had been revealed by Orthodox lay intellectuals. Both Soloviev and Nesterov had presented modern Old Believers as true bearers of Russia's religious character. Representatives of the official clergy were all but silenced by this challenge, as they had praised medieval religiosity consistently in the years since 1888. As the official Church's cultural mission disseminated a model of the national community constituted solely by the national faith, therefore, intellectuals from various Old Believer denominations (*soglasii*) emerged to challenge the clergy's model of the nation. And while restricted from expressing this challenge publicly before 1905, after the Paschal Edict they gained the freedom to contest the true nature of Russian Orthodoxy.

While the activities of Old Believers in the late imperial period are receiving increased attention today, their contribution to a broader Russian culture remains obscure. This is not due to an absence of contemporary sources. Both James West and Roy Robson have used a wide variety of publications to study the social thought and ecclesial organization of Old Believers after 1905.[102] West's articles on the industrialist Paul Riabushinsky and the patriotic program of journals such as *Tserkov* (*The Church*) and *Utro Rossii* (*The Dawn of Russia*) represent a good effort to place one peculiar Old Believer voice in the context of Russia's changing social order. However, no historian has attempted to trace the connections between Old Believer intellectuals and the official Church. Riabushinsky and his circle were not alone among the Old Believers in promoting an Orthodox vision of nationality. The claims made by Old Believer intellectuals were often shaped as an answer and even a challenge to the official clergy. Therefore, Old Believer intellectuals should be considered in light of the definition of the national faith made both by the clergy and by other religious intellectuals.

The literature published by the Old Believer press in the years after 1905 expressed a self-conscious challenge to the canonical Church, especially its internal mission. *Tserkov* carried a column titled "Among the Missionaries" that provided reports on polemical encounters between the two branches of Russian Orthodoxy. Old Believers consistently claimed that Russia's contemporary troubles had arisen from a degeneration of native religious standards. This, after all, was what clerical Orthodox patriots had been claiming since the 1880s. The Old Believer F. E. Melnikov, a leading figure in this debate, opened one of his most influential books by declaring that "all the theology of the ruling Church—its system, direction, and spirit—is permeated with the principles of Latinism, Protestantism, and even atheism."[103] Suddenly, then, the canonical Church found that Orthodox patriotism was a knife that cut both ways.

Thus, what might be called an Old Believer counter-mission, an effort to reverse the standard polemics of the official Church and appropriate them to serve Old Belief, became a regular feature in the press after the Paschal Edict. This was especially true when discussing the argument about the national faith. Here Old Believers seized the discourse directly out of the hands of official missionaries. The editors of *Staroobriadcheskaia mysl* (*Old Believer Thought*) did this in 1910, for instance, when they attacked the patriotic missionary John Vostorgov for what they regarded as his erroneous characterization of "the Russian God." His activities against Old Belief and his links to the Union of the Russian People caused him to distort true Russian patriotism into a political rather than a religious movement.[104] By carrying their polemics into the sphere of patriotism, Old Believer intellectuals entered a debate that they believed they could master.

Two elements of their contribution to Orthodox patriotism were emphasized especially. The first was medieval historical memory. Like those official priests who organized historical commemorations and led pilgrimages to the past, Old Believer patriots extolled the history of medieval Rus and presented it as the history of the formation of a primeval national community. As they described this history, however, they claimed it as a possession of Old Belief. An example of their argument is found in the works of a convert from the canonical Church, V. Senatov. As an authority on the schism, he had been an occasional writer for the inner mission's chief organ, *Missionerskoe obozrenie.* After the Paschal Edict, however, he abandoned his hostile stance and entered the *belokrinitskoe* denomination. He came to believe that Old Belief alone was the form of Orthodoxy that could serve the nation in its troubled revolutionary condition. With this religious and cultural vision, he established himself as the chief historian of Old Belief. His two-volume *Philosophy of the History of Old Belief* (1908) and numerous articles in journals constituted some of the most sustained counter-narratives of the national faith.[105]

His works describe a form of Russian Orthodoxy that emerged from a purely popular spirit. This faith assimilated the people's native customs and proved itself to be incorruptible when alien doctrine and theology were imported to Rus from the West. "The national faith," he stated, "is not the artificial dissemination of any kind of teaching, a fixed school, or a formal theology. It is an autonomous phenomenon, detached from any kind of external human agency. It is, as it were, the breath of the Holy Spirit in the Church." Old Belief, he claimed, represented this national faith and as a result had sustained the people throughout its history. His argument did not stop here, however, but followed the logic of Old Believer patriotism to its conclusion. The national faith, he claimed, had been opposed throughout modern history by an alien faith—that of the official Church. Here he was using almost exactly the same argument of clerical Orthodox patriots, but with arguably greater consistency. After all, it was the official Church that had embraced "alien," that is, non-Russian, forms of worship by authorizing the Greek-based Nikonian reforms in the seventeenth century and Italian style naturalistic iconography in the eighteenth century. Its cosmopolitan hierarchy, Senatov argued, had thus rejected the national faith and was responsible for the nation's continued disintegration. From the official Church's alien faith, he concluded, "springs all the modern religious problems of the Russian people and in it is found our modern church disunity."[106]

The national faith of Old Belief, on the other hand, has acted in history as a force of national integration. For him and other Old Believer intellectuals, the Time of Troubles that preceded the schism provided excellent proof for this claim. Here again the logic of official Orthodox patriotism was appropriated. Like clerical Orthodox patriots such as Vostorgov, Senatov regarded the Time of Troubles as an experience similar to the 1905 Revolution, believing it revealed the secret for a restored national unity. Ultimately, he found that it was a popular "devotion to the fatherland and to a love for the true faith of the Christian Church" that "unified the whole of the multimillion Russian

people." Also like official Orthodox patriots, he argued that medieval patriotism was essentially nonpolitical. "In all phases of the Time of Troubles," he
stated, "purely political motives did not stand in the first place. Above statist
motives stood religious ones." This truth was witnessed in the defense of
the Trinity-Sergius Lavra, which more than any other symbol rallied pious
patriots. At this juncture, he said, "the defense of the fatherland assumed a
holy and religious character. Leaders of the national troubles showed themselves to be not only enemies of the fatherland, but of the faith as well." In
the eyes of the people, in fact, "these traitors were secret apostates." With
Trinity-Sergius Lavra and other national holy places such as the Moscow
Kremlin finally recovered, then, the Old Believer nation called upon Michael
Romanov (r. 1613–1645), "the last tsar of the medieval Orthodox confession,"
to rule. Michael was characterized as the "first Russian tsar from the house
of Romanov and the last of its Old Believers." Thus his successor, Alexei
Mikhailovich, "fell under the influence of Greek and Kievan renegades" to
become a "New Believer" (*novoobriadets*). Nevertheless, the national faith did
not die. "Up to our day," Senatov concluded, "its traditions have been preserved in Old Believer identity" (*v litse staroobriadchestva*).[107]

Historical memory was only one of two main elements of Old Believer
patriotism. In appropriating the official Church's formula of the national
faith, intellectuals like Senatov also sought to form a modern national culture with the faith of old Rus at its center. One journal, *Staraia Rus (Old Rus)*,
played an especially active role in this program. As with most Old Believer
journals that appeared in the wake of the Paschal Edict, it did not stay in
print long. But during 1912 it attracted influential contributors such as N. F.
Kapterev and a renowned convert from the official Church, Bishop Mikhail.
It also attracted the talent of Ivan Kirillov. In the inaugural issue, the editors
devoted themselves to help establish a "cultural path" that would lead toward
Russia's renewal and called upon Old Believers of all denominations, both
popovtsy and *bespopovtsy,* to form a united core of patriots to pursue this goal.
Old Belief, as the national faith, alone possessed the power "to develop within
itself the pure Russian, Slavic principle" that would unite the nation.[108]

Staraia Rus established a forum for Old Believer contributions to Orthodox patriotism. Many of its writers employed the same symbols of the national
faith as the official Church. They agreed that medieval culture embodied
the national faith, but their conclusion was that the official Church, not Old
Belief, stood condemned in the early twentieth century by the standards of
that faith. One of the many articles that discussed religious life in the seventeenth century claimed that "Old Belief constituted the symbol of the Russian

man and included within itself his entire spiritual character." The customs of Old Belief "represented in the eyes of contemporary Russian people the paths by which walked in Rus the hosts of saintly people of the Orthodox Russian land, who constituted its might. Because of them, Rus was transfigured into 'Holy Rus.'" The lesson of the seventeenth century, according to this view, was that national unity was based in an Orthodox patriotism of Old Belief. The "most energetic force to draw Russian people to the Old Belief," the author continued, "was a feeling of patriotism." In the medieval atmosphere, "ecclesial self-consciousness" came to encompass "all spheres of life." So closely were Old Belief and patriotism linked that "the very word 'Russian' became a synonym for 'Orthodox.'" But the patriotism of old Rus, the author insisted, was not a political one. "If we were to search the Old Belief of the seventeenth century for a feeling of patriotism in the modern sense, then we very likely would not find it. For its patriotism consisted only in this: a bold faith in the great calling of the Russian people and in its great mission. The patriotism of the seventeenth century was constituted solely by Old Belief."

Criticizing the official Church's internal mission, the author summoned all of the "cultural forces of Old Belief."[109] This cultural counter-mission included a revival of seventeenth-century icon painting and church singing. The Old Believer art patron Sergei Riabushinsky, for instance, promoted interest in old Russian art and even patronized a major exhibition in 1913 that featured medieval icons.[110] More humble intellectuals wrote articles in various culturally engaged journals or gave public lectures. Y. A. Bogachenko, for example, delivered a lecture on the topic of "Old Believer spiritual poetry and psalms" to a full audience gathered in Moscow's Historical Museum in 1912. A sympathetic reviewer writing in *Staraia Rus* described the event as "a serious and bold step toward acquainting Old Believers and the public generally with a purely Russian national art." Bogachenko's theme was the formation of a specifically Russian style of church singing in a period when Orthodoxy in Rus was threatened by paganism in the East and Roman Catholicism in the West. His argument thus resembled that made by the cultural missionaries, who claimed that authentic national art was found only in the medieval period. These songs, Bogachenko argued, were an important source in defining the religious culture of the primeval nation. As such, they represented "monuments of national poetry and national art."[111] His argument was based on the theory, common to both dissenting and official forms of Orthodox patriotism, that Christian art attained its highest level of expression when it embodied particular national principles. In the process of national formation, then, art occupied a "special significance" by providing the "backdrop

from which the spiritual life of a given people emerges." In light of the Old
Believer project to form a modern Russian nation, Bogachenko therefore discussed the significance of what he considered Russia's modern art. "Do our
people in the present time possess art?" he asked. "No, Russian high society
broke away from its people in the time of Peter I. . . . The people continued
to live and were nourished only by that very art that by degrees began to
decline, then dissolve, and was in the end forgotten." As we saw in Chapter
3, members of official missionary societies such as Trenev had stated virtually
the same thing, though with less consistency in light of their defense of the
official faith. In the present case, however, the author assured his audience
that national church singing could still be heard among village communities
of Old Believers.[112]

The cultural program of Old Believer intellectuals was thus designed to
disseminate historical memory and cultural symbols tailored to promote their
vision of an Orthodox national destiny. The goal was not only to promote the
formation of a national community, but also to secure for themselves a leading position within it. The contributors to *Staroobriadcheskaia mysl, Tserkov,
Staraia Rus,* and other journals that appeared after 1905 shared this common
goal. One of these writers, however, went further than others in leading the
cultural counter-mission.

Ivan Kirillov, a lay intellectual who wrote prolifically in a diversity of
journals, collaborated with other leaders of Old Belief such as F. E. Melnikov and Bishop Mikhail to create a unified Old Believer Church.[113] His
publishing labors included two books, *The Third Rome* (1914) and *The Truth
of Old Belief* (1916), that outlined the relationship of Old Belief to modern
Russian culture. Kirillov's work represents the culmination of Old Believer
patriotism before the Revolution, and his vision of Russia's national destiny
deserves attention here.

While *The Truth of Old Belief* appeared in a time of war, Kirillov had
expressed the thoughts contained in it much earlier. *The Third Rome,* for
instance, had been published serially in the journal *Staroobriadcheskaia
mysl* in 1913, and his journal contributions and other minor works in the
years after 1905 presented similar intellectual themes. Therefore, the patriotic message that dominated his later work should not be read as merely a
response to the patriotic feeling that accompanied the early stages of the war.
Rather, it was an expression of a complex relationship between Old Believer
and official forms of Orthodox patriotism. Kirillov appropriated the formula of the national faith to serve his vision of a Russian nation restored by
Old Belief.

Both works were conceived as Old Believer apologetics. This fact was most evident in the 546-page *The Truth of Old Belief,* which included extended refutations of what Kirillov stated were misconceptions held by the secular public and the official Church about Old Belief. Most of all, he sought to answer attacks claiming that Old Belief manifested an "exclusive focus upon nationality."[114] He argued strenuously that the nationality it preserved "is not a sharp, blind nationality, but one that declares the highest principles of humanity deposited by the Creator himself within all peoples." Old Belief embodied a nationality that would "preserve the truth of God and maintain the purity of the Christian Church," while at the same time giving modern Russia cultural unity.[115]

Like clerical Orthodox patriots, Kirillov repeatedly emphasized the Christian nature of Russian nationality. As a practicing *popovets*[116] committed to the expansion of his ecclesial community, he was sensitive to claims that patriotism was inherently subversive to Christian universality.[117] As we have seen, this problem was integral to Orthodox patriotism as a whole. To elaborate his solution, Kirillov naturally did not turn to leaders of the official Church who had addressed the problem, despite the fact that Archbishop Antony's essay "On Nationalism and Patriotism," for instance, had begun to circulate within the religious press and might have served as a source for reference.[118] Instead, Kirillov turned to the thought of Vladimir Soloviev, who, as we have seen, not only defined Orthodox patriotism in distinction from political nationalism but also held a favorable attitude toward the Old Believers. Kirillov borrowed explicitly from Soloviev's thought in both of his works. Like Soloviev, he was repelled by the competitive nature of secular nationalism. He criticized Katkov and Danilevsky in particular, accusing them of lowering Russia's national calling to one of "pagan self-sufficiency."[119] Echoing Soloviev's emphatic distinction between patriotism and nationalism, he employed the word "nationalism" rarely and with reluctance.

We use the term "Old Believer nationalism" only to contrast it with the principles of cosmopolitanism common to educated society. If we were to take Old Belief by itself, without any comparisons, then it would in no way be possible to speak about Old Believer nationalism, as about a "program" or "movement" of any kind. . . . Old Believer nationalism is constituted by a special religious, Christian spirit, in which "nationalism" in a partisan or political sense is absent. Such is the distinction of Old Believer nationalism from nationalism as a program of political parties. The first shares no relationship with the second.[120]

Not only was Kirillov critical of the secular nationalism of Russia's modern political parties, but he also completely rejected the tripartite model of nationality formulated by the imperial state and endorsed by the official clergy. Official Nationality, he argued, denied the national faith because it was designed first of all to serve a state structure that was multinational and secular. Here he began to articulate the radical potential that Orthodox patriotism had possessed since 1888 but had been concealed by the official clergy with its ideal of the apostle-like tsar. "Why did our government in its history acquire the alien system of Official Nationality?" he asked. "The answer can only be that since the time of Peter the government has torn itself away from the Russian people. It has ceased to be national, and accordingly lacks the ability to perceive the Russian people's particularity."[121] Orthodox patriotism was now moving beyond even the critical statements of other lay intellectuals. It was not only an apostle-like tsar who stood condemned by the national faith, but also the entire imperial system of government. Kirillov's sweeping critique of the official order encompassed the entire history of modern Russia, all the way back to the time of the schism, when "the national faith became distorted."[122]

The history of modern Russia therefore expressed a conflict between two forces, "national Rus" (*narodnaia Rus*) and the "Russian Empire" (*Rossiiskaia Imperiia*).[123] "In what direction," Kirillov asked, "are we to search for the true nationality of the Russian people today? The historical government has deviated from the national principle, and the intelligentsia has even more fully rejected all that is native." What was needed, he stated, was a "powerful shove" that would cause Russia "to return to a path of true national self-consciousness."[124] The nation's unity, he claimed, awaited the triumph of Old Belief.

––––––––––––––––––––

In this chapter we have seen how religious intellectuals appropriated Orthodox patriotism to promote their own vision of Russia's national destiny. To varying degrees, their activities were conducted in relation to those of the official Church. Nesterov was the most clearly influenced by the Church's patriotic ideals, and Soloviev also sympathized with them on the occasion of the baptism festival in 1888. Bulgakov's sympathy appears to have grown only in the years after the Revolution of 1905, but it can also be measured by his interest in defining a "national faith" grounded in "Church self-consciousness." For their part, Kirillov and other Old Believer intellectuals had only a hostile relationship with the official Church. But this does not mean that they found nothing redeeming in its activities. The Old Believers' appropriation of the national faith shows their sympathy for the creation of an Orthodox national community.

In all cases, however, religious intellectuals fundamentally altered the clergy's model of Holy Rus. None of them supported the autocracy or, with the possible exception of Soloviev, the image of the apostle-like tsar. All of them criticized the official clergy and revealed that the national faith was not the same as the official faith. Whether critical of imperial state tradition for using its authority to punish heterodoxy (in the case of Bulgakov), or for exchanging the national faith for an alien "New Belief" (in the case of Senatov), religious intellectuals used Orthodox patriotism to challenge the state system defended with such energy by their clerical rivals. To illustrate the irrelevance of the tsar and the autonomy of the people, each held up Old Belief as a model form of Russian national self-consciousness, despite the obvious contradiction this presented to the Christian principle of universality.

And thus, perhaps better than the clergy, Russia's religious intellectuals revealed the fundamental inconsistencies of Orthodox patriotism. Taken to its logical conclusion, Holy Rus was constituted by its national faith alone, and neither the tsar nor even the official clergy could ultimately defend their status in the face of its primacy. Furthermore, the Church's principle of universality, though defended warmly by each of these intellectuals, was ultimately obscured as the effort to form a national community took the leading place. Again Soloviev might be an exception, but even his sincere effort to uphold an ecumenical ideal was confounded by a rhetorical defense of the religious traditions of Old Belief. In the end, the lessons of lay Orthodox patriotism went unnoticed, both among intellectuals and the official clergy. It was left to the clergy to advance Orthodox patriotism one step further before war and revolution brought the movement to an end. This it did with the Germogen canonization festival of 1913.

CHAPTER 8

⟶ ✦ ⟵

The Germogen Canonization
Festival of 1913

The last act of prerevolutionary clerical Orthodox patriotism was played out in the Moscow Kremlin in 1913 during the canonization festival of Patriarch Germogen. For more than thirty years the influence of Orthodox patriotism within the Church had been growing steadily. In 1888 it was mainly the lower clergy and a small number of prelates such as Archbishop Nikanor and Metropolitan Platon who had made the boldest claims about the national faith and the apostle-like tsar. As the cultural mission took shape thereafter, it attracted members of the Church's younger generation, who, drawing upon theological traditions and images to address an empire-wide audience, began to forge a national community based on Orthodox ecclesial self-consciousness. Then, in the "second time of troubles" that followed 1905, the influence of Orthodox patriotism surged among apprehensive elements of the conservative clergy. Young priests and disconcerted prelates looked to the contemporary example of Vostorgov, Skvortsov, Nikon, and Antony as they confronted Russia's impending social, political, and spiritual disaster. The Germogen canonization festival of 1913, occurring on the eve of the war that would precipitate this disaster, was an expression of this influence.

By this time, Vostorgov controlled a considerable publishing network, including a press and two journals, *Vernost* and *Pravoslavnyi blagovestnik*. Skvortsov, in addition to being the Holy Synod's leading missionary authority, maintained control of *Missionerskoe obozrenie* as well as the newspaper *Kolokol*. Archbishop Antony and Bishop Nikon had both become members of the Holy Synod. Finally, in addition to these leading Orthodox patriots there existed a growing number of priests and missionaries whose writings appeared regularly on the pages of Church publications and who were eager to enter public life. They believed that the canonization of Germogen would demonstrate the enhanced vitality of Orthodox patriotism within the Church and, like the baptism festival of 1888, attract a large response from the Russian public.

In fact, it would prove to be the Church's last opportunity to promote the movement within Russia until the end of the twentieth century. The First World War disrupted its ability to organize large public commemorations, and the Revolution that followed brought a violent end to its public activities. Only in 1988, as the communist system itself began to disintegrate, did Church leaders again have the opportunity to stage a large commemoration in the form of the millennium baptism festival.

Thus, in some ways the canonization festival of 1913 was the prerevolutionary clergy's final contribution to the making of a Holy Russia. Indeed, for Bishop Nikon it represented the "triumph of Russian Orthodox patriotism" (*torzhestvo russkago pravoslavnago patriotizma*).[1] More than two hundred thousand people came to the Kremlin to participate in the festival, ten times the number that had assembled on the shores of the Dnieper River a generation earlier. During the divine services and festal addresses, these pilgrims to the past listened attentively as the clergy praised the patriotic deeds of Germogen, Russia's newly recognized national saint.

In another sense, however, the festival represented the movement's limitations. While it received enormous support from the ecclesiastical press, the ideals of the national faith and the apostle-like tsar that it was designed to propagate failed to elicit a broader response. Secular newspapers did not for the most part take up the model of Holy Rus presented by it. Old Believers publicly contested the Church's claim to embody the national faith of the seventeenth-century patriarch. Perhaps most disappointingly, the tsar himself declined to participate in the celebration. By the time Russia went to war the following year, a number of Church leaders were even questioning the value of nationality in the life of the Orthodox Church.

THE STRUGGLE TO DEFINE GERMOGEN'S IMAGE

Like the baptism festival a quarter of a century earlier, the canonization festival was designed from the beginning as a national commemoration. Its clerical organizers believed that historical memory of Germogen could be used to disseminate their model of Holy Rus to a large public audience. As in 1888, then, it represented an effort to recover a usable past. We have seen how members of the clergy had consistently traced the origin of the Russian nation to medieval Rus. This was true especially for the seventeenth century, which had commenced with the Time of Troubles (1598–1613). In the wake of the Revolution of 1905, the Time of Troubles gained additional symbolic importance in the eyes of Church leaders. It demonstrated that in a time of civil unrest and military catastrophe the Church served as the main source of national unity. Writer-priests called upon their readers "to remember our historical past" and used the history of the Time of Troubles as a lesson for modern Russia.[2]

More than any other figure from this past, the holy Germogen represented a model of Orthodox patriotism. He had served as the missionary archbishop of Kazan, bringing the Orthodox faith to the Muslim peoples of the empire's eastern borderlands. After being elected patriarch of Moscow, he had served to strengthen Church authority in the aftermath of its decline under Ivan the Terrible. Finally, as a zealous preacher during the invasions of Roman Catholic Poland, he had helped preserve the national faith and the institution of an apostle-like tsar.

Germogen had long been regarded as one of Russia's most holy men. Less than half a century after his death, Tsar Alexei had ordered that his relics be taken from the Chudov Monastery, where he had perished of hunger in 1612, to Uspensky Cathedral. There they were placed in a sarcophagus that, by the beginning of the nineteenth century, began to attract common pilgrims. Germogen thereafter became associated with a number of miracles, most of which were recorded after the turn of the century when the desire to canonize him began to take hold.

It was at this time that Church authorities began to take an active interest in the historical image of Germogen. This was not due exclusively to his renewed relevance in the wake of the Revolution of 1905. For at this time leaders of secular public opinion also began to recognize Germogen as a symbol of Russian national strength. Such interest was of course welcomed by the clergy, especially those, like Archbishop Antony of Volynia, who were eager to revive the patriarchate. Yet the public appropriation of Germogen's image threatened to diminish the leadership it had been seeking to exercise for the past generation.

The issue became heated in 1910, when the Imperial Moscow Archeological Society decided to raise funds to erect a statue of Germogen and his contemporary Dionisii. The place the society selected was Red Square, where they hoped to complement the famous images of Minin and Pozharsky, two lay heroes of the Time of Troubles. While the society was prepared from the start to cooperate with the Holy Synod (largely because it sought donations that were to be collected primarily in churches) several conservative members of the Church were alarmed at the possible effects a lay commemoration of Germogen would have.[3] Such fears may have been justified, for one petition sent by the society to the Ministry of the Interior suggested that "the central figure of the monument" should in fact not be the patriarch, but Tsar

Michael Feodorovich (r. 1613–1645).[4] Accordingly, the Synod rejected the society's request, though Nicholas II, as Michael's descendent, was himself pleased to donate 2,000 rubles.[5]

The defense of the Church's prerogative in leading the commemoration of medieval national heroes was assumed with particular energy by Bishop Nikon. A powerful prelate in 1910, he would become a member of the Holy Synod in 1912 and an archbishop in 1913. In his journal *Troitskoe slovo*, published from Trinity-Sergius Lavra, he followed the Archeological Society's proposal closely. Since the calamities of 1905 he had regularly compared "the time of troubles three hundred years ago to our own."[6] Both periods, he stated, had witnessed a crisis in the destiny of "Holy Rus."[7] Unexpectedly, he saw little difference between the proposal to erect an image of Germogen and the erection of an image of the Buddha in St Petersburg, which had earlier aroused his zealous opposition. Both images, he claimed, were signs that Russia was being overcome by paganism. Why? He feared that the responsibility for erecting monuments and of observing national holidays was passing out of the hands of the official Church and into the hands of state authorities and secular nationalists. This was troubling enough, but the proposal to build a statue of Germogen next to the Kremlin, the "altar of Orthodox Rus," was a symbolic challenge to the Church's cultural leadership. He explained his objections to the use of secular statues as monuments with reference to the statue of Tsar Alexander II, which, like the proposed statue of Germogen, stood outside the Kremlin. "The people," he claimed, "understand true monuments as churches. Statues cannot be monuments, and it was therefore a wise decision to place the great Tsar-Liberator *outside* the national altar, the Kremlin. There he reverently contemplates from a distance, as it were, the holy object of Orthodox Rus. Let the Imperial Archeological Society and those artists involved with the proposed Germogen statue reflect upon this."

Nikon called upon the official clergy under the authority of the Holy Synod to counter the influence of the lay public by assuming control of its own Germogen monument project and, if possible, the construction of other national monuments in Russia. For it to be an authentic expression of the national spirit, he claimed, a national monument must be a consecrated holy object such as a temple. As he explained, "a monument-statue [*pamiatnik-statuia*] does not conform to our Russian national self-consciousness and our national ideals. The Orthodox Church does not accept sculpture as a form of church art, or if it tolerates it does so contrary to the general rules. Sculpture too much resembles that very pagan cult which so aggravated the first Christians." He blamed the "Western Church" for the degeneration of national feeling into the proliferation of secular monument-statues. By degrees, its alien faith "brought sculpture into its form of worship because it was, however unconsciously, consistently under the influence of the pagan idea." As a result, Western Christianity and the pagan nationalism it had spawned had "placed the keys of the heavenly kingdom into the hands of Perun."

Pagan nationalism had even begun to penetrate Holy Rus. Nikon also criticized the statue of St Vladimir standing in the hills of Kiev as a betrayal of the saint's true spiritual legacy. The only true monument to him and every other clerical figure from the Russian past was a church. Thus, he praised St Vladimir Cathedral that Vasnetsov and Nesterov had completed in 1896. Likewise, the only fitting monument to Patriarch Germogen would be a "temple-monument" (*khram-pamiatnik*). This would identify national glory with a holy place, and could even be executed in the "Russian style." What is more, a monument-temple would also foster national integration because it could be used as a site at which donations could be collected for activities such as the publication of pamphlets "with a strictly Orthodox and patriotic content."[8]

Nikon was sensitive to the idea of monument-statues because he associated them with efforts within Russian society to define a model of nationality that was secular. In a previous issue of *Troitskoe slovo* he had taken up this theme when he criticized the lay intellectual Menshikov for promoting "nationalism" at the expense of "nationality." Only the latter in an Orthodox guise, the prelate argued, was legitimate.[9] Likewise, monuments that were not sanctified by the presence of the Holy Church became idols to "man and his genius" in which God Himself "is forgotten."[10] The threat of an educated public developing a secular model of Russian nationality had always been a leading motivation for the clergy to embrace Orthodox patriotism. In 1888 the St Petersburg Slavic Philanthropic Society had proposed a baptism anniversary celebration to advance its secular model of the nation. Likewise now, as the Imperial Moscow Archeological Society sought to appropriate the image of Germogen to pursue its secular goals, Church leaders rose up to assert their cultural influence. These were the circumstances under which the Church decided to canonize Germogen as a national saint in 1913.

THE GERMOGEN TERCENTENARY

The decision to canonize Germogen in 1913 grew out of unsuccessful efforts during the previous year to present him to the Russian public as a symbol of national unity. The year 1912 marked the three-hundred-year anniversary of his death, and prelates such as Nikon used the occasion to highlight the

Church's role in Russian life. The decision to commemorate the tercentenary of Germogen's death was made by the clergy in the immediate wake of the Germogen monument dispute. The year 1912 witnessed the addition to the Holy Synod of Nikon and another Orthodox patriot, Archbishop Antony of Volynia. They both strongly supported the dissemination of historical memory about the Time of Troubles, and they were met with sympathy from other conservatives on the Synod such as Metropolitan Macarius (Nevskii, 1836–1918) of Moscow and the future New Martyr Vladimir (Bogoiavlenskii, 1848–1918), then Metropolitan of St Petersburg. They were conscious of the fact that within the past few years only minor efforts to commemorate the Church's leadership during the Time of Troubles had been made. In 1910, for instance, Skvortsov's *Kolokol* had commemorated the tercentenary of the liberation of Trinity-Sergius Lavra from the Poles with articles about the heavenly assistance offered to patriotic Russians by St Sergius.[11] Though Germogen was not yet a saint, his stature as an ecclesiastical figure appealed strongly to the conservative members of the Synod. Furthermore, in light of the upcoming Romanov tercentenary of 1913, they were eager to ensure that the Church's vision of Russia's destiny would not be eclipsed by the state's secular supporters.[12]

The Germogen tercentenary celebration of 1912 occurred on February 17 and included a memorial liturgy in Uspensky Cathedral, where Germogen's remains lay. The event itself was not very notable and failed to attract a large audience. Among those who did turn out, notably, were representatives of Russia's patriotic unions.[13] Commemorative events were also scheduled in the capital and in Kazan, where Germogen's ministry had begun, but these also drew very few participants.[14] Thus participation in the tercentenary was almost solely an affair for the clergy. Nikon, Vostorgov, Skvortsov, and several minor Church figures all wrote articles and addresses that proclaimed the patriarch's significance for modern Russians. Clearly anticipating a formal canonization in the near future, Nikon emphasized Germogen's relationship to the rest of Russia's national saints. They had been given by Providence, he stated, "to rouse in the heart of the Russian people a faith in their intercessor during our much troubled times." Germogen was represented as a force for unity in the present. "The Rus of the twentieth century," Nikon claimed, "looks back to its distant past of the seventeenth century and sees among the living heroes of faith and patriotism the great man who led them."[15] Vostorgov made similar claims about the patriarch's virtual status as a national saint.[16] Skvortsov's *Kolokol* portrayed him as a "sufferer for the Russian land" and printed an icon-like image of him.[17] Despite these and a few other commemorative works, however, the ecclesiastical press had little to say about Germogen during the tercentenary year.[18]

The most interesting contribution was that of an obscure missionary priest from the Riga diocese named V. Shchukin who wrote a tribute that not only embodied the rich imagery of Orthodox patriotism but also revealed its theological roots.[19] It also revealed the close relationship between clerical Orthodox patriots and proponents of Russification in the borderlands. For Shchukin, the Germogen tercentenary offered an occasion to explore the character of Russia's "national religiosity" (*natsionalnaia religioznost*). Interestingly, his pamphlet was organized not around the holy man's piety, but around a question that in itself might seem quite extraneous to the matter of salvation. "In what," he asked, "does our primordial Russian Orthodoxy consist?" Such a question might have found an answer in the holy tradition of the universal Orthodox Church. To answer it under the present circumstances, however, Shchukin stated that it was first necessary to examine Russia's "national character."[20]

Russians possessed a tendency toward cross-cultural exchanges, he stated, and cited historical cases of seeking contacts with the Varangians and the Greeks. But Russia's expansive national destiny was now justified only by the fact that her people bore the universal faith. Russia was distinct, therefore, from other European nations such as Germany, whose national faith of Protestantism lacked a universal character. What justified a nation's destiny, Shchukin stated, was its ability to disseminate the "kingdom of God." This mission was possible for the Russian people because "they have concentrated all of their attention upon those visible and tangible manifestations of [the kingdom of God] on earth, to which the Orthodox faith has guided them." In short, Shchukin's definition of Russian nationality was eschatological.

It also bore traces of the Church's pneumatological tradition. By directing their faith toward the visible and tangible elements of this nationality, he claimed, Russians had sanctified it. As a result, God had manifested His presence in the Russian land. "The Russian people have directed their attention not toward a personal ascension to God but toward the footprints [*sledy*] of divine grace imprinted upon the earth. Very much is revealed about the purpose of the Russian people in these footprints of grace."[21] Here he listed the Church's holy objects such as icons and holy places such as temples as the only true expressions of Russian nationality. He asked his readers to turn their attention to "medieval Orthodox Rus," which was "entirely covered" by such footprints of grace and, therefore, authentic nationality. In the medieval past "every old Russian person maintained consciousness of himself as a dweller of Holy Rus in the presence of God, in the ground of the genuine kingdom of God."[22] His conclusion, then, was that "Holy Rus in actuality was the kingdom of God descended to earth."[23]

In the present, the remnant of this national community was called to preserve their faith by strengthening their nationality. Here Shchukin suggested that it was impossible to define faith without reference to nationality, for the latter manifested the former in particular cases of "materialization."[24] Like the ancient Israelites, modern Russians must not sacrifice their faith by intermixing with non-Russians. "Holy Rus," Shchukin argued, "cannot remain faithful to herself and fraternize with non-Orthodox neighbors on earth." Nevertheless, as the new Israel she bore a missionary responsibility to disseminate her faith. "The acceptance of the Russian Orthodox faith by itself," he added, "assimilates any non-Orthodox person to the best features of the Slavic-Russian people." Thus Russian nationality in Shchukin's argument came to play a crucial role in the dissemination of the universal faith. "By inserting their essential character and, as it were, their national soul into Orthodox Christianity, the Russian people transmuted [*prevratil*] this very Christianity in their soul, in their Russian character, and in their standard of Russian nationality."[25] Thus the answer to his opening question about the character of a specifically Russian form of the Christian faith was reached. Orthodoxy was powerless without a national culture in which to become "materialized." He was then prepared to turn to Germogen, who up until this point had been totally ignored, as the "great religious nationalist of our Holy Rus" (*velikii religioznyi natsionalist nashei sviatei Rusi*).[26] Germogen's example of a "holy nationalism" offered the means of bringing unity to Russia during her present time of troubles. After reviewing his deeds to preserve and disseminate the national faith, Shchukin closed with an appeal for "new Germogens" to enter public life.[27]

Shchukin's unusually dense expression of Orthodox patriotism is noteworthy for its appropriation of the term "nationalist," something the clergy such as Antony had for the most part preferred to exchange for "patriot." Apart from this work, however, the Germogen tercentenary of 1912 produced very little of interest from the official clergy. On the other hand, the year had witnessed an outburst of patriotic feeling among the secular public in association with the commemoration of the Fatherland War of 1812. To the clergy's consternation, some secular nationalists even used the Fatherland War commemoration to promote a model of nationality based upon Duma politics and European culture.

A striking example of such a secular model was found in a book published by N. I. Gerasimov titled *In Defense of Russian Nationalism*.[28] This book claimed that "the spirit of the times in Europe is nationalism," and that it was thus obligatory to "open in Russia an era of nationalism" as well.[29] While celebrating Russia's "national bravery" in "standing up against Europe" in the past, the present "so-called time of troubles" revealed that national self-consciousness remained weak. Significantly, Gerasimov bestowed virtually no credit at all to the official Church or even to the autocratic tradition when describing the forces that shaped the national community. In fact, the Church's Christian model of a Holy Rus that embodied the "kingdom of heaven" was dismissed as a "poetic dream." His ideal, rather, was the constitutional national state of England under William Gladstone.[30] Despite the secular nature of this ideal, he could not avoid discussing Russia's "national faith."[31] This was not what clerical Orthodox patriots promoted, however, but a nonecclesial embodiment of a vaguely Christian "national spirit."[32] Russia, he claimed, could be transformed into a strong national community only with the expansion of the Duma's authority and the consolidation of religious freedom.[33]

The Germogen tercentenary of 1912 proved a disappointment for clerical Orthodox patriots. When Skvortsov looked back on the year, he was forced to acknowledge that "only the Church" had taken an interest in it. The contrasting success of the Fatherland War commemoration indicated that the clergy were failing to assert the cultural leadership needed to guide Russia toward an ecclesial national integration. "In a time when all states recognize the necessity of promoting national feeling and national memory," he claimed, the Church must also make its influence felt.[34]

Perhaps even more troubling than the public's secular model of nationality, however, was the challenge that Old Believers made against the tercentenary. Patriarch Germogen, official Church leaders were acutely aware, had lived before the time of the schism and therefore could be claimed by Russia's other adherents to the national faith. In 1903 some of them had satirized the canonization of the "New Believer" Seraphim of Sarov, but the official Church's claim to the "Old Believer" Germogen made their attitude in 1912 much more volatile.[35] As a result, the tercentenary year also witnessed a nonconformist commemoration of the seventeenth-century patriot.

Ivan Kirillov himself, for instance, published a pamphlet that year in which he attacked Russia's modern secularized culture and blamed the official Church and the imperial state for supporting it. Titled *The True Church*, it looked to the Old Belief of the seventeenth century for an example of "religious national feeling."[36] It was this "spiritual life of medieval Rus," he claimed, "that gave birth to the great patriot Patriarch Germogen."[37] Kirillov's views were shared by others such as Paul Riabushinsky, whose liberal newspaper *Utro Rossii* published several illustrated articles to commemorate the tercentenary. One presented Germogen as the bearer of a "healthy patriotism" based in the Christian faith and political liberalism. "Just as the revolution of 1905 produced the State Duma," it noted optimistically, "so the seventeenth century bore the first land council [*zemsky sobor*] consisting of all estates." Then as now, however, the most important matter was to heed the example of Germogen's "native faith."[38] Another article was illustrated with the seventeenth-century patriarch crossing himself with two fingers. For those among Riabushinsky's liberal audience who would not have noted the significance of this themselves, a caption below explained. It emphasized that spurious representations of Germogen presently being circulated by missionaries of the official Church showed him using three fingers, a historical impossibility before the Nikonian reforms!

Even mainstream Old Believers participated in the nonconformist commemoration. One writing in the Pomorskii journal *Shchit very* recognized Germogen as an Old Believer missionary "among the Tatars." As in *Utro Rossii,* the patriarch's activities during the Time of Troubles were shown to demonstrate a devotion to the national faith that was inherently democratic. Seeing the state fall apart, "the hierarch appealed for assistance to that keeper of medieval piety, the great and powerful Russian people." And, even though this people had begun to succumb to secularization in modern times, their national faith had been preserved among Old Believers. This is why, the author claimed, the "memory about the most holy Germogen is especially dear for us Christian Old Believers." He even went on to claim that the "alien faith" finally embraced by the official Church under Nikon was that very faith "against which the patriarch-martyr fought."[39] Finally, the interest shown by the priestless Pomorskie was also shared by the Belokrinitskoe leadership. It scheduled its own services at the Rogozhskoe Cemetery in Moscow, celebrated by Old Believer Archbishop John of Moscow and other priests on the very day the official clergy were celebrating their version of the commemoration across the city in Uspensky Cathedral.[40]

THE DECISION TO CANONIZE

The lack of enthusiasm shown for the official canonical Germogen tercentenary was a disappointment for the clergy who supported it. Nevertheless, during the months following the commemoration, the first definite steps were taken toward the canonization of the saint. The official account of how the decision came about was buried in an article published by the missionary journal *Vera i razum* stating that a petition had been received by a member of the Synod, Metropolitan Vladimir, on the very day the tercentenary of Germogen's death was commemorated. It bore no fewer than twenty thousand signatures from a variety of faithful Muscovites, and it requested that the holy man finally be recognized formally as a saint. In light of the Synod's patriotic membership in 1912 and its desire to counter the secular forces of leadership anticipated from the state and nationalists during the following year, the decision was made to proceed with an inquiry into Germogen's sanctity. After scores of miracles had been confirmed, the Synod issued its official order for canonization.[41]

In the Orthodox Church, recognition of saints was generally less formal than in contemporary Roman Catholicism, and the standards for official canonization less exacting. The Church taught that the popular veneration of a deceased believer was sufficient for recognizing him or her as a saint informally.[42] In the case of Germogen, popular veneration had long occurred, and the decision to canonize was fully in accord with this fact. Yet the saint's reputation among the clergy who now influenced Church life in Russia was clearly significant as well.

The text of the order for canonization revealed that Orthodox patriotism was an important force behind the glorification. First of all, the order used the medieval orthography "Ermogen" in the place of the customary "Germogen." Freeze has claimed that this spelling represented an effort to dissociate the saint from the disgraced Bishop Germogen of Saratov, who was widely regarded in the secular press as an example of clerical obscurantism.[43] In light of the fact that Bishop Germogen had been defrocked more than a year earlier, and that in the meantime the Germogen tercentenary had been celebrated without altering the conventional spelling of his name, it seems to me more probable that the Church leadership was simply using a visual device to emphasize the fact that the saint represented a national faith that was medieval in origin. This was, after all, a time when medieval forms of orthography were being revived not only by the Church but also in the secular arts. Interestingly, some Old Believers had also used the medieval orthography when commemorating the tercentenary the previous year.[44] They surely had little reason to fear being associated with the disgraced "New Believer" bishop of Saratov.

The synodal order began its explanation for the canonization by discussing Patriarch Germogen's service in the Orthodox mission. It described his leadership in the religious life of Kazan and his work toward the "Christian enlightenment of those who stagnated in the darkness and delusions as faithless non-Russians." What is more, with the passage of years he succeeded in "uniting around himself all of the leaders of the mission." As his reward, he was blessed with two important portentous events. He was one of the first to discover the uncorrupted relics of St Gurii, an apostle to pagans along the Volga, and to witness the appearance of the Kazan Icon of the Mother of God in the sky after a city fire. Such extraordinary experiences prepared him for a life of service to Holy Rus.

Therefore, the order praised Germogen's patriotism more than any other single feature of his character, including personal piety. "He stood as a guardian of the holy faith and the dear customs of native Russian antiquities [*rodnoi russkoi stariny*], bravely reserving them from the encroachment of enemies of Church and native land." Among the holy objects that he helped to defend during the Time of Troubles were the Moscow Kremlin and Trinity-Sergius Lavra. But most importantly, it was his service as a heavenly intercessor for Holy Rus during the modern time of troubles that justified his glorification. "The fusion of the national faith in the holiness of Patriarch Germogen and reverence shown for him has been strengthened during recent years of sorrow and national troubles. In painful anxiety, Russia's sons have sought consolation for their heavy thoughts about the destiny of the native land by the sepulcher of the martyr who lived long ago during similar years of national upheaval." As a "great intercessor for Holy Rus," then, Germogen deserved to be elevated to the status of a national saint.[45]

The place chosen for the canonization ceremony was Uspensky Cathedral. It was scheduled for May 12 and was to be accompanied by a festival lasting five days.

GERMOGEN AND PATRIOTIC HAGIOGRAPHY

The level of clerical mobilization for the canonization festival was much higher than during the Germogen tercentenary, registered in part by the number of saints' lives of Germogen that began to appear in the months after the 1912 commemoration. While recording much about the clergy's patriotic intentions in staging the festival, they indicate that Germogen was intended above all to represent an image of Holy Rus.

To my knowledge, no effort to study these saints' lives or the others that proliferated in late imperial Russia has even been undertaken. For the most part, they were written by clerical writers to shape the self-consciousness of their intended popular audience. As such, their value in determining the beliefs of that audience is limited. Nevertheless, they can offer valuable insights into the meaning that Church leaders behind the canonization festival attached to Germogen's memory. In this they are superior to sources (such as synodal reports) that were directed toward a purely clerical audience. What is most striking about them is the influence of Orthodox patriotism. While numerous inexpensive and simple accounts of Orthodox saints were issued by the ecclesiastical press in the decades before the Revolution, most stressed individual piety and the role of the saint in promoting salvation within the universal Church. The lives that accompanied the canonization of Germogen, on the other hand, stressed national character without exception.

The Church's cultural mission had influenced this change of direction. National commemorations and the pilgrimages to the past that accompanied them had often been accompanied by lives emphasizing an individual saint's relationship to the national community and the collective historical experience that unified it. In 1888 a number of publications appeared treating the life of St Vladimir, and in 1892 many about St Sergius did also. Even when the modern St Seraphim was canonized in 1903, lives appeared to honor his reputed role in the nation's history.

This new direction in the content of saints' lives in Russia paralleled developments within the Roman Catholic Church in contemporary western Europe. In France, for instance, the Catholic clergy promoted pilgrimages to shrines such as Lourdes that emphasized not only salvation and healing but also participation in a collective national experience. "Using the political rhetoric of nationalism and other forms of mass democratic propaganda in the organization of large-scale pilgrimages," Suzanne Kaufman has written, the Roman Catholic Church "reoriented the meaning of the Lourdes pilgrimage, recasting the experience of a local religious event into a national battle over the meaning of French identity."[46] The pilgrimages to the past organized in late imperial Russia were thus part of a larger effort by the churches of modern Europe to adapt Christianity to the challenge of secular nationalism.

The Germogen canonization festival was accompanied by the most emphatic examples of Orthodox patriotic hagiography to appear before the Revolution. Expressing the same rhetoric as the synodal order of canonization, many saints' lives focused particular attention on Germogen's vocation as a "missionary."[47] His early years in Kazan figured prominently. Conquered only a generation before he arrived there, Kazan symbolized Russia's national destiny to disseminate the universal faith to other peoples in Asia. The fact that Germogen witnessed the Kazan Icon of the Mother of God in the sky over the city was taken as a sign that his life would contribute to "the victory of the Gospel over the Koran."[48] But his personal experience was intimately connected to that of the Christian national community. "Thus in the appearance of the icon there was displayed the greatness of Christianity. From that time to the present this icon has represented a symbol of the triumph over other religions not only in Kazan but in all of Orthodox Russia. It served as a victorious sign under which Rus departed from an era of troubles."[49]

While Germogen contributed to the fulfillment of the Russian Church's external mission, he was also confronted, like modern missionaries, by the people's lapses into faithlessness. Lives usually described his ability to discern an inseparable relationship between Russian nationality and ecclesial self-consciousness. For instance, he had been confronted by the fact that many newly baptized Tatars who continued to live "among their former religious brothers" had ultimately returned to their native faith. Likewise, "many Russians, living near Tatars or Germans in the suburbs, also broke away from Orthodoxy."[50] Observing these cases of apostasy, the cultural missionary began to promote Russian nationality in the region. He even ensured that "only Russians" would be settled in some areas.[51] Nor was the mission in the East, of course, the only focus of Germogen's patriotic missionary work. The internal mission to preserve Orthodoxy against the alien faith of Roman Catholicism came to occupy his chief activities. As time passed, hagiographers claimed, he became engrossed in the problems of Orthodox Russians living in the western borderlands. "In his heart, he felt compassion for the Russian people as it was confronted by the power of Poland during those times, for in this primordial Russian region it was ruled by the Poles. He understood that a terrible oppression of both the Orthodox faith and Russian nationality existed there."[52]

Germogen's example of preserving the national faith was even used to warn modern Russians against sympathizing with efforts to reunite Christendom. Referring to a "cunning enemy of our time," one life described proposals for "the assimilation of our holy mother Orthodox Church with the Anglicans." It described the presence of Anglican priests in Petersburg who were seeking to lure Russians away from the national faith. "The unity of Christians is very desirable," it admitted, "and people should be allowed to regard one another as brothers. But the unification of the Church is a different matter. Jesus Christ said, 'not peace but a sword I bring.' Our dogma of faith is that sword, and true Orthodox people are in danger of mistaking it."[53] Thus Germogen's defense of the national faith could even be used as an example to Orthodox Christians in the face of the nascent ecumenical movement.

With his devotion to the Orthodox mission, then, Germogen was spiritually prepared to lead the nation through its troubles. His defense of Russian national unity constituted the second greatest feature of his character according to the saints' lives. His example of self-sacrifice for the native land was described as a virtue that all true Russians should embrace. "There was a time when it appeared as if the very existence of Russia as a great power had reached its end," explained one life. "The people, seeing no possibility for salvation, began to despair. Then, from the midst of the people themselves, there appeared spirited leaders who inspired others to perform deeds for the salvation of the native land." Since Germogen was the greatest of these patriots, collective "memory" about him "must be preserved in sanctity and reverence by those who value the greatness of the native land."[54]

Above all, Germogen's devotion to Holy Rus and its national faith served as a witness to the most basic features of a timeless national character.[55] Some saints' lives went so far as to use Germogen as a vehicle for propagating an Orthodox model of Russian nationality almost exclusively, to the point that they read like nationalistic manifestos. "A Russian by birth who accepts another faith ceases to be a Russian," declared one. "Russia, accepting another faith in the place of Orthodoxy, ceased to be Russia. Therefore, there is a great significance for our fatherland on the day of the canonization of Saint Germogen."[56] Another baldly stated that "without his deeds Great Russia would not exist and in her place there would be only Polish and Swedish provinces filled by Catholicism and Lutheranism. There would be no Russian state, there would be no Russian nationality."[57]

THE CANONIZATION FESTIVAL

The canonization festival reflected the conservative clergy's continued attachment both to the ideal of a national faith and to the ideal of an apostle-like tsar. Originally, Nicholas II was expected to attend and participate in the liturgy of glorification in Uspensky Cathedral. The clergy's warm praise for him during the festival indicates that they believed his participation would add prestige to the Church as a force for national leadership. There was also the hope that an equally warm response by him would signal an interest in recovering the status of Orthodoxy as the empire's predominant and ruling faith. They remembered his participation in the Seraphim canonization festival of 1903 and hoped that the canonization of Germogen would remind him how incongruous the Paschal Edict was with the ideals of seventeenth-century statecraft. Significantly, however, Nicholas ultimately decided to cancel his attendance at the festival. Soon before it commenced he was compelled to make a diplomatic trip to Germany. From the start, then, the commemoration's image of a Holy Rus led by an apostle-like tsar was undermined. Church leaders had to make do with a telegram of sympathy from Nicholas and a symbol of bureaucratic Church administration in the person of Chief Procurator Vladimir Sabler.

Thus, the long-held ideal of an apostle-like tsar was again frustrated during the festival. Ironically, this frustration did not shake the persistence of that ideal. The conservatives who participated had made the tsar such an inseparable element of the national community that they were unable to imagine Holy Rus without him. Freeze has argued that the canonization actually represented an effort by the Church to define a more independent status for itself in relationship to the tsar. He notes especially the implicitly subversive message behind the image of Germogen as the savior of the Russian state after its collapse during the Time of Troubles. He even goes so far as to claim that the example of Germogen as an independent patriot and patriarch "tacitly condensed the famous formula 'Orthodoxy, Autocracy, Nationality' at the expense of the middle term."[58] However, while the canonization act and the festival that accompanied it expressed the Church's efforts to place itself before the tsar and any other secular image of the nation, I believe it is a mistake to perceive in its activities a diminution of the status of the tsar. Germogen was hailed by virtually all clerical participants as a defender of autocracy, not a critic of it, and when attention was directed to his role in saving the state from collapse it was intended to emphasize the symphony of Church and state rather than their competition. There were many priests and a few prelates in the years after 1905 who had begun to criticize autocracy and the Russian state tradition, but they were not the ones who organized the canonization festival.[59]

Indeed, I have seen no evidence to suggest that the conservative Church leadership who came to the Moscow Kremlin in 1913 ever questioned the formula of Official Nationality. It was frequently voiced by the priests who attended, and, despite the obvious anachronism, it was even ascribed to the seventeenth-century saint. "Germogen," asserted one work, "stood for our Russian ideals of Orthodoxy, Autocracy, and Nationality."[60]

During the festival the Moscow Kremlin was assigned a national symbolism similar to that of Kiev's Pecherskaia Lavra in 1888. The Kremlin contained some of the most revered holy objects of Holy Rus and, more significantly, was both the site of Germogen's repose in 1612 and the place where his relics were preserved. He had died in Chudov Monastery, and his remains had been moved to Uspensky Cathedral later in the seventeenth century. According to celebrants, the cathedral represented a "depository for proponents of the national faith."[61] During the festival week, pilgrims who had come to the city attended various services and listened to the addresses of the clergy. Judging by the accounts of both ecclesiastical and secular sources, the festival generated less enthusiasm than the baptism festival of 1888. While attracting more pilgrims (estimates were imprecise but claimed as many as two hundred thousand), the event was not punctuated with as many religious services and processions.[62] More significantly, secular newspapers generally gave only passing accounts of the event and lacked the interest shown in 1888.[63] The exception to the educated public's lack of interest was the prominent participation of patriotic unions, which, since the Paschal Edict of 1905, the conservative clergy had done so much to court. For its part, the Union of the Russian People warmly praised Germogen for his "great patriotism."[64]

The Church itself was the only institutional group that seems wholeheartedly to have participated. In contrast to the tercentenary commemoration of 1912, this time it was fully prepared to stage a large and widely documented event. Metropolitan Vladimir of St Petersburg attended along with Metropolitan Macarius of Moscow. Bishop Nikon and Vostorgov both came and delivered addresses along with a number of other priests and prelates. In an interesting resemblance to the baptism festival, a foreign representative of the universal Church was also on hand. Patriarch Gregory (r. 1906–1928) of Antioch arrived in Moscow just before the festival began, participated in the glorification liturgy in Uspensky Cathedral, and walked in the religious procession afterward. However, the fact that he had come to Russia primarily to participate in the Romanov tercentenary commemoration later in the month must have dampened the effect of his presence.[65]

What is more, the icon that the clergy walked behind during the processional was a symbol of how the canonization was less a celebration of the universal Church than of Holy Rus. It had been painted by the most famous artist of the Russian national style alive at the time, Victor Vasnetsov. He had been commissioned to execute this, the very first official icon of St Germogen, in light of his patriotic contributions to St Vladimir Cathedral in Kiev and the Temple of the Resurrection of Christ in St Petersburg.[66] Finally, the Patriarch of Antioch and other Church members who thought primarily about a universal faith might have been puzzled as they filed underneath the electrically illuminated patriotic message running up the side of the Ivan the Great Bell Tower: "Rejoice in the Holy Martyr Germogen, an Intercessor for the Russian Land!"[67] The latest canonization of a Russian national saint, in light of the rhetoric that surrounded it, appeared as a national affair with only minor relevance for the universal Church.

The articles and addresses published before and after the festival are a record not only of the model of nationality disseminated during the festival, but also of the growing dissonance from which clerical Orthodox patriotism suffered on the eve of the Revolution. As in 1888, the mission served as a backdrop to the national commemoration. Now some of the clergy responded to the glorification of another national saint by reflecting on the example of statecraft established by the nation's founding ruler, St Vladimir Equal-to-the-Apostles.[68] This did not convey a sense that all was well in modern Holy Rus, however, for the Paschal Edict was still in place and many missionaries continued to resent the fact that pagan services were conducted in the nation's capital. Skvortsov's *Missionerskoe obozrenie,* for instance, brought attention to the "Mongol and Tibetan flags" that now waved above the Neva River from the Buddhist temple.[69] Skvortsov himself spoke of "dark enemies" at large in Russia who continue "more powerfully and powerfully" to assail the Church.[70]

With the national faith in danger, clerical participants presented Germogen as a prophet sent to the Russian state. Some compared him to Samuel, the prophet of ancient Israel, who had discharged Saul from his duties as tsar in order to install the more pious David. As a prophet to the new Israel, Germogen showed the importance of preserving and disseminating the national faith. Three hundred years after the election of Michael Romanov, one observer remarked, Russia has not forgotten its national prophet "as ancient Israel forgot Samuel."[71]

This was the main lesson of the seventeenth-century Time of Troubles. "The grand princes of Moscow," one writer claimed, "understood well as the gatherers of Rus that political centralization alone could not unify a single homogeneous state. For this the consolidating bond [*podpochva*] of spiritual unity was required. The national bond of religious self-consciousness, cultivated by Russia's medieval shrines and towns, has always served as this consolidating bond." Thus secular power was insufficient to unite the divided nation. Only a form of the universal faith grounded in a particular collective experience and defined by tangible cultural artifacts could preserve national unity. Germogen had borne witness to this faith and therefore deserved to be recognized as a prophet of apostle-like statecraft the way Samuel served as a prophet to the founding tsars of ancient Israel. "If at the present moment the unparalleled historical significance of Patriarch Germogen is being evaluated, then it shows to all of Rus that until our time the Orthodox Church has lived according to a national faith." Indeed, "if Germogen had not perished in the cloistered underground of Chudov Monastery . . . perhaps the Russian people long ago would have been absorbed by non-Russians and there would not be a powerful Russian state. Even more, there would be no Holy Rus."[72]

By showing the Russian tsars the importance of preserving the national faith, Germogen thus symbolized the ideal of an apostle-like tsar. Two of the most active leaders of the canonization festival were Nikon and Vostorgov, and in their articles and addresses they especially stressed the legacy of St Vladimir. Nikon opened one article with a reference to what he considered a model of apostle-like statecraft, the Edict of Milan of St Constantine Equal-to-the-Apostles. The edict had established Christianity as a legal faith in the Roman Empire. It had reputedly been issued by the Christian emperor in the year 313, and for the conservative Church leaders who gathered in the Kremlin in 1913, the association of anniversaries was more than a coincidence. "Not in a single country in the world," Nikon began, "since that time sixteen hundred years ago when Constantine the Great declared in Milan his edict about the freedom of the Christian faith, has the holy Orthodox faith had such a vital connection to the life of the national soul than we have in Rus." What is more, Russia's past revealed her status as the successor to ancient Israel. "Our Russian history," he affirmed, "reminds one of the history of the Jewish people." But in the same way the national faith of ancient Israel and Byzantium had once begun to succumb to the forces of apostasy, so Holy Rus was presently overwhelmed by "wild sects and heresies." It was "living through a time of struggle for all the holy objects of the national heart," he claimed. "And here, from the heights of heaven and from the depths of past centuries has risen before us . . . the great holy man of medieval Rus, glorious Saint Germogen the Patriarch."

This latest saint of Holy Rus, he stated, was especially significant because he was "native to us not only according to faith, but according to the flesh." Thus Nikon claimed that the continued vitality of the Orthodox Church in Russia was closely tied to the influence of ethnic nationality. "I repeat: this is especially significant to us in our time of troubles," he stated. Russia's ethnic self-consciousness was challenged by non-Russians and by Russian cosmopolitan intellectuals. Even more, it was distorted by secular nationalists who sought only national unity, regardless of ecclesial self-consciousness. Therefore, Germogen was even more significant as a newly glorified national saint. He offered modern Russians a model of both ethnic national self-consciousness and ecclesial identity. The greater the number of saintly witnesses to the national faith in modern times, he suggested, the more unified Russia would become. "In the course of the ten years since the days of the Sarov festival," he observed, "the Lord has glorified and sent to our assistance St Seraphim, St Ioasaf, and now St Germogen." He continued by stating that there was every reason to expect that the canonizations of more national saints were on the way, looking to Anna Kashinskaia, Efrosin Sineozerskii, and Pitirim Tambovskii especially. Russia's present "coldness to the native faith," he concluded, would be overcome through the assistance of the national saints.[73]

Germogen's witness to the national faith was recognized by Vostorgov also. In fact, Vostorgov had been one of the conservative Church leaders most determined to see Germogen canonized. He had served on the synodal commission designed to evaluate Germogen's status as a miracle worker, and when the canonization decision was reached, he was invested with the responsibility for composing the liturgical prayers prescribed by the Church for the veneration of a new saint. The central role he played had resulted from a long interest in Germogen. After the Revolution of 1905 he had begun preparing special sermons on the anniversaries of Germogen's death and had commemorated the holy man in pamphlets and in his journal *Vernost*. As early as 1907 he expressed frustration that the patriarch "still had not been glorified" as a national saint.[74] Not only did the national prophet understand that "Orthodoxy is the foundation of Russian national self-consciousness," but he also showed how it constituted the "justification for the Russian state and its statecraft." Germogen also indicated that the Church alone "sanctified Russian patriotism."[75]

To support the revival of a form of statecraft directed toward the service of Orthodoxy, it was fitting that Russia's patriotic unions participate in the canonization festival. Vostorgov's relations with the patriotic unions yielded one of its more remarkable features. With their participation and financial support, he organized the construction of Russia's very first "monument-temple" to St Germogen, located on the site in Chudov Monastery where the saint was said to have died in 1612.[76] This was indeed a triumph of Nikon's ideal (discussed above) of Church rather than state leadership of national commemorations. And according to the taste of Orthodox patriotism, it was designed "in the medieval style."[77]

Perhaps better than any other feature of the canonization festival, the participation of monarchistic and nationalistic political unions in the construction of Russia's first church of St Germogen indicates how far clerical Orthodox patriotism had become entangled in ethnic nationalism, and how dissonant its claims to defend the Church's principle of universality could sound. Anticipating some dismay from less conservative members of the Church, Vostorgov defended the highly unusual involvement of ethnic nationalists in the construction of the new holy place. "The Russian monarchistic movement," he explained, "stands as the loyal guardian of our native historical state system and finds in the life and activity of St Germogen a perfect example for imitation."[78] Implicit here was the claim that the patriotic unions were left alone in the political sphere to defend the principle of apostle-like statecraft.

Completed on schedule, the temple was consecrated during the canonization festival. Vostorgov himself served at the altar, and as he did so representatives of the patriotic unions who had helped finance the temple assembled in the small, tightly packed nave to look on. It was a triumphant scene. In 1910 Bishop Nikon had objected when Russia's secular nationalists had proposed building a statue of Germogen outside the Kremlin. Now those very nationalists had been drawn into the Kremlin by the Church leadership to venerate Germogen in a "monument-temple" dedicated to the newly glorified national saint. But it was also a scene full of irony. Did the presence of the patriotic unions indicate that ethnic nationalism had finally been converted to the ideals of the universal faith, or did it suggest that the Church had failed to bar her doors against the secular forces of division?

EPILOGUE

Thus the Germogen canonization festival of 1913 came to a close. And what of the absent tsar? He arrived in Moscow on May 23, over a week after the clergy had concluded the liturgy of glorification and departed from Uspensky Cathedral. Nicholas came not to participate in the canonization of Germogen, however, but to lead a three-hundred-year anniversary celebration of the Romanov Dynasty. Notwithstanding his absence from the canonization, conservative priests welcomed his belated arrival and hailed him as the modern successor to the seventeenth-century Michael Romanov.

ORTHODOX PATRIOTISM AND THE ROMANOV TERCENTENARY

Indeed, Nicholas had done much to associate the Romanov tercentenary commemoration of 1913 with the imagery of Holy Rus. He had overseen the construction of a commemorative church on Mt Carmel in Palestine, where pilgrims under the care of the Orthodox Palestine Society would now find shelter.[1] Closer to home, he had ordered the construction of yet another church in the increasingly multireligious city of St Petersburg. Like many others that had appeared in recent years, it was to be decorated in the medieval style.[2] And like the newly dedicated Feodorovskii Cathedral in Tsarskoe Selo, it was dedicated to the icon of the Feodorovskaia Mother of God before which Michael Romanov prayed when contemplating his acceptance of the crown. Described as a "temple-monument" (*khram-pamiatnik*), it was intended to symbolize the modern tsar's devotion to the national faith.[3] Nicholas also paid homage to the imagery of medieval Rus by traveling throughout central Russia on his way to Moscow.[4] His route, what Soviet tour guides would later call the "Golden Ring," took him through Kostroma (where Michael agreed to accept the crown) and other medieval towns such as Yaroslavl, Rostov, Suzdal, and Vladimir. At each stop he made a point of visiting the local holy places such as churches and monasteries. Before reaching Moscow, the imperial train even passed through Sergiev Posad, where Nicholas could be observed praying in front of the relics of St Sergius at Trinity-Sergius Lavra.[5]

The construction of a monument-temple and Nicholas's pilgrimage to medieval holy places helped ensure a warm greeting from the conservative clergy when he arrived at the Kremlin gates for his ceremonial entrance into the "altar of Holy Rus." Many of the priests on hand to meet him had been participants in the recent canonization festival, and they tended to view the two events as parts of a single commemoration of medieval Rus. One arch-conservative priest named Seraphim, for instance, wrote a five-hundred-page book chronicling the canonization festival and the Romanov festival together.[6]

The mood of the missionary clergy was recorded in a series of articles that appeared in the journal *Missionerskii sbornik*. Some writers celebrated the Romanov commemoration by describing Nicholas as a leader of the Orthodox mission, the successor to Vladimir and Constantine. His family ancestor Michael Feodorovich was said to have accepted the crown with a promise to preserve Orthodoxy "in its purity." Likewise, Nicholas could even be regarded as a leader of the modern mission, and his expressed thoughts about the faith should be remembered by pastors and missionaries during the Romanov tercentenary.[7] Metropolitan Vladimir of St Petersburg hailed the Romanovs' support of missionary work in places such as Siberia during a ceremony in the capital's Kazan Cathedral. "Beloved Sovereign," the prelate proclaimed, "you are the bearer of the heavy royal cross. And on many occasions you have borne witness to your people that only in close relationship with the Church can the good of the people be achieved. Only in Orthodoxy is there salvation for our nationality. Only in the inseparable union of Church and state is there strength and power for our native Rus."[8]

Behind these supportive pronouncements about Nicholas, there was the recognition that tsarist statecraft was becoming disengaged from the historical goals of the mission. Yet clerical Orthodox patriots continued to hail him as an apostle-like leader. Even Pavel Svetlov, a liberal theologian, commemorated the Romanov Dynasty by calling autocracy the "logical consequence of Christian teaching about earthly authority." Like others, he considered the status of the Russian tsar in light of the example of ancient Israel. But what justified the Russian tsar's rule above all was the fact that he served the Church. He is "raised and will always dwell beneath the canopy of the Orthodox Church, its prayers, blessings, and grace." In consideration of the

Romanov tercentenary, then, Russians were reminded "that at the basis of our way of life must be placed the foundation of Christian truth and justice. That which is truly useful and beneficial for the Russian state organism can be only such activity which is established upon the basis of agreement and not discord with the Orthodox Church." A tsar who served the goals of the Church was thus an essential element of "Russian national self-consciousness."[9]

By far the most enthusiastic supporter of autocracy and the image of the apostle-like tsar was Abbot Seraphim. A monk from the Perm diocese of Siberia, he came to assume an active career in publishing and wrote a book on the First All-Russian Congress of Monks in 1912. This event was not as obscure as it might seem. It was organized by Bishop Nikon and other Orthodox patriots such as Skvortsov to discuss how monasticism might be strengthened to serve as a force for cultural leadership in modern Russia. Seraphim researched the public's response to the congress and claimed to find considerable interest among both conservative and liberal newspapers.[10] He also supported missionary affairs and attended the First All-Russian Congress of the External Mission in Kazan.[11] In 1913, he participated personally in the commemorations of Germogen and the Romanovs. He attended the canonization festival in the Kremlin and then followed reports about the tsar's trip through central Russia.

Abbot Seraphim's experiences of 1913 were recorded in the long book titled *A Festival of Duty*.[12] In a detailed hagiographical discussion of Germogen, he likened the seventeenth-century patriarch to the prophets of ancient Israel. In particular, he noted, the patriarch's role in facilitating Michael Romanov's accession to the throne resembled that of Samuel. He had blessed Saul and expected that the Israelite tsar would maintain loyalty to the will of God, disregarding "his own considerations and the will of the people."[13] When Saul forgot his responsibilities to God, Samuel was called to install David as a new tsar. This lesson was directly applicable to the new Israel. "The Church teaches that all authority is from God," Seraphim stated. "But to the Russian tsar is given a special significance, distinguishing him from the other authorities of the world. He is not only the sovereign of his own country and the leader of his people. He is established by God as the guardian and preserver of the Orthodox Church."[14] In making these claims, Seraphim referred to the works of the late Archbishop Nikanor of Kherson, who had helped to organize the baptism festival of 1888 and had described Russia as the new Israel.[15]

As he was concerned mainly with outlining an Orthodox vision of the national community in his chronicle, Seraphim, like so many clerical

Orthodox patriots before him, inevitably came to the inconvenient teaching about the universal Church. Without tarrying with New Testament passages such as Colossians or the Good Samaritan, he selected a small number of quotations that in his mind proved that "Jesus Christ was Himself the greatest patriot." Christ's teachings, in fact, demonstrated that He "cared most of all for members of his own nationality."[16] This was proven by Gospel passages such as Matt 15:24, where Christ spoke of being sent only to the house of Israel. This passage, serving as the epigraph for Skvortsov's journal *Missionerskoe obozrenie,* had long been interpreted by clerical Orthodox patriots as a summons to promote a national self-consciousness based on ecclesial identity. In light of such passages, asked Seraphim, "How can one not be a patriot? For patriotism is love for the fatherland in which we live, love toward our own people, love toward our national customs and manners. This love is the air of the soul, which God has placed in our heart beside that for family and humanity. It is thus understandable why all who have forgotten God appear as enemies of their native fatherland."[17] Examples in Russian history of this Orthodox patriotism included the national saints. In particular, he praised both Sergius of Radonezh and Vladimir Equal-to-the-Apostles.

After these patriotic prolegomena, Seraphim moved into the events that marked the twin commemorations of May. He provided a long narrative and commentary on the Germogen canonization, including some disparaging remarks about the "suffering Church of Antioch," from which Patriarch Gregory had arrived.[18] Most of his attention was not directed to the universal Church, however, but to Russia's national faith. Much of his text rambled from the example of Old Testament Israel to accounts of Russia's national saints.[19] His general conclusion after describing the Germogen canonization liturgy, and the thousands of native pilgrims who gathered outside of Uspensky Cathedral during it, was that "in truth our Orthodox Holy Rus still lives."[20] The latter half of the work was taken up by a long description of the tsar's journey to Moscow. While it added very little of interest, it did emphasize Nicholas's obligation as an apostle-like tsar. Seeing him as the defender of the faith, Seraphim claimed, the Russian people must honor autocracy "without limits."[21]

Seraphim also noted that Russia's Old Believers had commemorated the Germogen tercentenary the year before. He was especially sensitive to the fact that they were now making derogatory remarks about the official Church's separation from the national faith of the seventeenth century. Indeed, he and other leaders of the official Church had good reason to be defensive. Old Believer intellectuals were particularly critical about the official Church's

dramaturgical efforts to revive medieval Rus during the Germogen canonization festival. Some spoke scornfully about the contrived appearance
of "Holy Rus" in modern Moscow, stating that the festival atmosphere
appeared to have emerged "from a painting by Nesterov."[22] In the face of this
challenge, Seraphim insisted that the canonization demonstrated that official Orthodox patriotism possessed a national vision equally as vital as Old
Belief. He claimed that "schismatic Old Believers" had been misled by their
leadership into thinking that Germogen represented only a medieval form
of the national faith. On the contrary, his glorification by the modern official
Church "should demonstrate that the Orthodox Church did not break (and
never even thought to break) its connection with the pre-Nikonian Church.
It preserves precisely that faith which the first Muscovite patriarchs maintained."[23] In light of such patriotic protestations and a selective exegesis of
the New Testament, Seraphim thus produced a book that revealed as much
about the weaknesses of clerical Orthodox patriotism as its strengths.

Abbot Seraphim's book is one illustration of how efforts made to retain
the image of an apostle-like tsar approached a level of despair during the
festival year of 1913. On the eve of war, clerical Orthodox patriots made
virtually no effort to revise their commitment to autocracy, unmoved by or
oblivious to the alternative logic of the national faith that had been expressed
by religious intellectuals such as Soloviev, Nesterov, and Bulgakov. Their
desire to have the protection of the state had thus led them to an impasse.
Nicholas II, despite the encouraging words of missionary leaders, was not
going to mark the commemoration year with a repeal of the Paschal Edict.

As the summer passed and the memories of the Kremlin ceremonies
faded, then, clerical Orthodox patriots were again reminded of what they
had lost in 1905. In September, the Church organized still one more commemoration, this time of an event that long had preceded the formation of
Holy Rus but had always, until 1905, symbolized the status of the apostle-
like tsar.

IN THE TWILIGHT OF APOSTLE-LIKE STATECRAFT

The year 1913 marked sixteen hundred years since the date when St Constantine Equal-to-the-Apostles had issued the Edict of Milan. This edict, as
Nikon had noted during the Germogen canonization festival, was the event
that had established the Christian faith as a legal faith in the ancient Roman
Empire. It had been remembered by Russian missionaries as the moment
when the universal Church was given an apostle-like state to protect it.
Between 313 and 1905, Orthodox Christendom had possessed an apostle-like

tsar—first in Byzantium, then in Russia—who pledged to use the authority of the state to protect and even to disseminate the faith. The commemoration of an event that symbolized "the victory of Christianity over paganism" (as the Synod's order for the Edict of Milan commemoration stated) was a bitter reminder to many conservative missionaries and priests that the vital stream of Christian statecraft issuing from Byzantium had finally run into the sand of modern Russia.[24]

Despite this apparent *fait accompli,* a number of clerical writers marked the Edict of Milan commemoration with a renewed effort to recover apostle-like statecraft. A writer in the missionary journal *Vera i razum* acknowledged that Constantine's edict "was only about religious tolerance." Nevertheless, he claimed, "in the wake of this the legislative measures of Constantine, who within ten years became autocrat of the Roman Empire, step by step brought Christianity to the status of the predominant [*gospodstvuiushchei*] religion." The Edict of Milan, he claimed, "made Christianity a political force." What is more, it undermined "zoological divisions" between nationalities within the empire, allowing it to become unified around a single national faith. Thus its legacy was inherited centuries later by Russia. "Our Rus became the fruit of Constantine the Great's activity. From his successors (the Byzantine emperors), our princes—and first before all others St Vladimir—accepted Christianity as the new logic of statecraft. They thereby accepted the responsibility for the dissemination of Christianity to the people who, along with the community of Rus, were joined by a family of other peoples."[25]

Bishop Nikon, who had helped to organize the Holy Synod's Milan Edict anniversary commission, brought special attention to the decline of the Constantinian state legacy in modern Russia. In his commemorative article, he mournfully referred to "that freedom that our Sovereign has given us" in the Paschal Edict of 1905 and asked if it was really consistent with the intentions of the Milan Edict of 313. He did not refer personally to Tsar Nicholas, but any reference to the Russian nation by clerical Orthodox patriots necessarily included him.[26] As a leading missionary within the Church, Skvortsov also used the commemoration to reexpress his ideals for the tsar. In his interpretation the edict had given Christianity not only "freedom," but also "the right to be the predominant religion." He even took the occasion of this universal Church holiday to attack Roman Catholics for being "aliens" to the Orthodox within Christendom. Holy Rus, on the other hand, had the primary obligation to observe the anniversary faithfully. This obligation applied to its tsar also, for he was inseparable from the national community. The initiative for honoring Constantine, Skvortsov asserted, "should rest with the authority of the ruling Church. The Russian state, however, nursing the mother Church with love and care, should also demonstrate before all other peoples and states that it is not indifferent to the honoring of this great moment."[27]

Vostorgov's Edict of Milan commemoration was one of the most detailed. Interestingly, he used the Church's principle of universality to justify the state's protection of an official national faith. Because it embraced the Church's teaching that there was "neither Jew nor Greek" (here he was quoting Gal 3:28), Constantine's state was able to promote national integration the moment it acted to establish Christianity as the state religion. In contrast to the pious yet timid Nicholas, Constantine the Great in Vostorgov's mind was an ideal ruler, in whom "was felt a huge and indestructible force of will power." In fact, Constantine's apostle-like statecraft could be reduced to a simple slogan: "one God, one Church, one empire." Thus he was able to overcome the opposition of pagan political forces in his kingdom and promote the spread of Orthodoxy. In a reflection that had much to do with Vostorgov's view of the contemporary relationship between Nicholas and the State Duma, the archpriest stated that "Constantine knew that pagans were still more powerful than Christians, but he also knew that the truth is not located on the side of the majority."[28] Had there been patriotic unions in ancient Rome, one is tempted to speculate, Vostorgov might have taken this opportunity to praise them too.

Thus the Church's Orthodox patriots refused to jettison the principle of apostle-like statecraft even when there was little hope of retaining it. And, as if to scorn their reflections on the legacy of St Constantine, some of Russia's secular nationalists also entered the Edict of Milan commemoration. For them, the occasion provided an opportunity to emphasize the fact that the Russian nation was no longer defined by religious conformity. They saw the new Russia that had emerged from the medieval system of autocracy and religious uniformity as potentially much stronger, as the process of national integration now depended mainly on the more consistent force of ethnicity. For instance, the same publicist named Menshikov who had been criticized by clerical Orthodox patriots such as Nikon and Skvortsov for his indifference to the question of ecclesial self-consciousness actually appropriated the commemoration to promote religious freedom. Observing that some "Russians of the twentieth century" were claiming that an official faith must be protected by the state, he claimed that "Constantine Equal-to-the-Apostles adhered to another view." The ancient emperor's goal, he argued, had been nothing short of "freedom of religion."[29]

THE UNIVERSALISTIC ALTERNATIVE

And so the year 1913 ended, leaving clerical Orthodox patriotism in a state of confusion. As 1914 began, some among the clergy concluded that hopes of forming a national community under the missionary leadership of the Church were unrealistic. Furthermore, the presuppositions of this entire project were increasingly called into question. A leading journal such as *Tserkovnyi vestnik* drew attention to the fact that the year had been plagued by ongoing troubles. As the editors noted, the Germogen festival had been a potentially bright moment. "But this saint with his love of the holy faith and Holy Rus . . . lived in such a remote time when the Russian Church did not suffer her modern illnesses." The presence of the Patriarch of Antioch also highlighted Church issues that could not be solved by patriotism. Instead of paying homage to the pinnacle of Orthodox Christendom, Gregory had found a national Church sinking under the weight of an apostasy that "within the past year contin-ued to develop with remarkable speed in comparison with former times." Finally, the tsarist state, instead of serving the Church as the preserver and disseminator of the faith, continued to repress efforts to recover "the invio-lable canonical Church structure" lost under Peter the Great.[30]

Though most of the conservative Church leaders who had participated in the commemorations of 1913 maintained their attachment to the tsar and the memory of his apostle-like rule, others among the clergy had by now begun to look to other ways of defining modern Russia. Even those who sought to advance the ideals of the spiritual mission could propose alternatives to the formula of a national faith. One writer opened his commemoration of the Edict of Milan by lamenting that modern Russians "are beginning to return to the dissipated customs of the pagan world." His purpose, however, was to cause contemporaries to appreciate the universal significance of the anniver-sary. Both the West and the East had shared in the errors of history, he stated. But "the cross of Golgotha was raised for all of the world." Therefore the anniversary of Christianity's triumph should be an inspiration for both the Orthodox and the heterodox.[31]

An Orthodox priest in the western borderlands also rejected the ideals of the national faith and the apostle-like tsar. In his case, the Romanov tercente-nary served as an occasion to disseminate what he called "true patriotism." In his account, Russia could not be unified by a national faith, because the Chris-tian faith by definition is universal. "True Orthodoxy," he told his parish-ioners, "must not exclude respect for other Christian confessions." What is more, he noted, the tsar had recently shown that he was prepared to honor religious differences in modern Russia. Since the Paschal Edict, Nicholas had himself marked the passing of apostle-like statecraft by occasionally visiting Roman Catholic churches. He had even gone so far, the priest claimed, as to accept the "blessing of a Catholic priest."[32] Whether this was true or not, it is noteworthy that some Church leaders could use the commemorations of 1913 to promote a universalistic and even ecumenical alternative to the ideals of clerical Orthodox patriotism.

And as some came to question the image of Holy Rus, they even began to consider whether its union of ecclesial self-consciousness and national self-consciousness was not, in the end, unholy. In an article titled "Nationalism and the Moral Ideals of Christianity," written in 1914 less than three months before the beginning of the First World War, a priest named V. Beliaev challenged the very foundation of clerical Orthodox patriotism. He opened by noting the phenomenal success of nationalism and the rise of national self-consciousness in the modern world, especially in "our state and social life." The influence of this force was not limited to the laity, he noted, but had even found its way "into the life of the Church." After discussing the origins of nationalism in the French Revolution and its tendency to isolate collective communities from one another, he turned to its value measured from the view of Orthodox Christianity. "Moralists," he claimed, were wrong to defend the principle of national loyalty by invoking the Christian principles of sacrifice and love for others. The Christian, he claimed, must "struggle against national inclinations."

Beliaev was very conscious of the arguments of clerical Orthodox patriots—from Archbishop Nikanor in 1888 to Abbot Seraphim in 1913—that the New Testament prescribes national self-consciousness and patriotism. He even took the time to discuss the writings of Archbishop Antony of Volynia. Many had argued that Christ's command to love others as oneself justified the promotion of national self-consciousness and a feeling of patriotic loyalty. The commandment to love others, Beliaev argued to the contrary, actually called one to love those of other nationalities just as much as one's own. Furthermore, he argued, the use of highly selective biblical quotations was misleading. The teaching of Christ about love, when considered from more than one dimension, could not rightfully be used by the Church's Orthodox patriots. "Christ the Savior declared unambiguously that he was sent first of all to the lost sheep of the house of Israel. But from a larger perspective, from the entire content of Christian revelation and the history of the Church, it is perfectly clear that his words do not express a moral principle or a commandment." Having dismantled one of the key arguments of patriotic exegesis, Beliaev turned to the New Testament passage that he believed was much more relevant for the Church to consider when evaluating the significance of national self-consciousness.

His words, with which I will conclude this narrative, indicated an entirely different approach to the problems of the modern Church than that which had been promoted, with such persistence, by Russia's prerevolutionary clerical Orthodox patriots. "The significance of St Paul's teaching comes immediately to mind," he wrote. "It states that within the Church there is 'neither Greek nor Jew.' In regard to national differences, this principle has nothing less than the same significance as the commandment to love one's neighbor as oneself. Holding this principle, Christianity therefore represents the moral opposite to any teaching that excessively promotes a natural feeling of love toward one's own nationality."[33]

Illustrations: Part II

Fig. 2.1 *Alexander III Receiving Rural District Elders in the Yard of Petrovsky Palace in Moscow* by Ilya Repin, 1886. Alexander (r. 1881–1894), the son of assassinated Emperor Alexander II (r. 1855–1881) and father of the last tsar, Emperor Nicholas II (r. 1881–1917), represented a sharp turn toward conservatism in late imperial Russian statecraft.

Fig. 2.2 Metropolitan Antony (Krapovitsky) was a leading figure in the Orthodox Church both before and after the Revolution.

Fig. 2.3 Archpriest John Vostorgov was known to have stated, "Russia . . . is Holy Russia."

Fig. 2.4 Tsar Nicholas II and Tsaritsa Alexandra at the Petersburg Bicentennial Ball of 1903. Unlike his English relative Queen Victoria, Nicholas preferred costumes that suggested the Russian Empire's national unity.

Fig. 2.5 Participants in the St Petersburg Bicentennial Ball of 1903. This event marked the two-hundred-year anniversary of the founding of the city, Peter the Great's "window on the West." Paradoxically, instead of costumes from the Westernized Russian court, the imperial organizers chose those from the era of Peter's father, Tsar Alexei (r. 1645–1676).

Fig. 2.6 Nicholas II helps carry the reliquary during the canonization of St Seraphim in 1903. The last tsar was devoutly Orthodox and a strong supporter of the revival of the Church as evidenced by his role in the saint's canonization ceremonies in Sarov.

Fig. 2.7 Nicholas II blesses troops in 1905. In this photo, Tsar Nicholas, who had participated actively in the canonization ceremonies of St Seraphim of Sarov in 1903, offers an icon of the newly glorified Russian saint for veneration by soldiers departing from Peterhof (near St Petersburg) for the Far East during the Russo-Japanese War.

Fig. 2.8 Procession at the consecration of the Resurrection of Christ Church (popularly known as the Church of the Savior on Spilled Blood) in St Petersburg, 1907. This was the most dramatic of all efforts to architecturally "medievalize" the modern empire's capital. Nicholas II personally participated in the consecration ceremonies.

Fig. 2.9 Church of the Savior on the Waters in St Petersburg is another good example of Orthodox patriotism and the medievalization of the capital on the eve of the Revolution. Vasnetsov was commissioned to paint many of its icons.

Fig. 2.10 Feodorovsky Cathedral (also known as the Romanov Tercentenary Cathedral) in St Petersburg. Completed in 1913, this church was built to commemorate the Romanov Dynasty, which celebrated its three-hundred-year anniversary that year.

Fig. 2.11 Church of Saints Nicholas and Alexander Nevsky in St Petersburg. Built by the Imperial Orthodox Palestine Society in the Russian medieval style that also characterized the Church of Mary Magdalene in Jerusalem, this church's design supported the view of Orthodox patriots that a close bond existed between Holy Russia and the Holy Land. It represented architecturally the connection between Russian nationality and the universal mission of the Orthodox Church.

Fig. 2.12 A procession of the Union of the Russian People in 1907. Patriotic unions appeared in the wake of the October Manifesto of 1905 and the challenge presented by radical parties in the newly created State Duma. In this photograph, a priest is leading a public procession of the patriotic union.

Fig. 2.13 Portrait of Vladimir Soloviev. The preeminent philosopher of his time, Soloviev exercised enormous influence on the prerevolutionary generation of Russian intellectuals.

Fig. 2.14 Portrait of Sergei Bulgakov. A philosopher and economist, Bulgakov was a supporter of Marxism until the early twentieth century, when he turned first to idealism and then to Orthodox Christianity. What he called "Holy Russia" was a nation in which there was no need for autocracy.

Fig. 2.15 *Philosophers* by Mikhail Nesterov, 1917. The artist Nesterov took a keen interest in the development of what he considered a particularly Russian expression of philosophy and theology. Here he depicts the philosopher Sergei Bulgakov and the theologian and future New Martyr Pavel Florensky.

Fig. 2.16 *Holy Russia* (*Svyataya Rus*) by Mikhail Nesterov. This, the artist's most ambitious and explicit effort to depict the ideals of Orthodox patriotism, was completed in the revolutionary year of 1905. It shows Christ flanked on one side by saints of Russia and the broader universal Church, and on the other side by representatives of modern Russia. Among the latter are pious Orthodox believers and, in their Western dress (a top hat is visible), religious scoffers.

Fig. 2.17 Icon of St Germogen. Canonized in connection with the Romanov tercentenary of 1913, St Germogen had long been revered for his defense of an Orthodox Russia during the Time of Troubles. The lay Orthodox patriot Vasnetsov was commissioned to paint the first icon of the saint.

Fig. 2.18 Patriarch Germogen's cell in Chudov Monastery, Moscow Kremlin. St Germogen died in this cell in 1612 at the hands of Roman Catholic Poles, who had invaded Russia and captured the capital city during the Time of Troubles.

Fig. 2.19 Icon of the Council of New Martyrs of Russia Who Suffered under the Communist Yoke (ROCOR). This icon, commissioned for canonization ceremonies in 1981, includes Orthodox patriots such as Nicholas II and John Vostorgov.

Fig. 2.20 Icon of the Council of New Martyrs and Confessors of Russia Known and Unknown (Moscow Patriarchate). In 2000 the Moscow Patriarchate formally canonized the New Martyrs and Confessors of Russia. This icon, commissioned for the event, likewise depicts Nicholas II and John Vostorgov.

CONCLUSION

In this study I have tried to show how the Orthodox Church exhibited a burst of vitality and ambition in the final decades of the Russian Empire. Clerical Orthodox patriots were only one element in the resurgence that characterized Church life after the Great Reforms. I have made only passing reference, for instance, to the efforts made to reform Church administration and governance during these decades. The period between 1905 and 1917 especially was characterized by a strong though ultimately incomplete movement to reform the Church in order to help it minister more effectively to Russia's increasingly restless society. The most notable activities centered on efforts to reform liturgical life, to convene a national Church council, and to reestablish the patriarchate. This direction in Church activity was often dominated by liberals. It is their activities that historians have usually considered when assessing the strength of the Church on the eve of the Revolution.

My study has addressed another group of Church leaders. Clerical Orthodox patriots were in almost all cases conservative and resisted change in both society and the Church. There were some exceptions, such as Pavel Svetlov, who supported liberal reforms in the Church and promoted the position of the white clergy. Archbishop Antony (Khrapovitsky) also sought limited reforms such as the restoration of the patriarchate. On the whole, however, it was conservative missionary priests and prelates who most shaped debates about Russian nationality. Seeking a means for strengthening ecclesial loyalty and reeling from the specter of a religious free-for-all after the Paschal Edict, their attitudes toward the encroachments of the modern world were mostly negative. For this reason historians have been inclined to dismiss their contribution to history as unproductive, at best.

There is some justification for this, to be sure. Their uncompromising defense of the failing autocracy may have been short sighted, and in any case only served to isolate them further from much of society. More problematic was their aversion to anything that resembled novelty or foreign invention. Their attack on "rootless cosmopolitanism" especially, though never clearly articulated, revealed their reluctance to address productively the forces that were beginning to confront modern Russia. Most troubling of all was the occasional use of anti-Semitic rhetoric that found a place in their movement. Archbishop Antony, it should be said, distinguished himself (along with St John of Kronstadt) by vehemently denouncing pogroms as un-Christian. Likewise, Nikon monitored the anti-Semitic movement among Russia's secular nationalists and more than once intervened to chastise them with a pastoral "word of truth."[1] Nevertheless, many conservative Church figures such as Vladimir Skvortsov injured the Church's reputation by issuing angry and unreasonable words against the Jews. After the Revolution, it was often this misbehavior that was used by the communists to justify the new persecution. Lenin, in his infamous order to launch the Church valuables persecution of 1922, spoke explicitly of what he and others called the "black hundred clergy."

For all of their conservative and in some cases reactionary character, however, the clergy who embraced Orthodox patriotism demonstrated a considerable amount of vision and energy. Less open-minded than the liberal clergy, they were far more ambitious in shaping the public's collective consciousness and establishing a model of community that would help Russia as she entered the twentieth century. For this effort, I would argue, they deserve as much consideration as famous liberals such as Metropolitan Antony of St Petersburg or the Group of Thirty-Two Petersburg Priests.[2] Having harnessed the power of nationality during the baptism festival of 1888, they consciously entered public life as actively as, or more actively than, any other discernible clerical group of the time. From their example it is possible to conclude that the Church was not always a victim to the advance of modern history. Rather than shrink from or capitulate to this advance, Church leaders took the lead in trying to shape the troubled empire into a better and more united community.

Like the liberals, of course, they failed to win all of Russia over to the Orthodox Church. In the 1913 Germogen canonization festival, clerical Orthodox patriotism did not mobilize the public as effectively as it had during the baptism festival of 1888. What is more, other elements external to the movement emerged during that year that called its viability into doubt. Tsar Nicholas II, while remaining deeply pious and devoted to the Church, could no longer offer it protection from an increasingly hostile and revolutionary society. For their part the nationalists proved to offer little more than verbal support for the Church's goals. The construction of the Temple of St Germogen in the Kremlin and a warm response in *Russkoe znamia* were the limits of support provided by the patriotic unions, who had never been deeply committed to the principle of ecclesial universality. Thus the making of Holy Russia remained an unfinished project on the eve of the Revolution.

Nevertheless, the achievements of clerical Orthodox patriotism were considerable. In the short term, the clergy were able to win broad acceptance for the model of nationality it called Holy Rus. Like an icon, this model was designed to provoke a change of heart in those who encountered it. Any effort to gauge the influence of Holy Rus on the mind of the public, as I have noted throughout, must remain tentative. Nevertheless, in many cases substantial results clearly seem to have been achieved. What is more, in the long term Holy Rus survived in the face of alternative models of the nation that often sought to destroy it. Buried by the faithful martyrs who perished in Russia under communism or carried abroad by faithful exiles, the icon was preserved and cherished. At the Russian Orthodox St Serge Theological Institute in Paris, for instance, the clergy's model of Holy Rus was preserved and reproduced by such theologians as George Fedotov, whose studies of medieval Rus and topical essays repeatedly employed the rhetoric of Orthodox patriotism.[3] For its part, the Russian Orthodox Church Outside of Russia continued the legacy of 1888 by establishing an annual St Vladimir festival in its adopted home of Yugoslavia (where the exiled Antony served as First Hierarch), and when forced to move its headquarters to the United States after the Second World War, brought the liturgical arts of Orthodox patriotism with it. Holy Trinity Monastery in Jordanville, New York, became a "temple-monument" to the same vision of an authentically Russian form of Orthodox architecture promoted in St Petersburg under the last tsar. In 1982 the Church Abroad canonized several clerical Orthodox patriots, including John Vostorgov as well as Tsar Nicholas II and his immediate family.

And finally, during the decline and fall of communism, Holy Rus would again be elevated as an icon before the Russian public by a liberated Orthodox clergy. The millennium baptism festival of 1988 was clearly an effort to restore the national faith celebrated one hundred years earlier in 1888, and it self-consciously emulated its late-imperial precedent, far exceeding it in cultural and political impact.[4] The Church's support for the law "on historical religions" passed by the State Duma in 1997 also signaled a revival in efforts to establish a kind of apostle-like statecraft, even if the institution of a true apostle-like tsar had long ago perished with the murder of Nicholas II.

Indeed, the canonization of hundreds of new martyrs by the Moscow Patriarchate in 2000 was profoundly shaped by Orthodox patriotism. The statement titled "The Social Principles of the Russian Orthodox Church," issued by the Bishops Council to accompany the canonization festival in Moscow, represents one of the most significant documents in the history of the Orthodox Church in modern times. It gave a full account of clerical Orthodox patriotism by quoting the now familiar key passages of Scripture, by pointing to the example of Old Testament Israel, and by upholding the example of Russia's national saints. In full consistency with their prerevolutionary predecessors, the Orthodox Church's postcommunist clerical leadership invoked the universalistic principle to challenge and restrain the renewed force of post-Soviet ethnic nationalism. "The Church," claimed the Bishops Council, "unites within herself the universal and the national." Accordingly, it condemned "interracial enmity" and other expressions of secular nationalism simply as "sinful."[5]

The festal icon commissioned for the canonization resembled that produced by the Church Abroad in 1982, and it offered a remarkable visual witness to the continued life of Holy Rus in the twenty-first century. In this icon, new martyrs who had advanced clerical Orthodox patriotism before the Revolution, such as John Vostorgov and Nicholas II, were joined in communion with some of the movement's most beloved national saints, including Vladimir Equal-to-the-Apostles, Sergius of Radonezh, Seraphim of Sarov, and Patriarch Germogen. And thus, leaving the troubled twentieth century behind, Russia's Orthodox clergy returned to the making of Holy Russia.

ACKNOWLEDGMENTS

This book was completed with the assistance of various persons and institutions, and I would like to acknowledge them here. The majority of my research was conducted in Russia through a Research Fellowship from the International Research and Exchanges Board (IREX) in 1995 and 1996. Additional research and much of the writing were supported with a Reed-Smith Dissertation Fellowship from the University of California at Davis in 1996 and 1997. A travel grant from Davis in 1997 enabled me to participate in a conference and share my research with several other scholars.

My research in Russia was made much easier by the friendly and able staffs of the Russian National Library, the Russian State Historical Archive (RGIA), and the St Petersburg Spiritual Academy. At the Russian National Library two bibliographers, Sergei Yurevich Baranov and Nikita Lvovich Yeliseev, were especially helpful to me in locating publications and discussing Russian intellectual history. At the Russian State Historical Archive, I was greatly assisted in the reading room by Serafima Igorevna Varekhova and Tamara Yegorova, who both endured my poor command of the Russian language and helped me locate useful files. My work in the archive's catalog room was aided by the eager and friendly assistance of Slava Nosov and Vladimir Vyacheslavovich Bersenev. Outside of libraries and archives I benefited from the original views of Sergei Firsov and Nikolai Pokrovsky on the place of the Orthodox Church in Russian history. Finally, I would like especially to acknowledge the generous support of Boris Mironov, whose warmth and humor were a great blessing to me during my first weeks in St Petersburg.

In the United States my work benefited from the advice of many professors, friends, and colleagues. At a number of professional conferences, I have gained valuable insights into Russian history and the place of my topic within it from Aaron Michaelson, Jennifer Wynot, Jennifer Hedda, George

Kosar, Scott Kenworthy, Steve Duke, William Comer, Nicholas Breyfogle, Heather Coleman, Greg Gaut, John Basil, Geoffrey Hosking, Theophilus Prousis, Nadieszda Kizenko, and Theofanis Stavrou. While I was a lecturer at Fordham University, Bernice Rosenthal was kind enough to read the entire manuscript and make extensive comments upon it. The V. Rev. Thomas Hopko, Dean Emeritus of St Vladimir's Orthodox Theological Seminary in New York and the Rev. Vadim Pismenny also offered valuable assistance and encouragement. At Davis, Carl Sjovold offered a very sharp eye in reading my chapters, and his comments about the direction of my research, made in some cases across a chessboard, were very helpful. My friend Daniel McMahon offered encouragement by mail from distant Taiwan during much of the research and writing. I am especially grateful for the support of my friend David Foote, whose approach to history, while concentrated in a field very different from my own (early medieval Italy), was a great encouragement to me.

I want also to express my gratitude to the editorial staff of Holy Trinity Publications in Jordanville, New York. Having shelved this work after entering the priesthood, I might never have presented it for publication without the encouragement of Nicholas Chapman, whom I literally bumped into at a church conference in Seattle, Washington. His wife Nina Chapman was instrumental in helping me prepare the manuscript, and both of them worked very hard to assure that it met the high standards of the press. Archimandrite Luke (Murianka) was also involved in every stage of the manuscript's preparation, and I would like to thank him for his support and patience.

I am also indebted to my students at Fordham, Davis, California State University at Sacramento, Northwest University, Seattle University, Loyola Marymount University, and, most recently, Saint Katherine College for giving me the opportunity to develop my arguments within the context of lectures and directed readings on Russian history and Orthodox Church history.

My dissertation committee offered many useful observations and insights. The late Nicholas V. Riasanovsky of the University of California at Berkeley was kind enough to sit on the committee despite his retirement, and his command of Russian intellectual history and nationalism helped me to develop several of my arguments. Robert Crummey of Davis was extraordinarily helpful. At all times he showed a ready interest in my topic, provided sympathetic advice, and offered personal encouragement. The late Daniel Brower of Davis served as the committee chairman and met with me regularly during all stages of the work. Above all, I wish to thank my dear friend John Farrell. His critical evaluation of several chapters resulted in substantial improvements to the text, and his intelligent comments helped shape the overall argument. His generosity and sympathy have been inexhaustible, and I shall always feel deeply indebted to him.

It is impossible to acknowledge adequately the contributions made to my work by my wife Yelena. Entering my life during the book's earliest stages, she became a constant source of intellectual inspiration and emotional strength, contributing enormously to its ultimate completion. In my mind I simply cannot separate its creative development from the strolls she and I made through the streets of St Petersburg, often during breaks from research at the library, nor can I imagine the writing process in Davis without remembering her sympathy and unwavering love.

Finally, I wish to express deep gratitude to my parents, Gordon and Jananne Strickland. My professional training in history would have been inconceivable without their unconditional love and support, and it is to them that I dedicate this book.

NOTES

Introduction

1. The tsar's war manifesto was printed in most major newspapers and journals. See, for instance, *Novoe vremia* 13777 (July 21, 1914).

2. The most recent effort to provide a comprehensive history of Orthodox patriotism is Wil van den Bercken, *Holy Russia and Christian Europe: East and West in the Religious Ideology of Russia*, trans. John Bowden (London: SCM Press, 1999). An interesting introduction to the rise of national self-consciousness during the medieval period can be found in Paul Bushkovich, "The Formation of a National Consciousness in Early Modern Russia," *Harvard Ukrainian Studies* 10 (1986): 355–76. The origins of the Third Rome doctrine are treated with adequate attention to their religious context in Dimitri Stremooukhoff, "Moscow the Third Rome: Sources of the Doctrine," in *The Structure of Russian History: Interpretive Essays*, ed. Michael Cherniavsky (New York: Random House, 1970), 108–25. Also of interest is Joel Raba, "Moscow—The Third Rome or the New Jerusalem?" *Forshungen zur osteuropaischen Geschichte* 50 (1995): 297–307. For an account of Metropolitan Macarius's role in shaping Muscovite political ideology under Ivan IV, see David B. Miller, "The Velikie Minei Chetii and the Stepennaia Kniga of Metropolitan Macarius and the Origins of Russian National Consciousness," *Forschungen zur osteuropaeischen Geschichte* 26 (1979): 263–382. Macarius's ideological and literary activities are also set in their sixteenth-century religious context in Robert O. Crummey, *The Formation of Muscovy, 1304–1613* (London: Longman, 1987), 137–39.

3. According to Nicholas Riasanovsky, Orthodoxy served early Slavophiles such as Khomiakov as "the content and gauge of Russia, Russian culture, and the Russians." Nicholas V. Riasanovsky, *Russia and the West in the Teaching of the Slavophiles: A Study in Romantic Ideology* (Cambridge, Mass.: Harvard University Press, 1952), 75. Dostoevsky's use

of Orthodoxy to define Russian character has been widely studied. For an interesting account, see Wayne Dowler, *Dostoevsky, Gregor'ev, and Native Soil Conservatism* (Toronto: University of Toronto Press, 1982).

4. Fyodor Dostoevsky, *Demons*, trans. Richard Pevear and Larissa Volokhonksy (New York: Vintage Press, 1994), 250–52.

5. Michael Cherniavsky, *Tsar and People: Studies in Russian Myths,* 2nd ed. (New York: Random House, 1969).

6. Matt 28:19. This passage is read, significantly, at every Orthodox baptism, as well as every year on Holy and Great Saturday.

7. Col 3:11. Paul makes a similar statement in Gal 3:28.

8. The standard teaching about the universal Church before the period of the Great Reforms can be found in the two-volume study of Orthodox theology by Archbishop Macarius (Bulgakov). D. B. Macarius, *Pravoslavno-dogmaticheskoe bogoslovie,* 2nd ed. (St Petersburg: 1857), 2:144–48.

9. The Great Reforms were a series of far-reaching measures implemented during the reign of Tsar Alexander II with the aim of improving the conditions of Russian life. The best known of these was the emancipation of the serfs.

10. Geoffrey Hosking, *Russia: People and Empire, 1552–1917* (Cambridge, Mass.: Harvard University Press, 1997).

11. The Church's frustrated experience with the reforms is discussed in Gregory L. Freeze, *The Parish Clergy in Nineteenth-Century Russia: Crisis, Reform, Counter-Reform* (Princeton: Princeton University Press, 1983).

12. See Donald Treadgold, "Russian Orthodoxy and Society," in *Russian Orthodoxy under the Old Regime,* ed. Robert L. Nichols and Theofanis George Stavrou (Minneapolis: University of Minnesota Press, 1978), 21–43.

13. Gregory L. Freeze, "Handmaiden of the State? The Church in Imperial Russia Reconsidered," *Journal of Ecclesiastical History* 36:1 (January 1985): 82–102.

14. Robert L. Nichols, "Church and State in Imperial Russia," *The Donald W. Treadgold Papers* 102 (February 1995): 7–22.

15. The Church's concerns with socialism are summarized in Gerhard Simon, "Church, State and Society," in *Russia Enters the Twentieth Century*, ed. Erwin Oberlaender et al. (New York: Schocken Books, 1971), 199–235. For its interest in educated public opinion, see Gregory L. Freeze, "'Going to the Intelligentsia': The Church and Its Urban Mission in Post-Reform Russia," in *Between Tsar and People: Educated Society and the Quest for*

Public Identity in Late Imperial Russia, ed. Edith W. Clowes et al. (Princeton: Princeton University Press, 1991), 215–32.

16. Michael Cherniavsky, "'Holy Russia': A Study in the History of an Idea," *American Historical Review* 63:3 (April 1958): 617–37.

17. The Time of Troubles was a period of social upheaval, dynastic crisis, and foreign invasion during the period 1598–1613.

18. Ibid.

19. In a letter discussing revolutionary developments during the upheavals in Europe in 1848, Aksakov claimed that "the reason Russia is called Holy Rus" is that unlike with Western nations, her national history traveled along "the truly Orthodox road of our Christian faith." Quoted in Peter K. Christoff, *K. S. Aksakov: A Study in Ideas* (Princeton: Princeton University Press, 1982), 134.

20. Anthony Smith, *National Identity* (Reno: University of Nevada Press, 1991), 38.

21. I. I. Vostorgov, "Molitva," in *Polnoe sobranie sochinenii* (Moscow: 1914–1916), 2:404–10; and "Pravoslavie v istorii Rossii," ibid., 3:147–57.

22. Some missionaries working among the latter were inclined to claim that sectarians were "in essence" members of Holy Rus, but so long as they maintained allegiance to their sect they could not participate fully in the national community. For a discussion of the image of Baptists as a foreign confessional community, see Heather J. Coleman, *Russian Baptists and Spiritual Revolution, 1905–1929* (Bloomington: Indiana University Press, 2005), 92–108. Orthodox missionaries regarded Russian Baptists as having "succumbed to a foreign deviation from the true Christian faith that was preserved in the Russian Orthodox Church." See Coleman, *Russian Baptists and Spiritual Revolution,* 101. The case of the Dukhobors is treated in Nicholas B. Breyfogle, *Heretics and Colonizers: Forging Russia's Empire in the South Caucasus* (Ithaca, N.Y.: Cornell University Press, 2005).

23. I. I. Vostorgov, "Rus sviataia," in *Polnoe sobranie sochinenii,* 3:602–6.

24. The ideal of medieval Rus for Slavophiles is discussed in Paul Bushkovitch, "Orthodoxy and 'Old Rus' in the Thought of S. P. Shevyrev," *Forschungen zur osteuropaeischen Geschichte* 46 (1992): 203–20.

25. Cherniavsky, *Tsar and People,* 1–4.

26. Richard S. Wortman, *Scenarios of Power: Myth and Ceremony in Russian Monarchy* (Princeton: Princeton University Press, 2000), 2:242.

27. E. J. Hobsbawm, *Nations and Nationalism since 1780: Programme, Myth, Reality* (Cambridge: Cambridge University Press, 1990), 67–73.

28. Steve Bruce, ed., *Religion and Modernization: Sociologists and Historians Debate the Secularization Thesis* (Oxford: Clarendon Press, 1992); and David Martin, *The Religious and the Secular: Studies in Secularization* (New York: Taylor and Francis, 1969).

29. Hans Kohn, *The Idea of Nationalism: A Study of Its Origins and Background* (New York: Macmillan, 1961), 574.

30. Benedict Anderson, *Imagined Communities: Reflections on the Origins and Spread of Nationalism*, 2d ed. (London: Verso, 1991), 7.

31. Carlton J. H. Hayes, *Nationalism: A Religion* (New York: Macmillan, 1960), 15.

32. Salo Wittmayer Baron, *Modern Nationalism and Religion* (New York: Harper, 1947).

33. See Carolyn Ford, *Creating the Nation in Provincial France: Religion and Political Identity in Brittany* (Princeton: Princeton University Press, 1993); and Suzanne K. Kaufman, "Miracles, Medicine and the Spectacle of Lourdes: Popular Religion and Modernity in Fin-de-Siecle France" (Ph.D. diss., Rutgers University, 1996). For the case of Catholic priests in Prussian Poland, see William W. Hagen, "National Solidarity and Organic Work in Prussian Poland, 1815–1914," *Journal of Modern History* 44:1 (1972): 38–64. Though concerned mainly with lay intellectuals, another work to discuss Catholic patriotic ideals is Andrzej Walicki, *Philosophy and Romantic Nationalism: The Case of Poland* (Oxford: Oxford University Press, 1982), 232–36.

34. N. Rozanov, "Liubov k otechestvu s khristianskoi tochki zreniia," *Moskovskiia tserkovnyiia vedomosti* 2 (January 14, 1896): 15–19.

Chapter 1

1. Though the Church had observed St Vladimir's feast day (July 15) for centuries, and had used the feast of the Procession of the Cross (August 1) as an occasion to remember Vladimir's birthday, no empire-wide celebration of the baptism event itself had ever been undertaken, through either religious or secular authority. This fact was not lost on the festival's celebrants. For a contemporary discussion of Vladimir and the baptism in the historical memory of Russians throughout the ages, see N. Petrov, "Chestvovanie pamiati sv. Vladimira na iuge Rossii v chastnosti v Kieve," in *Vladimirskii sbornik v pamiat deviatisotletiia kreshcheniia Rossii* (Kiev: 1888), 1–24.

2. "If I were to name the single historical event most significant for Russian identity and Russian nationalism, I would propose not Napoleon's invasion of Russia in 1812, not Stalin's turn to a limited and strictly

controlled nationalism in the late 1930s, not even the emancipation of the serfs in 1861, but the so-called baptism of the Rus in 988. . . . With the baptism, Orthodoxy became a central element in Russian history and culture, whether in the days of the Kievan princes, of the quasi-medieval appanage Rusia, of the Orthodox tsardom of Muscovy, of the Orthodoxy empire of the Romanovs, or even, as the enemy, during the communist regime, which tried desperately but failed to eradicate it." Nicholas V. Riasanovsky, *Russian Identities: A Historical Survey* (Oxford: Oxford University Press, 2005), 4–5.

3. For accounts of the baptism, see Nicholas Mikhailovich Karamzin, *Istoriia gosudarstva rossiiskogo* (Moscow: Kniga, 1989), 1:151–54; and S. M. Soloviev, *Istoriia Rossii s drevneishikh vremen* (Moscow: n.p. 1962), 184–86. Karamzin's history, which never reached the era of Peter, was supplemented by his famous unpublished "memoir" on medieval and modern Russian history, which assigned considerable significance to the medieval state. See *Karamzin's Memoir on Ancient and Modern Russia,* trans. Richard Pipes (New York: n.p. 1966). For opinions about Peter among Karamzin, Soloviev, and other nineteenth-century historians, see Nicholas V. Riasanovsky, *The Image of Peter the Great in Russian History and Thought* (Oxford: Oxford University Press, 1985).

4. John R. Gillis, "Memory and Identity: The History of a Relationship," in *Commemorations: The Politics of National Identity*, ed. John R. Gillis (Princeton: Princeton University Press, 1994), 3–26. Though very different national ideals were involved, the Russian commemoration of 1888 can be compared to the American commemoration of 1876. For the latter, see Lyn Spillman, *Nation and Commemoration: Creating National Identities in the United States and Australia* (Cambridge: Cambridge University Press, 1997).

5. Richard S. Wortman, *Scenarios of Power: Myth and Ceremony in Russian Monarchy* (Princeton: Princeton University Press, 1995–2000), 2:80.

6. For the argument that nationalists contrived the national traditions they disseminated, see Eric Hobsbawm, "Introduction: Inventing Traditions," in *The Invention of Tradition*, eds. Eric Hobsbawm and Terence Ranger (Cambridge: Cambridge University Press, 1983), 1–14.

7. Anthony Smith, "The 'Golden Age' and National Renewal," in *Myths and Nationhood*, eds. Geoffrey Hosking and George Schoepflin (London: Routledge in association with the School of Slavonic and East European Studies, University of London, 1997), 36–59.

8. For the imagery of a "faithful remnant" of Israel amid religious apostasy and national catastrophe, see, for example, Isa 1.

9. Nikanor's scholarly contribution to the mission was unusually productive. His publications included *Opisanie nekotorykh sochinenii napisannykh russkimi raskolnikam v polzu raskola*, 2 vols. (St Petersburg: 1861); *Mozhno li pozitivnym filosofskim metodam dokazivat bytie* (Kazan: 1871); and *Pravoslavie v istorii Rossii i shtunda* (Chernigov: 1884).

10. I. Kargopoltsov, *Vysokopreosviashchennyi Platon* (St Petersburg: 1894), 20.

11. F. Grachev, ed., *Pamiati Vysokopreosviashchennago Nikanora* (Moscow: 1891), 4; and A. S. Przheborovskii, "Rech," in *Pamiati Vysokopreosviashchennago Nikanora* (Kazan: 1891), 52–56.

12. Archbishop Nikanor, "Tserkov i gosudarstvo," *Tserkovnyia vedomosti* 1 (January 1, 1888): 8–16; *Tserkovnyia vedomosti* 2 (January 9, 1888): 25–31; and *Tserkovnyia vedomosti* 3 (January 16, 1888): 51–60.

13. Col 3:11. See also Gal 3:28.

14. Archbishop Nikanor, "Pouchenie," in *Poucheniia, besedy, rechi, vozzvaniia i poslaniia* (n.p.), 3:252–60.

15. The office of Chief Procurator was created under Peter the Great following the abolition of the patriarchate as part of his effort to bring the Church under greater state control.

16. Rossiiskaia Natsionalnaia Biblioteka (RNB), Otdel Rukopisei, f. 631, 1888 (August/December), l. 7.

17. Michael F. Hamm, *Kiev: A Portrait, 1800–1917* (Princeton: Princeton University Press, 1995).

18. On the rise of Ukrainian nationalism in the late nineteenth century, see Thomas M. Prymak, *Mykola Kostomarov: A Biography* (Toronto: University of Toronto Press, 1996).

19. This aspiration was expressed in "K chestvovaniiu 900-letiia kreshcheniia Rusi," *Tserkovnyia vedomosti* 20 (May 14, 1888): 538–40. Despite such hopes, St Vladimir Cathedral was not formerly opened until 1896.

20. Pobedonostsev, in a letter written after the festival, remarked upon the strong impression made by Vasnetsov's contributions to the cathedral's interior. RNB, Otdel Rukopisei, f. 631, 1888 (April/July), lines 195–96.

21. Rossiiskii Gosudarstvennyi Istoricheskii Arkhiv (RGIA), f. 796, op. 209, d. 1866, lines 400–403.

22. Its membership had included figures such as M. P. Pogodin and Ivan Aksakov. For a list of members as early as 1883, see *Pervye*

15 let sushchestvovaniia S-Peterburgskago Slavianskago Blagotvoritelnago Obshchestva (St Petersburg: 1883). For the history of the contemporary pan-Slavic movement, see Hans Kohn, *Pan-Slavism: Its History and Ideology*, 2nd ed (New York: Vintage Books, 1960); and Michael Boro Petrovich, *The Emergence of Russian Panslavism, 1856–1870* (New York: Columbia University Press, 1956).

23. *Den* 98 (July 17, 1888). The editors of *Syn otechestva* likewise noted that the society's emphasis contradicted some of the religious themes promoted by clerical organizers. *Syn otechestva* 185 (July 15, 1888).

24. I. I. Malyshevskii, *Zhitie sviatago ravnoapostolnago kniaza Vladimira* (St Petersburg: 1888). For some of the other saints' lives published on the occasion of the anniversary, see G. S. Debolskii, *Zhitie Ravnoapostolnago kniazia Vladimira* (St Petersburg: 1888); E. De-Witte, *Ravnoapostolnyi kniaz Vladimir Sviatoi* (Kovna: 1888); and M. Rubtsov, *O tom, kak zhili nashi dedy i kak kniaz Vladimir krestil Russkii narod* (Voronezh: 1887).

25. Malyshevskii, *Zhitie sviatago ravnoapostolnago kniaza Vladimira*, 46.

26. The society's activities in the 1888 celebration are discussed in *Kratkii ocherk deiatelnosti S-Peterburgskago Slavianskago Blagotvoritelnago Obshchestva za 25 let ego sushchestvovanii, 1868–1893 gg.*, ed. F. M. Istomin (St Petersburg: 1893), 66f.

27. The synod's special order for the celebration there was printed in *Tserkovnyia vedomosti* 8 (February 20, 1888): 40–41; and *Kievskiia eparkhialnyia vedomosti* 9–10 (March 1–8, 1888): 137–41.

28. *Vladimirskii sbornik v pamiat deviatisotletiia kreshcheniia Rossii.*

29. For the effect of the Great Reforms on municipal government during the period, see Daniel R. Brower, *The Russian City between Tradition and Modernity, 1850–1900* (Berkeley: University of California Press, 1990), 92–139.

30. A total of fifteen thousand rubles was raised. *Izvestiia kievskoi gorodskoi dumy* 6 (1888).

31. The role of the Kiev municipal government in organizing the festival is discussed in the editorial comments of *Trudy kievskoi dukhovnoi akademii* 9–10 (September/October): 1–7.

32. These appear throughout the commemorative volume *Prazdnovanie deviatisotletiia kreshcheniia russkago naroda v Kieve* (Kiev: 1888).

33. The telegram's long list of signatories began thus: "We, the undersigned, peasants of various districts, stock traders of Moscow, artels of the railroad—in sum about 10,000 people—and then other persons from other estates living in Moscow. . . ." When the long list was finally

completed, the names of the actual authors (who were not peasants or workers, but clergy and municipal authorities) brought the final total to more than twenty thousand. *Prazdnovanie,* 164–65.

34. The term appeared in many of the newspapers. By invoking it, participants were borrowing, in a way similar to Nikanor's use of the new Israel metaphor, a recognizable construction from the medieval past. For historic references to Kiev as a Russian Jerusalem, see R. Stupperich, "Kiev— das zweite Jerusalem," *Zeitschrift fuer Slavische Philologie* 12 (1935): 332–54.

35. "Dni iubileinago torzhestva v Kieve," *Trudy kievskoi dukhovnoi akademii* 9–10 (September/October 1888): 8–56.

36. Estimates of attendance for the St Seraphim canonization festival in Sarov vary greatly. Citing newspaper reports, Gregory Freeze has calculated the number to be approximately 300,000. Gregory L. Freeze, "Subversive Piety: Religion and the Political Crisis in Late Imperial Russia," *Journal of Modern History* 68 (June 1996), 308–50. Some ministerial documents reporting on the ceremonies issued more modest estimates. I myself have seen figures as low as 100,000 and 70,000. RGIA, f. 565, op. 5, d. 20284; and RGIA, f. 797, op. 73, 2 otd., 3 st., d. 389.

37. One of these was the metropolitan of Serbia. "Dni iubileinago torzhestva v Kieve," *Trudy kievskoi dukhovnoi akademii* 9–10 (September/ October 1988): 8–56.

38. *Trudy kievskoi dukhovnoi akademii* 9–10 (September/October 1888): 100–102.

39. "Privetstvie ot iaponskoi pravoslavnoi tserkvi," *Prazdnovanie,* 294–99.

40. V. Pevnitskii, "Slovo," *Prazdnovanie*, 65–80.

41. Virtually all religious periodicals and major newspapers reported on the ceremonies and addresses of Kiev in the weeks surrounding the festival. Photographs were published in *Prazdnovanie*.

42. *Prazdnovanie 900-letiia kreshcheniia Rusi: Vserossiiskoe torzhestvo* (Moscow: 1888), 35–36. Pamphlets such as this were usually short, inexpensive, and aimed at a simple audience holding a reverence for religious places and artifacts. Some, however, were purely mercenary. One inexpensive example contained little more than advertisements of city services. *V pamiat deviatisotletiia kreshcheniia Rusi* (Kiev) [no date]. On estimates of public attendance, see "Dni iubileinago torzhestva v Kieve," *Trudy kievskoi dukhovnoi akademii* 9–10 (September/October 1888): 8–56.

43. *Moskovskiia vedomosti* 199 (July 20, 1888).

44. He identified only two new saints since the time of Peter the Great: Mitrofan and Tikhon of Voronezh.

45. Metropolitan Platon, "Slovo," *Prazdnovanie,* 58–64.

46. M. Zlatoverkhovnikov, "Slovo," *Prazdnovanie,* 90–100. Archbishop Nikanor had also spoken of a transcendent and timeless national community in his *Tserkovnyia vedomosti* article. "The fatherland," he stated there, "is the name for that entity into which we were born and raised. It includes the entire aggregate of our fathers, who continue to inhabit it." Archbishop Nikanor, "Tserkov i gosudarstvo."

47. V. Pevnitskii, "Slovo," *Prazdnovanie,* 65–80.

48. N. Favorov, "Slovo," *Prazdnovanie,* 81–89.

49. The text of Pobedonostsev's speech and an account of the banquet are found in *Prazdnovanie,* 136–42. Additional information about the banquet and his speech can be found in *Moskovskiia tserkovnyiia vedomosti* 30 (July 24, 1888): 378–82.

50. Nicholas V. Riasanovsky, *Nicholas I and Official Nationality in Russia, 1825–1855* (Berkeley: University of California Press, 1959). Official Nationality is a conception of the Russian Empire favored by the state in response to the rise of revolutionary ideologies.

51. The cantata's text was printed in V. M. Buzni, ed., *Imperator Aleksandr III v russkoi poezii* (St Petersburg: 1912).

52. For the text of the tsar's telegram, which was printed in most of the journals reporting on the celebration, see *Prazdnovanie,* 145.

53. The parade terminated at the Neva, where the city's main river was itself sanctified. For descriptions of the capital's celebration, see *S-Peterburgskiia vedomosti* 193 (July 15, 1888); *Den* 98 (July 17, 1888); and *Syn otechestva* 185 (July 15, 1888).

54. After a pilgrimage to the Holy Land, Grand Duke Sergei Alexandrovich offered to serve as the society's official patron. For an account of the tsar's personal role in promoting the Palestine Society, see A. A. Dmitrievskii, ed., *Imperatorskoe Pravoslavnoe Palestinskoe Obshchestvo i ego deiatelnost za itekushchuia chetvert veka (1882–1907)* (St Petersburg: 1907).

55. The ceremonial opening of the chapter is described in *Moskovskiia tserkovnyiia vedomosti* 21 (May 22, 1888).

56. Archbishop Macarius, "Slovo v den prazdnovaniia deviatisotletiia kreshcheniia Rusi," *Donskiia eparkhialnyia vedomosti* 15 (August 1, 1888): 587–93.

57. I. Novitskii, "Slovo v den prazdnovaniia 900-letiia kreshcheniia Rusi—15 iiulia 1888 goda," *Kurskiia eparkhialnyia vedomosti* 29 (July 23, 1888): 461–73.

58. T. Butkevich, "Slovo v den chestvovaniia deviatisotletiia kreshcheniia Rusi," *Vera i razum* 14 (July 1888): 69–78.

59. *Privetstvennyi adres po cluchaiu 900-letiia prosveshcheniia Russkago naroda Pravoslavnoiu veroiu* (Petrozavodsk: 1888).

60. The society had been organized in 1849. Its purpose was to promote the unity of Christians across confessional boundaries, a program that came to be known as ecumenism. For the text of its appeal, see "Adres Evangelicheskago Soiuza Ego Imperatorskomu Velichestvu Aleksandru III," *Tserkovnyiia vedomosti* 7 (February 13, 1888): 165–67. The petition was accompanied by the Chief Procurator's rebuttal.

61. *Tserkovnyiia vedomosti* 7 (February 13, 1888): 167–71.

62. Quoted in "Torzhestvo 900-letiia kreshcheniia sv. kniazia Vladimira i vsei Rusi v Khersone tavricheskom," *Pravoslavnoe obozrenie* (October 1888): 340–407.

63. Detailed discussions of addresses appeared in *Syn otechestva* 185 (July 15, 1888); *Russkiia vedomosti* 193 (July 15, 1888); *Den* 98 (July 17, 1888); *Moskovskiia vedomosti* 196 (July 17, 1888); and *Novoe vremia* 4446 (July 16, 1888).

64. Louise McReynolds, *The News under Russia's Old Regime: The Development of a Mass-Circulation Press* (Princeton: Princeton University Press, 1991), 44.

65. The coverage of *Strannik* was the most exhaustive. Its summer issues surveyed a vast amount of literature that had appeared during the year to honor the anniversary, including newspaper stories, journal articles, sermons, lives of St Vladimir, poems, and even historical novels.

66. *Den* 98 (July 17, 1888); *Novoe vremia* 4446 (July 16, 1888); and *Syn otechestva* 185 (July 15, 1888).

67. *Sankt-Peterburgskiia vedomosti* 196 (July 18, 1888).

68. *Moskovskiia vedomosti* 196 (July 17, 1888).

69. This theme inspired frequent use of the Third Rome doctrine. For one example, see *Novoe vremia* 4446 (July 16, 1888).

70. *Den* 97 (July 15, 1888).

71. *Russkie vedomosti* 193 (July 15, 1888).

72. V. S. Soloviev, "Vladimir Sviatoi i Khristianskoe Gosudarstvo," in *Sobranie sochinenii*, eds. S. M. Solovev and E. L. Radlov, 2nd ed. (St Petersburg: 1911–1914), 11:121–35; and "Otvet na korrespondentsiiu iz Krakova," ibid., 135–38.

73. For the fullest treatment of the proposal by Kireev himself, written after the affair had subsided, see his article "Po voprosu o sozdanii

vselenskago sobora," *Moskovskiia tserkovnyia vedomosti* 37 (September 11, 1888): 473–76. He had first floated the idea at the end of the preceding year. His qualifications for making such a recommendation were not as impertinent as they might seem. The general had made a reputation for himself as a leading advocate for reestablishing ties with Old Catholics, adherents of the Catholic faith who had broken with the papacy after its declaration of infallibility. For Kireev's research and essays on this topic, see A. A. Kireev, *Sochineniia* (St Petersburg: 1912), vol. 2. For a good survey of Kireev's interest in Slavophilism, see John D. Basil, "Alexander Kireev: Turn-of-the-Century Slavophile and the Russian Orthodox Church, 1890–1910," *Cahiers du Monde russe et sovietique* 32:3 (July/September 1991): 337–48.

74. The Church's antischismatic missionaries were naturally some of the first to object. For the reaction of the Brotherhood of St Peter the Metropolitan, see *Bratskoe slovo* 13 (September 1, 1888): 215–30.

75. *Moskovskiia tserkovnyia vedomosti* 27 (July 3, 1888): 333–40.

76. See, for example, the summer issues of *Tserkovnyia vedomosti.*

77. For a brief account of this event by one of the official Church's journals, see *Moskovskiia tserkovniia vedomosti* 37 (September 11, 1888). It is unclear whether the anniversary year played a symbolic role or not.

78. *Bratskoe slovo* 13 (September 1, 1888), 215–30.

79. S. O., "Pastyrskoe vrazumlenie staroobriadtsem," *Moskovskiia tserkovnyiia vedomosti* 33 (August 8, 1888): 422–23.

80. *Prazdnovanie,* 362–71.

81. Quoted in "Dni iubileinago torzhestva v Kieve," *Trudy kievskoi dukhovnoi akademii* 9–10 (September/October 1888): 8–56.

Chapter 2

1. The Russian word *ekklesiologiia* did not enter the lexical mainstream until the twentieth century, and the term most often used for this branch of theology in the nineteenth century was the simple construction "dogma about the Church" (*dogma o tserkvi*).

2. Vladimir Troitskii, *Ocherki iz istorii dogmata o tserkvi* (Sergiev Posad: 1912), 8.

3. Troitskii's textbook noted that the Holy Spirit and not human psychology is ultimately responsible for Church unity. Ibid., 30.

4. Ibid., iv.

5. Ibid., iii.

6. E. E. Golubinskii, *Istoriia kanonizatsii sviatykh v russkoi tserkvi* (Moscow: 1902), 90.

7. Ibid., 92–109. The sixteenth-century canonization of Russian saints is also discussed in Paul Bushkovitch, *Religion and Society in Russia: The Sixteenth and Seventeenth Centuries* (New York: Oxford University Press, 1992), 88 and passim; Robert O. Crummey, *The Formation of Muscovy, 1304–1613* (London: Longman, 1987), 131–39; and Nicholas V. Riasanovsky, *A History of Russia*, 4th ed. (Oxford: Oxford University Press, 1984), 36.

8. According to its autocephalous status, the Russian Church was free to conduct canonizations without the participation of the larger universal Church. For a discussion of the Church's rules for canonization, see "Kanonizatsiia," in *Khristianstvo: Entsiklopedicheskii slovar* (Moscow: Nauch, 1993), 1:673–79.

9. Robert Nichols, "The Friends of God: Nicholas II and Alexandra at the Canonization of Seraphim of Sarov, July 1903," in *Religious and Secular Forces in Late Tsarist Russia*, ed. Charles Timberlake (Seattle: University of Washington Press, 1992), 206–29.

10. Gregory L. Freeze, "Subversive Piety: Religion and the Political Crisis in Late Imperial Russia," *Journal of Modern History* 68 (June 1996): 308–50.

11. Rossiiskaia Natsionalnaia Biblioteka (RNB), russkii fond, call number 34.82.6.1665.

12. Most of these publications about St Seraphim were anonymous. See, for instance, *Zhitie prepodobnago ottsa nashego Serafima, sarovskago chudotvortsa i novyia chudesa sovershivshiiasia pri otkrytii sviatykh moshchei ego*, 5th ed. (St Petersburg: 1903).

13. *Zhitie prepodobnago ottsa nashego Serafima sarovskago* (Moscow: 1903), 36–37.

14. M. V. Sabashnikova, *Sviatoi Serafim* (Moscow: 1913), 52–53.

15. Ibid., 90.

16. *Zhitie prepodobnago Serafima i opisanie sarovskoi pustyni* (St Petersburg: 1903), no pagination.

17. I. Mikhail, "19 iiulia," *Tserkovnyi vedomosti* 30 (July 24, 1903): 932–35.

18. Hieromonk Aleksandr, *Nazidatelnoe znachenie blagodatnoi lichnosti prepodobnago Serafima sarovskago dlia nashego vremeni* (St Petersburg: 1905), 5.

19. Kiev's Pecherskaia monastery was one of four to be given the supreme rank of *lavra*. The three others were the Trinity-Sergius Lavra

north of Moscow, the Alexander Nevsky Lavra in St Petersburg, and the Pochaevskaia-Uspenskaia Lavra in Volynia.

20. Aleksandr, *Nazidatelnoe znachenie blagodatnoi lichnosti prepodobnago Serafima sarovskago dlia nashego vremeni,* 8.

21. Ibid., 22.

22. The term *kingdom of heaven* is used particularly in the Gospel of Matthew, and the equivalent *kingdom of God* mainly in the other gospels. Most biblical scholars agree that the terms are synonymous.

23. I. Ivantsov, *Pravoslavnoe obozrenie* (1878).

24. G. Borkov, *Tserkov Khristovo i tsarstvo Bozhie* (Kazan: 1910), 43–44.

25. Georges Florovsky provides a particularly favorable account of the archbishop's history of the Church. Georges Florovsky, *Puti russkago bogosloviia* (Paris: 1937), 365–66.

26. Archbishop Macarius, *Pravoslavno-dogmaticheskoe bogoslavie* (3d ed.; St Petersburg: 1868), 1:62.

27. P. Y. Svetlov, *Ideia tsarstva Bozhiia v eia znachenii dlia khristianskago mirosozertsaniia* (Sergiev Posad: 1905), 9.

28. Ibid., 89.

29. Ibid., 134.

30. Ibid., 327.

31. Ibid., 242.

32. Ibid., 132.

33. Ibid., 217.

34. Ibid., 238.

35. Ibid., 146.

36. Ibid.

37. The influence of the work is witnessed by subsequent interest in his ideas among other theologians. See, for example, G. Borkov, *Tserkov Khristovo i tsarstvo Bozhie* (n.p.).

38. P. Butsinskii, "Venchanie Tsarei na tsarstvo," *Vera i razum* 8 (April 1896): 446–88.

39. V. Skvortsov, "Torzhestvo Pravoslaviia i tserkovnosti na koronatsionnykh moskovskikh prazdnestvakh," *Missionerskoe obozrenie* (May/June 1896): 104–37.

40. *Missionerskoe obozrenie* (June/July 1896).

41. A. D. Beliaev, "Vozmozhno-li soedinenie Pravoslavnoi Tserkvi s Latinskago?" *Vera i razum* 6 (March 1896): 297–320; 9 (May 1896): 532–52; 11 (June 1896): 631–56; 13 (July 1896): 19–46; 15 (August 1896): 142–63; and 16 (August 1896): 218–34.

42. S. O., "Inoslavnye svideteli istiny Pravoslaviia," *Missionerskoe sbornik* 1 (January/February 1896): 24–32.

43. Quoted in *Moskovkiia vedomosti* 128 (May 11, 1896). The reference here, of course, is to the confrontation between Church and state in sixteenth-century Muscovy, in which the leader of the former was suppressed and executed by the tsar.

44. *Sviashchennoe koronovanie russkikh Gosudarei*, ed. S. Dedov, 4th ed. (St Petersburg: 1911), 1.

45. The very first canon of the Seventh Ecumenical Council of 787 emphatically asserted that both the apostles and subsequent authoritative councils had been "illumined by the same Spirit." *Nicene and Post-Nicene Fathers of the Christian Church*, eds. Philip Schaff and Henry Wace, 2nd ed. (Grand Rapids: Eerdmans, 1997), 14:555. Later local Church councils were opened customarily by the corporate singing of the Orthodox hymn to the Holy Spirit, "O Heavenly King."

46. In particular, see St Gregory's sermon on the day of Pentecost, "Slovo 41" in Grigorii Bogoslov, *Tvoreniia uzhe vo sviatykh ottsa nashego Grigoriia Bogoslova* (St Petersburg: 1912), 1:575–86.

47. This point is made, for instance, by Timothy Ware in *The Orthodox Church* (London: Penguin, 1964), 235. See also Michael Pomazansky, *Orthodox Dogmatic Theology* (Platina, Calif.: Saint Herman of Alaska Brotherhood, 1984), 86–91.

48. Vladimir Lossky, *The Mystical Theology of the Eastern Church* (Crestwood, N.Y.: St Vladimir's Seminary Press, 1957), 9.

49. Pomazansky, *Orthodox Dogmatic Theology,* 214–15.

50. Quoted in Leonid Ouspensky and Vladimir Lossky, *The Meaning of Icons*, trans. G. E. H. Palmer and E. Kadloubovsky (Crestwood, N.Y.: St Vladimir's Seminary Press, 1982), 43.

51. Quoted in Ware, *Orthodox Church,* 42.

52. "The Meaning and Language of Icons," in Ouspensky and Lossky, *Meaning of Icons,* 23–50.

53. George P. Fedotov, *Kievan Christianity.* Vol. 1 of *The Russian Religious Mind* (Belmont, Mass.: Nordland, 1975), 410. Also see his essays on the terrestrial nature of religious culture in Rus in the two-volume collection *Sudba i grekhi Rossii: Izbrannye stati po filosofii russkoi istorii i kultury*, ed. V. F. Boikov (St Petersburg: n.p. 1991).

54. Fedotov, *Russian Religious Mind,* 408.

55. Crummey, *Formation of Muscovy,* 189.

56. For a recent account of Soloviev's "theology of culture," see Paul Valliere, "The Theology of Culture in Late Imperial Russia," in *Sacred Stories: Religion and Spirituality in Modern Russia*, eds. Mark D. Steinberg and Heather J. Coleman (Bloomington: Indiana University Press, 2007), 377–95.

57. This, for instance, is the judgment of Svetlov, *Ideia tsarstva Bozhiia.*

58. Archbishop Antony, "Prevoskhodstvo pravoslaviia nad ucheniem papizma v ego izlozhenii Vl. Solovievym," in *Polnoe sobranie sochinenii*, 2nd ed. (St Petersburg: 1911), 3:125–53.

59. Florovsky, *Puti russkago bogosloviia,* 322–30.

60. *Beseda startsa Serafima s N.A. Motovilovym o tseli khristianskoi zhizni* (Sergiev Posad: 1911); repr. in *Sviatoi prepodobnyi Serafim sarovskii chudotvorets* (Moscow: n.p. 1991), 42–79.

61. N. G. Popov, *O bozhestve i chelovechestvo* (Sergiev Posad: 1908), 169.

62. John Sergiev, *Polnoe sobranie sochinenii* (St Petersburg: 1905), 6: 106–7.

63. Ibid., 111.

64. Vera Shevzov, *Russian Orthodoxy on the Eve of Revolution* (Oxford: Oxford University Press, 2004), 54.

65. Ibid., 130.

66. Bishop Nikon, *Chto nam nuzhnee vsego* (Sergiev Posad: 1905), 4.

Chapter 3

1. Recent accounts of the late imperial missionary movement's contact with the nationality issue include Robert P. Geraci and Michael Khodarkovsky, eds., *Of Religion and Empire: Missions, Conversion, and Tolerance in Tsarist Russia* (Ithaca, N.Y.: Cornell University Press, 2001); Paul W. Werth, *At the Margins of Orthodoxy: Mission, Governance, and Confessional Politics in Russia's Volga-Kama Region, 1827–1905* (Ithaca, N.Y.: Cornell University Press, 2002); and Robert P. Geraci, *Window on the East: National and Imperial Identities in Late Tsarist Russia* (Ithaca, N.Y.: Cornell University Press, 2001). For the missionary movement as such, see Aaron Michaelson, "The Russian Orthodox Missionary Society, 1970–1917: A Study in Religious and Educational Enterprise" (Ph.D. dissertation, University of Minnesota: 1999).

2. For some of the earliest experiences of secularization among the workers in cities, see Reginald E. Zelnik, "'To the Unaccustomed Eye':

Religion and Irreligion in the Experience of St Petersburg Workers in the 1870s," *Russian History* 16:2–4 (1989): 297–326.

3. In 1895 one history of the Orthodox Missionary Society lamented that "hundreds of thousands" of non-Orthodox inhabited Russia, an estimate that the census would show to be naive in the extreme. Alexander Nikolskii, *Pravoslavnoe missionerskoe obshchestvo* (Moscow: 1895), 3. Missionaries regularly expressed dismay at what they considered the large size of the non-Orthodox population. The period's missionary congresses, for instance, often opened with warnings that sectarianism and Old Belief were not waning but on the contrary rising. When the census was published, it revealed no fewer than thirty-six million non-Orthodox subjects, a figure that itself was frequently considered underestimated. For a discussion of the results, see John Shelton Curtiss, *Church and State in Russia: The Last Years of the Empire, 1900–1917* (New York: Columbia University Press, 1940), 71n.

4. One of the best examples of the Church's dialogic method among those from Orthodox backgrounds—in this case apostate—was the institution of missionary "conversations" (*besedy*) that were regularly conducted among local sectarians and Old Believers. Transcripts and discussions of these appeared in contemporary spiritual journals.

5. For the source of the epigraph, see Matt 10:6.

6. "Nashe delo i ego zadachi," *Missionerskoe obozrenie* 1 (January 1896): iii–xvii.

7. In all, 198 attended the congress. This figure was considerably higher than those of the two preceding all-Russian congresses, held in 1887 and 1891. I. M. Gromoglasov, *Tretii vserossiiskii missionerskii sezd* (Sergiev Posad: 1898), 15.

8. B. M. Skvortsov, *Deianiia 3-go vserossiiskago missionerskago sezd v Kazani* (Kiev: 1897), 196.

9. Ibid., 208.

10. Ibid., 209.

11. Ibid., 226–27.

12. Ibid., 225.

13. Skvortsov even made a point of thanking Sabler and Pobedonostsev for the state's support of the mission in his opening speech. For Sabler's address, see Gromoglasov, *Tretii vserossiiskii missionerskii sezd,* 18–22.

14. Skvortsov, *Deianiia,* 24.

15. Ibid., 33.

16. Gary Marker has shown that such a public had been formed well before the turn of the eighteenth century. His evidence includes publications such as the newspaper *Sankt-Peterburgskiia vedomosti* (1727–1917), whose content frequently offended the state. Even more challenging from the Church's perspective was the periodical *Zapiski* (1728–1742), which sought particularly to foster the formation of a secular culture. Gary Marker, *Publishing, Printing, and the Origins of Intellectual Life in Russia, 1700–1800* (Princeton: Princeton University Press, 1985).

17. Jeffrey Brooks, *When Russia Learned to Read: Literacy and Popular Literature, 1861–1917* (Princeton: Princeton University Press, 1985), 330.

18. Ibid., 333.

19. *Svod zakonov Rossiiskoi imperii* (St Petersburg: 1904), vol. 1, part 1, art. 40.

20. One estimate of nearly a 40 percent level of literacy is given by A. G. Rashin, "Gramatnost i narodnoe obrazovanie v Rossii XIX i nachale XX v.," *Istoricheskie zapiski* 37 (1951): 50.

21. Charles Taylor, *Sources of the Self: The Making of the Modern Identity* (Cambridge, Mass.: Harvard University Press, 1989), 27. Taylor is concerned mainly with the individual moral self, though, as he frequently notes, community and nationality can be framed in the same way.

22. See John Eugene Clay, "Antisectarian and Antischismatic Missions of the Russian Orthodox Church," *The Modern Encyclopedia of Religions in Russia and the Soviet Union*, ed. Paul D. Steeves (Gulf Breeze, Fla.: Academic International Press, 1988–1997), 2:93–101; Gregory L. Freeze, ed., *Forschungen zur osteuropaeischen Geschichte*, Vol. 2 of *Geschichte der russischen Kirche,* ed. Igor Smolitsch (Leiden: E. J. Brill, 1991), 246–345; and N. A. Smirnov, "Missionerskaia deiatelnost tserkvi (Vtoraia polovina XIX v.-1917g.)," in *Russkoe pravoslavie: Vekhi istorii* (Moscow: Izd-vo polit. lit-ry, 1989), 438–62.

23. *Tserkovnyi vestnik* 17 (April 29, 1910). 504–8. For a discussion of the "cultural mission" to Orthodox peoples of European Russia, see *Tserkovnyi vestnik* 14 (April 8, 1910): 424–28.

24. Stolypin's program is treated in Donald Treadgold, *The Great Siberian Migration: Government and Peasant in Resettlement from Emancipation to the First World War* (Princeton: Princeton University Press, 1957), 153–83.

25. Treadgold's figures indicate that Vostorgov's estimate was exaggerated. Ibid., 159–60.

26. The articles were later reprinted in his *Polnoe sobranie sochinenii* (Moscow: 1916), 4:450–70.

27. *Khronologicheskii katalog izdanii Pravoslavnago Missionerskago Obshchestva* (Kazan: 1910).

28. The historical department of the commission's catalogs was usually the largest. Among the favored representatives of Russian national art were the composer Mikhail Glinka and the painter V. M. Vasnetsov. Listings of the catalog were included in the commission's individual publications. An example can be found in I. Fudel, *Sviatai Rus* (Moscow: 1902).

29. *Moskovskiia tserkovnyiia vedomosti* 14 (April 3, 1905): 163–66. The topics of these "public theological readings" were listed in the society's annual reports published in the journal.

30. It established a "historical-archeological department" and an "iconological department" in 1896, both of which served in the future to organize the society's historical pursuits. *Moskovskiia tserkovnyia vedomosti* 5 (February 2, 1897): 63–66.

31. For a brief description of the Vernost publishing house, see P. N. Zyrianov, *Pravoslavnaia tserkov v borbe s revoliutsiei, 1905–1907* (Moscow: Izd-vo "Nauka," 1984), 119.

32. John Vostorgov, *Pravoslavie v istorii Rossii* (Moscow: 1910), 6–7. Also see his *Patriotizm i khristianstvo* (Moscow: 1909).

33. Vostorgov, *Patriotizm i khristianstvo,* 5.

34. See, for instance, "Velikoe prizvanie Russkago naroda," *Polnoe sobranie sochinenii,* 1:69–72; "Russkaia ideia," ibid., 336–42; "Rossiia i vostok," ibid., 2:45–50; "Rus sviataia," ibid., 3:602–6; and "Missionerskoe prizvanie Rossii," ibid., 611–15.

35. John Vostorgov, "Kultura," *Polnoe sobranie sochinenii,* 1:316–19.

36. Seymour Becker, "The Muslim East in Nineteenth-Century Russian Popular Historiography," *Central Asian Survey* 5:3–4 (1986): 25–47. Another interesting account of the public's cultural leadership by the author is "Russia between East and West: The Intelligentsia, Russian National Identity, and the Asian Borderlands," *Central Asian Survey* 10:4 (1991): 47–64.

37. The Church's historiographical interests can be traced in the manuals it published for use in public education. See, for instance, A. Dobroklonskii, *Rukovodstvo po istorii russkoi tserkvi* (Moscow: 1884–1893), 4 vols.

38. K. Evseev, "O sovremennom tserkovnom samosoznanii," *Khristianin* (January 1912): 50–59.

39. Ibid.

40. A. Beliaev, *Illiustrirovannaia istoriia russkoi tserkvi* (Moscow: 1894), 1:155.

41. Ibid., 1:167–68.

42. Ibid., 2:3.

43. Ibid., 2:191.

44. Ibid., 2:194.

45. Ibid., 2:198–208.

46. M. I. Khitrov, *Drevniaia Rus v velikie dni* (St Petersburg: 1899), 67.

47. Scott M. Kenworthy, *The Heart of Russia: Trinity-Sergius Lavra, Monasticism, and Society after 1825* (Oxford: Oxford University Press, 2010), 187.

48. Because of an illness, the historian's address was actually read by an assistant. For the text, see E. E. Golubinskii, "O znachenii prepodobnago Sergiia Radonezhskago v istorii nashego monashestva," *Bogoslovskii vestnik* (November 1892): 173–89.

49. Quoted in Vasily Kliuchevsky, *Sochinenii v deviati tomakh*, ed. V. L. Yanin (Moscow: Mysl, 1987), 1:6.

50. Robert F. Byrnes, *V. O. Kliuchevsky, Historian of Russia* (Bloomington: University of Indiana Press, 1995).

51. V. O. Kliuchevsky, "Znachenie prep. Sergiia Radonezhskago dlia russkago naroda i gosudarstva," *Bogoslovskii vestnik* (November 1892): 190–204. Kliuchevsky's mention of the kingdom of God is obscure here. When he quotes the construction "Tsarstvo Bozhie podobno zakvaske," he appears to be referring to Matthew 13 or 16, or perhaps Luke 12. He does not cite the source for the quotation.

52. This is the conclusion of Byrnes's research. The absence of such religiously loaded terms and Kliuchevsky's focus on social and economic experience led Byrnes to argue that the Orthodox religious tradition played little role in his otherwise ambitious project to formulate Russian nationality. See Byrnes, *V. O. Kliuchevsky,* 174. Byrnes does not analyze the text of the St Sergius address.

53. *Tserkovnyia vedomosti* 40 (October 10, 1892): 1377–89. Kenworthy confirms this figure in *Heart of Russia,* 187.

54. A. S., "Moskva, 27 sentiabria," *Moskovskiia tserkovnyia vedomosti* 39 (September 27, 1892): 527–28.

55. Geoffrey Hosking, *Russia: People and Empire, 1552–1917* (Cambridge, Mass.: Harvard University Press, 1997), 292.

56. Ibid., 293.

57. One of his earliest efforts seems to have been in 1881, when he lamented the death of Dostoevsky. See Archbishop Nikanor, *Poucheniia, besedy, rechi, vozzvaniia i poslaniia Nikanora Arkhiepiskopa Khersonskago i Odesskago*, 3rd ed. (Odessa: 1890), 1:212–22.

58. I. I. Vostorgov, "Pamiati A.S. Pushkina," *Polnoe sobranie sochinenii,* 1:266–86. See also three other addresses from the year printed in ibid., 287–95.

59. The history behind Tolstoy's excommunication is treated in P. N. Zyrianov, "Tserkov v period trekh rossiiskikh revoliutsii," *Russkoe pravoslavie: Vekhi istorii* (Moscow: n.p. 1989), 381–437.

60. It was first published abroad in 1894. Though it quoted the New Testament only in conclusion, it used what the author regarded as a Christian standard of community to reject all divisive political models. In light of this standard, he argued, "patriotism in our time presents to mankind nothing but the most terrible future." For the text, see L. N. Tolstoy, *Polnoe sobranie sochinenii* (Moscow: n.p. 957), 39:27–80.

61. General comments and praise about Dostoevsky's utility for the Church appeared frequently in the spiritual journals. For two articles on his religious and moral views, see Vasily Shingarov, "Osnovnyia idei pravoslaviia v izlozhenii F. M. Dostoevskago," *Vera i razum* 20 (October 1904): 391–415; and I. Rozanov, "Religiozno-nravstvennaia zhizn v khudozhestvennom osveshchenii F. M. Dostoevskago," *Strannik* (April 1905): 555–79. Some writers used Dostoevsky's views on political affairs such as the Balkans crisis to help formulate the Church's position. See V. Azbukhin, "Dostoevskii i vostochnoi vopros," *Khristianin* (January 1913): 184–94.

62. For his intellectual background and training, see James W. Cunningham, *A Vanquished Hope: The Movement for Church Renewal in Russia, 1905–1906* (Crestwood, N.Y.: St Vladimir's Seminary Press, 1981), 59–66.

63. He attended many of the abortive St Petersburg religious-philosophical meetings in the first years of the century, and there encountered leading secular intellectuals such as Dmitry Merezhkovsky (1865–1941).

64. Antony (Khrapovitsky), *Polnoe sobranie sochinenii*, 2nd ed. (St Petersburg: 1911), 2:463–95.

65. Ibid., 3:369–77.

66. An example of the public medieval revival was the four-story building of the Petersburg Credit Society (1875), placed prominently

in the capital on the corner of the Alexandriinsky park between the
Alexandriinsky theater and the Imperial Public Library. It still stands today.
A few other examples are the Income Bank (1880s) on Theater Square, also
in St Petersburg, the Historical Museum (1883) on Red Square in Moscow,
Moscow's Merchant Trading Rows (1891), the building of the Moscow City
Duma (1892), and the Main Market building (1890) in Nizhny-Novgorod.

67.   A concise characterization of the "Russian style" of architecture can
be found in E. A. Borisova, *Russkaia arkhitektura vtoroi poloviny XIX veka*
(Moscow: Nauka, 1979), 220–70. For a broad application of the term, see
Evgenia Kirichenko, *The Russian Style* (London: L. King, 1991).

68.   See the inaugural issue, especially D. Solovev, "O pravoslavnom
tesrkovnom penii," *Baian* 1 (January 10, 1888): 5–7.

69.   Vladimir Morosan, "Liturgical Singing or Sacred Music?
Understanding the Aesthetic of the New Russian Choral School," in
Christianity and the Arts in Russia, eds. William C. Brumfield and Milos M.
Velimirovic (Cambridge: Cambridge University Press, 1991), 124–30.

70.   See Leonid Ouspensky and Vladimir Lossky, *The Meaning of
Icons*, trans. G. E. H. Palmer and E. Kadloubovsky (Crestwood, N.Y.: St
Vladimir's Seminary Press, 1982), 42.

71.   "Otchet sostoianii Obshchestva Liubitelei Dukhovnago
Prosveshcheniia v 1904 godu," *Moskovskiia tserkovnyia vedomosti* 13 (March
27, 1905): 151–54.

72.   D. K. Trenev, *Russkaia ikonopis i eia zhelaemoe razvitie* (Moscow:
1902), 5.

73.   Ibid., 9.

74.   Ibid., 11.

75.   D. K. Trenev, *Neskolko slov o drevnei i sovremennoi russkoi ikonopisi*
(Moscow: 1904), 2.

76.   Ibid., 5.

77.   Apparently, the initiative came from Metropolitan Filaret
(Drozdov, 1782–1867) himself. For accounts of the construction project,
see I. V. Alexandrovskii, *Sobor sv. Vladimira v Kieve* (Kiev: 1897); and
N. I. Petrov, *Iz istorii kievskago Vladimirskago sobora* (Kiev: 1898). For
photographs of the cathedral's interior, see *Kievskii Vladimirskii Sobor* (Kiev:
1896).

78.   V. L. Dedlov, *Kievskii Vladimirskii Sobor i ego khudozhestvennye
tvortsy* (Moscow: 1901), 9.

79.   This was the opinion of the period's highest authority about Russian
national art, V. V. Stasov. See V. V. Stasov, "Victor Mikhailovich Vasnetsov

i ego rabota," *Iskusstvo i khudozhestvennaia promyshlennost'* 1–2 (October/ November 1898): 65–98.

80. A. Rusakova, *Mikhail Nesterov* (Leningrad: Aurora, 1990), 7.

81. Dedlov, *Kievskii Vladimirskii Sobor,* 10.

82. Ibid., 26.

83. Ibid., 48.

84. Ibid., 57. At a later point he noted approvingly that both Vasnetsov and Nesterov were "ardent readers of Dostoevsky." Ibid., 76.

85. N. V. Rozhdestvenskii, "O znachenii Kievskago Vladimiraskago sobora v russkom religioznom iskusstve," *Vera i tserkov* 1 (1900): 84–100; 4 (1900): 589–607; and 5 (1900): 741–59.

86. Ibid.

Chapter 4

1. For a brief account of the controversy, see Henry Chadwick, *The Early Church* (London: Pelican Books, 1967), 38–40.

2. Robert O. Crummey, *The Formation of Muscovy* (New York: Longman, 1987), 126–28.

3. Rom 9:8.

4. Rom 11:16.

5. G. S. Debolskii, *Ustanovlenie vekhtozavetnoi tserkvi i khristianskiia*, 2nd ed. (St Petersburg: 1894), 7. One of the author's leading concerns in this work was the self-consciousness of ancient Israel as God's chosen people, who received considerable reinforcement from their regular national-religious holidays.

6. See especially Dan 12, which records the prophecy that the archangel, as Israel's protector, will lead it to victory and redemption at the end of time. This prophecy continued to resonate in the New Testament. See Rev 12:7 for the image of Michael in an early Christian context. Contemporary Russian Church leaders accepted this teaching and even integrated it into a claim that all the world's peoples enjoy the patronage of personal angel-protectors in heaven. This, for instance, was the claim of Archbishop Macarius in his standard theology. He used both the terms "angel-protector" (*angel-khranitel*) and "angel-ruler of a people" (*angel-narodopravitel*) to refer to Michael. Bishop Macarius, *Pravoslavno-dogmaticheskoe bogoslovie*, 3rd ed. (St Petersburg: 1868), 1:536–50.

7. The title also encompassed the other main archangel, Gabriel.

8. N. N. Efimov, *Rus—novyi Izrail* (Kazan: 1912).

9. According to Rowland, Efimov's study is the only other extant treatment. The closest medieval churchmen seem to have come to a cultural definition is in their vocabulary for discussing the community constituted under the state. Here they used the word *iazyk,* which implied a tribal continuity with the Muscovite people's ancestors. Daniel R. Rowland, "Moscow: The Third Rome or the New Israel?" *The Russian Review* 55 (October 1996): 591–614. For another account of Old Testament imagery in medieval Rus, see Joel Raba, "Moscow—the Third Rome or the New Jerusalem?" *Forschungen zur osteuropaeischen Geschichte* 50 (1995): 297–307.

10. As a posthumous admirer put it, Nikanor believed that "the Russian clergy is greatly harmed by insufficient knowledge and understanding of the history that infuses the flesh and blood of our consciousness." A. N., *Mysli Nikanora, Arkhiepiskop Khersonskago, o vozvelichenii pravoslaviia* (Kazan: 1910), 2–3.

11. Quoted in A. Krylov, *Apkhiepiskop Nikanor kak pedagog* (Novocherkassk: 1893), 46.

12. Archbishop Nikanor, *Poucheniia, besedy, rechi, vozzvaniia i poslaniia,* 3rd ed. (Odessa: 1890), 1:390–401.

13. His lifetime interest in research and scholarship brought significant distinctions, such as the award of a doctorate in theology in 1869 and election to membership in the Imperial Academy of Sciences.

14. E. N. A., "Kratkiia biogrificheskiia svedeniia o Vysokopreosviashchennom Nikanore," in *Pamiati Vysokopreosviashchennago Nikanora arkhiepiskop khersonskago i odesskago,* ed. N. Beliaev (Kazan: 1891), 1–3.

15. Some of his reminiscences about these experiences can be found in Archbishop Nikanor, *Biograficheskie materially,* ed. S. Petrovskii (Odessa: 1900), especially 325–46.

16. After his death he was nevertheless remembered as both a leading preacher and great administrator. See *Novoe vremia* 5327 (December 28, 1890).

17. For a brief account of his early writing career, see I. K., *Vysokopreosviashchennyi Nikanor, Arkhiepiskop Khersonskii* (Moscow: 1891), 4–5.

18. *Moskovskii listok* 361 (December 29, 1890).

19. Alexander B., *Opisanie nekotorykh sochinenii napisannykh russkimi raskolnikam v polzy raskola,* 2 vols. (St Petersburg: 1861). As the author stated in his preface, the study was intended to inform the synodal clergy about the intellectual sources and culture of Old Belief, and thus serve as a "weapon" in the service of the mission. It is significant that in conducting his polemic

with Old Believers, the priest was frequently drawn to emphasize the universal nature of the "Greco-Russian Church," in contrast to his sermons defining Russia as the new Israel. See especially his polemical addresses of the 1880s. Bishop Nikanor, *Pouchenie revniteliam starago obriada* (no place of publication or date). Here Nikanor nevertheless affirmed in principle the modern use of some Old Believer Church rituals.

20. N. Beliaev, "Kharakteristiki uchenoi, propovednicheskoi i administrativnoi deiatelnosti Vysokopreosviashchennago Nikanora," in *Pamiati Vysokopreosviashchennago Nikanora*, 3–11.

21. In fact, memory of the Russians' defeat at Sevastopol by the British and French at the beginning of the Crimean War seems never to have left his consciousness. References to the event repeatedly appeared in his addresses, beginning with the 1860 address about the new Israel discussed above.

22. I. K., *Vysokopreosviashchennyi Nikanor*, 13.

23. An argument from silence is admittedly ambiguous. It may be justified, though, by a review of Nikanor's published sermons and addresses, which were collected in two different publications of five volumes and four volumes, respectively, with each volume containing approximately five hundred pages of text. This mass of homiletical literature is for the most part devoted to moral preaching. But many of the addresses reveal the author's own philosophical reflections, and the occasional references, whether sustained or passing, to Western intellectuals and the character of modern culture offer interesting glimpses of the priest's intellectual development. A sermon of 1860, for instance, was solely concerned with "fanciful German philosophy" and the "anti-Christian worldview of our time." Though perhaps thinking of the left-wing Hegelians (in other works he cited Strauss and Feuerbach), he did not object to the principle of ethnic nationality for which German intellectuals such as Hegel and at that time in Russia were famous. In fact, he thought it germane to review the "purpose of nationality" revealed in world history, including particularly ancient Israel's, and concluded with an admonition to his audience not to betray the "Russian God" (*Russkii Bog*). See Archbishop Nikanor, "Pouchenie," in *Besedy i poucheniia* (Odessa: 1884), 1:1–15. In 1882, an audience gathered to hear a New Year's sermon listened to a discussion of "Renan in Russian translation" that characterized the problems and evils of modern Western biblical study. The author, apparently referring to the French writer's *Life of Jesus* and *History of Old Testament Israel*, nevertheless had nothing to criticize about the ethnic theories contained in *What Is the*

Nation?, which also went into Russian translation during the period. See Archbishop Nikanor, "Pouchenie," *Besedy i poucheniia,* 1:27–44. For the reception of Ernest Renan (1823–1892) in late imperial national thought, see I. A. Sikorskii, *Chto takoe natsiia i drugiia formi etnicheskoi zhizni?* (Kiev: 1915).

24. The focus on Tolstoy seems to have been powerful and nearly universal. For an account of Nikanor's anti-Tolstoy campaigns, see *Pamiati Vysokopreosviashchennago Nikanora,* 45–65.

25. Archbishop Nikanor, *Poucheniia, besedy, rechi, vozzvaniia i poslaniia,* vol. 1, 212–22.

26. See his address on the fiftieth anniversary of Pushkin's death in 1887 in ibid., 1:234–39.

27. This essay was never published in his lifetime, perhaps because of its highly critical remarks about the empire's cultural order. See Archbishop Nikanor, "Rasprostranenie idei neveriia v Rossii so vremeni Petra Velikago," in *Biograficheskie materialy,* 325–46.

28. Ibid.

29. The affair, which took place in 1874, is related in Krylov, *Arkhiepiskop Nikanor kak pedagog,* 48.

30. Once installed as the archbishop of Kherson, he led the diocesan program to establish a primary schooling system there. See I. K., *Vysokopreosviashchennyi Nikanor,* 10. For an account of late imperial reading patterns and tastes, see Jeffrey Brooks, *When Russia Learned to Read: Literacy and Popular Literature, 1861–1917* (Evanston, Ill.: Northwestern University Press, 2003). For accounts of the efforts of social elites and clerics to shape popular morality, see ibid. and Daniel R. Brower, *The Russian City between Tradition and Modernity, 1850–1900* (Berkeley: University of California Press, 1990).

31. Archbishop Nikanor, *Poucheniia, besedy, rechi, vozzvaniia i poslaniia,* 1:494–508. In another sermon, he repeated this critique of imperial Russia's culture. From Vladimir to Peter, he stated, "there lay in the soul of the Russian people an immutable striving, that each Russian person would be Russian first of all according to the faith." Since Peter, however, the people had steadily fallen away from the faith, despite their continued enforcement in the code of laws. See ibid., 3:9–21.

32. An interesting example is an address delivered on the occasion of the consecration of a chapel in a commercial school in which 70 percent of the students were said to be Jewish. Acknowledging this fact and reviewing the relationship of ancient Israel to the "new branch that grew from the old

root," he expressed hope that the close relations of Jews with Russians would lead the former toward the "Russian Orthodox faith," emphasizing especially their ever-growing ethnic connection to the "Russian tribe." By "the special conditions of the Russian way of life," he stated, "in three or four generations they [Jews living in Russia] in appearances of body and external features are Russian of a tribal type and are connected to the Russian people." See Bishop Nikanor, "Pouchenie," in *Besedy i poucheniia,* 3:134–52.

33. Archbishop Nikanor, *Poucheniia,* 3:252–60. This address appears to have made a strong impression upon other celebrants of the baptism anniversary, indicated by the fact that it was reprinted for an empire-wide audience. For two contemporary editions of the text, see the collection of addresses in *Pravoslavnoe obozrenie* (October 1888): 340–407; and *Strannik* (October 1888): 216–25.

34. In fact, following the example of Metropolitan Platon, Nikanor also used the baptism commemoration to launch a missionary challenge against the Old Believers. See *Poucheniia, besedy, rechi, vozzvaniia i poslaniia,* 3:261–82. Notably, he took this occasion to emphasize the difference between a commemoration of statehood, represented by the anniversary of the Rurik house celebrated in Novgorod in 1862, with a commemoration of nationality, which the present anniversary represented.

35. *Moskovskii listok* 361 (1890).

36. *Pamiati Vysokopreosviashchennago Nikanora,* 26.

37. The icon's prototype was discovered in Kazan at the time of Ivan the IV's conquest, and it subsequently served as the focus of prayers in times of national military emergency. Alexander I prayed before it in 1812; Nicholas II did so in 1914. In the latter case, it had become the central icon of Kazan Cathedral, built in the capital especially in honor of the icon. The present sermon was delivered in Moscow.

38. Shevzov quotes one priest in 1893 who used the feast of the Kazan Icon as an opportunity for claiming the Mother of God's special protection of the Russian people from the day Vladimir was baptized in 988 to the present, setting "Rus" apart from "all nations and kingdoms and peoples." Vera Shevzov, "Scripting the Gaze: Liturgy, Homilies, and the Kazan Icon of the Mother of God in Late Imperial Russia," in *Sacred Stories,* (Bloomington: Indiana University Press, 2007), 61–92.

39. The Patriotic War of 1812 is the Russian name for the Napoleonic invasion of Russia in 1812.

40. P. Smirnov, "Novyi Izrail," *Moskovskiia tserkovnyiia vedomosti* 45 (November 9, 1903): 567–71.

41. The body that organized the addresses was the Commission for the Establishment of General Educational Readings for the Industrial Workers of Moscow. I. Fudel, *Sviataia Rus* (Moscow: 1902), 10–12. In the address Fudel made reference to Nikanor's addresses, indicating that the archbishop's thought served as inspiration for subsequent cultural missionaries. Interestingly, he also cited Soloviev's *The National Question in Russia* to the workers.

42. Addressed to "noble sons of the holy Russian land," it included the following passage: "As older brothers, as the best and foremost servitors of this holy people, this new Israel, you stand upon the summit of your calling and can bear in your hearts and express in your life activities the best of its characteristics." Metropolitan Antony, "Rech," in *Rechi, slova i poucheniia*, 3rd ed. (St Petersburg: 1912), 340–44. In other passages the hierarch used Old Testament imagery that was more consistent with the Orthodox canon, but he continued to describe Russia as the modern fulfillment of Orthodox universality. In an address delivered to celebrate the one-thousand-year anniversary of the mission of Saints Cyril and Methodius in 1885, he focused particular attention on the eschatological succession of Israel's status from the Old Testament, through the Eastern Church as a whole, and finally to Rus in particular. To do so, he also invoked Old Testament images of the holy temple of Jerusalem and the Archangel Michael. See "Rech," ibid., 176–83.

43. Some of the more influential honorary members, after the tsar and imperial family, were Metropolitan Platon, John Sergiev, and Count Witte. The society also recognized Archbishop Nikanor as a source of inspiration. On this, see *Pamiati Vysokopreosviashchennago Nikanora, 7.*

44. Theofanis George Stavrou, *Russian Interests in Palestine, 1882–1914: A Study of Religious and Educational Enterprise* (Thessalonika: Institute for Balkan Studies, 1963).

45. The member of the imperial family who served as its formal patron was Grand Duke Sergei Alexandrovich, who, following the death of Alexander II in 1881, made a much publicized pilgrimage to Jerusalem and returned to offer his support to the nascent society. For a thorough history of the society's early experiences, see A. A. Dmitrievskii, *Imperatorskoe Pravoslavnoe Palestinskoe Obshchestvo i ego deiatelnost za itekshuiu chetvert veka (1882–1907)* (St Petersburg: 1907). This study and others like it offered considerable praise to Alexander III for the society's existence and prestige. For an account of the society's services to local non-Russian Orthodox, see F. Paleolog, *Imperatorskoe Pravoslavnoe Palestinskoe Obshchestvo: Ocherki ego deiatelnosti* (St Petersburg: 1891). The leading act of charity performed

by the society in Palestine was the construction and support of Orthodox parish schools.

46. V. M. Skvortsov, *Deianiia 3-go Vserossisskago Missionerskago Sezda v Kazani* (Kiev: 1897), 212.

47. Here the argument usually emphasized the indifferent attitude toward relics and shrines of the so-called rationalistic sects.

48. This was the reasoning of one defender of the society in an address before the Kiev missionary congress in 1908. See Hieromonk Viktor, *Ierusalimskaia missiia* (Kharkov: 1909), 24–28.

49. This is evidenced in the guidebook literature that was published to promote interest in and ultimately facilitate pilgrimages. Guidebooks usually included a wealth of information about the history of ancient Israel and descriptions of related points of interest. For an especially thorough example, see *Putovoditel vo sviatom grad Irusalim ko gradu Gospodniu i prochnim sviatym mestam vostoka, i na Sinai* (Moscow: 1908). Typical of many, this publication carries supplementary information about the Palestine Society and travel requirements for the common pilgrim. The subject of Old Testament history itself was considered by the Orthodox Missionary Society to be a suitable object for popular study. For a list of books and brochures on the topic, see *Khronologicheskii katalog izdanii Pravoslavnago Missionerskago Obshchestva* (Kazan: 1910).

50. V. N. Khitrovo, "Pravoslavie v Sviatoi Zemle," in *Pravoslavnyi palestinskii sbornik* 1 (St Petersburg: 1881), 1–98.

51. For accounts of increased rates of pilgrimage, see Chris J. Chulos, *Converging Worlds: Religion and Community in Peasant Russia, 1861–1917* (DeKalb: Northern Illinois University Press, 2003); Robert H. Greene, *Bodies like Bright Stars: Saints and Relics in Orthodox Russia* (DeKalb: Northern Illinois University Press, 2010); Roy Robson, "Transforming Solovki: Pilgrim Narratives, Modernization, and Late Imperial Monastic Life," in *Sacred Stories,* 44–60.

52. Ibid.

53. For a general estimation of the figure, see his *Russkie palomniki Sviatoi zemli* (St Petersburg: 1905), 27 and 55.

54. As he put it: "Eleven days after departure from Petersburg you can already be praying at the tomb of our Lord." Khitrovo, "Pravoslavie v Sviatoi Zemle."

55. The church was named after St Mary Magdalene, in honor of Alexander III's mother, Maria Nikolaevna. It was founded in 1882 and completed in 1888, the year of the baptism anniversary.

56. Khitrovo, *Russkie palomniki,* 93.

57. The society enjoyed a very wide and well-financed range of literature. Each year reports about the empire-wide activities were published in a collection titled *Soobshcheniia Imperatorskago Pravoslavnoe Palestinskoe Obshchestvo* (1886–1917). An infrequent periodical devoted mainly to scholarly study and titled *Pravoslavnyi Palestinskii sbornik* (1881–1922) also appeared. The society financed a large variety of publications ranging from guidebooks and pamphlets to full-scale archeological and historical works on the Holy Land. Most of these were published by the publishing house of V. Kirshbaum in St Petersburg.

58. The number of chapter members could range widely. In 1901, for instance, the Arkhangelsk diocesan chapter contained 38 members, that at Odessa 85, and that at Ekaterinburg 183. *Deiatelnost otdelov Imperatorskago Pravoslavnago Palestinskago Obshchestva v 1900–1901 godu* (St Petersburg: 1901).

59. The chapter in Odessa had an especially wide outreach, as embarkation for Palestine on steamers most often occurred there. One educated pilgrim later reflected how the Palestine Society's local leaders made a point of providing outgoing pilgrims with free literature about the society's activities. He even noted the inspirational passages from the Psalms printed therein. See E. F. Muiaka, *V Ierusalim!* (St Petersburg: 1903), 8.

60. "Deiatelnost otdelov Imperatorskago Pravoslavnago Palestinskago Obshchestva v 1895–1896 godu," *Soobshcheniia Imperatorskago Pravoslavnago Palestinskago Obshchestvo* (August 1896): 400–447. The average public turnout for the readings, which were often held in churches on specially scheduled "Palestine evenings," was no doubt quite small. However, many chapters reported sizable individual gatherings of hundreds and sometimes thousands.

61. As one priest put it: "We call the Palestine Society national because its tasks embody the striving of the Russian man. But this society is also national because it is composed exclusively of public contributions, if the 30,000 rubles contributed through His Majesty's will is not considered." Nicholas Letnitskii, *Rech* (Astrakhan: 1907), 9.

62. A. A. Dmitrievskii, *Tipi sovremennykh russkikh palomnikov v Sviatuiu Zemliu,* 2nd ed. (St Petersburg: 1912), 3. The first edition of this work was published in 1903.

63. Ibid., 4.

64. Ibid., 8.

65. Ibid., 28. He also recommended a follow-up journey to Athens on the return trip to Russia.

66. E. Efimov, *Rech o religiozno-vospitatelnom znachenii palomnichestva vo Sviatuiu Zemliu* (no place of publication: 1908), 5.

67. Peter Smirnov, *Sudba Ierusalima i russkie palomniki* (St Petersburg: 1896), 3. Whether this was the same P. Smirnov who delivered the new Israel address in Moscow in 1903 is impossible to determine from the text. Both authors held the rank of *protoierei*.

68. Ibid., 17–18.

69. Though he spoke of the "liberation of Jerusalem," the author explicitly rejected a political role for Russia in the region, and in fact accused Western Christians of using pilgrimages as a pretext for expansion. Ibid., 21.

70. Bishop Nikanor, "Beseda o sodeistvii Pravoslavnym v Sviatoi Zemle," in *Izdanie Imperatorskoe Pravoslavnoe Palestinskoe Obshchestvo* (St Petersburg: 1899), 1–8.

71. See, for example, M. S. Palmov, "Beseda o znachenii Sviatoi Zemli dlia khristianskago mira," in *Izdanie Imperatorskago Pravoslavnago Palestinskago Obshchestva* (St Petersburg: 1899), 1–14. Here the author cited two passages in particular:

And the Lord will take possession of Judah as his inheritance in the Holy Land, and will again choose Jerusalem. (Zech 2:12)

"And you shall be to Me a kingdom of priests, and a holy nation." These are the words which you shall speak to the children of Israel. (Exod 19:6)

Both of these passages, Palmov claimed, spoke to ancient Israel's role in the "dissemination of the Kingdom of God among the Gentiles." Ibid.

72. Efimov, *Rech o religiozno-vospitatelnom znachenii sviatoi zemli* (Chernigov: 1902), 1–2. For a contemporary account of the Zionist movement, see *Novoe vremia* 9405 (May 12, 1902).

73. An exception was Bishop Macarius of Tomsk, who invoked recognizable anti-Judaic terms such as the "murder of Christ" (*Khristoubiistvo*) when characterizing the passing of Jerusalem from the ancient Jews to the new Israel after the crucifixion. Even so, most of his attention was directed toward the history of modern Christendom. See Bishop Macarius, *Beseda o Sviatoi Zemli i Imperatorskom Pravoslavnom Palestinskom Obshchestve* (St Petersburg: 1898).

74. Stavrou refers to Soloviev in only three instances and generally does not include his activities and vision within the scope of his study.

75. An example of his borderline opinion regarding the question of Russian challenges to the Turkish Empire is found in two articles in *Moskovskiia vedomosti* in 1895. As the year opened he described the "two struggles" that exist for Russia in Palestine, one of a military nature with Turkey, and the other of a religious nature with Catholicism. In November, however, he made a point of stating that Russia did not want and should not seek an end to the "sick man of Europe." *Moskovskiia vedomosti* 11 (January 11, 1895); and *Moskovskiia vedomosti* 306 (November 6, 1895).

76. M. P. Soloviev, *Istoricheskoe prizvanie Rossii v Sviatoi Zemle* (Tobolsk: 1894); *Po Sviatoi Zemle* (St Petersburg: 1897); *Sviataia Zemlia i Imperatorskoe Pravoslavnoe Palestinskoe Obshchestvo* (St Petersburg: 1895); and *Sviataia Zemlia i Rossiia* (St Petersburg: 1900).

77. "Obshchee sobranie Imperatorskago Pravoslavnago Palestinskago Obshchestva," *Soobshcheniia Imperatorskago Pravoslavnago Palestinskago Obshchestva* 1 (1901): 4–22.

78. The ambiguity of these terms grows from the two words for "Russia" in the Russian language. *Narod* means people or nation. *Russkii* derives from the ethnic identity of early Russian civilization. *"Rossiiskii,"* however, was invented much later to denote the ethnically mixed population of the Russian Empire.

79. Rowland, "Moscow: The Third Rome or the New Israel?"

Chapter 5

1. James W. Cunningham, *A Vanquished Hope: The Movement for Church Renewal in Russia, 1905–1906* (Crestwood, N.Y.: St Vladimir's Seminary Press, 1981), 270.

2. Gregory L. Freeze, ed., *Forschungen zur osteuropaeischen Geschichte*, vol. 2 of *Geschichte der russischen Kirche,* ed. Igor Smolitsch (Leiden: E. J. Brill, 1991), 180.

3. Robert F. Byrnes, *Pobedonostsev: His Life and Thought* (Bloomington: Indiana University Press, 1968), 165–209.

4. K. P. Pobedonostsev, "Moskovskii sbornik*,"* in *Sochineniia,* ed. L. A. Karpova (St Petersburg: n.p.1996), 264–471. A very good treatment of Pobedonostev's views is found in John D. Basil, "Konstantin Petrovich Pobedonostsev: An Argument for a Russian State Church," *Church History* 64:1 (March 1995): 44–61.

5. E. N., *O sviatom ravnoapostolnom tsare Konstantine velikom i o tsarskoi vlasti*, 2nd ed. (Orel: 1899). The church celebrated the miraculous survival of the tsar each year on October 17.

6. Ibid., 18.

7. Ibid., 19–20.

8. Ibid., 37–38.

9. Ibid., 43.

10. Ibid., 44.

11. For a discussion of Alexander's image as a national ruler, see Richard S. Wortman, *Scenarios of Power: Myth and Ceremony in Russian Monarchy* (Princeton: Princeton University Press, 1995–2000), 2:177–88.

12. John Vostorgov, *Pamiati Imperatora Alexandra III-go* (Tiflis: 1905), 2.

13. Ibid., 16.

14. Ibid., 18.

15. Sergei Firsov, *Russkaia Tserkov nakanune peremen (konets 1890-kh-1918 gg.)* (Moscow: n.p. 2002), 54.

16. A. Elchaninov, *Tsarstvovanie Gosudaria Imperatora Nikolaia Alexandrovicha* (St Petersburg: 1913), 66.

17. Ibid., 68.

18. Ibid., 70.

19. V. M. Skvortsov, *Tsarskoe palomnichestvo Ikh Imperatorskikh Velichestv na poklonenie vekovym sviatyniam Kieva* (Kiev: 1896), 4.

20. Ibid., 18.

21. For a collection of articles and reports describing the official organization of the coronation ceremony, see RGIA, f. 1574, op. 2, d. 72.

22. *Moskovskiia tserkovnyia vedomosti* 20 (May 19, 1896).

23. "Vysokoe znachenie sviashchennago venchaniia," *Missionerskoe obozrenie* (May 1896): 58–67.

24. *Moskovskiia vedomosti* 122 (May 5, 1896).

25. *Moskovskiia vedomosti* 125 (May 8, 1896).

26. A discussion of Saul's role in the history of Old Testament Israel and the selection of David as its tsar is found in "Otvety iz slova Bozhiia voproshaiushchim o nashem upovanii o Tsarskoi vlasti," *Missionerskoe obozrenie* (May 1896): 68–83. For a later treatment of the matter, see A. Tyshko, *O samoderzhavnoi tsarskoi vlasti i eia bozhestvennom ustanovlenii* (Peterograd: 1915), 45–65.

27. *Svod Zakonov Rossiiskoi imperii* (St Petersburg: 1857), I, article 34. At the Third All-Russian Missionary Congress the following year, the image of Saul was again raised. Delegates agreed to integrate the example

of the failed Israelite tsar into missionary handbooks on the Old Testament that would teach Russians how "Saul was no different than apostates and opponents of the holy church." V. M. Skvortsov, *Deianiia 3-go Vserossiiskago Missionerskago Sezda v Kazani* (Kiev: 1897), 260.

28. Ibid. 198.

29. His speech was printed in ibid., 23–33.

30. *Polnoe sobranie zakonov Rossiiskoi Imperii* (St Petersburg: 1905), vol. 1, art. 22581. A brief treatment of the issues surrounding the decision to grant religious toleration is found in Peter Waldron, "Religious Toleration in Late Imperial Russia" in *Civil Rights in Imperial Russia*, eds. Olga Crisp and Linda Edmondson (Oxford: Clarendon Press, 1989), 103–19.

31. V. Skvortsov, "So skrizhalei serdtsa," *Missionerskoe obozrenie* 5 (March 1903): 798–18.

32. *Polnoe sobranie zakonov Rossiiskoi Imperii* (St Petersburg: 1907), vol. 1, art. 25495.

33. Bloody Sunday on January 9/22, 1905, was a protest of petitioners led by Priest Gapon who were blocked in their route to the Winter Palace in St Petersburg by armed Cossacks who fired on them, leading to fatalities.

34. *Polnoe sobranie zakonov Rossiiskoi Imperii* (St Petersburg: 1908), vol. 1, art. 26125.

35. Ibid.

36. A. Ivanov, "Svoboda i sovest," *Missionerskoe obozrenie* 12 (August 1903): 173–84; D. Tsvetaev, "Polozhenie inoveriia v Rossii," *Missionerskoe obozrenie* 1 (January 1904): 41–55; N. Griniakin, "Ne staroobriadets i ne starover, no raskolnik," *Missionerskoe obozrenie* 2 (January 1904): 224–30; V. Skvortsov, "So skrizhalei serdtsa," *Missionerskoe obozrenie* 14 (September 1904): 593-608.

37. V. Skvortsov, "So skrizhalei serdtsa," *Missionerskoe obozrenie* 3 (February 1905): 538–42.

38. Ibid.

39. V. Skvortsov, "So skrizhalei serdtsa," *Missionerskoe obozrenie* 7–8 (May 1905): 1251–71.

40. Ibid.

41. Some priests were arrested for participating in the affairs of the Social Democrats. For one case, see RGIA, f. 796, op. 188, 1 stol, 5 otd., d. 6991. The radical political activities of parish priests is treated in Edward E. Roslof, *Red Priests: Renovationism, Russian Orthodoxy, and Revolution,*

1905–1946 (Bloomington: Indiana University Press, 2002); and John Shelton Curtiss, *Church and State in Russia: The Last Years of the Empire, 1900–1917* (New York: Columbia University Press, 1940), 198–202.

42. The reaction of the Church hierarchy is discussed in P. S. Troitskii, *Tserkov i gosudarstvo v Rossii* (Moscow: 1909), 188. Metropolitan Antony of St Petersburg was one of the few who welcomed religious toleration. For his response, see Metropolitan Antony, "Rech," *Tserkovnyia vedomosti* 46 (November 12, 1905): 1043–44.

43. Archimandrite Nikon, *Za kogo govorit istoriia? K voprosu o monashestve* (Moscow: 1903), 3.

44. Information about the life of Nikon can be found in his autobiography. See Bishop Nikon, *Chem zhiva nasha russkaia pravoslavnaia dusha* (Trinity-Sergius Lavra: 1909). Scott M. Kenworthy gives considerable attention to the bishop in *The Heart of Russia: Trinity-Sergius, Monasticism, and Society after 1825* (New York: Oxford University Press, 2010), 227. See also *Khristianstvo: Entsiklopedicheskii slovar* (Moscow: Nauch, 1993), 219.

45. *Chem zhiva nasha russkaia pravoslavnaia dusha*, 13–14.

46. Hiermonk Nikon, *Zhitie i podvigi prepodobnago i bogonosnago ottsa nashego Sergiia*, 2nd ed. (Moscow: 1891).

47. Bishop Nikon, *Chto nam nuzhnee vsego,* 6.

48. Bishop Nikon, *Gde zhe nashe khristianstvo?* (Trinity-Sergius Lavra: 1910), 4.

49. Bishop Nikon, *V zashchitu prazdnikov* (St Petersburg: 1909), 1.

50. Ibid., 2.

51. Ibid., 5.

52. *Troitskoe slovo* 1 (February 7, 1910): 1–4.

53. E. Nikon, "Moi dnevnik," *Troitskoe slovo* 2 (July 14, 1910): 29–31.

54. E. Nikon, "Moi dnevnik," *Troitskoe slovo* 34 (September 26, 1910): 541–44.

55. *Troitskoe slovo* 50 (December 31, 1910): 794–95.

56. Tishaishii Tsar is a popular title meaning "a most peaceful ruler," stemming from the reign of Alexei I (1645–1682).

57. RGIA, f. 797, op. 73, 2 otd., 3 st., d. 98, lines 3–4.

58. Ibid., lines 19–21.

59. Ibid., line 2.

60. Quoted in Waldron, "Religious Toleration."

61. Igor Smolitsch, *Geschichte der russischen Kirche, 1700–1917* (Leiden: E. J. Brill, 1964), 1:215.

62. I. M. Gromoglasov, *Tretii Vserossiiskii Missionerskii sezd* (Sergiev Posad: 1898), 18–22.

63. Cunningham, *A Vanquished Hope,* 80–81.

64. Ibid., 323–24.

65. Curtiss, *Church and State in Russia,* 346. A large percentage was allocated especially for clerical salaries and the mission.

66. Smolitsch, *Geschichte der russischen kirche,* 1:709.

67. The church and its construction are described in *Khram Voskreseniia Khristova* (St Petersburg: 1907); and *Kratkoe opisanie khrama vo imia Voskreseniia Khristova* (St Petersburg: 1909).

68. Many commented upon this effect at the time, though as experienced historians of architecture noted, the tent roofs and other features looked more toward the seventeenth-century churches of Kostroma and Yaroslavl for inspiration.

69. An official account of the costs is found in *Otchet po sooruzheniiu khrama vo imia Voskreseniia Khrista na meste smertelnago raneniia Imperatora Aleksandra II* (St Petersburg: 1907).

70. N. Pokrovskii, "Novyi Khram Voskreseniia Khristova na Ekaterinskom kanale v S.-Peterburge," *Tserkovnyiia vedomosti* 33 (August 18, 1907): 1363–69; and "Khram Voskreseniia Khristova," *Strannik* (September 1907): 297–300.

71. N. V., "Khram-pamiatnik Tsariu-Osvoboditeliu," *Dobroe slovo* 34 (August 26, 1907): 1098–11.

72. Quoted in Viacheslav Mukhin, *Tserkovnaia kultura Sankt-Peterburga* (St Petersburg: I. Fyodorov, 1994), 229.

73. See, for instance, V. G. Isachenko et al., *Arkhitektory-stroiteli Peterburga nachala XX veka: Katalog vystavki* (Leningrad: VOOPIK, 1982).

74. Wortman, *Scenarios of Power,* 2:244–56.

75. A. V. Bertash, E. I. Zherikhina, and M. G. Talalai, *Khramy Peterburga: Spravochnik-putevoditel* (St Petersburg: n.p. 1992).

76. Quoted in *Tserkovnyi vestnik* 43 (October 27, 1905): 1347–53.

77. To my knowledge, no such effort has ever been made. Most accounts of the missionary priest's life are brief and were published to denounce or to defend him in light of one of several controversies that arose during the height of his career after 1905. See N. N. Durnovo, *Protoierei Ioann Ioannovich Vostorgov i ego politicheskaia deiatelnost* (Moscow: 1908); N. N. Durnovo, *Novye podvigi protoiereia I. I. Vostorgova i ego opravdaniia* (Moscow: 1909); and K. F. Kostiukhin, *Pravda o protoieree Vostorgove*

(Moscow: 1910). For a recent and unbiased account of his life, see the bibliographical article in *Khristianstvo: Entsiklopedicheskii slovar,* 1:377 78.

78. His involvement in the courses yielded publications designed for use by the inner mission. See, for instance, I. I. Vostorgov, *Sviashchennoe samosoznanie* (Moscow: 1911); and I. I. Vostorgov, ed., *Opyt protivosotsialisticheskago katakhizisa* (Moscow: 1911).

79. I. I. Vostorgov, "Smysl Tsarskago koronovaniia," in *Polnoe sobranie sochinenii* (Moscow: 1914–1916), 2:263–70. This address was issued in 1903 after the February Manifesto.

80. "Pastyrskii golos vo dni revoliutsii," ibid., 2:497–533.

81. Ibid.

82. John Meyendorff, *Byzantium and the Rise of Russia: A Study of Byzantino-Russian Relations in the Fourteenth Century* (Crestwood, N.Y.: St Vladimir's Seminary Press, 1989), 11.

83. Jonn Ilich Sergiev, *Novyia groznyia slova o. Ioanna Kronshtadtskago* (St Petersburg: 1908), 6.

84. Ibid., 8.

85. I. I. Vostorgov, "Osviashchenie gosudarstva i vlasti," in *Polnoe sobranie sochinenii,* 3:571–78.

86. "Zavety istorii o vernosti pravoslaviiu i samoderzhaviiu," ibid., 579–87.

Chapter 6

1. Studies of western European nationalism that offer some insights into late imperial Russia are Benedict Anderson, *Imagined Communities: Reflections on the Origin and Spread of Nationalism*, 2nd ed. (London: Verso, 1991); E. J. Hobsbawm, *Nations and Nationalism since 1780: Programme, Myth, Reality* (Cambridge: Cambridge University Press, 1990); and John Breuilly, *Nationalism and the State*, 2nd ed. (Chicago: University of Chicago Press, 1994).

2. Geoffrey Hosking, *Russia: People and Empire, 1552–1917* (Cambridge, Mass.: Harvard University Press, 1997), 319. A more recent survey with much insight into Russian nationalism is Nicholas V. Riasanovsky, *Russian Identities: A Historical Survey* (Oxford: Oxford University Press, 2005). Another recent work that addresses the contrast between civic and ethnic models of the nation is Laura Engelstein, *Slavophile Empire: Imperial Russia's Illiberal Path* (Ithaca, N.Y.: Cornell University Press, 2009). For an effort to explore the varieties of ethnic nationality in modern Russia, see Simon Franklin and Emma Widdis,

eds., *National Identity in Russian Culture: An Introduction* (Cambridge: Cambridge University Press, 2004).

3. A study of efforts to create an ethnically united national community is Theodore R. Weeks, *Nation and State in Late Imperial Russia: Nationalism and Russification on the Western Frontier, 1863–1914* (DeKalb: Northern Illinois University Press, 1996).

4. Miliukov's civic nationalism was expressed in statements to the State Duma such as the following: "The nation is not a race, the nation is not the totality of physical features which remain unchanging over centuries." Quoted in Melissa Kirschke Stockdale, *Paul Miliukov and the Quest for a Liberal Russia, 1880–1918* (Ithaca, N.Y.: Cornell University Press, 1996), 188.

5. Quoted in Hans Rogger, "Russia," in *The European Right: A Historical Profile*, eds. Hans Rogger and Eugen Weber (Berkeley: University of California Press, 1965), 443–501.

6. The Octobrist Party took its name from the October Manifesto that called for the creation of a representative assembly called the Duma. In contrast to more radical parties, they tended to support the regime within the Duma.

7. Hosking, *Russia,* 439.

8. *Tserkovnyi vestnik* 47 (November 24, 1905): 1477–80.

9. Quoted in Don C. Rawson, *Russian Rightists and the Revolution of 1905* (New York: Cambridge University Press, 1995), 28.

10. *Tserkovnyi vestnik* 13 (March 30, 1906): 399–402.

11. Petr Struve, "Intelligentsiia i natsionalnoe litso," in *Patriotica: Politika, kultura, religiia, sotsializm* (St Petersburg: 1911), 370–74.

12. A. K., "Russkaia tserkov v 1904 godu," *Tserkovnyi vestnik* 1 (January 6, 1905): 2–10. See also the editorial column in *Tserkovnyi vestnik* 6 (February 10, 1905): 164–68. Metropolitan Antony of St Petersburg also supported the edict. See Metropolitan Antony, "Rech," *Tserkovnyia vedomosti* 46 (November 12, 1905): 1043–44.

13. V. Yablonskii, "K voprosu o veroterpimosti," *Strannik* (March 1905): 442–62.

14. Sergei Firsov, *Russkaia Tserkov nakanune peremen (konets 1890-kh-1918 gg.)* (Moscow: n.p. 2002), 251.

15. "Ot redaktsii," *Tserkovno-obshchestvennaia zhizn* 1 (December 16, 1905): 4–5.

16. N. Nikolskii, "Chto delat?" *Tserkovno-obshchestvennaia zhizn* 2 (December 23, 1905): 58–59.

17. Kadets were a party favoring liberal reforms and were frequently at odds with the regime.

18. John Shelton Curtiss, *Church and State in Russia: The Last Years of the Empire, 1900–1917* (New York: Columbia University Press, 1940), 280–83.

19. This change in electoral law that reduced the radical and liberal membership of the Duma was initiated by Prime Minister Peter Stolypin.

20. Ibid., 322–28.

21. Ibid., 342–43.

22. John Vostorgov, *Gosudarstvennaia Duma i pravoslavno-russkaia tserkov* (Moscow: 1906).

23. Ibid., 5.

24. Ibid., 31.

25. Ibid., 32.

26. *Russkii Narodnyi Soiuz imeni Mikhaila Arkhangela: Programma i ustav* (St Petersburg: 1908), 1. For the symbolic importance of the Archangel Michael among Orthodox patriots, see Chapter 4.

27. Ibid., 8.

28. See, for example, RGIA, f. 796, op. 188, otd. 6, st. 3, d. 7771.

29. RGIA, f. 796, op. 197, otd. 6, st. 3, d. 323.

30. The Stundists were a religious group inspired by Western forms of Christianity such as the Baptists.

31. I have been unable to locate the original document of this petition in the synodal archive. The text was later published in "Glavnyi sovet soiuza russkago naroda," in *V Sviateishii Pravitelstvuiushchii Sinod* (St Petersburg: 1909).

32. *Katakhizis Soiuza Russkago Naroda* (Pochaev: 1910).

33. RNB, catalog 37.55.3.215.

34. Quoted in Curtiss, *Church and State in Russia,* 271–72.

35. A highly biased and polemical account of the Pochaev Monastery's activities after 1905 can be found in a brief work issued by the League of Militant Godless. See Boris Kandidov, *Krestom i nagaikoi: Pochaevskaia lavra i chernosotennoe dvizhenie* (Moscow: 1928). The monastery's political activities and affiliation with the Union of the Russian People are discussed briefly in Rawson, *Russian Rightists,* 92–95.

36. *Otchet staritskago otdela Soiuza russkago naroda o chteniiakh religiozno-nravstvennago i patriot10cheskago soderzhaniia* (Staritsa: 1911), 5.

37. James W. Cunningham, *A Vanquished Hope: The Movement for Church Renewal in Russia, 1905–1906* (Crestwood, N.Y.: St Vladimir's Seminary Press, 1981), 215–16. For Svetlov's theological contributions to Orthodox patriotism, see Chapter 3 of the present dissertation.

38. Many of his collected addresses demonstrate this. See Metropolitan Antony, "Rech," in *Rechi, slova i poucheniia*, 3rd ed. (St Petersburg: 1912), 44–46, 116–18, 176–83, 340–44.

39. A. Dubrovin, *Otkrytoe pismo Predsedatelia Glavnago Soveta Soiuza Russkago Naroda* (St Petersburg: 1906), 5.

40. Firsov, *Russkaia Tserkov,* 296.

41. *Khristianstvo: Entsiklopedicheskii slovar,* 1:92–93.

42. Cunningham, *A Vanquished Hope,* 64.

43. Archbishop Antony, "Slova v den soshestviia Sviatago Dukha," in *Polnoe sobranie sochinenii*, 2nd ed. (St Petersburg: 1911), 1:18–20.

44. "Slovo pri otkrytii pamiatnika Imperatoru Aleksandru II," ibid., 68–72.

45. "Slovo v den sviashchennago koronovaniia Ikh Imperatorskikh Velichestv," ibid., 79–82; and "Slovo v den otrytiia Sviatykh Moshchei Sviatitelia Feodosiia Chernigovskago," ibid., 93–96. Feodosii had lived in the seventeenth century, and the occasion of his canonization was used as an opportunity by missionaries to promote reconciliation with the Old Believers. For an appeal to the Old Believers by an official priest, see N. N. Esipov, *Sviatitel i Chudotvorets Arkhiepiskop Chernigovskii Feodosii Uglitskii* (St Petersburg: 1897), 254–56.

46. Archbishop Antony, "Slovo," in *Polnoe sobranie sochinenii,* 1: 135–43.

47. "Pismo na K.P. Pobedonostseva," ibid Volume 1, 540–47.

48. "O svobode veroispovedanii," ibid., 3:442–47.

49. Ibid.

50. "Vselenskaia Tserkov i narodnost," ibid., 2:31–42.

51. Ernest Renan was a nineteenth-century French author whose book *Life of Jesus* challenged traditional Christian beliefs.

52. Ibid.

53. "O natsionalizme i patriotizme," ibid., 1:220–25.

54. Ibid.

55. Ibid.

56. I. I. Vostorgov, "Blagodarnost," in *Polnoe sobranie sochinenii,* 2:448–52; "Palestina dlia Rossii i Gruzii," ibid., 88–96; and "Osnovatel Pravoslavnago Palestinskago Obshchestva," ibid., 3:350–53.

57. "Pravoslavie v istorii Rossii," ibid., 3:147–57; "Pravoslavno-russkoe gosudarstvennoe mirovozzrenie," ibid., 20–31; "Patrioticheskie soiuzy i ikh otnoshenie k religii," ibid., 124–30; and "Molitva," ibid., 2:404–10.

58. "Rus Sviataia," ibid., 3:602–7; "Missionerskoe prizvanie Rossii," ibid., 611–16; "Istoricheskoe prizvanie Rossii," ibid., 1:175–80; and "Znachenie sviatoi very," ibid., 2:187–94.

59. "Raspiatie rodiny," ibid., 3:16–20; "Chudesa very pravoslavnoi," ibid., 1:73–77; "Sviashchennoi pamiati nebesnago pokrovitelia zemli russkoi," ibid., 3:73–76; and "Zavety patriarkha Germogena," ibid., 187–93.

60. "Duma i dukhovenstvo, ibid., 4:389–408.

61. "Patrioticheskoe nachinanie," ibid., 505–7.

62. He quoted Rom 9:3–4.

63. "Patriotizm i khristianstvo," ibid., 3:236–40.

64. "Patrioticheskie soiuzy i ikh otnoshenie k religii," ibid., Vol. 3, 124–30.

65. Ibid.

66. For two recent accounts of Russification, see Hosking, *Russia,* 367–98; and Weeks, *Nation and State in Late Imperial Russia,* 10–15.

67. I. I. Vostorgov, "Kultura," in *Polnoe sobranii sochinenii,* 1:316–19.

68. Franklin and Widdis, *National Identity in Russian Culture,* 7.

69. "Rus Sviataia," in *Polnoe sobranii sochinenii*, 3:602–7.

70. "Pravoslavie v istorii Rossii," ibid., 147–57.

71. For a complete account of the scandalous theft of the icon, see "Russkaia tserkov v 1904 godu," *Tserkovnyi vestnik* 1 (January 6, 1905): 2–10.

72. I. I. Vostorgov, "Mirovoe prizvanie Rossii," in *Polnoe sobranie sochinenii,* 3:241–49.

73. See the journal's stated program in the inaugural issue, *Vernost* 1 (April 1, 1909).

74. Olga Ivanova, "Sviataia Rus," *Vernost* 16 (August 1, 1909): 26–31; A. Kruglov, "Prepodobnyi igumen Sergii Radonezhskii," *Vernost* 59 (July 1, 1910): 20–28; D. Iurin, "Paskha v Sviatoi Zemli," *Vernost* 49 (Easter, 1910): 25–35; A. Beliaev, "Sviatoi blagovernyi kniaz Aleksandr Nevskii i Aleksando-Nevskaia lavra," *Vernost* 67 (August 26, 1910): 31–40; I. I. Vostorgov, "Dragotsennaia zhemchuzhina," *Vernost* 16 (August 1, 1909): 3–13.

75. *Vernost* 132 (January 6, 1912).

76. I. I. Vostorogov, "Edinenie," *Vernost* 61 (July 15, 1910): 2–14.

77. I. I. Vostorgov, "Dobroe slovo pereselentsu," supplement to *Vernost* 61 (July 15, 1910).

78. I. I. Vostorgov, "Chto Dukh glagolaet Tserkvam?" *Vernost* 68 (September 2, 1910): 3–15.

79. Ibid.
80. Here he was quoting Rev 2:2, 4–5.
81. *Kolokol* 311 (February 8, 1907).
82. *Kolokol* 1 (December 24, 1905).
83. *Kolokol* 283 (January 4, 1907).
84. *Kolokol* 1165 (January 31, 1910).
85. Ibid.
86. *Kolokol* 285 (January 6, 1907).
87. *Kolokol* 291 (January 14, 1907).
88. *Kolokol* 307 (February 2, 1907).
89. *Kolokol* 313 (February 10, 1907).
90. *Kolokol* 320 (February 18, 1907).
91. *Kolokol* 344 (March 21, 1907).
92. *Kolokol* 352 (March 30, 1907).
93. *Kolokol* 324 (February 23, 1907).
94. *Kolokol* 414 (June 20, 1907).
95. V. M. Skvortsov, *Tserkovnyi svet i gosudarstvennyi razum*, 2 vols. (St Petersburg: 1912–1913).
96. Ibid., 1:ii–iii.
97. Ibid., 48–49.
98. Ibid., 24 (appendix).
99. Ibid., 2:3.
100. Ibid., 5.
101. Ibid., 14.
102. Ibid., 15.
103. Ibid., 18–21.
104. Ibid., 31–32.
105. Ibid., 148.
106. I. I. Vostorgov, "Zavety patriarkha Germogena," in *Polnoe sobranie sochinenii*, 3:187–93.

Chapter 7

1. V. M. Skvortsov, *Tserkovnyi svet i gosudarstvennyi razum* (St Petersburg: 1912–1913), ii.
2. P. N. Zyrianov, "Tserkov v period trekh rossiiskikh revoliutsii," in *Russkoe pravoslavie: Vekhi istorii* (Moscow: Izd-vo polit. lit-ry, 1989), 381–437.
3. Gregory L. Freeze, "'Going to the Intelligentsia': The Church and Its Urban Mission in Post-Reform Russia," in *Between Tsar and People:*

Educated Society and the Quest for Public Identity in Late Imperial Russia,
eds. Edith W. Clowes et al. (Princeton: Princeton University Press, 1991),
215–32.

4. *Missionerskoe obozrenie* regularly commented on lay intellectual
affairs. A few representative articles from 1903 are Iromonakh Mikhail,
"Novoe khristiantsvo Merezhkovskago," *Missionerskoe obozrenie* 5 (March
1903), 576–95; Ivan Aivazov, "Novyi put v ego otnoshenii k starym putiam i
k pravoslavnoi tserkvi," *Missionerskoe obozrenie* 8 (May 1903): 1214–19; and
P. Kozitskii, "Intelligentsiia i narod," *Missionerskoe obozrenie* 15 (October
1903): 524–43.

5. Zyrianov, "Tserkov v period trekh rossiiskikh revoliutsii."

6. Nicholas V. Riasanovsky, *Russia and the West in the Teaching of the
Slavophiles: A Study in Romantic Ideology* (Cambridge, Mass.: Harvard
University Press, 1952).

7. I. A. Fedotova, "Bogoslovskoe nasledie A. S. Khomiakova i
pravoslavnaia akademicheskaia mysl vtoroi poloviny XIX v.," *Veche* 8
(November 1996/January 1997), 64–72.

8. "Nashi zadachi," *Khristianin* (January 1907): 1–26.

9. Ibid.

10. "Sredi gazet," *Khristianin* (August 1910): 684–700.

11. Nicholas Berdiaev, *Novoe religioznoe soznanie i obshchestvennost* (St
Petersburg: 1907).

12. The reports from meetings of the society were published in issues of
Novyi put. For the debate about freedom of conscience in which Skvortsov
participated, see *Novyi put* (March 1903): 113–55. For a discussion of
Merezhkovsky's involvement in the society, see Bernice Glatzer Rosenthal,
*Dmitri Sergeevich Merezhkovsky and the Silver Age: The Development of a
Revolutionary Personality* (The Hague: Martinus Nijhoff, 1975).

13. The influence of Kireevsky is evident in Soloviev's first major work,
The Crisis of Western Philosophy, published in 1874. Soloviev's intellectual
development is treated in K. Mochulskii, *Vladimir Soloviev: Zhizn i
uchenie,* in *Gogol, Solovev, Dostoevskii* (Moscow: Izd-vo "Respublika,"
1995), 63–216; D. Stremooukhoff, *Vladimir Soloviev and His Messianic
Work*, trans. Elizabeth Meyendorff (Belmont, Mass.: Nordland, 1980);
S. M. Solovev, *Vladimir Solovev: Zhizn i tvorcheskaia evoliutsiia* (Moscow:
n.p. 1997); and Nicolas Zernov, *Three Russian Prophets* (London: S. C. M.
Press, 1944).

14. The full text of Soloviev's letter to Alexander III appears in V.
Solovev, *Pisma*, ed. E. L. Radlov (Petrograd: n.p. 1923), 149–50.

15. V. S. Solovev, "O dukhovnoi vlasti v Rossii," in *Sobranie sochinenii*, eds. S. M. Solovev and E. L. Radlov, 2nd ed. (St Petersburg: 1911–1914), 3:227–42; "O raskole v russkom narode i obshchestve," ibid., 3:245–80; "O tserkovnom voprose po povodu starokatolikov," ibid., 4:123–32; "Kak probudit nashi tserkovnyia sily?" ibid., 4:203–6; "Novozavetnyi Izrail," ibid., 4:207–20; "Pervobytnoe iazychesvto," ibid., 6:174–233; "Polskaia natsionalnaia tserkov," ibid., 9:63–70; and "Ideia sverkhcheloveka," ibid., 9:265–74. Some of his published letters to governmental authorities and Church prelates also addressed the issues of the mission and religious freedom. See "Arkhimandritu A. Vadkovskomu," *Sobranie sochinenii*, 11:369–71; "Imperatoru Nikolaiu II," ibid., 11:452–56; and "Pismo k K. P. Pobedonostsevu," ibid., 12:287–89.

16. E. L. Radlov, "V. S. Solovev," *Sobranie sochinenii*, 10:vii–li.

17. For a discussion of the theological underpinnings of Soloviev's interest in Christian reunion, see Paul Valliere, *Modern Russian Theology: Bukharev, Soloviev, Bulgakov* (Grand Rapids, Mich.: Eerdmans, 2000).

18. Solovev, *Sobranie sochinenii*, 4:3.

19. V. S. Solovev, "Soglashenie s Rimom i moskovskiia gazety," in *Sobranie sochinenii*, 4:117–22.

20. Ibid., 63.

21. Greg Gaut, "Can a Christian Be a Nationalist? Vladimir Solov'ev's Critique of Nationalism," *Slavic Review* 57:1 (Spring 1998): 77–94.

22. The clergy's lack of sympathy for Soloviev's ecumenism is seen, for example, in I. A., "V. S. Solovev kak zashchitnik papstva po kn. 'La Russie et L'eglise Universelle,'" *Vera i razum* 12 (June 1904): 614–38.

23. N. Preobrazhenskii, "K voprosu o sblizhenii mezhdu pravoslaviem i anglikanstvom," *Bogoslovskii vestnik* (December 1888): 662–72; "Inoslavnye svideteli istiny Pravoslaviia," *Missionerskii sbornik* 1 (January/February 1896): 24–32; V. A. Sokolov, "Mozhno-li ili dolzhno-li nam molitsia v tserkvi za usopshikh-inoslavnykh?" *Bogoslovskii vestnik* (January 1906): 1–31; and I. P. Sokolov, "O deistvitelnosti anglikanskoi ierarkhii," *Khristianskoe chtenie* (February 1913).

24. The second part of the work appeared in 1891. V. S. Solovev, "Natsionalnyi vopros v Rossii," in *Sobranie sochinenii*, 5:3–401.

25. Ibid., 13.

26. Ibid., 12:607–8.

27. Ibid., 10:252–54.

28. Ibid., 4:243.

29. Ibid., 4:259–60.

30. Ibid., 4:244.

31. Ibid., 4:257.

32. Ibid., 4:271.

33. Ibid., 4:266.

34. Ibid., 4:268.

35. Ibid., 4:284.

36. Ibid., 4:470.

37. Ibid., 4:526.

38. Ibid., 4:531.

39. Ibid., 4:533.

40. Ibid., 4:567.

41. Because of its provocative tone and criticism of the official Church, this work had to be published abroad in France. Though it appeared in 1889, Soloviev stated in the preface that he had been engaged in writing it for the past seven years.

42. He spoke, for instance, of Constantinople as the "second Rome." *Sobranie sochinenii,* 4:151. In other works Soloviev emphasized the egocentric nature of the Third Rome doctrine. See "Vizantizm i Rossiia," *Sobranie sochinenii,* 7:285–328.

43. Solovev, *Sobranie sochinenii,* 11:169.

44. Ibid.

45. Ibid., 11:178.

46. Ibid., 11:181.

47. Ibid., 11:185.

48. Ibid., 11:187.

49. Ibid., 11:186–87.

50. V. S. Solovev, "O raskole v russkom narode i obshchestve," *Sobranie sochinenii,* 3:245–82.

51. Like *Russia and the Universal Church,* it was published illicitly in France.

52. Passing references can also be found in Mochulskii, *Vladimir Soloviev,* 167; Stremooukoff, *Vladimir Soloviev and His Messianic Work,* 185–86; and Zernov, *Three Russian Prophets,* 127.

53. Martin George, "Die 900-Jahr-Feier der Taufe Russlands im Jahr 1888 und die Kritik Vladimir Sergeevic Solovevs am Verhaeltnis von Staat und Kirche in Russland," *Jahrbuecher fuer Geschichte Osteuropas* 36:1 (1988): 15–36.

54. It may be worth noting that Soloviev did not explicitly use the construction "national faith" in the commemoration essay. He did,

however, speak of the "national faith" (*narodnaia vera*) in an open letter he later wrote in order to clarify some of his arguments there. The occasion for doing so was a disagreement with a reviewer of the essay who claimed that the faith of Russia's earliest Christians was actually Catholic. See V. S. Soloviev, "Otvet na korrespondentsiiu iz Krakova," in *Sobranie sochinenii,* 11:135–38.

55. *The Chronicle of Nestor* is one of the earliest written accounts of Russian history recorded in the twelfth century.

56. V. S. Solovev, "Vladimir Sviatoi i Khristianskoe Gosudarstvo," in *Sobranie sochinenii,* 11:121–35.

57. A. Rusakova, *Mikhail Nesterov*, trans. Andrew Bromfield and Natalia Rogovskaya (Leningrad: n.p. 1990), 7.

58. M. V. Nesterov, *Davnie dni* (Moscow: Iskusstvo, 1959), 15.

59. A lengthy description of the circumstances surrounding the painting is found in S. Durylin, *Nesterov* (Moscow: n.p. 1976), 63–71.

60. I. Nikonova, *Mikhail Vasilevich Nesterov* (Moscow: Iskusstvo, 1979), 20–21.

61. Quoted in Durylin, *Nesterov,* 70.

62. A letter dated July 17—the last day of the festival—makes a sarcastic reference to "Kievan idols." See *Pisma izbrannoe,* 34–35.

63. Ibid., 95.

64. Rusakova, *Mikhail Nesterov,* 159.

65. *Pisma izbrannoe,* 54.

66. Nesterov's first experiences with Bastien-Lepage's *Joan d'Arc* are related in *Davnie dni,* 199–200.

67. It is true that in one letter from Pompei dated in 1889 Nesterov spoke of Danilevsky's *Russia and Europe* as a "good book," but this hardly constitutes an endorsement of its overall message. In general, his letters lacked much commentary upon political affairs. See M. V. Nesterov, *Pisma izbrannye*, ed. A. A. Rusakova (Moscow: n.p. 1988), 50.

68. Quoted in Rusakova, *Mikhail Nesterov,* 158.

69. For an interesting discussion of the significance of central and local or even private initiative in the construction and use of temples and chapels at the time, see Vera Shevzov, *Russian Orthodoxy on the Eve of Revolution* (Oxford: Oxford University Press, 2004), 54–130. Shevzov cautions against assuming a strong opposition between the official and popular, noting that even in the matter of local "chapel culture," for instance, "chapels in general seem to have contributed to the cohesion of the Orthodox community at large." Ibid., 130.

70. *Pisma izbrannoe,* 41.

71. Durylin, *Nesterov,* 93.

72. Like *Holy Rus,* this latter painting was a religious representation of the nation. It depicted a large crowd of people standing by a river. Among them were symbolical figures ranging from a holy fool to prominent novelists such as Dostoevsky and even Tolstoy.

73. Michael Cherniavsky, *Tsar and People: Studies in Russian Myths* (New York: Random House, 1969), 218–19.

74. A. Kruglov, "Svetilnik svetleishii," *Vernost* 52 (May 15, 1910): 15–24.

75. P. Muratov, "Tvorchestvo M. V. Nesterova," *Russkaia mysl* 4 (April 1907): 151–58.

76. Maksimilian Voloshin, "Vystavka M. Nesterova," *Vesy* 3 (March 1907): 105–8.

77. "M. V. Nesterov i ego tvorchestvo," *Niva* 20 (May 19, 1907): 322–25.

78. V. V. Rozanov, "Moliashchaiasia Rus," *Novoe vremia* 11087 (January 23, 1907).

79. V. V. Rozanov, "Gde zhe 'religiia molodosti,'" *Russkoe slovo* 36 (February 15, 1907).

80. V. V. Rozanov, "M. V. Nesterov," *Zolotoe runo* 2 (1907): 3–7.

81. Catherine Evtuhov, *The Cross and the Sickle: Sergei Bulgakov and the Fate of Russian Religious Philosophy* (Ithaca, N.Y.: Cornell University Press, 1997), 29.

82. Arsenii Gulyga, *Russkaia ideia i ee tvortsy* (Moscow: "Soratnik," 1995), 179.

83. S. N. Bulgakov, "Chto daet sovremennomu soznaniiu filosofiia Vladimira Soloveva?" in *Ot marksisma k idealizmu* (St Peterburg: 1903).

84. Evtuhov, *The Cross and the Sickle,* 118.

85. Quoted in ibid., 120.

86. Quoted in ibid., 119.

87. Quoted in ibid., 122.

88. D. M. Merezhkovskii, *Polnoe sobranie sochinenii Dmitriia Sergeevicha Merezhkovskago* (Moscow: 1914), vols. 9–12. Merezhkovsky's research was not primarily concerned with nationality. Nevertheless, he took special interest in Dostoevsky's claim that "the Russian people is constituted by Orthodoxy" (*russkii narod ves v pravoslavii*) and used this as an angle of interpretation. See *Polnoe sobranie sochinenii,* 12:68. In discussing Tolstoy, he echoed the arguments of cultural missionaries by stating that "Tolstoy does not believe in God, does not believe in the Son of God, does not believe in Christ." *Polnoe sobranie sochinenii,* 11:236.

89. S. N. Bulgakov, "Ivan Karamazov kak filosoficheskii tip," in *Ot Marksizma k idealizmu* (St Petersburg: 1903), 83–112.

90. The address was later published as an article in the journal *Svoboda i kultura*. For the text, see Sergei Bulgakov, "Venets ternovyi (pamiati F. M. Dostoevskoago)," in *Dva grada* (Moscow: 1911), 2:223–43.

91. It appeared as a publication of the Religious-Philosophical Library. See *F. M. Dostoevskii, kak propovednik khristianskago vozrozhdeniia i vselenskago pravoslaviia* (Moscow: 1908). Interestingly, the text of Vladimir Soloviev's *Three Speeches in Memory of Dostoevsky* was also included.

92. S. N. Bulgakov, "Geroizm i podvizhnichestvo: Iz razmyshlenii o religioznykh idealakh russkoi intelligentsii," in *Vekhi* (Moscow: 1909), 176–222.

93. Ibid.

94. See Antony's open letter reprinted in Archbishop Antony, *Polnoe sobranie sochinenii*, 2nd ed. (St Petersburg: 1911), 3:552–54. The archbishop's interest in lay Orthodox patriotism was not limited to the authors of *Vekhi*. He also maintained amiable relations with Mikhail Nesterov, and in 1917 the artist painted a memorable portrait of him.

95. Archbishop Antony, *Polnoe sobranie sochinenii*, 3:554–68.

96. Evtuhov, *The Cross and the Sickle*, 141.

97. For the text, see S. N. Bulgakov, "Pervokhristianstvo i noveishii sotsializm," in *Dva grada* (Moscow: 1911), 2:1–50.

98. Sergei Bulgakov, "Razmyshleniia o natsionalnosti," in *Dva grada*, 2:278–303.

99. Sergei Bulgakov, "Tserkov i kultura," in *Dva grada*, 2:303–13.

100. Bulgakov, "Razmyshleniia o natsionalnosti."

101. Ibid.

102. For the role of the industrialist Paul Riabushinsky in financing *Tserkov*, and the journal's vision of a modern Russian national identity, see James L. West, "The Neo-Old Believers of Moscow: Religious Revival and Nationalist Myth in Late Imperial Russia," *Canadian-American Slavic Studies* 26:1–3 (1992): 5–28; James L. West, "The Riabushinsky Circle: Burzhuaziia and Obshchestvennost' in Late Imperial Russia," in *Between Tsar and People: Educated Society and the Quest for Public Identity in Late Imperial Russia*, eds. Edith W. Clowes et al. (Princeton: Princeton University Press, 1991), 41–56; and James L. West, "The Rjabushinsky Circle: Russian Industrialists in Search of a Bourgeoisie, 1909–1914," *Jahrbuecher fuer Geschichte Osteuropas* 32:3 (1984): 358–77. On Old Believer efforts to create an empire-wide community, see Roy Robson, *Old Believers in Modern Russia* (DeKalb: Northern Illinois University Press, 1995).

103. F. E. Melnikov, *Bluzhdaiushchee bogoslovie* (Moscow: 1911), 1.

104. *Staroobriadcheskaia mysl* 6 (June 1910): 409–10.

105. V. G. Senatov, *Filosofiia istorii staroobriadchestva* (Moscow: 1908). Also see his contributions in *Tserkov.*

106. V. Senatov, "Dve tserkvi," *Tserkov* 9 (1910): 297–300.

107. V. Senatov, "Kak russkaia zemlia soedinilas," *Tserkov* 6 (1913): 129–34; *Tserkov* 7 (1913): 153–56.

108. "O nashikh tseliakh," *Staraia Rus* (December 1911): 1–3.

109. I. Vedi, "Chto nuzhno sovremennomu staroobriadchestvu?" *Staraia Rus* (December 1911): 8–12.

110. The exhibition was scheduled to commemorate the founding of the Romanov Dynasty. *Vystavka drevne-russkago iskusstva, ustroennaia v 1913 godu v oznamenovanie chestvovaniia 300-letiia tsarstvovaniia Doma Romanovykh* (Moscow: 1913).

111. I. K., "Lektsiia Y.A. Bogachenko," *Staraia Rus* 1 (1912): 17–19.

112. Ibid.

113. A brief account of Kirillov's career is found in *Staroobriadchestvo: Opyt entsiklopedicheskogo slovaria* (Moscow: n.p. 1996), 140–41.

114. I. A. Kirillov, *Pravda staroi very* (Moscow: 1916), 29.

115. Ibid., 47.

116. *Popovets:* a member of an Old Believer community that had a priesthood and sacraments.

117. For his own confessional views and his effort to unify all of Old Belief, see I. Kirillov, *Istinnaia tserkov* (Moscow: 1912).

118. *Khristianin* (August 1910): 536–43.

119. I. A. Kirillov, *Tretii Rim* (Moscow: 1914), 87.

120. Kirillov, *Pravda staroi very,* 59.

121. Ibid., 32.

122. Kirillov, *Tretii Rim,* 39.

123. Kirillov, *Pravda staroi very,* 40.

124. Ibid., 42.

Chapter 8

1. Bishop Nikon, *Pamiati velikago sviashchennomuchenika za otechestvo* (Sergiev Posad: 1912), 56.

2. Feodosii Ivanov, *Tserkov v epokhu smutnago vremeni na Rusi* (Ekaterinoslav: 1906), 276.

3. RGIA, f. 799, op. 6, d. 48, lines 1–2.

4. RGIA, f. 472, op. 43, d. 145, line 3.

5. RGIA, f. 468, op. 17, d. 1773, line 1.

6. Bishop Nikon, *Chto nam nuzhnee vsego* (Sergiev Posad: 1905), 3. Nikon's inaugural article for *Troitskoe slovo* also compared the present to the Time of Troubles. *Troitskoe slovo* 1 (February 7, 1910): 1–4.

7. Nikon, *Chto nam nuzhnee vsego,* 46.

8. Bishop Nikon, "Moi dnevnik," *Troitskoe slovo* 22 (July 4, 1910): 348–52.

9. Bishop Nikon, "Moi dnevnik," *Troitskoe slovo* 14 (May 9, 1910): 221–24.

10. Bishop Nikon, "Moi dnevnik," *Troitskoe slovo* 23 (July 11, 1910): 366–68.

11. *Kolokol* 1148 (January 12, 1910).

12. Evidence of the Synod's consciousness about the impending dynastic celebration is found in the many articles and announcements of *Tserkovnyia vedomosti* throughout 1912.

13. "Chestvovanie pamiati sviateishago patriarkha Germogena v Moskve," *Tserkovnyia vedomosti* 8 (February 25, 1912): 327–32.

14. *Tserkovnyia vedomosti* 8 (February 25, 1912): 332–34.

15. Bishop Nikon, "Nam li molitsia za nego?" *Tserkovnyia vedomosti* 9 (March 3, 1912): 348–51.

16. I. Vostorgov, "Slovo pokhvalnoe Germogenu," *Tserkovnyia vedomosti* 7 (February 18, 1912): 233–36; and "Sluzhenie vechnomu," *Tserkovnyia vedomosti* 8 (February 25, 1912): 275–79.

17. *Kolokol* 1754 (February 11, 1912); *Kolokol* 1755 (February 12, 1912); *Kolokol* 1756 (February 14, 1912); *Kolokol* 1759 (February 17, 1912); and *Kolokol* 1760 (February 18, 1912).

18. For other articles, see P. Skubachevskii, "Germogen patriarkh Moskovskii i vseia Rusi i ego sluzhenie otechestvu v Smutnoe vremia," *Vera i razum* 4 (February 1912): 449–66; and P. Nevskii, "Tserkovno-politicheskie deiateli smutnago vremeni XVII-go veka," *Khristianin* (February 1912): 388–408.

19. V. Shchukin, *Patriarkh Germogen kak predstavitel i pobornik natsionalnoi religioznosti* (Riga: 1912).

20. Ibid., 3.

21. Ibid., 4.

22. Ibid., 6–7.

23. Ibid., 8.

24. Ibid., 5.

25. Ibid., 10.

26. Ibid., 16.

27. Ibid., 17.

28. N. I. Gerasimov, *V zashchitu russkago natsionalizma* (Moscow: 1912).

29. Ibid., 15.

30. Ibid., 24–25.

31. Ibid., 35.

32. Ibid., 39.

33. Ibid., 25.

34. *Kolokol* 2014 (January 1, 1913).

35. "Stikhtvorenie na otrytie ostankov o. Serafima Sarovskago," *Staroobriadets* 5 (May 1907). This poem, the editors claimed, had originally been written in 1903.

36. I. Kirillov, *Istinnaia tserkov* (Moscow: 1912), 11.

37. Ibid., 9–10.

38. *Utro Rossii* 39 (February 12, 1912).

39. V. Iaksanov, "Velikii sviatitel," *Shchit very* 2 (February 1912): 99–105.

40. *Utro Rossii* 39 (February 17, 1912).

41. *Vera i razum* 4 (February 1913), 559–60. See also *Strannik* (March 1913): 467–75.

42. *Khristianstvo: Entsiklopedicheskii slovar* (Moscow: 1993), 1:673–79.

43. Gregory L. Freeze, "Subversive Piety: Religion and the Political Crisis in Late Imperial Russia," *Journal of Modern History* 68 (June 1996): 308–50.

44. V. Iaksanov, "Velikii sviatitel," *Shchit very* 2 (Februrary 1912): 99–105.

45. *Tserkovnyia vedomosti* 15–16 (April 14, 1913): 143–50 (official section).

46. Suzanne K. Kaufman, "Miracles, Medicine, and the Spectacle of Lourdes: Popular Religion and Modernity in Fin-De-Siecle France" (Ph.D. diss., Rutgers University, 1996).

47. F. G. Titov, *Sviateishii patriarkh vserossiiskii Germogen kak revnitel pravoslaviia, missioner i velikii patriot* (Kiev: 1912).

48. S. Kedrov, *Zhineopisanie Sviateishago Germogena Patriarkha Moskovskago i vseia Rossii* (Moscow: 1912), 16.

49. Ibid.

50. *Stradalets za rodinu: Patriarkh Germogen* (St Petersburg: 1912), 9.

51. V. V. Nazarevskii, *Sviateishii Germogen, patriarkh vseia Rossii* (no place, date, or pagination).

52. V. V. Nazarevskii, *Sviateishii Germogen, patriarkh vseia Rossii.*

53. *Sviatitel Ermogen* (St Petersburg: 1913), 4. A more sympathetic response to Anglican efforts to promote Christian unity was found during the same year in a work that said nothing about Germogen and his example. See I. P. Sokolov, "O deistvitelnosti anglikanskoi ierarkhii," *Khristianskoe chtenie* (February 1913): 153–74.

54. *Sviatitel Germogen, Patriarkh Moskovskii i vseia Rusi* (Moscow: 1913), 5.

55. *Sviateishii Patriarkh Germogen i mesto ego zakliucheniia* (Moscow: 1913), 33.

56. *Sviatitel Ermogen,* 2.

57. I. Solovev, *Kakoi smysl i znachenie imeet prichtenie Sviateishago Patriarkha Ermogena k liku sviatykh?* (Sergiev Posad: 1913), 4.

58. Gregory Freeze, "Subversive Piety."

59. The attitudes of the liberal clergy are treated well in James W. Cunningham, *A Vanquished Hope: The Movement for Church Renewal in Russia, 1905–1906* (Crestwood, N.Y.: St Vladimir's Seminary Press, 1981).

60. N. Milovanov, *Proslavlenie patriarkha Ermogena* (St Petersburg: 1914), 14. Interestingly, this work was written by a priest and published by Skvortsov.

61. D. Vvedenskii, "Dukhovnyi strazh zemli russkoi," *Moskovskiia tserkovnyia vedomosti* 19 (May 11, 1913): 368–71.

62. *Moskovskiia tserkovnyia vedomosti* 20 (May 18, 1913): 387–89.

63. The newspaper *Russkiia vedomosti* limited its coverage of the festival to a few details, while the more remote *Kievlianin* reported nothing at all. *Russkiia vedomosti* 109 (May 12, 1913). Most conservative newspapers, on the other hand, provided more substantial coverage. Those that took the greatest interest did not always interpret the festival in the way intended by Church organizers, however. *Moskovskiia vedomosti,* for instance, declared Germogen's glorification a "religious-state festival," though it did emphasize the role of Germogen's "national faith." *Moskovskiia vedomosti* 108 (May 11, 1913). For other accounts, see *Novoe vremia* 13347 (May 10, 1913); and *Moskovskii listok* 109 (May 12, 1913).

64. *Russkoe znamia* 107 (May 15, 1913).

65. *Moskovskiia tserkovnyia vedomosti* 18 (May 4, 1913): 353–54.

66. *Moskovskiia tserkovnyia vedomosti* 18 (May 4, 1913): 352–53.

67. *Moskovskiia tserkovnyia vedomosti* 20 (May 18, 1913): 389–96.

68. V. Parkhomenko, "K voprosu o kreshchenii Vladmira Sviatago i khristianizatsii pri nem Rusi," *Vera i razum* 11 (June 1913): 648–58.

69. *Missionerskoe obozrenie* 3 (March 1913).

70. V. Skvortsov, "Pravoslavnaia missiia v 1912 godu," *Missionerskoe obozrcnic* 1 (January 1913): 132–41.

71. I. Solovev, *Kakoi smysl i znachenie imeet prichtenie Sviateishago Patriarkha Ermogena k liku sviatykh?*, 4.

72. D. Vvedenskii, "Dukhovnyi strazh zemli russkoi," *Moskovskiia tserkovnyia vedomosti* 19 (May 11, 1913): 368–71.

73. Bishop Nikon, "Urok s neba," *Tserkovnyia vedomosti* 15–16 (April 14, 1913): 698–702.

74. I. Vostorgov, *Vo slavu sviatago Germogena, Patriarkha vserossiiskago* (Moscow: 1913), 6.

75. Ibid., 10–11.

76. Two umbrella organizations were mentioned by name, Russkii Monarkhicheskii Soiuz and Russkoe Monarkhicheskoe Sobranie v Moskve.

77. Ibid., 46.

78. Ibid., 42.

Epilogue

1. RGIA, f. 797, op. 83, otd. 2, stol 3, d. 562.

2. Nicholas had ordered the construction of a temple in the medieval style in Tsarskoe Selo dedicated to St Seraphim. It was consecrated in 1911. D. N. Loman, *Poiasnitelnaia zapiska po oborudovleniiu tserkvi prepodovnago Serafima Sarovskago chudotvortsa* (St Peterburg: 1912).

3. "Khram-pamiatnik 300-letiia tsarstvovaniia Doma Romanovykh," *Tserkovnyia vedomosti* 17 (April 27, 1913): 772–74.

4. For a detailed analysis of the ceremonies that accompanied the tsar's journey, see Richard S. Wortman, "'Invisible Threads': The Historical Imagery of the Romanov Tercentenary," *Russian History* 16:2–4 (1989): 389–408.

5. "Iubileinyia torzhestva," *Tserkovnyia vedomosti* 22 (June 1, 1913): 1007–49.

6. Hegumen Seraphim, *Torzhestvo dolga* (Kungur: 1914).

7. "Pravoslavnaia Tserkov i missiia pravoslavnago dukhovenstva v slovakh Gosudaria Imperatora po sluchaiu Vserossiiskago torzhestva 'Trekhsotiletiia tsarstvovaniia Doma Romanovykh,'" *Missionerskii sbornik* 3 (March 1913): i–ix. Also see V. Smirnov, "Gosudar Imperator i Pravoslavie," *Missionerskii sbornik* 3 (March 1913): x–xii.

8. B. G., "Romanovskie iubileinye dni," *Istoricheskii vestnik* (March 1913): 1–64 (supplement).

9. P. Y. Svetlov, "Chem silno, slavno i veliko russkoe tsarstvo?" *Tserkovnyia vedomosti* 18–19 (May 6, 1913): 784–88.

10. Hieromonk Seraphim, *Pervyi vserossiiskii inocheskii sezd* (Kungur: 1912).

11. Hieromonk Seraphim, *Pervyi v Rossii po vneshnei missii kazanskii missionerskii sezd*, 3 vols. (Nizhny-Novgorod: 1911–1912). In this work also, the author examined a great many reports about the mission published in the secular press.

12. Hegumen Seraphim, *Torzhestvo dolga.*

13. Ibid., 68.

14. Ibid., 74.

15. Seraphim identified several past and present Orthodox patriots among the clergy. In addition to Nikanor, he admired Archbishop Antony of Volynia, Bishop Nikon, Skvortsov, and Vostorgov.

16. Hegumen Seraphim, *Torzhestvo dolga*, 88.

17. Ibid., 89.

18. Ibid., 136.

19. Indeed, the carelessness with which he quoted other sources makes it unclear at times whether passages in his text are original.

20. Ibid., 184.

21. Ibid., 277.

22. *Utro Rossii* 109 (May 12, 1913).

23. Hegumen Seraphim, *Torzhestvo dolga,* 234.

24. For the Synod's order to observe the anniversary, see *Tserkovnyia vedomosti* 11 (March 16, 1913): 125–26 (official section). Many journals offered space for the discussion of the commemoration. *Pravoslavnyi sobesednik,* for instance, devoted its entire September issue to the edict's significance.

25. V. Parkhomenko, "Istoricheskii moment izdaniia Milanskago edikta i ego znachenie," *Vera i razum* 18 (September 1913): 732–37.

26. Archbishop Nikon, "Iubilei pobedy kresta nad iazychestvom," *Tserkovnyia vedomosti* 35 (August 31, 1913): 1550–52.

27. *Kolokol* 2035 (January 26, 1913).

28. I. Vostorgov, "Torzhestvo kresta Khristova," *Tserkovnyia vedomosti* 35 (August 31, 1913): 1553–71.

29. *Novoe vremia* 13473 (September 14, 1913).

30. "Russkaia tserkovnaia zhizn v 1913 godu," *Tserkovnyi vestnik* 1 (January 2, 1914): 10–17.

31. K. Fomenko, "Slovo," *Tserkovnyia vedomosti* 37 (September 14, 1913): 1652–55.

32. RGIA, f. 797, op. 83, 2 otd., 3 stol, d. 302, line 1.

33. V. Beliaev, "Natsionalizm i nravstvenno khristianskie idealy," *Tserkovnyi vestnik* 21 (May 22, 1914): 618–21.

Conclusion

1. Archbishop Nikon, "Slovo pravdy nashim patriotam-antisemitam," *Tserkovnyia vedomosti* 28:25 (June 20, 1915): 745–48.

2. The story of left-leaning clergy is told in part by Jennifer Hedda, *His Kingdom Come: Orthodox Pastorship and Social Activism in Revolutionary Russia* (DeKalb: Northern Illinois University Press, 2008).

3. See, for instance, G. P. Fedotov, *Sudba i grekhi Rossii*, 2 vols. (St Petersburg: n.p. 1991).

4. Nathaniel Davis, *A Long Walk to Church: A Contemporary History of Russian Orthodoxy* (Boulder, Colo.: Westview Press, 1995), 59–69.

5. The text of the document is appended to *O sotsialnoy kontseptsii russkogo pravoslaviya* (Moscow: n.p. 2002), 250–393.

BIBLIOGRAPHY

UNPUBLISHED SOURCES

I. ARCHIVAL MATERIALS

Rossiiskaia natsionalnaia biblioteka, Otdel rukopisei, St Petersburg

f. 631   S. A. Rachinskii
f. 738   V. V. Stasov
f. 773   V. M. Vasnetsov

Rossiiskii gosudarstvennyi istoricheskii arkhiv, St Petersburg

f. 468   Kabinet Ego Imperatorskogo Velichestva
f. 472   Kantseliariia Ministerstva Imperatorskogo Dvora
f. 796   Kantseliariia Sinoda
f. 797   Kansteliariia Ober-Prokuropa Sinoda
f. 799   Khoziaistvennoe Upravlenie Sinoda
f. 812   Pribaltiiskoe Pravoslavnoe Bratstvo
f. 1284   Departament Obshchikh Del Ministerstva Vnutrennikh Del
f. 1574   K. P. Pobedonostsev

II. DISSERTATIONS AND UNPUBLISHED PAPERS

Bushkovich, Paul. "What Is Russia? Russian National Consciousness and the State, 1500–1917." Unpublished paper.

Clay, J. Eugene. "Priestly Old Belief in the Early Twentieth Century: The Conversion of Archbishop Nikola (Pozdnev) of Saratov and the Creation of a New Old Believer Hierarchy." Unpublished paper.

Comer, William J. "The Evolution of a Liberal Cleric: The Path of Archimandrite Mikhail from Orthodoxy to the Christianity of Golgotha." Unpublished paper.

Geekie, J. L. H. "The Church and Politics in Russia, 1905–1917: A Study of the Political Behavior of the Russian Orthodox Clergy in the Reign of Nicholas II." Ph.D. dissertation, University of East Anglia: 1976.

Geraci, Robert Paul. "Window on the East: Ethnography, Orthodoxy, and
    Russian Nationality in Kazan, 1870–1914." Ph.D. dissertation, University
    of California, Berkeley: 1995.
Kasinic, E. and Irina V. Pozdeeva. "Sources, Bibliography, and Historiog-
    raphy of the Old Belief of the Modern Period: System and Structure."
    Unpublished paper.
Kaufman, Suzanne K. "Miracles, Medicine and the Spectacle of Lourdes:
    Popular Religion and Modernity in Fin-De-Siecle France." Ph.D. dis-
    sertation, Rutgers University: 1996.
Michaelson, Aaron. "The Russian Orthodox Missionary Society, 1970–1917:
    A Study in Religious and Educational Enterprise." Ph.D. dissertation,
    University of Minnesota: 1999.
Poe, Marshall. "'Moscow, the Third Rome': The Origins and Transforma-
    tion of a Pivotal Moment." Unpublished paper.
Pozdeeva, I. "'Serebrianyi vek' russkogo staroobriadchestva, 1905–1917."
    Unpublished paper.

PUBLISHED SOURCES

I. PRIMARY LITERATURE

A. NEWSPAPERS
Den
Grazhdanin
Kievkianin
Kolokol
Moskovskaia kopeika
Moskovskii listok
Moskovskiia vedomosti
Novoe vremia
Russkii invalid
Russkiia vedomosti
Russkoe slovo
Russkoe znamia
S-Peterburgskiia vedomosti
Strela
Syn otechestva
Utro Rossii

B. JOURNALS

Astrakhanskiia eparkhialnyia vedomosti
Baian
Bogoslovskii vestnik
Bozhiia niva
Bratskoe slovo
Dobroe slovo
Donskiia eparkhialnyia vedomosti
Golos dolga
Istoricheskii vestnik
Istoricheskoe obozrenie
Izvestiia kievskoi gorodskoi dumy
Khersonskiia eparkhialnyia vedomosti
Khristianin
Khristianskoe chtenie
Kievskiia eparkhialnyia vedomosti
Kurskiia eparkhialnyia vedomosti
Minskiia eparkhialnyia vedomosti
Missionerskii sbornik
Missionerskoe obozrenie
Moskovskiia tserkovnyia vedomosti
Niva
Novyi put
Pochaevskii listok
Pravoslavnii sobesednik
Pravoslavnoe obozrenie
Pravoslavno-russkoe slovo
Pravoslavnyi blagovestnik
Priamoi put
Rizhskiia eparkhialnyia vedomosti
Rodnaia niva
Russkaia mysl
Russkii inok
Russkoe obozrenie
Shchit very
Slovo tserkvi
Staraia Rus
Staroobriadcheskaia mysl
Staroobriadcheskii pastyr

Staroobriadcheskii pomorskii zhurnal

Staroobriadets

Strannik

Troitskoe slovo

Trudy kievskoi akademii

Tserkov

Tserkov i obshchestvo

Tserkovno-obshchestvennaia zhizn

Tserkovnyi vestnik

Tserkovnyiia vedomosti

Vera i razum

Vera i tserkov

Vernost

Vestnik russkago sobraniia

Vestnik soiuza russkago naroda

Vesy

Vladimirskiia eparkhialnyia vedomosti

Voprosy filosofii i psikhologii

C. BOOKS AND BROCHURES

Aivazov, I. G. *Novoe vselenskoe khristianstvo—religiia kontsa.* Kharkov, 1904.

Aleksandrovskii, I. V. *Sobor sv. Vladimira v Kieve.* Kiev, 1897.

Antonov, N. P. *Russkie svetskie bogoslovy i ikh religiozno-obshchestvennoe mirosozertsanie.* St Petersburg, 1912.

Antony (Khrapovitskii). *Polnoe sobranie sochinenii.* 2nd ed. 3 vols. St Petersburg, 1911.

———. *Russkaia pravda.* Moscow, 1912.

Antony (Vadkovsky). *Rechi, slova i poucheniia.* 3rd ed. St Petersburg, 1912.

Beliaev, A. *Illiustrirovannaia istoriia russkoi tserkvi.* 2 vols. Moscow, 1894.

Beliaev, N., ed. *Pamiati Vysokopreosviashchennago Nikanora arkhiepiskop khersonkago i odesskago.* Kazan, 1891.

Belliutsin, I. S. *Description of the Clergy in Rural Russia.* Edited and translated by Gregory L. Freeze. Ithaca, N.Y., 1985.

Berdiaev, Nicholas. *Aleksei Stepanovich Khomiakov.* Tomsk, 1996.

———. *Novoe religioznoe soznanie i obshchestvennost.* St Petersburg, 1907.

———. *Sudba Rossii.* Moscow, 1918.

Billington, James H. *Russia in Search of Itself.* Washington, D.C., 2004.

Borkov, G. *Tserkov Khristovo i tsarstvo Bozhie.* Kazan, 1910.

Bulgakov, Sergei. *Dva grada.* 2 vols. Moscow, 1911.

———. *Ot marksizma k idealizmu.* St Petersburg, 1903.

Buzni, V. M., ed. *Imperator Aleksandr III v russkoi poezii.* St Petersburg, 1912.

Chepik, Mikhail. *Patrioticheskaia khrestomatiia.* Sergiev Posad, 1913.

Chirkov, S. M., ed. *Kreshchenie russkago naroda.* Kazan, 1888.

Christoff, Peter K. *K. S. Aksakov: A Study in Ideas.* Princeton, N.J., 1982.

Debolskii, G. S. *Kratkoe obozrenie bogosluzheniia pravoslavnoi tserkvi.* St Petersburg, 1886.

———. *O liubvi k otechestvu i trude po slovu Bozhiiu.* St Petersburg, 1890.

———. *Ustanovleniia vetkhozavetnoi tserkvi i khristianskoi.* 2nd ed. St Petersburg, 1894.

———. *Zhitie Ravnoapostolnago kniazia Vladimira.* St Petersburg, 1888.

Dedlov, V. L. *Kievskii Vladimirskii sobor i ego khudozhestvennye tvortsy.* Moscow, 1910.

Dedov, S., ed. *Sviashchennoe koronovanie russkikh Gosudarei.* 4th ed. St Petersburg, 1911.

De-Witte, E. *Ravnoapostolnyi kniaz Vladimir Sviatoi.* Kovna, 1888.

Dmitrievskii, A. A. *Imperatorskoe Pravoslavnoe Palestinskoe Obshchestvo i ego deiatelnost za itekushchuia chetvert veka (1882–1907).* St Petersburg, 1907.

———. *Sviateishii Patriarkh Germogen i russkoe dukhovenstvo v nikh sluzhenii otechestvu v smutnoe vremia.* St Petersburg, 1912.

———. *Tipi sovremenykh russkikh palomnikov v Sviatuiu Zemliu.* 2nd ed. St Petersburg, 1912.

Dobroklonskii, A. *Rukovodstvo po istorii russkoi tserkvi.* 4 vols. Moscow, 1884–1893.

Dubrovin, A. *Otrytkoe pismo Predsedatelia Glavnago Soveta Soiuza Russkago Naroda.* St Petersburg, 1906.

———. *Taina sudby.* St Petersburg, 1907.

Durnovo, N. N. *Novye podvigi protoiereia I.I. Vostorgova i ego opravdaniia.* Moscow, 1909.

———. *Protoierei Ioann Ioannovich Vostorgov i ego politicheskaia deiatelnost.* Moscow, 1908.

Elchaninov, A. *Tsarstvovanie Gosudaria Imperatora Nikolaia Aleksandrovicha.* St Petersburg, 1913.

Esipov, N. N. *Sviatitel i Chudotvorets Arkhiepiskop Chernigovskii Feodosii Uglitskii.* St Petersburg, 1897.

Filaret (Drozdov). *Monarkhicheskoe uchenie Filareta.* Moscow, 1907.

———. *Sochineniia Filareta Mitropolita Moskovskago i Kolomenskago.* 5 vols. Moscow, 1873.

Filosofov, D. V. *Neugasimaia lampada: Stati po tserkovnym i religioznym voprosam.* Moscow, 1912.

————. *Slova i zhizn* n.p. 1909.

Fudel, I. *Sviatai Rus*. Moscow, 1902.

Georgievskii, G. *Prazdnichnyia sluzhby i tserkovnyia torzhestva v staroi Moskve*. St Petersburg, 1899.

Gerasimov, N. I. *V zashchitu russkago natsionalizma*. Moscow, 1912.

Gershenzon, M., ed. *Vekhi*. Moscow, 1909.

Golubev, S. T. *Sekta Novyi Izrail*. St Petersburg, 1911.

Golubinskii, E. E. *Istoriia kanonizatsii sviatykh v russkoi tserkvi*. Moscow, 1902.

Grachev, F., ed. *Pamiati Vysokopreosviashchennago Nikanora*. Moscow, 1894.

Gromoglasov, I. M. *Tretii vserossiiskii missionerskii sezd*. Sergiev Posad, 1898.

Hedda, Jennifer. *His Kingdom Come: Orthodox Pastorship and Social Activism in Revolutionary Russia*. DeKalb, Ill., 2008.

Iablonskii, V. M. *Promysl Bozhii i pravoslavnaia tserkov v sudbakh Rossii smutnago vremeni*. St Petersburg, 1913.

Istomin, F. M. *Kratkii ocherk deiatelnosti S-Peterburgskago Slavianskago Blagotvoritelnago Obshchestva za 25 let ego sushchestvovanii, 1868–1893*. St Petersburg, 1893.

Ivanov, A. *Istoricheskii ocherk po povodu prazdnovaniia 900 letiia kreshcheniia russkago naroda*. Kaluga, 1888.

Ivanov, Feodosii. *Tserkov v epokhu smutnago vremia na Rusi*. Ekaterinoslav, 1906.

Kargopoltsov, I. *Vysokopreosviashchennyi Platon*. St Petersburg, 1894.

Kedrov, S. *Zhizneopisanie Sviateishago Germogena Patriarkha Moskovskago i vseia Rossii*. Moscow, 1912.

Kenworthy, Scott M. *The Heart of Russia: Trinity Sergius, Monasticism, and Society after 1825*. Oxford, 2010.

Khitrovo, V. N. *Russkie palomniki Sviatoi zemli*. St Petersburg, 1905.

Kireev, A. A. *Sochineniia*. 2 vols. St Petersburg, 1912.

Kirillov, I. A. *Istinnaia tserkov*. Moscow, 1912.

————. *Pravda staroi very*. Moscow, 1916.

————. *Tretii rim*. Moscow, 1914.

Koialovich, M. O. *Istoriia russkago samosoznaniia*. 4th ed. Minsk, 1997.

Kostiukhin, K. F. *Pravda o protoieree Vostorgove*. Moscow, 1910.

Krylov, A. *Arkhiepiskop Nikanor kak pedagog*. Novocherkassk, 1893.

Leisman, N. *Pribaltiiskoe Pravoslavnoe Bratstvo*. Riga, 1892.

Liderov, Aleksei. *O bozhestvennoi liturgii*. 3 vols. Kostroma, 1889–1890.

Loman, D. N. *Poiasnitelnaia zapiski po oborudovleniiu tserkvi prepodobnago Serafima Sarovskago chudotvortsa*. St Petersburg, 1912.

Macarius (Bulgakov). *Pravoslavno-dogmaticheskoe bogoslovie.* 2nd ed. 2 vols.
    St Petersburg, 1857.
Macarius (Nevskii). *Izbrannye slova, rechi, besedy, poucheniia.* Moscow, 1996.
————. *Polnoe sobranie propovednicheskikh trudov.* Sergiev Posad, 1914.
Malyshevskii, I. I. *Zapadnaia Rus v borbe za veru i narodnost.* St Petersburg,
    1897.
————. *Zhitie sviatago ravnoapostolnago kniazia Vladimir.* St Petersburg,
    1888.
Maslov, P. *Sviateishii Germogen, Patriarkh Vserossiiskii.* Simeropol, 1912.
Melnikov, F. E. *Bluzhdaiushchee bogoslovie.* Moscow, 1911.
Merezhkovskii, D. *Bolnaia Rossiia.* St Petersburg, 1910.
Milovanov, N. *Proslavlenie patriarkha Ermogena.* St Petersburg, 1914.
Muiaka, E. F. *V Ierusalim!* St Petersburg, 1903.
Nesterov, M. V. *Davnie dni.* Moscow, 1959.
————. *Izbrannye pisma.* Leningrad, 1988.
Nikanor (Brovkovich). *Besedy i poucheniia.* 2nd ed. 4 vols. Odessa, 1884–
    1887.
————. *Biograficheskie materialy.* Edited by S. Petrovskii. Odessa, 1900.
————. *Mozhno li poistivnym filosofskim metodam dakazivat bytie.* Kazan,
    1871.
————. *Opisanie nekotorykh russkimi raskolnikam v polzu raskola.* 2 vols. St
    Petersburg, 1861.
————. *Poucheniia, besedy, rechi, vozzvaniia i poslaniia.* 3rd ed. 5 vols.
    Odessa, 1890.
————. *Pravoslavie v istorii Rossii i shtunda.* Chernigov, 1884.
————. *Tserkov i gosudarstvo.* St Petersburg, 1888.
Nikanor (Kamenskii). *O sviatom ravnoapostolnom tsare Konstantine velikom i
    o tsarskoi vlasti.* 2nd ed. Orel, 1899.
Nikolskii, Aleksandr. *Pravoslavnoe missionerskoe obshchestvo.* Moscow, 1895.
Nikon (Rozhdestvenskii). *Chem zhiva nasha russkaia pravoslavnaia dusha.*
    Sergiev Posad, 1909.
————. *Chto nam nuzhnee vsego.* Sergiev Posad, 1905.
————. *Dostoslavnoe trekhsotletie.* Sergiev Posad, 1913.
————. *Gde zhe nashe khristianstvo?* Sergiev Posad, 1910.
————. *Kto kulturnee: oni ili my?* Sergiev Posad, 1912.
————. *Pamiati velikago sviashchennomuchenika za otechestvo.* Sergiev
    Posad, 1912.
————. *V zashchitu prazdnikov.* St Petersburg, 1909.
————. *Za kogo govorit istorii?* Moscow, 1903.

————. *Zavety sviateishago patriarkha Germogena nashemu vremeni.* Moscow, 1912.

————. *Zhitie i podvigi prepodobnago i bogonosnago ottsa nashego Sergiia.* 2nd ed. Moscow, 1891.

Paleolog, F. *Imperatorskoe Pravoslavnoe Palestinskoe Obshchestvo: Ocherki ego deiatelnosti.* St Petersburg, 1891.

Petrov, N. I. *Iz istorii kievskago Vladimirskago sobora.* Kiev, 1898.

Platon (Gorodetskii). *Izbrannyia slova i besedy Vysokopreosviashchennago Platona.* Kiev, 1892.

Pobedonostsev, K. P. *Sochineniia.* St Petersburg, 1996.

Pokrovskii, Aleksandr. *Znachenie pravoslavnoi tserkvi v Rossii.* St Petersburg, 1863.

Polianskii, I. *Staroobriadtsy i vysochaishii ukaz 17 aprelia 1905 g.* Moscow, 1905.

Pomazansky, Michael. *Orthodox Dogmatic Theology.* Platina, Calif., 1994.

Popov, N. G. *O bozhestve i chelovechestve.* Sergiev Posad, 1908.

Puchugin, L. F. *Starai Vera: Apologeticheskoe issledovanie.* Saratov, 1913.

Rossiev, Pavel. *Velikii pechalnik za rodinu: Patriarkh Germogen.* Moscow, 1912.

Roznatovskii, K. N. *Osnovy tserkovnago samosoznanie.* St Petersburg, 1908.

Rubtsov, M. *O tom, kak zhili nashi dedy i kak kniaz Vladimir krestil Russkii narod.* Voronezh, 1887.

Segiev, Ioann. *Novyia groznyia slova o. Ioanna Kronshtadtskago.* St Petersburg, 1908.

————. *Polnoe sobranie sochinenii Ioanna Sergieva (Kronshtadtskago).* 7 vols. St Petersburg, 1896–1904.

Senatov, V. G. *Filosofiia istorii staroobriadchestva.* 2 vols. Moscow, 1908.

————. *Vavilon, Izrail i Germaniia.* Petrograd, 1916.

Serafim (Igumen). *Pervyi v Rossii po vneshnei missii kazanskii missionerskii sezd.* 3 vols. Nizhni-Novgorod, 1911–1912.

————. *Pervyi vserossiiskii inocheskii sezd.* Kungur, 1912.

————. *Slova, besedy i rechi.* 11 vols. Kungur, 1908.

————. *Torzhestvo dolga.* Kungur, 1914.

Shchukin, V. *Patriarkh Germogen kak predstavitel i pobornik natsionalnoi religioznosti.* Riga, 1912.

————. *V sumerkakh nyneshnei zhizni.* Riga, 1912.

Sikorskii, I. A. *Chto takoe natsiia i drugiia formi etnicheskoi zhizni?* Kiev, 1915.

Skvortsov, V. M. *Deianiia 3-go vserossiiskago missionerskago sezd v Kazani.* Kiev, 1897.

————. *Missionerskii posokh.* 2 vols. St Petersburg, 1912.

————. *Torzhestvo pravoslaviia i tserkovnosti na koronatsionnykh moskovskikh prazdnestvakh.* Kiev, 1896.

————. *Tsarskoe palmomnichetvo Ikh Imperatorskikh Velichestv na poklonenie vekovym sviatyniam Kieva.* Kiev, 1896.

————. *Tserkovnyi svet i gosudarstvennyi razum.* 2 vols. St Petersburg, 1912–1913.

Smirnov, Petr. *Sudba Ierusalima i russkie palomniki.* St Petersburg, 1896.

Sobashnikova, M. V. *Sviatoi Serafim.* Moscow, 1913.

Sokolov, N. M. *Sviatye zemli russkoi.* St Petersburg, 1903.

Solovev, I. *Kakoi smysl i znachenie imeet prichtenie Sviateishago Patriarkha Ermogena k liku sviatykh?* Sergiev Posad, 1913.

Solovev, I. P. *Obiasnenie Bogosluzheniia pravoslavnoi tserkvi s tserkovnym ustavom.* St Petersburg, 1911.

Solovev, M. P. *Istoricheskoe prizvanie Rossii v Sviatoi Zemli.* Tobolsk, 1894.

————. *Po Sviatoi Zemle.* St Petersburg, 1897.

————. *Sviataia Zemlia i Imperatorskoe Pravoslavnoe Palestinskoe Obshchestvo.* St Petersburg, 1895.

————. *Sviataia Zemlia i Rossiia.* St Petersburg, 1900.

Solovev, V. S. *Pisma.* Edited by E. L. Radlov. Petrograd, 1923.

————. *Pisma Vladimira Sergeevich Soloveva.* Edited by E. L. Radlov. 3 vols. St Petersburg, 1908–1911.

————. *Sobranie sochinenii V.S. Soloveva.* Edited by S. M. Solovev and E. L. Radlov. 12 vols. Brussels, 1966.

Steletskii, N. *Patriotizm pri svete Khristianskago mirovozzreniia.* Kiev, 1908.

Struve, Petr. *Patriotica. Politika, kultura, religiia, sotsializm: Sbornik statei za piat let (1905–1910).* St Petersburg, 1911.

Svetlov, P. I. *Ideia tsarstva Bozhiia v eia znachenii dlia khristianskago mirosozertsaniia.* Sergiev Posad, 1905.

Tikhomirov, Lev. *Chto takoe otechestvo?* Moscow, 1907.

Titov, F. G. *Sviateishii patriarkh vserossiiskii Germogen kak revnitel pravoslaviia, missioner i velikii patriot.* Kiev, 1912.

Tolstoi, L. N. "Patriotizm i khristianstvo," in *Polnoe sobranie sochinenii,* vol. 39, 27–80. Moscow, 1957.

Trenev, D. K. *Neskolko slov o drevnei i sovremennoi russkoi ikonopisi.* Moscow, 1904.

————. *Russkaia ikonopis i eia zhelaemoe razvitie.* Moscow, 1902.

Troitskii, P. S. *Tserkov i gosudarstvo v Rossii.* Moscow, 1909.

Troitskii, Vladimir. *Ocherki iz istorii dogmata o tserkvi.* Sergiev Posad, 1912.

Tsarevskii, A. A. *Znachenie Pravoslaviia v zhizni i istoricheskoi sudbe Rossii.* Kazan, 1898.

Tyshko, A. *O samoderzhavnoi tsarskoi vlasti i eia bozhestvennom ustanovlenii.* Petrograd, 1915.

Uspenskii, A. I. *Viktor Mikhailovich Vasnetsov.* Moscow, 1906.

Ustinov, V. M. *Ideia natsionalnago gosudarstva.* Kharkov, 1906.

Volkov, E. *Patriarkh Germogen.* St Petersburg, 1913.

Vostorgov, I. I. *Gosudarstvennaia Duma i pravoslavnaia russkaia tserkov.* Moscow, 1906.

————. *Imperator Aleksandr III.* Moscow, 1908.

————. *Liubov k Sviatoi Zemli.* St Petersburg, 1911.

————. *Osviashchenie gosudarstvo i vlasti.* Moscow, 1909.

————. *Pamiati Imperatora Aleksandra III-go.* Tiflis, 1905.

————. *Pastyrskii golos vo dni smuty.* Moscow, 1917.

————. *Patrioticheskie soiuzy i ikh otnoshenie k religii.* Moscow, 1907.

————. *Patriotizm i khristianstvo.* Moscow, 1909.

————. *Polnoe sobranie sochinenii.* 5 vols. Moscow, 1914–1916.

————. *Pravoslavie v istorii Rossii.* Moscow, 1910.

————. *Sviashchennoe samosoznanie.* Moscow, 1911.

————. *Vo slavu sviatago Germogena, Patriarkha vserossiiskago.* Moscow, 1913.

————. *Zavety istorii.* Moscow, 1907.

Vostorgov, I. I., ed. *Opyt protivosotsialisticheskago katakhizisa.* Moscow, 1911.

Zhitrov, *Drevniaia Rus v velikie dni.* St Petersburg, 1899.

II. Secondary literature

Anderson, Benedict. *Imagined Communities: Reflections on the Origin and Spread of Nationalism.* 2nd ed. London, 1991.

Babakov, V. G. and V. M. Semenov. *Natsionaloe soznanie i natsionalnaia kultura.* Moscow, 1996.

Baehr, Stephen L. "From History to National Myth: *Translatio imperii* in Eighteenth-Century Russia." *Russian Review* 37:1 (January 1978), 1–13.

Balashov, Nicholas. *Na puti k liturgicheskomu vozrozhdeniiu.* Moscow, 2001.

Baron, Salo Wittmayer. *Modern Nationalism and Religion.* New York, 1947.

Basil, John D. "Alexander Kireev: Turn-of-the-Century Slavophile and the Russian Orthodox Church, 1890–1910." *Cahiers du Monde russe et sovietique* 32:3 (July–September 1991), 337–47.

————. "Konstantin Petrovich Pobedonostsev: An Argument for a Russian State Church." *Church History* 64:1 (March 1995), 43–61.

Becker, Seymour. "The Muslim East in Nineteenth-Century Russian Popular Historiography." *Central Asian Survey* 5:3–4 (1986), 25–47.

———. "Russia between East and West: The Intelligentsia, Russian National Identity and the Asian Borderlands." *Central Asian Survey* 10:4 (1991), 47–64.

Benois, Alexandre. *The Russian School of Painting.* Translated by Abraham Yarmolinsky. New York, 1916.

Berdiaev, Nicolas. *The Russian Idea.* Translated by R. M. French. Boston, 1962.

Bertash, E. I. et al. *Khramy Peterburga: Spravochnik-putevoditel.* St Petersburg, 1992.

Bodarskii, Y. E. "Zemlevladenie russkoi pravoslavnoi tserkvi i ee khoziaistvenno-ekonomicheskaia deiatelnost (XI—nachalo XX v.)." In *Russkoe pravoslavie: Vekhi istorii,* edited by A. I. Klibanov, 501–562. Moscow, 1989.

Bogolepov, Alexander. *Church Reforms in Russia, 1905–1918.* Berwick, Pa., 1966.

Borisova, E. A. *Russkaia arkhitektura vtoroi polovny XIX veka.* Moscow, 1979.

Breuilly, John. *Nationalism and the State.* 2nd ed. Chicago, 1993.

Breyfogle, Nicholas B. *Heretics and Colonizers: Forging Russia's Empire in the South Caucasus.* Ithaca, N.Y., 2005.

Brooks, Jeffrey. *When Russia Learned to Read: Literacy and Popular Literature, 1861–1917.* Princeton, N.J., 1985.

Brower, Daniel R. *The Russian City between Tradition and Modernity, 1850–1900.* Berkeley, 1990.

———. "Russian Roads to Mecca: Religious Tolerance and Muslim Pilgrimage in the Russian Empire." *Slavic Review* 55:3 (1996), 567–84.

Bruce, Steve, ed. *Religion and Modernization: Sociologists and Historians Debate the Secularization Thesis.* Oxford, 1992.

Buganov, A. V. *Russkaia istoriia v pamiati krestian XIX veka i natsionalnoe samosoznanie.* Moscow, 1992.

Bushkovitch, Paul. "The Formation of a National Consciousness in Early Modern Russia." *Harvard Ukrainian Studies* 10 (1986), 355–76.

———. "Orthodoxy and Old Rus' in the Thought of S. P. Shevyrev." *Forschungen zur osteuropaeischen Geschichte* 46 (1992), 203–220.

———. *Religion and Society in Russia: The Sixteenth and Seventeenth Centuries.* Oxford, 1992.

Byrnes, Robert F. "'Between Two Fires': Kliuchevskii on Religion and the Russian Orthodox Church," *Modern Greek Studies Yearbook* 6 (1990), 157–85.

———. *Pobedonostsev: His Life and Thought.* Bloomington, Ind., 1968.

———. *V. O. Kliuchevsky, Historian of Russia.* Bloomington, Ind., 1995.

Cherniavsky, Michael. "'Holy Russia': A Study in the History of an Idea." *American Historical Review* 63:3 (April 1958), 617–37.

———. "The Old Believers and the New Religion." *Slavic Review* 25:1 (March 1966), 1–39.

———. "Russia." In *National Consciousness, History, and Political Culture in Early-Modern Europe,* edited by Orest Ranum, 118–43. Baltimore, 1975.

———. *Tsar and People: Studies in Russian Myths.* 2nd ed. New York, 1969.

Clay, John Eugene. "Antisectarian and Antischismatic Missions of the Russian Orthodox Church." In *The Modern Encyclopedia of Religions in Russia and the Soviet Union* vol. 2, 93–101. Gulf Breeze, Fla., 1990.

Coleman, Heather J. *Russian Baptists and Spiritual Revolution, 1905–1929.* Bloomington, Ind., 2005.

Costello, David R. "*Novoe Vremia* and the Conservative Dilemma, 1911–1914." *Russian Review* 37:1 (January 1978), 30–50.

Craycraft, James. *The Church Reform of Peter the Great.* Stanford, Calif., 1971.

Crummey, Robert O. *The Formation of Muscovy, 1304–1613.* London, 1987.

———. *Old Believers and the World of Antichrist: The Vyg Community and the Russian State, 1694–1855.* Madison, Wis., 1970.

Cunningham, James W. *A Vanquished Hope: The Movement for Church Renewal in Russia, 1905–1906.* Crestwood, N.Y., 1981.

Curtiss, John Shelton. *Church and State in Russia: The Last Years of the Empire, 1900–1917.* New York, 1940.

Dowler, Wayne. *Dostoevsky, Grigor'ev, and Native Soil Conservatism.* Toronto, 1982.

———. "The Politics of Language in Non-Russian Elementary Schools in the Eastern Empire, 1865–1914." *Russian Review* 54:4 (October 1995), 516–38.

Duncan, Peter J. S. *Russian Messianism: Third Rome, Revolution, Communism and After.* London, 2000.

Durylin, S. *Nesterov v zhizni i tvorchestve.* Moscow, 1976.

Efimov, N. N. *Ru—novyi Izrail.* Kazan, 1912.

Engelstein, Laura. "Holy Russia in Modern Times: An Essay on Orthodoxy and Cultural Change." *Past and Present* 173:1 (November 2001), 129–56.

———. *Slavophile Empire: Imperial Russia's Illiberal Path.* Ithaca, N.Y., 2009.

Evtukov, Catherine. *The Cross and the Sickle: Sergei Bulgakov and the Fate of Russian Religious Philosophy.* Ithaca, N.Y., 1997.

Fedotov, G. P. *The Russian Religious Mind. Volume One: Kievan Christianity, the Tenth to the Thirteenth Centuries.* Cambridge, Mass., 1946.

———. *Sudba i grekhi Rossii: Izbrannye stati po filosofii russkoi kultury.* Edited by V. F. Boikov. 2 vols. St Petersburg, 1991.

Fedotova, I. A. "Bogoslovskoe nasledie A.S. Khomiakova i pravoslavnaia akademicheskaia mysl vtoroi poloviny XIX v." *Veche* 8 (1997), 64–72.

Ferenczi, Caspar. "Freedom of the Press under the Old Regime, 1905–1914." In *Civil Rights in Imperial Russia,* edited by Olga Crisp and Linda Edmondson, 191–214. Oxford, 1989.

Firsov, S. L. "Chelovek vo vremeni: shtrikhi k portretu Konstantina Petrovicha Pobedonostseva." In *K. P. Pobedonostsev: Pro et Contra,* edited by D. K. Burlaka, 6–27. St Petersburg, 1996.

———. *Russkaia Tserkov nakanune peremen (konets 1890-kh-1918gg.).* Moscow, 2002.

Florovskii, Georgii. *Puti russkogo bogosloviia.* Vilnius, 1991.

Ford, Carolyn. *Creating the Nation in Provincial France: Religion and Political Identity in Brittany.* Princeton, N.J., 1993.

Franklin, Simon, ed. and trans. *Sermons and Rhetoric of Kievan Rus'.* Cambridge, Mass., 1991.

Franklin, Simon and Emma Widdis. *National Identity in Russian Culture: An Introduction.* Cambridge, 2004.

Freeze, Gregory L. "Going to the Intelligentsia: The Church and Its Urban Mission in Post-Reform Russia." In *Between Tsar and People: Educated Society and the Quest for Public Identity in Late Imperial Russia,* edited by Edith Clowes et al., 215–32. Princeton, N.J., 1991.

———. "Handmaiden of the State? The Church in Imperial Russia Reconsidered." *Journal of Ecclesiastical History* 36:1 (January 1985), 82–102.

———. *The Parish Clergy in Nineteenth-Century Russia: Crisis, Reform, Counter-Reform.* Princeton, N.J., 1983.

———. *The Russian Levites: Parish Clergy in the Eighteenth-Century.* Cambridge, Mass., 1977.

———. "Subversive Piety: Religion and the Political Crisis in Late Imperial Russia." *Journal of Modern History* 68 (June 1996), 308–350.

Gaut, Greg. "Can a Christian Be a Nationalist? Vladimir Solov'ev's Critique of Nationalism." *Slavic Review* 57:1 (Spring 1998), 77–94.

Gellner, Ernest. *Nations and Nationalism.* Ithaca, N.Y., 1983.

George, Martin. "Die 900-Jahr-Feier der Taufe Russlands im Jahr 1888 und die Kritik Vladimir Sergeevic Solovevs am Verhaeltnis von Staat und Kirche in Russland." *Jahrbuecher fuer Gechichte Osteuropas* 36 (1988), 15–36.

Geraci, Robert P. *Window on the East: National and Imperial Identities in Late Tsarist Russia*. Ithaca, N.Y., 2001.

Geraci, Robert and Michael Khodarkovsky, eds. *Of Religion and Empire: Missions, Conversion, and Tolerance in Tsarist Russia*. Ithaca, N.Y., 2001.

Gerstein, Linda. *Nikolai Strakhov*. Cambridge, Mass., 1971.

Gillis, John R., ed. *Commemorations: The Politics of National Identity*. Princeton, N.J., 1994.

Gordienko, N. S. *"Kreshchenie Rusi": Fakty protiv legend i mifov*. Leningrad, 1984.

Greene, Robert H. *Bodies like Bright Stars: Saints and Relics in Orthodox Russia*. DeKalb, Ill., 2010.

Greenfeld, Liah. *Nationalism: Five Roads to Modernity*. Cambridge, Mass., 1992.

Grekulov, E. F., ed. *Religiia i tserkov v istorii Rossii*. Moscow, 1975.

Gulyga, Arsenii. *Russkaia ideia i ee tvortsy*. Moscow, 1995.

Hagen, William W. "National Solidarity and Organic Work in Prussian Poland, 1815–1914." *Journal of Modern History* 44:1 (1972), 38–64.

Hamant, Yves, ed. *The Christianization of Ancient Russia*. Paris, 1992.

Hamm, Michael F. *Kiev: A Portrait, 1800–1917*. Princeton, N.J., 1995.

Hayes, Carlton J. H. *Essays on Nationalism*. New York, 1926.

———. *Nationalism: A Religion*. New York, 1960.

Hedda, Jennifer. *His Kingdom Come: Orthodox Pastorship and Social Activism in Revolutionary Russia*. DeKalb, Ill., 2008.

Hitchens, Keith. *Orthodoxy and Nationality: Andreiu Saguna and the Rumanians of Transylvania, 1846–1873*. Cambridge, Mass., 1977.

Hobsbawm, E. J. *Nations and Nationalism since 1780: Programme, Myth, Reality*. Cambridge, 1990.

Hosking, Geoffrey. *The Russian Constitutional Experiment: Government and Duma, 1907–1914*. Cambridge, 1973.

———. *Russia: People and Empire, 1552–1917*. Cambridge, Mass., 1997.

Hosking, Geoffrey and George Schoepflin, eds. *Myths of Nationhood*. London, 1997.

Hosking, Geoffrey and Robert Service, eds. *Russian Nationalism Past and Present*. London, 1998.

Isachenko, V. G. et al., eds. *Arkhitektory-stroiteli Peterburga nachala XX veka: Katalog vystavki*. Leningrad, 1982.

Jahn, Humbertus F. *Patriotic Culture in Russia during World War I*. Ithaca, N.Y., 1995.

Kandidov, Boris. *Krestom i nagaikoi: Pochaevskaia lavra i chernosotennoe dvizhenie.* Moscow, 1928.

Karpovich, Michael. "Vladimir Soloviev on Nationalism." *Review of Politics* 8 (1946), 183–91.

Kartashev, A. V. *Ocherki po istorii russkoi tserkvi.* 2 vols. Moscow, 1991.

Kenworthy, Scott M. *The Heart of Russia: Trinity-Sergius, Monasticism, and Society after 1825.* Oxford, 2010.

Klibanov, A. I. "Narodnye protivotserkovnye dvizhenii." *Russkoe pravoslavie: Vekhi istorii,* edited by A. I. Klibanov, 562–615. Moscow, 1989.

Kohn, Hans. *The Idea of Nationalism.* New York, 1961.

———. *Panslavism: Its History and Ideology.* 2nd ed. New York, 1960.

Kopanitsa, M. M. *Sovremennye sotsialnye kontseptsii russkogo pravoslaviia.* Kharkov, 1988.

Lazuko, A. K. *Viktor Mikailovich Vasnetsov.* Leningrad, 1990.

Liaglina, G. S. "Tsenzurnaia politika tserkvi v XIX—nachale XX v." *Russkoe pravoslavie: Vekhi istorii,* edited by A. I. Klibanov, 463–500. Moscow, 1989.

Lievan, Dominic. *Nicholas II: Twilight of the Empire.* New York, 1993.

Lincoln, Bruce. *The Great Reforms.* DeKalb, Ill., 1990.

Litvak, B. G., "Russkoe pravoslavie v XIX veke." *Russkoe pravoslavie: Vekhi istorii,* edited by A. I. Klibanov, 309–380. Moscow, 1989.

Lossky, Vladimir. *The Mystical Theology of the Eastern Church.* London, 1957.

MacMaster, Robert E. *Danilevsky: A Russian Totalitarian Philosopher.* Cambridge, Mass., 1967.

Maloney, George A. *A History of Orthodox Theology since 1453.* Belmont, Mass., 1976.

Marker, Gary. *Publishing, Printing, and the Origins of Intellectual Life in Russia, 1700–1800.* Princeton, N.J., 1985.

Martin, David. *A General Theory of Secularization.* Oxford, 1978.

———. *The Religious and the Secular: Studies in Secularization.* New York, 1969.

McReynolds, Louise. *The News under Russia's Old Regime: The Development of a Mass-Circulation Press.* Princeton, N.J., 1991.

Meyendorff, John. *Byzantine Theology: Historical Trends and Doctrinal Themes.* New York, 1979.

———. *Byzantium and the Rise of Russia.* Crestwood, N.Y., 1989.

———. *The Orthodox Church.* Translated by John Chapin. New York, 1962.

————. *Rome, Constantinople, Moscow: Historical and Theological Studies.* Crestwood, N.Y., 1996.

————. "Universal Witness and Local Identity in Russian Orthodoxy (988–1988)." *California Slavic Studies* 16 (1993), 11–29.

Miller, David B. "The Cult of Saint Sergius of Radonezh and Its Political Uses." *Slavic Review* 52:4 (Winter 1993), 698–99.

————. "The Velikie Minei Chetii and the Stepennaia Kniga of Metropolitan Makarii and the Origins of Russian National Consciousness." *Forschungen zur osteuropaeischen Geschichte* 26 (1979), 263–382.

Mochulskii, K. "Vladimir Solovev: Zhizn i uchenie." In *Gogol, Solovev, Dostoevskii.* Moscow, 1995.

Morosan, Vladimir. "Liturgical Singing or Sacred Music? Understanding the Aesthetic of the New Russian Choral School." *Christianity and the Arts in Russia,* edited by William C. Brumfield and Milos M. Velimirovic, 124–30. Cambridge: 1991.

Mukhin, Viacheslav. *Tserkovnaia kultura Sankt-Peterburga.* St Petersburg, 1994.

Munzer, Egbert. *Solovyev: Prophet of Russian-Western Unity.* London, 1956.

Nichols, Robert L. "Church and State in Imperial Russia." *Donald W. Treadgold Papers* 102 (February 1995), 7–24.

————. "The Friends of God: Nicholas II and Alexandra at the Canonization of Serafim of Sarov, July 1903." In *Religious and Secular Forces in Late Tsarist Russia,* edited by Charles Timberlake, 206–9. Seattle, 1992.

Nichols, Robert L. and Theofanis George Stavrou, eds. *Russian Orthodoxy under the Old Regime.* Minneapolis, 1978.

Nikolskii, N. M. *Istoriia russkoi tserkvi.* 3rd ed. Moscow, 1983.

Nikonova, I. *Mikhail Vasilevich Nesterov.* Moscow, 1979.

Ouspensky, Leonid and Vladimir Lossky. *The Meaning of Icons.* Translated by G. E. H. Palmer and E. Kadloubovsky. Crestwood, N.Y., 1989.

Petrovich, Michael Boro. *The Emergence of Russian Panslavism, 1856–1870.* New York, 1956.

Pipes, Richard. *Struve: Liberal on the Right, 1905–1944.* Cambridge, Mass., 1980.

Plokhy, Serhii. *The Origins of the Slavic Nations: Premodern Identities in Russia, Ukraine, and Belarus.* Cambridge, 2006.

Pushkarev, S. G. *Rol pravoslavnoi tserkvi v istorii Rossii.* 2nd ed. New York, 1985.

Putnam, George F. *Russian Alternatives to Marxism.* Knoxville, Tenn., 1977.

Raba, Joel. "Moscow—The Third Rome or the New Jerusalem?" *Forschungen zur osteuropaeischen Geschichte* 50 (1995), 297–307.

Rawson, Don C. *Russian Rightists and the Revolution of 1905.* Cambridge, 1995.

Reed, Christopher. *Religion, Revolution, and the Russian Intelligentsia, 1900–1912.* London, 1979.

Reyburn, Hugh Y. *The Story of the Russian Chruch.* London, 1924.

Riabushinskii, Vladimir. *Staroobriadchestvo i russkoe religioznoe chuvstvo.* Moscow, 1994.

Riasanovsky, Nicholas V. "The Emergence of Eurasianism." *California Slavic Studies* 4 (1967), 39–72.

———. *A History of Russia.* 4th ed. Oxford, 1984.

———. *The Image of Peter the Great in Russian History and Thought.* Oxford,1985.

———. "Khomiakov and Sobornost." In *Continuity and Change in Russian and Soviet Thought,* edited by Ernest Simmons, 183–96. Cambridge, Mass., 1955.

———. *Nicholas I and Official Nationality in Russia, 1825–1855.* Berkeley, 1959.

———. "Pogodin and Sevyrev in Russian Intellectual History." In *Russian Thought and Politics,* edited by Hugh McLean et al., 149–67. Cambridge, Mass., 1957.

———. *Russia and the West in the Teaching of the Slavophiles: A Study in Romantic Ideology.* Cambridge, Mass., 1952.

Ridenour, Robert. *Nationalism, Modernism, and Personal Rivalry in Nineteenth-Century Russian Music.* Bloomington, Ind., 1977.

Robson, Roy. *Old Believers in Modern Russia.* DeKalb, Ill., 1995.

Rogger, Hans. *National Consciousness in Eighteenth-Century Russia.* Cambridge, Mass., 1960.

———. "Russia." In *The European Right,* edited by Hans Rogger and Eugen Weber, 443–500. Berkeley, 1966.

Rosenthal, Bernice Glatzer. *Dmitri Sergeevich Merezhkovsky and the Silver Age: The Development of a Revolutionary Mentality.* The Hague, 1975.

Roslof, Edward E. *Red Priests: Renovationism, Russian Orthodoxy, and Revolution, 1905–1946.* Bloomington, Ind., 2002.

Rowland, Daniel B. "Moscow—The Third Rome or the New Israel?" *Russian Review* 55 (October 1996), 591–614.

Rusakova, A. *Mikail Nesterov.* Leningrad, 1990.

Sakharova, A. M., ed. *Religiia i tserkov v istorii Rossii.* Moscow, 1975.

Scheibert, P. "Die Petersburger religioes philosophischen Zusammenkuenfte von 1902 und 1903." *Jahrbuecher fuer Geschichte Osteuropas* 12 (1964), 513–60.

Scherrer, Jutta. *Die Petersburger Religioez-Philosophischen Vereinigunen: Die Entwicklung des religioezen Selbstverstandnisses ihrer Intelligencija-Mitgleider (1901–1917).* In *Forschungen zur osteurpaeischen Geschichte* 19 (1973).

Shestakov, V. P. *Eskhatalogiia i utopia.* Moscow, 1995.

Shevzov, Vera. *Russian Orthodoxy on the Eve of Revolution.* Oxford, 2004.

Shnirelman, V. A. "Natsionalisticheskii mif: Osnovye kharakteristiki." *Slavianovedenie* 6 (November–December 1995), 3–13.

Simon, Gerhard. "Church, State and Society." In *Russia Enters the Twentieth Century,* edited by Erwin Oberlaender et al., 199–235. New York, 1971.

Smirnov, N. A., ed. "Missionerskaia deiatelnost tserkvi (Vtoraia polovina XIX v.—1917 g.)." *Russkoe pravoslavie: Vekhi istorii,* edited by A. I. Klibanov, 438–62. Moscow, 1989.

———. *Tserkov v istorii Rossii (IX v.—1917 g.): Kriticheskie ocherki.* Moscow, 1967.

Smith, Anthony. *National Identity.* Reno, Nev., 1991.

———. *Theories of Natonalism.* New York, 1971.

Smolitsch, Igor. *Geschichte der russischen Kirche, 1700–1917,* vol. 1. Leiden, 1964.

———. *Geschichte der russischen Kirche. Volume Two.* Edited by Gregory L. Freeze. In *Forschungen zur osteuropaeischen Geschichte* 45 (1991).

Solovev, S. M. *Vladimir Solovev: Zhizn i tvorcheskaia evoliutsiia.* Moscow, 1997.

Soloviev, Alexander V. *Holy Russia: The History of a Religious-Social Idea.* S-Gravenhage, 1959.

Spillman, Lyn. *Nation and Commemoration: Creating National Identities in the United States and Australia.* Cambridge, 1997.

Spinka, Matthew. *The Church and the Russian Revolution.* New York, 1927.

Stavrou, Theofanis George. *Russian Interests in Palestine, 1882–1914: A Study of Religious and Educational Enterprise.* Thessalonika, 1963.

Steinberg, Mark D. and Heather Coleman. *Sacred Stories: Religion and Spirituality in Modern Russia.* Bloomington, Ind., 2007.

Stockdale, Melissa Kirschke. *Paul Miliukov and the Quest for a Liberal Russia, 1880–1918.* Ithaca, N.Y., 1996.

Stremooukhoff, Dimitri. "Moscow the Third Rome: Sources of the Doctrine." *Speculum* 28 (1953), 84–101.

———. *Vladimir Soloviev and His Messianic Work.* Translated by Elizabeth Meyendorff. Belmont, Mass., 1980.

Stupperich, R. "Kiev—das zweite Jerusalem: Ein Beitrag zur Geschichte des ukrainisch-russischen Nationalbewusstseins." *Zeitschrift fuer Slavische Philologie* 12 (1935), 332–54.

Taylor, Charles. *Sources of the Self: The Making of the Modern Identity.* Cambridge, Mass., 1989.

Thaden, Edward C. *Conservative Nationalism in Nineteenth-Century Russia.* Seattle, 1964.

Till, Barry. *The Churches Search for Unity.* Harmondsworth, England, 1972.

Treadgold, Donald. *The Great Siberian Migration: Government and Peasant in Resettlement from Emancipation to the First World War.* Princeton, N.J., 1957.

Tsurikov, Vladimir, ed. *Philaret, Metropolitan of Moscow 1782–1867. Perspectives on the Man, His Works, and His Times.* Jordanville, N.Y., 2003.

Ulianov, N. "Kompleks Filofeia." *Novyi zhurnal* 45 (1956), 249–73.

Valkenier, Elizabeth Kridl. "Politics in Russian Art: The Case of Repin." *Russian Review* 37:1 (January 1978), 14–39.

Vallier, Paul. *Modern Russian Theology: Bukharev, Soloviev, Bulgakov.* Grand Rapids, Mich., 2000.

Van den Bercken, Wil. *Holy Russia and Christian Europe: East and West in the Religious Ideology of Russia.* Translated by John Bowden. London, 1999.

Veniamin (Fedchenkov). *Nebo na zemle.* Moscow, 1994.

Vernadsky, George. *A History of Russia. Volume Two: Kievan Russia.* New Haven, Conn., 1948.

Waldron, Peter. "Religious Reform after 1905: Old Believers and the Orthodox Church." *Oxford Slavonic Papers* 20 (1987), 110–39.

———. "Religious Toleration in Late Imperial Russia." In *Civil Rights in Imperial Russia,* edited by Olga Crisp and Linda Edmondson, 103–119. Oxford, 1989.

Walicki, Andrzej. *Philosophy and Romantic Nationalism: The Case of Poland.* Oxford, 1982.

———. *The Slavophile Controversy: History of a Conservative Utopia in Nineteenth-Century Russian Thought.* Translated by Hilda Andrews-Rusiecka. Notre Dame, Ind., 1989.

Weeks, Theodore R. "Defending Our Own: Government and the Russian Minority in the Kingdom of Poland, 1905–1914." *Russian Review* 54:4 (October 1995), 539–51.

―――. "Defining Us and Them: Poles and Russians in the 'Western Provinces,' 1863–1914." *Slavic Review* 53:1 (Spring 1994), 26–41.

―――. *Nation and State in Late Imperial Russia: Nationalism and Russification on the Western Frontier, 1863–1914.* DeKalb, Ill., 1996.

Werth, Paul W. *At the Margins of Orthodoxy: Mission, Governance, and Confessional Politics in Russia's Volga-Kama Region, 1827–1905.* Ithaca, N.Y., 2002.

West, James. "The Neo-Old Believers of Moscow: Religious Revival and Nationalist Myth in Late Imperial Russia." *Canadian-American Slavic Studies* 26:1–3 (1992), 5–28.

―――. "The Rjabusinskij Circle: Russian Industrialists in Search of a Bourgeoisie, 1909–1914." *Jahrbuecher fuer Geschichte Osteuropas* 32 (1984), 358–77.

―――. "The Riabushinsky Circle: *Burzhuaziia* and *Obshchestvennost'* in Late Imperial Russia." In *Between Tsar and People: Educated Society and the Quest for Public Identity in Late Imperial Russia,* edited by Edith Clowes et al., 215–32. Princeton, N.J., 1991.

Whittaker, Cynthia H. "The Ideology of Sergei Uvarov: An Interpretative Essay." *Russian Review* 37:2 (April 1978), 158–76.

Wortman, Richard. "'Invisible Threads': The Historical Imagery of the Romanov Tercentenary." *Russian History* 16:2–4 (1989), 389–408.

―――. *Scenarios of Power: Myth and Ceremony in the Russian Monarchy. Volume One: From Peter the Great to the Death of Nicholas I.* Princeton, N.J., 1995.

―――. *Scenarios of Power: Myth and Ceremony in the Russian Monarchy. Volume Two: From Alexander II to the Abdication of Nicholas II.* Princeton, N.J., 2000.

Young, Glennys. *Power and the Sacred in Revolutionary Russia: Religious Activists in the Village.* University Park, Penn., 1997.

Zelnik, Reginald E. "'To the Unaccustomed Eye': Religion and Irreligion in the Experience of St Petersburg Workers in the 1870s." *Russian History* 16:2–4 (1989), 297–326.

Zenkovskii, V. V., ed. *Pravoslavie i kultura.* Berlin, 1923.

Zernov, Nicolas. *Eastern Christendom.* London, 1961.

―――. *Three Russian Prophets.* London, 1944.

Zyrianov, P. N. *Pravoslavnaia tserkov v borbe s revoliutsiei, 1905–1907 gg.* Moscow, 1984.

―――. "Tserkov v period trekh rossiiskikh revoliutsii." In *Russkoe pravoslvie: Vekhi istorii,* edited by A. I. Klibanov, 381–437. Moscow, 1989.

LIST OF ILLUSTRATIONS

ILLUSTRATIONS: PART I

Fig. 1.1 Photographer unknown, Emperor Nicholas II on the balcony of the Winter Palace at St Petersburg after the "Te Deum," 1914. Photograph from the personal archive of General S. P. Andolenko. Source: Marvin Lyons, *Nicholas II The Last Tsar* (New York: St Martin's Press, 1974), plate 246.

Fig. 1.2 Olexa Yur, Statue of Vladimir the Great, 2008. Color photograph, photographer's own archive. Source: http://commons.wikimedia.org/wiki/ File:StVolodymyrKyiv.jpg?uselang=ru (accessed April 5, 2013).

Fig. 1.3 Photographer unknown, Celebration of the baptism of Russia in Kiev in 1888. Scan of photograph, archive of Livejournal.com user andriy69, Kiev, Ukraine. Source: http://mysteriouskiev.com/storage/imglib/i/old/photogalleries/76557/77300/ s640x480-4.jpg (accessed April 5, 2013).

Fig. 1.4 Title page of *Missionerskoe obozrenie*, no. 1, 1907. Holy Trinity Seminary Archives, *Foundation of Russian History*, Jordanville, New York.

Fig. 1.5 Laurits Tuxen, *Coronation of Nicholas II / Krönung Nikolaus II. und Alexandra Fjdorownas von 1898*, 1898. Oil on canvas, 66.0 x 87.5 cm. Hermitage Museum, St Petersburg, Russia. Source: http://en.wikipedia.org/wiki/ File:Coronation_of_Nicholas_II.jpg (accessed April 5, 2013).

Fig. 1.6 Vasily Perov, *A Meal in the Monastery*, 1876. Oil on canvas, 84 x 126 cm. Museum of Russian Art, Kiev, Ukraine. Source: http://www.wikipaintings.org/en/ vasily-perov/a-meal-in-the-monastery-1876 (accessed April 5, 2013).

Fig. 1.7 Photographer unknown, Portrait of Russian historian Vasily Klyuchevsky (1841–1911). Scan of photograph, archive of Mariluna. Source: http://en.wikipedia .org/wiki/File:Vasily_Klyuchevsky_1893.jpg#filehistory (accessed April 5, 2013).

Fig. 1.8 Ilya Repin, *Lev Nikolayevich Tolstoy Shoeless*, 1901. Oil on canvas, 207 x 73 cm. State Russian Museum, St Petersburg, Russia. Source: http://en.wikipedia.org/wiki/File:Tolstoy_by_Repin_1901.jpg#filehistory (accessed April 5, 2013).

Fig. 1.9 Viktor M. Vasnetsov, *Self-Portrait*, 1873. State Tretyakov Gallery, Moscow, Russia. Source: http://en.wikipedia.org/wiki/File:Wiktor_Michajlowitsch_Wassnezow_003.jpg (accessed April 5, 2013).

Fig. 1.10 Vasily Perov, *Portrait of Fedor Dostoyevsky*, 1872. Oil on canvas, 99 x 80.5 cm. State Tretyakov Gallery, Moscow, Russia. Source: http://en.wikipedia.org/wiki/File:Vasily_Perov_-_Портрет_Ф.М.Достоевского_-_Google_Art_Project.jpg (accessed April 5, 2013).

Fig. 1.11 Viktor M. Vasnetsov, *Baptism of Saint Vladimir*, 1893. Oil on canvas, 71 x 58 cm. Cathedral of St Vladimir, Kiev, Ukraine. Source: http://uk.wikipedia.org/wiki/Файл:Vasnetsov_Bapt_Vladimir_fresco_in_Kiev.jpg (accessed April 5, 2013).

Fig. 1.12 Viktor M. Vasnetsov, *Cathedral of Saints of the Universal Church*, 1885–1896. Fresco, Cathedral of St Vladimir, Kiev, Ukraine. Source: http://uk.wikipedia.org/wiki/Файл:Собор_святителей_Вселенской_церкви_(2).jpg (accessed April 5, 2013).

Fig. 1.13 Viktor M. Vasnetsov, *Russian Bishops*, 1885–1896. Fresco, Cathedral of St Vladimir, Kiev, Ukraine. Source: http://uk.wikipedia.org/wiki/Файл:Vasnetsov_Russian_Bishops.jpg (accessed April 5, 2013).

Fig. 1.14 Sustructu, View of the Church of Mary Magdalene from the Temple Mount, 2008. Color photograph, photographer's own archive. Source: http://commons.wikimedia.org/wiki/File:Church_of_Mary_Magdalene1.jpg?uselang=ru (accessed April 5, 2013).

Fig. 1.15 F. M. Timon, Pascha, end of the nineteenth century. Photograph, Orthodox Pilgrim Center, Jerusalem, Israel. Source: http://commons.wikimedia.org/wiki/File:Pasha.jpg?uselang=ru (accessed April 5, 2013).

Fig. 1.16 Artist unknown, Icon of the Archangel Michael, c. 1410. Icon, Cathedral of the Archangel, Moscow Kremlin, Russia. Source: http://commons.wikimedia.org/wiki/File:Mikharkhangel2.jpg?uselang=ru (accessed April 5, 2013).

Fig. 1.17 Nikolai Naidenov, Cathedral of the Archangel, 1882. Photograph from *Naidenov's Moscow: Cathedrals, Monasteries and Churches*, vol 2, plate 2. (n.p.; 1883) Source: http://ru.wikipedia.org/wiki/Файл:Arkhsobor19cen.jpg (accessed April 5, 2013).

Fig. 1.18 Shakko (photographer), iconographer unknown, *The Russian Princes over Their Graves*. Fresco, Cathedral of the Archangel, Moscow Kremlin, Russia. Color photograph, 2009, archive of Wikipedia user Shakko. Source: http://commons .wikimedia.org/wiki/File:Archangelskiy_sobor002.JPG?uselang=ru (accessed April 5, 2013).

ILLUSTRATIONS: PART II

Fig. 2.1 Ilya Repin, *Alexander III Receiving Rural District Elders in the Yard of Petrovsky Palace in Moscow*, 1886. Oil on canvas, 293 x 490 cm. State Tretyakov Gallery, Moscow, Russia. Source: http://commons.wikimedia.org/wiki/ File:Alexander_III_reception_by_Repin.jpg?uselang=ru (accessed April 6, 2013).

Fig. 2.2 Photographer unknown, Metropolitan Anthony (Khrapovitsky) of Kiev and Galicia, 1936. Scan of photograph, archive of Черный человек. Source: http://commons.wikimedia.org/wiki/File:Metropolitan_Anthony_(Khrapovitsky). jpg?uselang=ru (accessed April 6, 2013).

Fig. 2.3 Photographer unknown, Archpriest Ioann Vostorgov, 1900. Scan of photograph, archive of Чръный человек. Source: http://ru.wikipedia.org/wiki/ Файл:Ioann_Vostorgov,_1900s.jpg (accessed April 6, 2013).

Fig. 2.4 Photographer unknown, Nicholas II of Russia and Alexandra Fyodorovna (Alix of Hesse) in Russian dress, 1903. Scan of photograph, archive of Crimea/ Munkalap, Hungary. Source: http://commons.wikimedia.org/wiki/File:Alix_and_ Nicky_in_Russian_dress.3.jpg?uselang=ru (accessed April 6, 2013).

Fig. 2.5 Photographer unknown, Portrait of participants at costume ball in 1903. Photograph, archive of Maris LEIPA Foundation, Moscow, Russia. Source: http://commons.wikimedia.org/wiki/File:1903_ball_-_01_group.jpg?uselang=ru (accessed April 6, 2013).

Fig. 2.6 Photographer unknown, His Majesty Emperor Nicholas II carrying the relics of Seraphim of Sarov in procession, 1903. Source: G. Malofeyev et al., eds., *Ventsenosnaya Sem'ya* [Imperial family] (Moscow: Kovcheg, 2006), p. 74.

Fig. 2.7 Photographer unknown, Nicholas II holding an icon of St Seraphim of Sarov while giving parting encouragement to Grand Duchess Anastasia Nikolayevna's 148th Infantry Caspian Regiment before its departure for the front in Manchuria; Peterhof, 1905. Source: Mikhail Pavlovich Iroshnikov, *Nikolai II, poslednii rossiiskii imperator*, Russian ed. (St Petersburg: Dukhovnoe prosveshchenie, 1992), p. 332.

Fig. 2.8 Photographer unknown, Procession at the consecration of the Church of the Resurrection from the south side of the building, 1907. Photograph, archive of Spas-Na-Krovi. Source: http://www.spas-na-krovi.ru/img/consecration/15.jpg (accessed April 6, 2013).

Fig. 2.9 Photographer unknown, Christ the Savior Church at the Angliiskaya Embankment, 1910. Scan of photograph, archive of Paul Kaganer, St Petersburg, Russia. Source: http://commons.wikimedia.org/wiki/File:Christ_the_Saviour_Church_(on_Waters)_1910s_1.jpg?uselang=ru (accessed April 6, 2013).

Fig. 2.10 S. S. Krichinsky, Cathedral of Our Lady of St Theodore [also know as the Fyodorovskaya Theotokos] and St Alexander Nevsky, 1913. Scan of photograph, archive of B. Guennadiev. Source: http://upload.wikimedia.org/wikipedia/commons/4/4e/ Фёдоровский_Собор_в_память_300-летия_царствования_Дома_Романовых_в_Санкт-Петербурге.jpg?uselang=ru (accessed April 11, 2013).

Fig. 2.11 Bulla Photographic Studio, Church of St Nicholas and the Blessed Alexander Nevsky, 1915. Scan of photograph, archive of AlexEleon. Source: http://commons.wikimedia.org/wiki/File:Nikolo_Bargradskaja_Chirch_in_Saint_Petersburg.JPG?uselang=ru (accessed April 6, 2013).

Fig. 2.12 Photographer unknown, The Black Hundred Procession, 1907. Scan of photograph, archive of Kristallstadt. Source: http://en.wikipedia.org/wiki/File:Black-hundred1907.jpg (accessed April 6, 2013).

Fig. 2.13 Photographer unknown, Vladimir Sergeyevich Solovyov, n.d. Scan of photograph, archive of Deodar. Source: http://commons.wikimedia.org/wiki/File:V.Solovyov.jpg?uselang=ru (accessed April 6, 2013).

Fig. 2.14 M. M. Boiovich, Sergei Nikolaevich Bulgakov, 1907. Scan of photograph, archive of Ctac. Source: http://commons.wikimedia.org/wiki/File:Sergey_Bulgakov.jpg?uselang=ru (accessed April 6, 2013).

Fig. 2.15 Mikhail Nesterov, *Philosophers*, 1917. Oil on canvas, 123 x 125 cm. State Tretyakov Gallery, Moscow, Russia. Source: http://commons.wikimedia.org/wiki/File:Nesterov_Florensky_Bulgakov.jpg?uselang=ru (accessed April 6, 2013).

Fig. 2.16 Mikhail Nesterov, *Holy Russia*, 1905. Oil on canvas, 233 x 375 cm. Russian Museum, St Petersburg, Russia. Source: http://commons.wikimedia.org/wiki/File:Nesterov_SaintRussia.JPG?uselang=ru (accessed April 6, 2013).

Fig. 2.17 Viktor Mikhaylovich Vasnetsov, Saint Germogen Patriarch of Moscow, 1915. Icon, State Museum of the History of Religion, St Petersburg, Russia. Source: http://commons.wikimedia.org/wiki/File:Patriarch_Germogen_icon_(1915) .jpg?uselang=ru (accessed April 6, 2013).

Fig. 2.18 Photographer unknown, The chapel located in the place where Patriarch Hermogenus of Moscow and All Russia was imprisoned between April 1611 and February 1612 and probably died of hunger, 1912. Scan of photograph from *Prawosławnaja Encikłopiedija*, vol. XVIII (Moscow: Cerkowno-Naucznyj Center, 2009), p. 646. Source: http://pl.wikipedia.org/wiki/Plik:Hermogen%27s_cell.jpg (accessed April 6, 2013).

Fig. 2.19 N. A. Papkov, The Holy New Martyrs, Confessors and Passion-Bearers of Russia, 1981. Icon, 92 x 122 cm. Holy Epiphany Church, Boston, Massachusetts. Source: Icon Studio of Holy Trinity Monastery, Jordanville, New York.

Fig. 2.20 St Tikhon's Orthodox Theological Institute Iconographers, The New Martyrs and Confessors of Christ of the Russian Church, 2001. Icon, St Tikhon's Orthodox Theological Institute, Moscow, Russia. Source: http://ru.wikipedia .org/wiki/ Файл:Икона Собор святых новомучеников и исповедников российских.jpg (accessed April 6, 2013).

INDEX

The citations in parentheses following the page numbers refer to note numbers; for example, 249(n23) refers to the text associated with note 23 on page 249. References to photographs in the illustration sections begin with "F"; for example, F2.3 refers to Figure 2.3.

medieval, 55
national commemorations in,
    4–5. *See also* baptism
    festival of 1888
national self-consciousness of,
    xviii, xx, 20–21, 38–39,
    43–44, 49–50, 194
nationalism in. *See* nationalism;
    Orthodox patriotism
as new Israel, xx, 7, 157. *See also*
    new Israel metaphor
non-Orthodox population in, 46,
    241(n3)
religious freedom in, 19–20, 22,
    93, 99–102, 105, 115–16
versus Rus, xv
Russian terms for, 88, 256(n78)
as Third Rome, 88–89
transfigured natural
    environment of, 41–42,
    166–67
Russian nationalism, identification
    with Orthodox faith. *See*
    Orthodox patriotism
russkii, 88, 119, 256(n78)

Sabler, Vladimir K., 16, 48, 109,
    241(n13)
saints
    canonization festival in 2000, 222
    commemoration of, 29–30
    as images of Holy Rus, 14, 164
    as symbols of Moscow's
        leadership in Orthodox
        world, 28–29, 237(n7–8)
sanctification, principle applied to
    objects/places, 43
sanctified national landscape,
    166–69

Saul, 99, 156–57, 211, 257(n26),
    257–58(n27)
Senatov, V., 181–82
Seraphim, Abbott, 211–13
Seraphim of Sarov, St, xiii, 3, 10,
    30–32, 42, 166, F2.6
Sergius of Radonezh, St, 3, 55,
    56–57, 164–66, F1.13
Shchukin, V., 194–95
Silence, 168
Skvortsov, Vladimir M.
    anti-Semitic rhetoric of, 220
    on coronation of Nicholas II,
        37–38
    on cultural-historical tasks of
        Russia, 48
    on Edict of Milan
        commemoration, 214–15
    as editor of *Kolokol,* 140
    in excommunication of Tolstoy,
        148
    on intellectuals, 148
    on Nicholas II, 97
    on Official Nationality, 140–41
    on religious toleration, 99–101
    on Third All-Russian Missionary
        Congress, 47–48
Slavophilism, 149
Smirnov, Peter, 78–80, 85, 260(n67)
"Social Principles of the Russian
    Orthodox Church, The,"
    222
Society for Religious-Moral
    Enlightenment, 112
Society of Lovers of Spiritual
    Enlightenment, 51–52, 63,
    243(n30)
Soloviev, M. P., 87, 256(n74),
    257(n75)